Windows®
NT®/2000
Native API
Reference

Gary Nebbett

800 East 96th Street, Indianapolis, IN 46240

Windows® NT®/2000 Native API Reference

Copyright © 2000 by MTP

International Standard Book Number: 1-57870-199-6

Library of Congress Catalog Card Number: 99-66351

Printed in the United States of America

First Printing: January 2000

06 05 04   7 6 5 4 3 2

Interpretation of the printing code: The rightmost double-digit number is the year of the book's printing; the rightmost single-digit number is the number of the book's printing. For example, the printing code 00-1 shows that the first printing of the book occurred in 2000.

Trademarks

Warning and Disclaimer

Publisher
David Dwyer

Executive Editor
Linda Ratts Engelman

Acquisitions Editor
Karen Wachs

Product Marketing Manager
Stephanie Layton

Managing Editor
Gina Brown

Development Editor
Leah Williams

Project Editor
Laura Loveall

Book Designer
Louisa Klucznik

Cover Designer
Aren Howell

Team Coordinator
Jennifer Garrett

Technical Reviewers
Michael W. Barry
Thomas L. Nowatzki

Indexer
Larry Sweazy

Proofreader
Debbie Williams

Compositor
Amy Parker

About the Author

Gary Nebbett first started working with operating systems when he joined the MultiMIRTOS development team at Standard Telecommunication Laboratories immediately after graduating from London University in 1982. (MultiMIRTOS was a real-time embedded operating system for the Intel 8086 processor.) An interest in operating systems having been awakened, Gary tried to develop tools to trace system calls, reconstruct deleted files, and capture network traffic whenever he subsequently encountered an operating system (such as, VMS, UNIX, or NT). Gary lives in Basel, Switzerland. In his free time he enjoys squash, cross-country skiing, walking in the Alps, mountain biking in the Black Forest, and tackling the occasional cryptic crossword. He has seldom been known to decline the offer of another glass of port (preferably accompanied by some more Stilton).

About the Technical Reviewers

Michael W. Barry has 18 years of programming experience. Upon receiving a B.S.E.E. from the University of Texas at Austin, Mike went to work for Datapoint Corporation, where he was involved in networking and desktop video conferencing. Mike holds over 14 patents ranging from video teleconferencing to color-image processing to cluster printing. He has been involved in NT Kernel and User mode programming since the Windows NT 3.1 beta and is considered an expert on the Windows NT operating system. Mike is a published author and technical reviewer for several technical book publishers. Currently, Mike is Senior Vice President of Development and Engineering at T/R systems, Inc. (the inventors of cluster printing), where he and his group are pioneering cluster printing systems based on Windows NT.

Mike lives in Atlanta, Georgia, with his lovely wife and two wonderful children. In his free time, he enjoys scuba diving, tennis, coaching soccer, water skiing and knee boarding.

Thomas L. Nowatzki has more than 25 years of professional software development experience on a variety of hardware and software platforms. For the past 5 years, he has been working in the areas of Intel architecture analysis, NT performance, and NT internals. His formal training includes a Masters of Science Degree in Electrical Engineering from the University of North Dakota. He co-holds two U.S. Patents and has had half a dozen more patent applications filed on his behalf related to the subject of computer technology.

Contents

Feedback Information

At MTP, our goal is to create in-depth technical books of the highest quality and value. Each book is crafted with care and precision, undergoing rigorous development that involves the unique expertise of members from the professional technical community.

Readers' feedback is a natural continuation of this process. If you have any comments regarding how we could improve the quality of this book, or otherwise alter it to better suit your needs, you can contact us at feedback@samspublishing.com. Please make sure to include the book title and ISBN in your message.

We greatly appreciate your assistance.

Introduction

The Windows NT native application programming interface is the set of system services provided by the Windows NT executive to both user mode and kernel mode programs. The native API routines are the equivalent of UNIX system calls or VMS system services.

The native API is little mentioned in the Windows NT documentation, so there is no well-established convention for referring to it. "native API" and "native system services" are both appropriate names, the word "native" serving to distinguish the API from the Win32 API, which is the interface to the operating system used by most Windows applications.

It is commonly assumed that the native API is not documented in its entirety by Microsoft because they wish to maintain the flexibility to modify the interface in new versions of the operating system without being bound to ensure backwards compatibility. To document the complete interface would be tantamount to making an open-ended commitment to support what may come to be perceived as obsolete functionality. Indeed, perhaps to demonstrate that this interface should not be used by production applications, Windows 2000 has removed some of the native API routines that were present in Windows NT 4.0 and has changed some data structures in ways that are incompatible with the expectations of Windows NT 4.0 programs.

This book describes the native API in the same style as is used to describe a subset of the native API in the Device Driver Kit (DDK) documentation. Although the names of the parameters of the native system services and the members of structures have been chosen "in the style of" the documented subset of the API, any resemblance to the actual names is coincidental. The systems observed were the free (retail) builds of Windows NT 4.0 Service Pack 3 and Windows 2000 Release Candidate 2 running on Intel processors. Some of the routines in the native API are not implemented on the Intel platform (such as support for Very Large Memory [VLM]) and are, therefore, not described in this book, and some other routines (such as support for Virtual DOS Machines [VDM]) are only briefly described. The graphical system services implemented by win32k.sys are not discussed at all.

Despite the stylistic similarity, there are major differences from DDK documentation. Foremost of these is that the information in this book has been deduced from observations of the behavior of Windows NT rather than access to its source code or development team.

Because the information provided here is based purely on rigorous deduction, there can be no guarantee that small errors do not exist within the text. These errors do not undermine the intention of the book, which is to provide a description of the native API satisfactory for use in developing "resource kit"-like utilities (that is, debugging and analysis tools) and other "unsupported" software *without encouraging its use in production applications.*

Explanations of topics that can be found in the DDK documentation and the book, *Inside Windows NT* (second edition), by David Solomon are not repeated in this book, and a knowledge of the Win32 API, C++ and the C++ standard libraries is assumed.

The purpose of this introduction is to provide some background on the native API before delving into the details. At the end of the introduction there is a brief description of the organization to help guide you in your reading.

Using the Native API

About 10 percent of the native API is documented in the DDK for use by device driver writers, and the definitions of these routines appear in the include file ntddk.h.

The native API routines defined in ntddk.h can be called by a Win32 program, but ntddk.h cannot simply be included in the same compilation unit as winnt.h (which is indirectly included by windows.h) because some identical data structures are defined in both files. The simple program that follows generates many type redefinition and macro redefinition warnings and errors when compiled:

```
#include <windows.h>
#include <ntddk.h>

int main()
{
    return 0;
}
```

There are many useful definitions in winnt.h and ntddk.h, and rather than copying one of the files and editing it to remove the duplicate definitions, the examples in this book use a feature of C++ to place the Win32 and native definitions in different namespaces:

```
#include <windows.h>

namespace NT {
    extern "C" {
#pragma warning(disable: 4005)   // macro redefinition
#include <ntddk.h>
#pragma warning(default: 4005)
    }
}
using NT::NTSTATUS;

int main()
{
    return 0;
}
```

This compiles without warning when using Version 11 of the Microsoft C++ compiler (distributed with Visual C++ Version 5), but it produces a large number of "notes" when compiled with Version 12 of the compiler (distributed with Visual C++ Version 6). These notes augment the information returned by the macro redefinition warning, but—unlike the warning—they cannot be suppressed.

As a consequence of this use of namespaces, all uses of type definitions from ntddk.h must be preceded by "NT::." An exception is made for NTSTATUS (via the "using" statement) so that the NT_SUCCESS macro continues to work.

For convenience, all the examples in the book use a single include file named ntdll.h, which includes windows.h, ntddk.h and all the definitions of native system services.

Relationship Between Win32 and the Native API

Many Win32 functions are simple wrappers around native API routines, and the descriptions of the native API routines in this book list the Win32 functions related to the native routine. The term "related" is interpreted to mean that the Win32 function uses the native routine to implement the bulk of its functionality. Because knowledge of the Win32 is assumed, a statement of the broad equivalence between a native system service and a Win32 function often serves as the sole explanation of the system service. Examples I.1 and I.2 show two typical Win32 wrappers around native system service.

Example I.1: Typical Win32 Wrapping Around a Native API Routine

```
HANDLE Win32RootDirectory()
{
    static HANDLE Handle;

    if (Handle == 0) {
        NT::UNICODE_STRING ObjectName;
        NT::RtlInitUnicodeString(&ObjectName, L"\\BaseNamedObjects");

        NT::OBJECT_ATTRIBUTES ObjectAttr = {sizeof ObjectAttr, 0,
                                            &ObjectName,
                                            OBJ_CASE_INSENSITIVE};

        ACCESS_MASK DesiredAccess = READ_CONTROL ¦ DIRECTORY_QUERY
                                  ¦ DIRECTORY_TRAVERSE
                                  ¦ DIRECTORY_CREATE_OBJECT
                                  ¦ DIRECTORY_CREATE_SUBDIRECTORY;

        NT::ZwOpenDirectoryObject(&Handle, DesiredAccess, &ObjectAttr);
    }
    return Handle;
}

HANDLE CreateMutexW(LPSECURITY_ATTRIBUTES SecAttr, BOOL InitialOwner,
                    PCWSTR Name)
{
    NT::UNICODE_STRING ObjectName;
    NT::OBJECT_ATTRIBUTES ObjectAttr = {sizeof ObjectAttr, 0, 0, OBJ_OPENIF};

    if (Name) {
        NT::RtlInitUnicodeString(&ObjectName, Name);
        ObjectAttr.RootDirectory = Win32RootDirectory();
        ObjectAttr.ObjectName = &ObjectName;
    }
    if (SecAttr) {
        if (SecAttr->bInheritHandle) ObjectAttr.Attributes ¦= OBJ_INHERIT;
        ObjectAttr.SecurityDescriptor = SecAttr->lpSecurityDescriptor;
    }

    HANDLE Handle;

    NTSTATUS rv = NT::ZwCreateMutant(&Handle, MUTANT_ALL_ACCESS,
                                     &ObjectAttr, InitialOwner);
    if (NT_SUCCESS(rv)) {
```

```
        SetLastError(rv == STATUS_OBJECT_NAME_EXISTS
                    ? ERROR_ALREADY_EXISTS : ERROR_SUCCESS);
        return Handle;
    }
    else {
        SetLastError(NT::RtlNtStatusToDosError(rv));
        return 0;
    }
}
```

The wrapping around **ZwCreateMutant** in the implementation of `CreateMutexW` in Example I.1 is typical of the Win32 wrapping around native system services that take an object name as parameter. First a `UNICODE_STRING` structure is created to hold the name. A `UNICODE_STRING` is defined thus:

```
typedef struct _UNICODE_STRING {
    USHORT Length;              // Length of string in bytes
    USHORT MaximumLength;
    PWSTR  Buffer;              // Pointer to Unicode string
} UNICODE_STRING, *PUNICODE_STRING;
```

This string makes it easier for the system service to check that accessing the name string will not cause an access violation because it initially just has to verify that `Buffer` and `Buffer + Length` are valid pointers. If the system service was not told the length of the string, it would have to carefully scan the string looking for the terminating `null` character.

```
typedef struct _OBJECT_ATTRIBUTES {
    ULONG Length;
    HANDLE RootDirectory;
    PUNICODE_STRING ObjectName;
    ULONG Attributes;
    PVOID SecurityDescriptor;
    PVOID SecurityQualityOfService;
} OBJECT_ATTRIBUTES, *POBJECT_ATTRIBUTES;
```

A pointer to the `UNICODE_STRING` is embedded in an `OBJECT_ATTRIBUTES` structure, which allows additional information about the name to be made available to the system service. This structure is described in more detail later, but for the present discussion the most important member is `RootDirectory`, which contains a handle to a "container" object; the `ObjectName` member is a name relative to this container. Ignoring complications related to Windows Terminal Server, kernel32.dll creates and caches a handle to the object directory named "\BaseNamedObjects," and uses this handle as the `RootDirectory` in most Win32 requests to create objects (files and registry keys being notable exceptions).

Example I.2: Simplest Win32 Wrapping Around a Native API Routine

```
BOOL ResetEvent(HANDLE Handle)
{
    NTSTATUS rv = NT::ZwClearEvent(Handle);

    return NT_SUCCESS(rv)
        ? TRUE : SetLastError(NT::RtlNtStatusToDosError(rv)), FALSE;
}
```

When the relationship between a Win32 function and a native API routine is like that of ResetEvent and ZwClearEvent in Example I.2, the remarks following the definition of the native note that "ResetEvent exposes the full functionality of ZwClearEvent," because ResetEvent can do everything that ZwClearEvent can do. The only difference between the two is the translation of the error code (from the native numbering scheme to the Win32 scheme) and the storage of the error code in the Thread Environment Block (TEB) for later retrieval by GetLastError if necessary.

Calling Native System Services from Kernel Mode

The routines that comprise the native API can usually be recognized by their names, which come in two forms: NtXxx and ZwXxx. (Xxx is the convention used in the DDK documentation for a wildcard.) For user mode programs, the two forms of the name are equivalent and are just two different symbols for the same entry point in ntdll.dll. The code at the entry point in ntdll.dll executes an instruction that causes the processor to enter kernel mode. The kernel mode code that executes in response to this instruction (the system service dispatcher) records the previous mode of the processor in the ETHREAD structure of the current thread before calling the function that implements the particular native system service.

Kernel mode code links against ntoskrnl.exe rather than ntdll.dll. The two different forms of the system service name point to different entry points: the ZwXxx format entry point contains a copy of the code from ntdll.dll, which re-enters the kernel and uses the system service dispatcher, and the NtXxx format entry point contains the actual implementation of the system service.

Example I.3 shows the typical preamble to a native system service and helps to explain the difference between using the ZwXxx and NtXxx forms of the system service name. If code that is already running in kernel mode calls the ZwXxx entry point, it re-enters the system service dispatcher, which updates the previous mode to be kernel mode, and then when the actual code of the system service is executed, much of the preamble is skipped. The code that is skipped includes checks for privileges, and the fact that the previous mode is kernel means that any subsequent attempt to open an object will succeed regardless of the Access Control List (ACL) attached to the object.

If, however, the kernel mode code calls the NtXxx entry point, the results depend upon the previous mode—over which the kernel mode code has little control—for example, the previous mode in a device driver dispatch routine could vary from call to call. If the system service has any parameters that are pointers and these pointers point to automatic or static variables in the kernel mode program, then a call to the system service will fail with STATUS_ACCESS_VIOLATION because the pointers fail the test of being less than MmUserProbeAddress if the previous mode is user mode.

If the system service does not have any pointer parameters, it is practical to use the NtXxx entry points, provided that the "privileges" of bypassing privilege and access control checks are not needed.

All the examples in this book use the ZwXxx form of the name.

Example I.3: Typical Preamble to a Native System Service

```
NTSTATUS
NTAPI
NtCreatePagingFile(
    IN PUNICODE_STRING FileName,
    IN PULARGE_INTEGER InitialSize,
    IN PULARGE_INTEGER MaximumSize,
    IN ULONG Reserved
    )
{
    KPROCESSOR_MODE PreviousMode = ExGetPreviousMode();

    __try {
        if (PreviousMode == UserMode) {

            if (SeSinglePrivilegeCheck(SeCreatePagefilePrivilege,
                                       PreviousMode) == FALSE)
                return STATUS_PRIVILEGE_NOT_HELD;

            if (FileName + 1 > MmUserProbeAddress)
                ExRaiseAccessViolation();

            if (PCHAR(FileName->Buffer)+FileName->Length >
MmUserProbeAddress)
                ExRaiseAccessViolation();

            if (ULONG(InitialSize) & 3)
                ExRaiseDatatypeMisalignment();

            if (InitialSize + 1 > MmUserProbeAddress)
                ExRaiseAccessViolation();

            if (ULONG(MaximumSize) & 3)
                ExRaiseDatatypeMisalignment();

            if (MaximumSize + 1 > MmUserProbeAddress)
                ExRaiseAccessViolation();
        }

        // Copy the arguments and file name string to kernel memory
    }
    __except(PreviousMode == UserMode
            ? EXCEPTION_EXECUTE_HANDLER : EXCEPTION_CONTINUE_SEARCH) {

        return GetExceptionCode();
    }

    // Create the page file

    return STATUS_SUCCESS;
}
```

The parameters in the definition of **NtCreatePagingFile** in Example I.3 are preceded by the string "IN," which is a macro that expands to an empty string. This is part of a convention used by the DDK documentation to indicate whether a parameter is an input parameter, an output parameter, or both. If the parameter is an output parameter, it is preceded by "OUT," and if it is both an input and an output parameter, it is preceded by "IN OUT." If a parameter is a pointer, the parameter name is sometimes followed by the string "OPTIONAL," which indicates that a null pointer may be used as argument.

Return Values of Native System Services

The descriptions of the native system services include information on the possible return values, which is a status code for most system services. The list of values is not normally complete, both because this is difficult to achieve and because there is little benefit in noting that many system services could fail with STATUS_INVALID_PARAMETER, for example. The values that are listed are intended to give an indication of the interesting ways in which the system service could fail.

Relative Frequency of Native System Services Use

When running a checked build of Windows NT, the system counts the number of invocations of each of the system services. Table I.1 contains these call counts sorted by frequency for a Windows NT 4.0 system, which ran for a few hours before the data was gathered.

Table I.1: Relative Frequency of Use of Native System Services

Call count	Service name
399236	NtWaitForSingleObject
245859	NtReplyWaitReceivePort
237888	NtRequestWaitReplyPort
78260	NtReadFile
50028	NtClose
44768	NtDeviceIoControlFile
34598	NtSetEvent
27512	NtClearEvent
23878	NtOpenThreadToken
22551	NtWaitForMultipleObjects
18441	NtOpenKey
14504	NtAllocateVirtualMemory
14361	NtProtectVirtualMemory
13975	NtQueryInformationToken
13335	NtEnumerateKey
12910	NtQueryValueKey
12273	NtOpenProcessToken
11261	NtSetInformationFile
9207	NtFlushInstructionCache
8906	NtQueryInformationFile
7198	NtFreeVirtualMemory
6987	NtReleaseMutant
6637	NtWriteFile

```
6227    NtQuerySecurityObject
5907    NtEnumerateValueKey
5763    NtOpenFile
5541    NtQueryDirectoryFile
5346    NtQueryDefaultLocale
5062    NtSetValueKey
4716    NtRequestPort
4335    NtQueryKey
3927    NtQueryAttributesFile
3805    NtMapViewOfSection
3787    NtCreateFile
3576    NtReadVirtualMemory
3007    NtReplyPort
2858    NtQuerySystemTime
2558    NtOpenSection
2477    NtReleaseSemaphore
2461    NtFsControlFile
2414    NtQueryVolumeInformationFile
2360    NtQueryVirtualMemory
2353    NtDuplicateObject
2127    NtWriteVirtualMemory
2095    NtSetInformationProcess
2091    NtQueryInformationProcess
1909    NtCreateSection
1897    NtCreateKey
1741    NtCreateEvent
1651    NtContinue
1645    NtGetContextThread
1590    NtSetContextThread
1232    NtDeleteKey
1106    NtUnmapViewOfSection
 980    NtTestAlert
 899    NtSetInformationThread
 869    NtQueryInformationThread
 809    NtQueryEvent
 717    NtQuerySystemInformation
 678    NtOpenProcess
 618    NtDelayExecution
 583    NtFlushBuffersFile
 582    NtQueryObject
 576    NtSetInformationObject
 568    NtCreateThread
 563    NtResumeThread
 555    NtRegisterThreadTerminatePort
 414    NtQuerySection
 385    NtTerminateProcess
 350    NtOpenSymbolicLinkObject
 305    NtOpenDirectoryObject
 290    NtLockFile
 287    NtUnlockFile
 269    NtTerminateThread
 234    NtAcceptConnectPort
 233    NtConnectPort
 232    NtCompleteConnectPort
 230    NtQuerySymbolicLinkObject
 209    NtCreateProcess
 166    NtImpersonateClientOfPort
 147    NtCreateNamedPipeFile
```

```
1        NtPrivilegeObjectAuditAlarm
1        NtQueryFullAttributesFile
1        NtSetDefaultHardErrorPort
1        NtSetIntervalProfile
1        NtSuspendThread
1        NtUnloadKey
0        NtAdjustGroupsToken
0        NtAlertResumeThread
0        NtAlertThread
0        NtCancelIoFile
0        NtCreateChannel
0        NtCreateEventPair
0        NtDeleteFile
0        NtDeleteObjectAuditAlarm
0        NtExtendSection
0        NtFlushWriteBuffer
0        NtGetPlugPlayEvent
0        NtGetTickCount
0        NtListenChannel
0        NtLoadKey2
0        NtLockVirtualMemory
0        NtOpenChannel
0        NtOpenEventPair
0        NtOpenIoCompletion
0        NtOpenMutant
0        NtOpenTimer
0        NtPlugPlayControl
0        NtPulseEvent
0        NtQueryEaFile
0        NtQueryInformationPort
0        NtQueryIntervalProfile
0        NtQueryIoCompletion
0        NtQueryMultipleValueKey
0        NtQueryMutant
0        NtQueryOleDirectoryFile
0        NtQuerySemaphore
0        NtQuerySystemEnvironmentValue
0        NtQueryTimer
0        NtQueueApcThread
0        NtReadFileScatter
0        NtReplaceKey
0        NtReplyWaitReplyPort
0        NtReplyWaitSendChannel
0        NtRestoreKey
0        NtSaveKey
0        NtSendWaitReplyChannel
0        NtSetContextChannel
0        NtSetEaFile
0        NtSetHighEventPair
0        NtSetHighWaitLowEventPair
0        NtSetHighWaitLowThread
0        NtSetInformationKey
0        NtSetInformationToken
0        NtSetIoCompletion
0        NtSetLdtEntries
0        NtSetLowEventPair
0        NtSetLowWaitHighEventPair
0        NtSetLowWaitHighThread
```

```
0    NtSetSystemEnvironmentValue
0    NtSetSystemPowerState
0    NtSetSystemTime
0    NtSetTimerResolution
0    NtSetVolumeInformationFile
0    NtShutdownSystem
0    NtSignalAndWaitForSingleObject
0    NtStopProfile
0    NtSystemDebugControl
0    NtUnlockVirtualMemory
0    NtVdmControl
0    NtW32Call
0    NtWaitHighEventPair
0    NtWaitLowEventPair
0    NtWriteFileGather
```

Organization of This Book

This book is divided into seventeen chapters and four appendices. Each chapter covers a group of (sometimes loosely) related system services, the final chapter, Chapter 17, bearing the catchall title "Miscellany." The description of each system service is intended to be understandable in isolation so that it is possible to locate an entry via either the table of contents, or the index and to find all of the relevant information there.

An attempt to ensure that system services are described before being used in an example determined the order of the chapters. For example, the chapter describing processes follows chapters on virtual memory and section objects because the virtual memory and section object system services are needed in the examples that demonstrate process creation.

The appendices cover additional material that is largely independent of particular system services (perhaps with the exception of Appendix C, "Exceptions and Debugging," which provides background information of relevance to the system services that raise and handle exceptions). Of particular importance to kernel mode programmers is Appendix A, "Calling System Services from Kernel Mode," which discusses techniques for making the full range of system services available to kernel mode programs.

1

System Information and Control

The system services described in this chapter operate on the system as a whole rather than on individual objects within the system. They mostly gather information about the performance and operation of the system and set system parameters.

ZwQuerySystemInformation

ZwQuerySystemInformation queries information about the system.

```
NTSYSAPI
NTSTATUS
NTAPI
ZwQuerySystemInformation(
    IN SYSTEM_INFORMATION_CLASS SystemInformationClass,
    IN OUT PVOID SystemInformation,
    IN ULONG SystemInformationLength,
    OUT PULONG ReturnLength OPTIONAL
    );
```

Parameters

SystemInformationClass

The type of system information to be queried. The permitted values are a subset of the enumeration SYSTEM_INFORMATION_CLASS, described in the following section.

SystemInformation

Points to a caller-allocated buffer or variable that receives the requested system information.

SystemInformationLength

The size in bytes of SystemInformation, which the caller should set according to the given SystemInformationClass.

ReturnLength

    Optionally points to a variable that receives the number of bytes actually returned to `SystemInformation`; if `SystemInformationLength` is too small to contain the available information, the variable is normally set to zero except for two information classes (6 and 11) when it is set to the number of bytes required for the available information. If this information is not needed, `ReturnLength` may be a null pointer.

Return Value

    Returns `STATUS_SUCCESS` or an error status, such as `STATUS_INVALID_INFO_CLASS`, `STATUS_NOT_IMPLEMENTED`, or `STATUS_INFO_LENGTH_MISMATCH`.

Related Win32 Functions

    `GetSystemInfo`, `GetTimeZoneInformation`, `GetSystemTimeAdjustment`, PSAPI functions, and performance counters.

Remarks

    ZwQuerySystemInformation is the source of much of the information displayed by "Performance Monitor" for the classes Cache, Memory, Objects, Paging File, Process, Processor, System, and Thread. It is also frequently used by resource kit utilities that display information about the system.

    The `ReturnLength` information is not always valid (depending on the information class), even when the routine returns `STATUS_SUCCESS`. When the return value indicates `STATUS_INFO_LENGTH_MISMATCH`, only some of the information classes return an estimate of the required length.

    Some information classes are implemented only in the "checked" version of the kernel. Some, such as `SystemCallCounts`, return useful information only in "checked" versions of the kernel.

    Some information classes require certain flags to have been set in `NtGlobalFlags` at boot time. For example, `SystemObjectInformation` requires that `FLG_MAINTAIN_OBJECT_TYPELIST` be set at boot time.

    Information class `SystemNotImplemented1` (4) would return `STATUS_NOT_IMPLEMENTED` if it were not for the fact that it uses `DbgPrint` to print the text "EX: `SystemPathInformation now available via SharedUserData`." and then calls `DbgBreakPoint`. The breakpoint exception is caught by a frame based exception handler (in the absence of intervention by a debugger) and causes **ZwQuerySystemInformation** to return with `STATUS_BREAKPOINT`.

ZwSetSystemInformation

ZwSetSystemInformation sets information that affects the operation of the system.

```
NTSYSAPI
NTSTATUS
NTAPI
ZwSetSystemInformation(
    IN SYSTEM_INFORMATION_CLASS SystemInformationClass,
    IN OUT PVOID SystemInformation,
```

```
    IN ULONG SystemInformationLength
    );
```

Parameters

SystemInformationClass
> The type of system information to be set. The permitted values are a subset of the enumeration SYSTEM_INFORMATION_CLASS, described in the following section.

SystemInformation
> Points to a caller-allocated buffer or variable that contains the system information to be set.

SystemInformationLength
> The size in bytes of SystemInformation, which the caller should set according to the given SystemInformationClass.

Return Value

> Returns STATUS_SUCCESS or an error status, such as STATUS_INVALID_INFO_CLASS, STATUS_NOT_IMPLEMENTED or STATUS_INFO_LENGTH_MISMATCH.

Related Win32 Functions

> SetSystemTimeAdjustment.

Remarks

> At least one of the information classes uses the SystemInformation parameter for both input and output.

SYSTEM_INFORMATION_CLASS

The system information classes available in the "free" (retail) build of the system are listed below along with a remark as to whether the information class can be queried, set, or both. Some of the information classes labeled "SystemNotImplementedXxx" are implemented in the "checked" build, and a few of these classes are briefly described later.

		Query	Set
typedef enum _SYSTEM_INFORMATION_CLASS {			
SystemBasicInformation,	// 0	Y	N
SystemProcessorInformation,	// 1	Y	N
SystemPerformanceInformation,	// 2	Y	N
SystemTimeOfDayInformation,	// 3	Y	N
SystemNotImplemented1,	// 4	Y	N
SystemProcessesAndThreadsInformation,	// 5	Y	N
SystemCallCounts,	// 6	Y	N
SystemConfigurationInformation,	// 7	Y	N
SystemProcessorTimes,	// 8	Y	N
SystemGlobalFlag,	// 9	Y	Y
SystemNotImplemented2,	// 10	Y	N
SystemModuleInformation,	// 11	Y	N

```
    SystemLockInformation,                 // 12      Y        N
    SystemNotImplemented3,                 // 13      Y        N
    SystemNotImplemented4,                 // 14      Y        N
    SystemNotImplemented5,                 // 15      Y        N
    SystemHandleInformation,               // 16      Y        N
    SystemObjectInformation,               // 17      Y        N
    SystemPagefileInformation,             // 18      Y        N
    SystemInstructionEmulationCounts,      // 19      Y        N
    SystemInvalidInfoClass1,               // 20
    SystemCacheInformation,                // 21      Y        Y
    SystemPoolTagInformation,              // 22      Y        N
    SystemProcessorStatistics,             // 23      Y        N
    SystemDpcInformation,                  // 24      Y        Y
    SystemNotImplemented6,                 // 25      Y        N
    SystemLoadImage,                       // 26      N        Y
    SystemUnloadImage,                     // 27      N        Y
    SystemTimeAdjustment,                  // 28      Y        Y
    SystemNotImplemented7,                 // 29      Y        N
    SystemNotImplemented8,                 // 30      Y        N
    SystemNotImplemented9,                 // 31      Y        N
    SystemCrashDumpInformation,            // 32      Y        N
    SystemExceptionInformation,            // 33      Y        N
    SystemCrashDumpStateInformation,       // 34      Y        Y/N
    SystemKernelDebuggerInformation,       // 35      Y        N
    SystemContextSwitchInformation,        // 36      Y        N
    SystemRegistryQuotaInformation,        // 37      Y        Y
    SystemLoadAndCallImage,                // 38      N        Y
    SystemPrioritySeparation,              // 39      N        Y
    SystemNotImplemented10,                // 40      Y        N
    SystemNotImplemented11,                // 41      Y        N
    SystemInvalidInfoClass2,               // 42
    SystemInvalidInfoClass3,               // 43
    SystemTimeZoneInformation,             // 44      Y        N
    SystemLookasideInformation,            // 45      Y        N
    SystemSetTimeSlipEvent,                // 46      N        Y
    SystemCreateSession,                   // 47      N        Y
    SystemDeleteSession,                   // 48      N        Y
    SystemInvalidInfoClass4,               // 49
    SystemRangeStartInformation,           // 50      Y        N
    SystemVerifierInformation,             // 51      Y        Y
    SystemAddVerifier,                     // 52      N        Y
    SystemSessionProcessesInformation      // 53      Y        N
} SYSTEM_INFORMATION_CLASS;
```

SystemBasicInformation

```
typedef struct _SYSTEM_BASIC_INFORMATION { // Information Class 0
    ULONG Unknown;
    ULONG MaximumIncrement;
    ULONG PhysicalPageSize;
    ULONG NumberOfPhysicalPages;
    ULONG LowestPhysicalPage;
    ULONG HighestPhysicalPage;
    ULONG AllocationGranularity;
    ULONG LowestUserAddress;
    ULONG HighestUserAddress;
    ULONG ActiveProcessors;
    UCHAR NumberProcessors;
} SYSTEM_BASIC_INFORMATION, *PSYSTEM_BASIC_INFORMATION;
```

Members

Unknown
Always contains zero; interpretation unknown.

MaximumIncrement
The maximum number of 100-nanosecond units between clock ticks. Also the number of 100-nanosecond units per clock tick for kernel intervals measured in clock ticks.

PhysicalPageSize
The size in bytes of a physical page.

NumberOfPhysicalPages
The number of physical pages managed by the operating system.

LowestPhysicalPage
The number of the lowest physical page managed by the operating system (numbered from zero).

HighestPhysicalPage
The number of the highest physical page managed by the operating system (numbered from zero).

AllocationGranularity
The granularity to which the base address of virtual memory reservations is rounded.

LowestUserAddress
The lowest virtual address potentially available to user mode applications.

HighestUserAddress
The highest virtual address potentially available to user mode applications.

ActiveProcessors
A bit mask representing the set of active processors in the system. Bit 0 is processor 0; bit 31 is processor 31.

NumberProcessors
The number of processors in the system.

Remarks

Much of the data in this information class can be obtained by calling the Win32 function `GetSystemInfo`.

SystemProcessorInformation

```
typedef struct _SYSTEM_PROCESSOR_INFORMATION { // Information Class 1
    USHORT ProcessorArchitecture;
    USHORT ProcessorLevel;
    USHORT ProcessorRevision;
    USHORT Unknown;
    ULONG FeatureBits;
} SYSTEM_PROCESSOR_INFORMATION, *PSYSTEM_PROCESSOR_INFORMATION;
```

Members

ProcessorArchitecture

The system's processor architecture. Some of the possible values are defined in winnt.h with identifiers of the form PROCESSOR_ARCHITECTURE_* (where '*' is a wildcard).

ProcessorLevel

The system's architecture-dependent processor level. Some of the possible values are defined in the Win32 documentation for the SYSTEM_INFO structure.

ProcessorRevision

The system's architecture-dependent processor revision. Some of the possible values are defined in the Win32 documentation for the SYSTEM_INFO structure.

Unknown

Always contains zero; interpretation unknown.

FeatureBits

A bit mask representing any special features of the system's processor (for example, whether the Intel MMX instruction set is available). The flags for the Intel platform include:

Intel Mnemonic	Value	Description
VME	0x0001	Virtual-8086 Mode Enhancements
TCS	0x0002	Time Stamp Counter
	0x0004	CR4 Register
CMOV	0x0008	Conditional Mov/Cmp Instruction
PGE	0x0010	PTE Global Bit
PSE	0x0020	Page Size Extensions
MTRR	0x0040	Memory Type Range Registers
CXS	0x0080	CMPXCHGB8 Instruction
MMX	0x0100	MMX Technology
PAT	0x0400	Page Attribute Table
FXSR	0x0800	Fast Floating Point Save and Restore
SIMD	0x2000	Streaming SIMD Extension

Remarks

Much of the data in this information class can be obtained by calling the Win32 function GetSystemInfo.

SystemPerformanceInformation

```
typedef struct _SYSTEM_PERFORMANCE_INFORMATION { // Information Class 2
    LARGE_INTEGER IdleTime;
    LARGE_INTEGER ReadTransferCount;
    LARGE_INTEGER WriteTransferCount;
    LARGE_INTEGER OtherTransferCount;
    ULONG ReadOperationCount;
    ULONG WriteOperationCount;
    ULONG OtherOperationCount;
    ULONG AvailablePages;
    ULONG TotalCommittedPages;
    ULONG TotalCommitLimit;
    ULONG PeakCommitment;
    ULONG PageFaults;
    ULONG WriteCopyFaults;
    ULONG TransitionFaults;
    ULONG Reserved1;
    ULONG DemandZeroFaults;
    ULONG PagesRead;
    ULONG PageReadIos;
    ULONG Reserved2[2];
    ULONG PagefilePagesWritten;
    ULONG PagefilePageWriteIos;
    ULONG MappedFilePagesWritten;
    ULONG MappedFilePageWriteIos;
    ULONG PagedPoolUsage;
    ULONG NonPagedPoolUsage;
    ULONG PagedPoolAllocs;
    ULONG PagedPoolFrees;
    ULONG NonPagedPoolAllocs;
    ULONG NonPagedPoolFrees;
    ULONG TotalFreeSystemPtes;
    ULONG SystemCodePage;
    ULONG TotalSystemDriverPages;
    ULONG TotalSystemCodePages;
    ULONG SmallNonPagedLookasideListAllocateHits;
    ULONG SmallPagedLookasideListAllocateHits;
    ULONG Reserved3;
    ULONG MmSystemCachePage;
    ULONG PagedPoolPage;
    ULONG SystemDriverPage;
    ULONG FastReadNoWait;
    ULONG FastReadWait;
    ULONG FastReadResourceMiss;
    ULONG FastReadNotPossible;
    ULONG FastMdlReadNoWait;
    ULONG FastMdlReadWait;
    ULONG FastMdlReadResourceMiss;
    ULONG FastMdlReadNotPossible;
    ULONG MapDataNoWait;
    ULONG MapDataWait;
    ULONG MapDataNoWaitMiss;
    ULONG MapDataWaitMiss;
    ULONG PinMappedDataCount;
    ULONG PinReadNoWait;
    ULONG PinReadWait;
    ULONG PinReadNoWaitMiss;
    ULONG PinReadWaitMiss;
    ULONG CopyReadNoWait;
    ULONG CopyReadWait;
    ULONG CopyReadNoWaitMiss;
```

```
        ULONG CopyReadWaitMiss;
        ULONG MdlReadNoWait;
        ULONG MdlReadWait;
        ULONG MdlReadNoWaitMiss;
        ULONG MdlReadWaitMiss;
        ULONG ReadAheadIos;
        ULONG LazyWriteIos;
        ULONG LazyWritePages;
        ULONG DataFlushes;
        ULONG DataPages;
        ULONG ContextSwitches;
        ULONG FirstLevelTbFills;
        ULONG SecondLevelTbFills;
        ULONG SystemCalls;
    } SYSTEM_PERFORMANCE_INFORMATION, *PSYSTEM_PERFORMANCE_INFORMATION;
```

Members

IdleTime
>   The total idle time, measured in units of 100-nanoseconds, of all the processors in the system.

ReadTransferCount
>   The number of bytes read by all calls to **ZwReadFile**.

WriteTransferCount
>   The number of bytes written by all calls to **ZwWriteFile**.

OtherTransferCount
>   The number of bytes transferred to satisfy all other I/O operations, such as **ZwDeviceIoControlFile.**

ReadOperationCount
>   The number of calls to **ZwReadFile**.

WriteOperationCount
>   The number of calls to **ZwWriteFile**.

OtherOperationCount
>   The number of calls to all other I/O system services, such as **ZwDeviceIoControlFile**.

AvailablePages
>   The number of pages of physical memory available to processes running on the system.

TotalCommittedPages
>   The number of pages of committed virtual memory.

TotalCommitLimit
>   The number of pages of virtual memory that could be committed without extending the system's pagefiles.

PeakCommitment
> The peak number of pages of committed virtual memory.

PageFaults
> The number of page faults (both soft and hard).

WriteCopyFaults
> The number of page faults arising from attempts to write to copy-on-write pages.

TransitionFaults
> The number of soft page faults (excluding demand zero faults).

DemandZeroFaults
> The number of demand zero faults.

PagesRead
> The number of pages read from disk to resolve page faults.

PageReadIos
> The number of read operations initiated to resolve page faults.

PagefilePagesWritten
> The number of pages written to the system's pagefiles.

PagefilePageWriteIos
> The number of write operations performed on the system's pagefiles.

MappedFilePagesWritten
> The number of pages written to mapped files.

MappedFilePageWriteIos
> The number of write operations performed on mapped files.

PagedPoolUsage
> The number of pages of virtual memory used by the paged pool.

NonPagedPoolUsage
> The number of pages of virtual memory used by the nonpaged pool.

PagedPoolAllocs
> The number of allocations made from the paged pool.

PagedPoolFrees
> The number of allocations returned to the paged pool.

NonPagedPoolAllocs
> The number of allocations made from the nonpaged pool.

NonPagedPoolFrees
The number of allocations returned to the nonpaged pool.

TotalFreeSystemPtes
The number of available System Page Table Entries.

SystemCodePage
The number of pages of pageable operating system code and static data in physical memory. The meaning of "operating system code and static data" is defined by address range (lowest system address to start of system cache) and includes a contribution from win32k.sys.

TotalSystemDriverPages
The number of pages of pageable device driver code and static data.

TotalSystemCodePages
The number of pages of pageable operating system code and static data. The meaning of "operating system code and static data" is defined by load time (`SERVICE_BOOT_START` driver or earlier) and does not include a contribution from win32k.sys.

SmallNonPagedLookasideListAllocateHits
The number of times an allocation could be satisfied by one of the small nonpaged lookaside lists.

SmallPagedLookasideListAllocateHits
The number of times an allocation could be satisfied by one of the small-paged lookaside lists.

MmSystemCachePage
The number of pages of the system cache in physical memory.

PagedPoolPage
The number of pages of paged pool in physical memory.

SystemDriverPage
The number of pages of pageable device driver code and static data in physical memory.

FastReadNoWait
The number of asynchronous fast read operations.

FastReadWait
The number of synchronous fast read operations.

FastReadResourceMiss
The number of fast read operations not possible because of resource conflicts.

FastReadNotPossible
> The number of fast read operations not possible because file system intervention required.

FastMdlReadNoWait
> The number of asynchronous fast read operations requesting a Memory Descriptor List (MDL) for the data.

FastMdlReadWait
> The number of synchronous fast read operations requesting an MDL for the data.

FastMdlReadResourceMiss
> The number of synchronous fast read operations requesting an MDL for the data not possible because of resource conflicts.

FastMdlReadNotPossible
> The number of synchronous fast read operations requesting an MDL for the data not possible because file system intervention required.

MapDataNoWait
> The number of asynchronous data map operations.

MapDataWait
> The number of synchronous data map operations.

MapDataNoWaitMiss
> The number of asynchronous data map operations that incurred page faults.

MapDataWaitMiss
> The number of synchronous data map operations that incurred page faults.

PinMappedDataCount
> The number of requests to pin mapped data.

PinReadNoWait
> The number of asynchronous requests to pin mapped data.

PinReadWait
> The number of synchronous requests to pin mapped data.

PinReadNoWaitMiss
> The number of asynchronous requests to pin mapped data that incurred page faults when pinning the data.

PinReadWaitMiss
> The number of synchronous requests to pin mapped data that incurred page faults when pinning the data.

CopyReadNoWait
> The number of asynchronous copy read operations.

CopyReadWait
> The number of synchronous copy read operations.

CopyReadNoWaitMiss
> The number of asynchronous copy read operations that incurred page faults when reading from the cache.

CopyReadWaitMiss
> The number of synchronous copy read operations that incurred page faults when reading from the cache.

MdlReadNoWait
> The number of synchronous read operations requesting an MDL for the cached data.

MdlReadWait
> The number of synchronous read operations requesting an MDL for the cached data.

MdlReadNoWaitMiss
> The number of synchronous read operations requesting an MDL for the cached data that incurred page faults.

MdlReadWaitMiss
> The number of synchronous read operations requesting an MDL for the cached data that incurred page faults.

ReadAheadIos
> The number of read ahead operations performed in anticipation of sequential access.

LazyWriteIos
> The number of write operations initiated by the Lazy Writer.

LazyWritePages
> The number of pages written by the Lazy Writer.

DataFlushes
> The number of cache flushes in response to flush requests.

DataPages
> The number of cache pages flushed in response to flush requests.

ContextSwitches
> The number of context switches.

FirstLevelTbFills
> The number of first level translation buffer fills.

SecondLevelTbFills
The number of second level translation buffer fills.

SystemCalls
The number of system calls executed.

Remarks

Slightly longer descriptions of many of the members of this structure can be found in the Win32 documentation for the NT Performance Counters.

SystemTimeOfDayInformation

```
typedef struct _SYSTEM_TIME_OF_DAY_INFORMATION { // Information Class 3
    LARGE_INTEGER BootTime;
    LARGE_INTEGER CurrentTime;
    LARGE_INTEGER TimeZoneBias;
    ULONG CurrentTimeZoneId;
} SYSTEM_TIME_OF_DAY_INFORMATION, *PSYSTEM_TIME_OF_DAY_INFORMATION;
```

Members

BootTime
The time when the system was booted in the standard time format (that is, the number of 100-nanosecond intervals since January 1, 1601).

CurrentTime
The current time of day in the standard time format.

TimeZoneBias
The difference, in 100-nanosecond units, between Coordinated Universal Time (UTC) and local time.

CurrentTimeZoneId
A numeric identifier for the current time zone.

Remarks

None.

SystemProcessesAndThreadsInformation

```
typedef struct _SYSTEM_PROCESSES { // Information Class 5
    ULONG NextEntryDelta;
    ULONG ThreadCount;
    ULONG Reserved1[6];
    LARGE_INTEGER CreateTime;
    LARGE_INTEGER UserTime;
    LARGE_INTEGER KernelTime;
    UNICODE_STRING ProcessName;
    KPRIORITY BasePriority;
    ULONG ProcessId;
```

```
        ULONG InheritedFromProcessId;
        ULONG HandleCount;
        ULONG Reserved2[2];
        VM_COUNTERS VmCounters;
        IO_COUNTERS IoCounters;   // Windows 2000 only
        SYSTEM_THREADS Threads[1];
    } SYSTEM_PROCESSES, *PSYSTEM_PROCESSES;

    typedef struct _SYSTEM_THREADS {
        LARGE_INTEGER KernelTime;
        LARGE_INTEGER UserTime;
        LARGE_INTEGER CreateTime;
        ULONG WaitTime;
        PVOID StartAddress;
        CLIENT_ID ClientId;
        KPRIORITY Priority;
        KPRIORITY BasePriority;
        ULONG ContextSwitchCount;
        THREAD_STATE State;
        KWAIT_REASON WaitReason;
    } SYSTEM_THREADS, *PSYSTEM_THREADS;
```

Members

NextEntryDelta
> The offset, from the start of this structure, to the next entry. A `NextEntryDelta` of zero indicates that this is the last structure in the returned data.

ThreadCount
> The number of threads in the process.

CreateTime
> The creation time of the process in the standard time format (that is, the number of 100-nanosecond intervals since January 1, 1601).

UserTime
> The sum of the time spent executing in user mode by the threads of the process, measured in units of 100-nanoseconds.

KernelTime
> The sum of the time spent executing in kernel mode by the threads of the process, measured in units of 100-nanoseconds.

ProcessName
> The name of the process, normally derived from the name of the executable file used to create the process.

BasePriority
> The default base priority for the threads of the process.

ProcessId
> The process identifier of the process.

InheritedFromProcessId

The process identifier of the process from which handles and/or address space was inherited.

HandleCount

The number of handles opened by the process.

VmCounters

Statistics on the virtual memory usage of the process. VM_COUNTERS is defined thus in ntddk.h:

```
typedef struct _VM_COUNTERS {
    ULONG PeakVirtualSize;
    ULONG VirtualSize;
    ULONG PageFaultCount;
    ULONG PeakWorkingSetSize;
    ULONG WorkingSetSize;
    ULONG QuotaPeakPagedPoolUsage;
    ULONG QuotaPagedPoolUsage;
    ULONG QuotaPeakNonPagedPoolUsage;
    ULONG QuotaNonPagedPoolUsage;
    ULONG PagefileUsage;
    ULONG PeakPagefileUsage;
} VM_COUNTERS, *PVM_COUNTERS;
```

IoCounters

Statistics on the I/O operations of the process. This information is only present in Windows 2000. IO_COUNTERS is defined thus:

```
typedef struct _IO_COUNTERS {
    LARGE_INTEGER ReadOperationCount;
    LARGE_INTEGER WriteOperationCount;
    LARGE_INTEGER OtherOperationCount;
    LARGE_INTEGER ReadTransferCount;
    LARGE_INTEGER WriteTransferCount;
    LARGE_INTEGER OtherTransferCount;
} IO_COUNTERS, *PIO_COUNTERS;
```

Threads

An array of SYSTEM_THREADS structures describing the threads of the process. The number of elements in the array is available in the ThreadCount member.

The members of SYSTEM_THREADS follow.

KernelTime

The time spent executing in kernel mode, measured in units of 100-nanoseconds.

UserTime

The time spent executing in user mode, measured in units of 100-nanoseconds.

CreateTime

The creation time of the thread in the standard time format (that is, the number of 100-nanosecond intervals since January 1, 1601).

WaitTime

The time at which the thread last entered a wait state, measured in clock ticks since system boot.

StartAddress

The start address of the thread.

ClientId

The client identifier of the thread, comprising a process identifier and a thread identifier.

Priority

The priority of the thread.

BasePriority

The base priority of the thread.

ContextSwitchCount

The number of context switches incurred by the thread.

State

The execution state of the thread. Permitted values are drawn from the enumeration THREAD_STATE.

```
typedef enum {
    StateInitialized,
    StateReady,
    StateRunning,
    StateStandby,
    StateTerminated,
    StateWait,
    StateTransition,
    StateUnknown
} THREAD_STATE;
```

WaitReason

An indication of the reason for a wait. Some possible values are defined in the enumeration KWAIT_REASON, but other values may also be used.

```
typedef enum _KWAIT_REASON {
    Executive,
    FreePage,
    PageIn,
    PoolAllocation,
    DelayExecution,
    Suspended,
    UserRequest,
    WrExecutive,
    WrFreePage,
    WrPageIn,
    WrPoolAllocation,
    WrDelayExecution,
    WrSuspended,
    WrUserRequest,
    WrEventPair,
```

```
        WrQueue,
        WrLpcReceive,
        WrLpcReply,
        WrVirtualMemory,
        WrPageOut,
        WrRendezvous,
        Spare2,
        Spare3,
        Spare4,
        Spare5,
        Spare6,
        WrKernel
    } KWAIT_REASON;
```

Remarks

The format of the data returned to the SystemInformation buffer is a sequence of SYSTEM_PROCESSES structures, chained together via the NextEntryDelta member. The Threads member of each SYSTEM_PROCESSES structure is an array of ThreadCount SYSTEM_THREADS structures. The end of the process chain is marked by a NextEntryDelta value of zero.

The Process Status API (PSAPI) function EnumProcesses uses this information class to obtain a list of the process identifier in the system.

A demonstration of the use of this information class to implement a subset of the Tool Help Library appears in Example 1.1.

The addition of the IoCounters member to SYSTEM_PROCESSES structure in Windows 2000 has the consequence that Windows NT 4.0 applications that access the Threads member fail when run under Windows 2000; for example, the pstat.exe resource kit utility suffers from this problem.

SystemCallCounts

```
typedef struct _SYSTEM_CALLS_INFORMATION { // Information Class 6
    ULONG Size;
    ULONG NumberOfDescriptorTables;
    ULONG NumberOfRoutinesInTable[1];
    // ULONG CallCounts[];
} SYSTEM_CALLS_INFORMATION, *PSYSTEM_CALLS_INFORMATION;
```

Members

Size

The size in bytes of the returned information.

NumberOfDescriptorTables

The number of system service dispatch descriptor tables for which information is available.

NumberOfRoutinesInTable

An array of the count of routines in each table.

Remarks

Information on the number of calls to each system service is only gathered if the "checked" version of the kernel is used and memory is allocated by the creator of the table to hold the counts.

The counts of calls to each system service follow the array `NumberOfRoutinesInTable`.

SystemConfigurationInformation

```
typedef struct _SYSTEM_CONFIGURATION_INFORMATION { // Information Class 7
    ULONG DiskCount;
    ULONG FloppyCount;
    ULONG CdRomCount;
    ULONG TapeCount;
    ULONG SerialCount;
    ULONG ParallelCount;
} SYSTEM_CONFIGURATION_INFORMATION, *PSYSTEM_CONFIGURATION_INFORMATION;
```

Members

DiskCount
The number of hard disk drives in the system.

FloppyCount
The number of floppy disk drives in the system.

CdRomCount
The number of CD-ROM drives in the system.

TapeCount
The number of tape drives in the system.

SerialCount
The number of serial ports in the system.

ParallelCount
The number of parallel ports in the system.

Remarks

This information is a subset of the information available to device drivers by calling `IoGetConfigurationInformation`.

SystemProcessorTimes

```
typedef struct _SYSTEM_PROCESSOR_TIMES { // Information Class 8
    LARGE_INTEGER IdleTime;
    LARGE_INTEGER KernelTime;
    LARGE_INTEGER UserTime;
    LARGE_INTEGER DpcTime;
```

```
    LARGE_INTEGER InterruptTime;
    ULONG InterruptCount;
} SYSTEM_PROCESSOR_TIMES, *PSYSTEM_PROCESSOR_TIMES;
```

Members

IdleTime

The idle time, measured in units of 100-nanoseconds, of the processor.

KernelTime

The time the processor spent executing in kernel mode, measured in units of 100-nanoseconds.

UserTime

The time the processor spent executing in user mode, measured in units of 100-nanoseconds.

DpcTime

The time the processor spent executing deferred procedure calls, measured in units of 100-nanoseconds.

InterruptTime

The time the processor spent executing interrupt routines, measured in units of 100-nanoseconds.

InterruptCount

The number of interrupts serviced by the processor.

Remarks

An array of structures is returned, one per processor.

SystemGlobalFlag

```
typedef struct _SYSTEM_GLOBAL_FLAG { // Information Class 9
    ULONG GlobalFlag;
} SYSTEM_GLOBAL_FLAG, *PSYSTEM_GLOBAL_FLAG;
```

Members

GlobalFlag

A bit array of flags that control various aspects of the behavior of the kernel.

Remarks

This information class can be both queried and set. SeDebugPrivilege is required to set the flags. Some flags are used only at boot time and subsequent changes have no effect. Some flags have an effect only when using a "checked" kernel.

The flags recognized by the "gflags" resource kit utility are:

```
FLG_STOP_ON_EXCEPTION           0x00000001
FLG_SHOW_LDR_SNAPS              0x00000002
FLG_DEBUG_INITIAL_COMMAND       0x00000004
FLG_STOP_ON_HUNG_GUI            0x00000008
FLG_HEAP_ENABLE_TAIL_CHECK      0x00000010
FLG_HEAP_ENABLE_FREE_CHECK      0x00000020
FLG_HEAP_VALIDATE_PARAMETERS    0x00000040
FLG_HEAP_VALIDATE_ALL           0x00000080
FLG_POOL_ENABLE_TAIL_CHECK      0x00000100
FLG_POOL_ENABLE_FREE_CHECK      0x00000200
FLG_POOL_ENABLE_TAGGING         0x00000400
FLG_HEAP_ENABLE_TAGGING         0x00000800
FLG_USER_STACK_TRACE_DB         0x00001000
FLG_KERNEL_STACK_TRACE_DB       0x00002000
FLG_MAINTAIN_OBJECT_TYPELIST    0x00004000
FLG_HEAP_ENABLE_TAG_BY_DLL      0x00008000
FLG_IGNORE_DEBUG_PRIV           0x00010000
FLG_ENABLE_CSRDEBUG             0x00020000
FLG_ENABLE_KDEBUG_SYMBOL_LOAD   0x00040000
FLG_DISABLE_PAGE_KERNEL_STACKS  0x00080000
FLG_HEAP_ENABLE_CALL_TRACING    0x00100000
FLG_HEAP_DISABLE_COALESCING     0x00200000
FLG_ENABLE_CLOSE_EXCEPTIONS     0x00400000
FLG_ENABLE_EXCEPTION_LOGGING    0x00800000
FLG_ENABLE_DBGPRINT_BUFFERING   0x08000000
```

SystemModuleInformation

```
typedef struct _SYSTEM_MODULE_INFORMATION { // Information Class 11
    ULONG Reserved[2];
    PVOID Base;
    ULONG Size;
    ULONG Flags;
    USHORT Index;
    USHORT Unknown;
    USHORT LoadCount;
    USHORT ModuleNameOffset;
    CHAR ImageName[256];
} SYSTEM_MODULE_INFORMATION, *PSYSTEM_MODULE_INFORMATION;
```

Members

Base

The base address of the module.

Size

The size of the module.

Flags

A bit array of flags describing the state of the module.

Index

The index of the module in the array of modules.

Unknown
   Normally contains zero; interpretation unknown.

LoadCount
   The number of references to the module.

ModuleNameOffset
   The offset to the final filename component of the image name.

ImageName
   The filepath of the module.

Remarks

The data returned to the SystemInformation buffer is a ULONG count of the number of modules followed immediately by an array of SYSTEM_MODULE_INFORMATION.

The system modules are the Portable Executable (PE) format files loaded into the kernel address space (ntoskrnl.exe, hal.dll, device drivers, and so on) and ntdll.dll.

The PSAPI function EnumDeviceDrivers uses this information class to obtain a list of the device drivers in the system. It is also used by the PSAPI functions GetDeviceDriverFileName and GetDeviceDriverBaseName.

The code in Example 1.3 uses this information class.

SystemLockInformation

```
typedef struct _SYSTEM_LOCK_INFORMATION { // Information Class 12
    PVOID Address;
    USHORT Type;
    USHORT Reserved1;
    ULONG ExclusiveOwnerThreadId;
    ULONG ActiveCount;
    ULONG ContentionCount;
    ULONG Reserved2[2];
    ULONG NumberOfSharedWaiters;
    ULONG NumberOfExclusiveWaiters;
} SYSTEM_LOCK_INFORMATION, *PSYSTEM_LOCK_INFORMATION;
```

Members

Address
   The address of the ERESOURCE structure.

Type
   The type of the lock. This is always RTL_RESOURCE_TYPE (1).

ExclusiveOwnerThreadId
   The thread identifier of the owner of the resource if the resource is owned exclusively, otherwise zero.

ActiveCount
The number of threads granted access to the resource.

ContentionCount
The number of times a thread had to wait for the resource.

NumberOfSharedWaiters
The number of threads waiting for shared access to the resource.

NumberOfExclusiveWaiters
The number of threads waiting for exclusive access to the resource.

Remarks

The data returned to the SystemInformation buffer is a ULONG count of the number of locks followed immediately by an array of SYSTEM_LOCK_INFORMATION.

The locks reported on by this information class are only available to kernel mode code. The locks support multiple reader single writer functionality and are known as "resources." They are initialized by the routine ExInitializeResourceLite and are documented in the DDK.

SystemHandleInformation

```
typedef struct _SYSTEM_HANDLE_INFORMATION { // Information Class 16
    ULONG ProcessId;
    UCHAR ObjectTypeNumber;
    UCHAR Flags;  // 0x01 = PROTECT_FROM_CLOSE, 0x02 = INHERIT
    USHORT Handle;
    PVOID Object;
    ACCESS_MASK GrantedAccess;
} SYSTEM_HANDLE_INFORMATION, *PSYSTEM_HANDLE_INFORMATION;
```

Members

ProcessId
The process identifier of the owner of the handle.

ObjectTypeNumber
A number which identifies the type of object to which the handle refers. The number can be translated to a name by using the information returned by **ZwQueryObject**.

Flags
A bit array of flags that specify properties of the handle.

Handle
The numeric value of the handle.

Object
The address of the kernel object to which the handle refers.

GrantedAccess

The access to the object granted when the handle was created.

Remarks

The data returned to the SystemInformation buffer is a ULONG count of the number of handles followed immediately by an array of SYSTEM_HANDLE_INFORMATION.

Examples of the use of this information class to implement utilities that list the open handles of processes appear in Example 1.2 and Example 2.1 in Chapter 2, "Objects, Object Directories, and Symbolic Links."

SystemObjectInformation

```
typedef struct _SYSTEM_OBJECT_TYPE_INFORMATION { // Information Class 17
    ULONG NextEntryOffset;
    ULONG ObjectCount;
    ULONG HandleCount;
    ULONG TypeNumber;
    ULONG InvalidAttributes;
    GENERIC_MAPPING GenericMapping;
    ACCESS_MASK ValidAccessMask;
    POOL_TYPE PoolType;
    UCHAR Unknown;
    UNICODE_STRING Name;
} SYSTEM_OBJECT_TYPE_INFORMATION, *PSYSTEM_OBJECT_TYPE_INFORMATION;

typedef struct _SYSTEM_OBJECT_INFORMATION {
    ULONG NextEntryOffset;
    PVOID Object;
    ULONG CreatorProcessId;
    USHORT Unknown;
    USHORT Flags;
    ULONG PointerCount;
    ULONG HandleCount;
    ULONG PagedPoolUsage;
    ULONG NonPagedPoolUsage;
    ULONG ExclusiveProcessId;
    PSECURITY_DESCRIPTOR SecurityDescriptor;
    UNICODE_STRING Name;
} SYSTEM_OBJECT_INFORMATION, *PSYSTEM_OBJECT_INFORMATION;
```

Members

NextEntryOffset

The offset from the start of the SystemInformation buffer to the next entry.

ObjectCount

The number of objects of this type in the system.

HandleCount

The number of handles to objects of this type in the system.

TypeNumber

A number that identifies this object type.

InvalidAttributes

A bit mask of the OBJ_Xxx attributes that are not valid for objects of this type. The defined attributes are

```
OBJ_INHERIT
OBJ_PERMANENT
OBJ_EXCLUSIVE
OBJ_CASE_INSENSITIVE
OBJ_OPENIF
OBJ_OPENLINK
OBJ_KERNEL_HANDLE          // Windows 2000 only
```

GenericMapping

The mapping of generic access rights to specific access rights for this object type.

ValidAccessMask

The valid specific access rights for this object type.

PoolType

The type of pool from which this object type is allocated (paged or nonpaged).

Unknown

Interpretation unknown.

Name

A name that identifies this object type.

The members of SYSTEM_OBJECT_INFORMATION follow.

NextEntryOffset

The offset from the start of the SystemInformation buffer to the next entry.

Object

The address of the object.

CreatorProcessId

The process identifier of the creator of the object.

Unknown

Normally contains zero; interpretation unknown.

Flags

A bit array of flags that specify properties of the object. Observed values include:

```
SINGLE_HANDLE_ENTRY        0x40
DEFAULT_SECURITY_QUOTA     0x20
PERMANENT                  0x10
EXCLUSIVE                  0x08
CREATOR_INFO               0x04
KERNEL_MODE                0x02
```

PointerCount

The number of pointer references to the object.

HandleCount
The number of handle references to the object.

PagedPoolUsage
The amount of paged pool used by the object.

NonPagedPoolUsage
The amount of nonpaged pool used by the object.

ExclusiveProcessId
The process identifier of the owner of the object if it was created for exclusive use (by specifying `OBJ_EXCLUSIVE`).

SecurityDescriptor
The security descriptor for the object.

Name
The name of the object.

Remarks

This information class is only available if `FLG_MAINTAIN_OBJECT_TYPELIST` was set in `NtGlobalFlags` at boot time.

The format of the data returned to the `SystemInformation` buffer is a sequence of `SYSTEM_OBJECT_TYPE_INFORMATION` structures, chained together via the `NextEntryOffset` member. Immediately following the name of the object type is a sequence of `SYSTEM_OBJECT_INFORMATION` structures, which are chained together via the `NextEntryOffset` member. The ends of both the object type chain and the object chain are marked by a `NextEntryOffset` value of zero.

The use of this information class to implement a utility that lists the open handles of processes appears in Example 1.2.

SystemPagefileInformation

```
typedef struct _SYSTEM_PAGEFILE_INFORMATION { // Information Class 18
    ULONG NextEntryOffset;
    ULONG CurrentSize;
    ULONG TotalUsed;
    ULONG PeakUsed;
    UNICODE_STRING FileName;
} SYSTEM_PAGEFILE_INFORMATION, *PSYSTEM_PAGEFILE_INFORMATION;
```

Members

NextEntryOffset
The offset from the start of the `SystemInformation` buffer to the next entry.

CurrentSize
The current size in pages of the page file.

TotalUsed

The number of pages in the page file that are in use.

PeakUsed

The peak number of pages in the page file that have been in use.

FileName

The filepath of the page file.

Remarks

None.

SystemInstructionEmulationCounts

```
typedef struct _SYSTEM_INSTRUCTION_EMULATION_INFORMATION { // Info Class 19
    ULONG SegmentNotPresent;
    ULONG TwoByteOpcode;
    ULONG ESprefix;
    ULONG CSprefix;
    ULONG SSprefix;
    ULONG DSprefix;
    ULONG FSPrefix;
    ULONG GSprefix;
    ULONG OPER32prefix;
    ULONG ADDR32prefix;
    ULONG INSB;
    ULONG INSW;
    ULONG OUTSB;
    ULONG OUTSW;
    ULONG PUSHFD;
    ULONG POPFD;
    ULONG INTnn;
    ULONG INTO;
    ULONG IRETD;
    ULONG INBimm;
    ULONG INWimm;
    ULONG OUTBimm;
    ULONG OUTWimm;
    ULONG INB;
    ULONG INW;
    ULONG OUTB;
    ULONG OUTW;
    ULONG LOCKprefix;
    ULONG REPNEprefix;
    ULONG REPprefix;
    ULONG HLT;
    ULONG CLI;
    ULONG STI;
    ULONG GenericInvalidOpcode;
} SYSTEM_INSTRUCTION_EMULATION_INFORMATION,
*PSYSTEM_INSTRUCTION_EMULATION_INFORMATION;
```

Remarks

The members of this structure are the number of times that particular instructions had to be emulated for virtual DOS machines. The prefix opcodes do not themselves require emulation, but they may prefix an opcode that does require emulation.

SystemCacheInformation

```
typedef struct _SYSTEM_CACHE_INFORMATION { // Information Class 21
    ULONG SystemCacheWsSize;
    ULONG SystemCacheWsPeakSize;
    ULONG SystemCacheWsFaults;
    ULONG SystemCacheWsMinimum;
    ULONG SystemCacheWsMaximum;
    ULONG TransitionSharedPages;
    ULONG TransitionSharedPagesPeak;
    ULONG Reserved[2];
} SYSTEM_CACHE_INFORMATION, *PSYSTEM_CACHE_INFORMATION;
```

Members

SystemCacheWsSize
   The size in bytes of the system working set.

SystemCacheWsPeakSize
   The peak size in bytes of the system working set.

SystemCacheWsFaults
   The number of page faults incurred by the system working set.

SystemCacheWsMinimum
   The minimum desirable size in pages of the system working set.

SystemCacheWsMaximum
   The maximum desirable size in pages of the system working set.

TransitionSharedPages
   The sum of the number of pages in the system working set and the number of shared pages on the Standby list. This value is only valid in Windows 2000.

TransitionSharedPagesPeak
   The peak of the sum of the number of pages in the system working set and the number of shared pages on the Standby list. This value is only valid in Windows 2000.

Remarks

This information class can be both queried and set. When setting, only the `SystemCacheWsMinimum` and `SystemCacheWsMaximum` values are used.

SystemPoolTagInformation

```
typedef struct _SYSTEM_POOL_TAG_INFORMATION { // Information Class 22
    CHAR Tag[4];
    ULONG PagedPoolAllocs;
    ULONG PagedPoolFrees;
    ULONG PagedPoolUsage;
    ULONG NonPagedPoolAllocs;
```

```
        ULONG NonPagedPoolFrees;
        ULONG NonPagedPoolUsage;
    } SYSTEM_POOL_TAG_INFORMATION, *PSYSTEM_POOL_TAG_INFORMATION;
```

Members

Tag
> The four character tag string identifying the contents of the pool allocation.

PagedPoolAllocs
> The number of times a block was allocated from paged pool with this tag.

PagedPoolFrees
> The number of times a block was deallocated to paged pool with this tag.

PagedPoolUsage
> The number of bytes of paged pool used by blocks with this tag.

NonPagedPoolAllocs
> The number of times a block was allocated from nonpaged pool with this tag.

NonPagedPoolFrees
> The number of times a block was deallocated to nonpaged pool with this tag.

NonPagedPoolUsage
> The number of bytes of nonpaged pool used by blocks with this tag.

Remarks

This information class is only available if FLG_POOL_ENABLE_TAGGING was set in NtGlobalFlags at boot time.

The data returned to the SystemInformation buffer is a ULONG count of the number of tags followed immediately by an array of SYSTEM_POOL_TAG_INFORMATION.

The data returned by this information class is displayed by the "poolmon" utility.

SystemProcessorStatistics

```
typedef struct _SYSTEM_PROCESSOR_STATISTICS { // Information Class 23
    ULONG ContextSwitches;
    ULONG DpcCount;
    ULONG DpcRequestRate;
    ULONG TimeIncrement;
    ULONG DpcBypassCount;
    ULONG ApcBypassCount;
} SYSTEM_PROCESSOR_STATISTICS, *PSYSTEM_PROCESSOR_STATISTICS;
```

Members

ContextSwitches
> The number of context switches performed by the processor.

DpcCount

The number of deferred procedure calls (DPC) that have been added to the processor's DPC queue.

DpcRequestRate

The number of DPCs that have been added to the processor's DPC queue since the last clock tick.

TimeIncrement

The number of 100-nanosecond units between ticks of the system clock.

DpcBypassCount

The number of DPC interrupts that have been avoided.

ApcBypassCount

The number of kernel APC interrupts that have been avoided.

Remarks

An array of structures is returned, one per processor.

The ReturnLength information is not set correctly (always contains zero).

SystemDpcInformation

```
typedef struct _SYSTEM_DPC_INFORMATION { // Information Class 24
    ULONG Reserved;
    ULONG MaximumDpcQueueDepth;
    ULONG MinimumDpcRate;
    ULONG AdjustDpcThreshold;
    ULONG IdealDpcRate;
} SYSTEM_DPC_INFORMATION, *PSYSTEM_DPC_INFORMATION;
```

Members

MaximumDpcQueueDepth

The maximum depth that the DPC queue should attain. If this depth is exceeded and no DPCs are active, a DPC interrupt is requested.

MinimumDpcRate

The minimum rate at which DPCs should be requested. If the current request rate is lower and no DPCs are active, a DPC interrupt is requested.

AdjustDpcThreshold

A parameter that affects the interval between retuning of the DPC parameters.

IdealDpcRate

The ideal rate at which DPCs should be requested. If the current rate is higher, measures are taken to tune the DPC parameters (for example, by adjusting the maximum DPC queue depth).

Remarks

This information class can be both queried and set. `SeLoadDriverPrivilege` is required to set the values.

These parameters only affect `MediumInportance` and `HighImportance` DPCs.

The `ReturnLength` information is not set correctly (always contains zero).

SystemLoadImage

```
typedef struct _SYSTEM_LOAD_IMAGE { // Information Class 26
    UNICODE_STRING ModuleName;
    PVOID ModuleBase;
    PVOID Unknown;
    PVOID EntryPoint;
    PVOID ExportDirectory;
} SYSTEM_LOAD_IMAGE, *PSYSTEM_LOAD_IMAGE;
```

Members

ModuleName
The full path in the native NT format of the module to load. Required on input.

ModuleBase
The base address of the module. Valid on output.

Unknown
Pointer to a data structure describing the loaded module. Valid on output.

EntryPoint
The address of the entry point of the module. Valid on output.

ExportDirectory
The address of the export directory of the module. Valid on output.

Remarks

This information class can only be set. Rather than setting any information (in a narrow sense of "setting"), it performs the operation of loading a module into the kernel address space and returns information on the loaded module.

After loading the module, `MmPageEntireDriver` (documented in the DDK) is called to make the entire module pageable. The module entry point is not called.

This information class is valid only when `ZwSetSystemInformation` is invoked from kernel mode.

SystemUnloadImage

```
typedef struct _SYSTEM_UNLOAD_IMAGE { // Information Class 27
    PVOID ModuleBase;
} SYSTEM_UNLOAD_IMAGE, *PSYSTEM_UNLOAD_IMAGE;
```

Members

ModuleBase
　　The base of a module.

Remarks

　　This information class can only be set. Rather than setting any information (in a narrow sense of "setting"), it performs the operation of unloading a module from the kernel address space.

　　Even if the module is a device driver, the `DriverUnload` routine is not called.

　　This information class is only valid when `ZwSetSystemInformation` is invoked from kernel mode.

SystemTimeAdjustment

```
typedef struct _SYSTEM_QUERY_TIME_ADJUSTMENT { // Information Class 28
    ULONG TimeAdjustment;
    ULONG MaximumIncrement;
    BOOLEAN TimeSynchronization;
} SYSTEM_QUERY_TIME_ADJUSTMENT, *PSYSTEM_QUERY_TIME_ADJUSTMENT;

typedef struct _SYSTEM_SET_TIME_ADJUSTMENT { // Information Class 28
    ULONG TimeAdjustment;
    BOOLEAN TimeSynchronization;
} SYSTEM_SET_TIME_ADJUSTMENT, *PSYSTEM_SET_TIME_ADJUSTMENT;
```

Members

TimeAdjustment
　　The number of 100-nanosecond units added to the time-of-day clock at each clock tick if time adjustment is enabled.

MaximumIncrement
　　The maximum number of 100-nanosecond units between clock ticks. Also the number of 100-nanosecond units per clock tick for kernel intervals measured in clock ticks.

TimeSynchronization
　　A boolean specifying that time adjustment is enabled when true.

Remarks

　　This information class can be both queried and set. `SeSystemtimePrivilege` is required to set the values. The structures for querying and setting values are different.

　　The `ReturnLength` information is not set correctly (always contains zero).

SystemCrashDumpInformation

```
typedef struct _SYSTEM_CRASH_DUMP_INFORMATION { // Information Class 32
    HANDLE CrashDumpSectionHandle;
    HANDLE Unknown;  // Windows 2000 only
} SYSTEM_CRASH_DUMP_INFORMATION, *PSYSTEM_CRASH_DUMP_INFORMATION;
```

Members

CrashDumpSectionHandle
A handle to the crash dump section.

Unknown
A handle to an unknown object. This information is only present in Windows 2000.

Remarks

If a crash dump section exists, a new handle to the section is created for the current process and returned in CrashDumpSectionHandle; otherwise, CrashDumpSectionHandle contains zero.

In Windows 2000, SeCreatePagefilePrivilege is required to query the values.

SystemExceptionInformation

```
typedef struct _SYSTEM_EXCEPTION_INFORMATION { // Information Class 33
    ULONG AlignmentFixupCount;
    ULONG ExceptionDispatchCount;
    ULONG FloatingEmulationCount;
    ULONG Reserved;
} SYSTEM_EXCEPTION_INFORMATION, *PSYSTEM_EXCEPTION_INFORMATION;
```

Members

AlignmentFixupCount
The numbers of times data alignment had to be fixed up since the system booted.

ExceptionDispatchCount
The number of exceptions dispatched since the system booted.

FloatingEmulationCount
The number of times floating point instructions had to be emulated since the system booted.

Remarks

None.

SystemCrashDumpStateInformation

```
typedef struct _SYSTEM_CRASH_DUMP_STATE_INFORMATION { // Information Class 34
    ULONG CrashDumpSectionExists;
    ULONG Unknown;   // Windows 2000 only
} SYSTEM_CRASH_DUMP_STATE_INFORMATION, *PSYSTEM_CRASH_DUMP_STATE_INFORMATION;
```

Members

CrashDumpSectionExists

A boolean indicating whether a crash dump section exists.

Unknown

Interpretation unknown. This information is only present in Windows 2000.

Remarks

In Windows 2000, this information class can also be set if `SeCreatePagefilePrivilege` is enabled.

SystemKernelDebuggerInformation

```
typedef struct _SYSTEM_KERNEL_DEBUGGER_INFORMATION { // Information Class 35
    BOOLEAN DebuggerEnabled;
    BOOLEAN DebuggerNotPresent;
} SYSTEM_KERNEL_DEBUGGER_INFORMATION, *PSYSTEM_KERNEL_DEBUGGER_INFORMATION;
```

Members

DebuggerEnabled

A boolean indicating whether kernel debugging has been enabled or not.

DebuggerNotPresent

A boolean indicating whether contact with a remote debugger has been established or not.

Remarks

None.

SystemContextSwitchInformation

```
typedef struct _SYSTEM_CONTEXT_SWITCH_INFORMATION { // Information Class 36
    ULONG ContextSwitches;
    ULONG ContextSwitchCounters[11];
} SYSTEM_CONTEXT_SWITCH_INFORMATION, *PSYSTEM_CONTEXT_SWITCH_INFORMATION;
```

Members

ContextSwitches

The number of context switches.

ContextSwitchCounters
Normally contains zeroes; interpretation unknown.

Remarks

The resource kit utility "`kernprof`" claims to display the context switch counters (if the "-x" option is specified), but it only expects nine `ContextSwitchCounters` rather than eleven. It displays the information thus:

```
Context Switch Information
    Find any processor            0
    Find last processor           0
    Idle any processor            0
    Idle current processor        0
    Idle last processor           0
    Preempt any processor         0
    Preempt current processor     0
    Preempt last processor        0
    Switch to idle                0
```

SystemRegistryQuotaInformation

```
typedef struct _SYSTEM_REGISTRY_QUOTA_INFORMATION { // Information Class 37
    ULONG RegistryQuota;
    ULONG RegistryQuotaInUse;
    ULONG PagedPoolSize;
} SYSTEM_REGISTRY_QUOTA_INFORMATION, *PSYSTEM_REGISTRY_QUOTA_INFORMATION;
```

Members

RegistryQuota
The number of bytes of paged pool that the registry may use.

RegistryQuotaInUse
The number of bytes of paged pool that the registry is using.

PagedPoolSize
The size in bytes of the paged pool.

Remarks

This information class can be both queried and set. `SeIncreaseQuotaPrivilege` is required to set the values. When setting, only the `RegistryQuota` value is used.

SystemLoadAndCallImage

```
typedef struct _SYSTEM_LOAD_AND_CALL_IMAGE { // Information Class 38
    UNICODE_STRING ModuleName;
} SYSTEM_LOAD_AND_CALL_IMAGE, *PSYSTEM_LOAD_AND_CALL_IMAGE;
```

Members

ModuleName
The full path in the native NT format of the module to load.

Remarks

This information class can only be set. Rather than setting any information (in a narrow sense of "setting"), it performs the operation of loading a module into the kernel address space and calling its entry point.

The entry point routine is expected to be a __stdcall routine taking two parameters (consistent with the DriverEntry routine of device drivers); the call arguments are two zeroes.

If the entry point routine returns a failure code, the module is unloaded.

Unlike ZwLoadDriver, which loads the module in the context of the system process, ZwSetSystemInformation loads the module and invokes the entry point in the context of the current process.

SystemPrioritySeparation

```
typedef struct _SYSTEM_PRIORITY_SEPARATION { // Information Class 39
    ULONG PrioritySeparation;
} SYSTEM_PRIORITY_SEPARATION, *PSYSTEM_PRIORITY_SEPARATION;
```

Members

PrioritySeparation
A value that affects the scheduling quantum period of the foreground application. In Windows NT 4.0, PrioritySeparation takes a value between zero and two (the higher the value, the longer the quantum period). In Windows 2000, the low order six bits of PrioritySeparation are used to configure the scheduling quantum.

Remarks

None.

SystemTimeZoneInformation

```
typedef struct _SYSTEM_TIME_ZONE_INFORMATION { // Information Class 44
    LONG Bias;
    WCHAR StandardName[32];
    SYSTEMTIME StandardDate;
    LONG StandardBias;
    WCHAR DaylightName[32];
    SYSTEMTIME DaylightDate;
    LONG DaylightBias;
} SYSTEM_TIME_ZONE_INFORMATION, *PSYSTEM_TIME_ZONE_INFORMATION;
```

Members

Bias
The difference, in minutes, between Coordinated Universal Time (UTC) and local time.

StandardName
> The name of the timezone when daylight saving time is not in effect.

StandardDate
> A SYSTEMTIME structure specifying when daylight saving time ends.

StandardBias
> The difference, in minutes, between UTC and local time when daylight saving time is not in effect.

DaylightName
> The name of the timezone when daylight saving time is in effect.

DaylightDate
> A SYSTEMTIME structure specifying when daylight saving time starts.

DaylightBias
> The difference, in minutes, between UTC and local time when daylight saving time is in effect.

Remarks

This structure is identical to the TIME_ZONE_INFORMATION structure returned by the Win32 function GetTimeZoneInformation.

SystemLookasideInformation

```
typedef struct _SYSTEM_LOOKASIDE_INFORMATION { // Information Class 45
    USHORT Depth;
    USHORT MaximumDepth;
    ULONG TotalAllocates;
    ULONG AllocateMisses;
    ULONG TotalFrees;
    ULONG FreeMisses;
    POOL_TYPE Type;
    ULONG Tag;
    ULONG Size;
} SYSTEM_LOOKASIDE_INFORMATION, *PSYSTEM_LOOKASIDE_INFORMATION;
```

Members

Depth
> The current depth of the lookaside list.

MaximumDepth
> The maximum depth of the lookaside list.

TotalAllocates
> The total number of allocations made from the list.

AllocateMisses
> The number of times the lookaside list was empty and a normal allocation was needed.

TotalFrees
> The total number of allocations made from the list.

FreeMisses
> The number of times the lookaside list was full and a normal deallocation was needed.

Type
> The type of pool from which the memory for the lookaside list is allocated. Possible values are drawn from the enumeration POOL_TYPE:

```
typedef enum _POOL_TYPE {
    NonPagedPool,
    PagedPool,
    NonPagedPoolMustSucceed,
    DontUseThisType,
    NonPagedPoolCacheAligned,
    PagedPoolCacheAligned,
    NonPagedPoolCacheAlignedMustS,
    MaxPoolType
    NonPagedPoolSession = 32,
    PagedPoolSession,
    NonPagedPoolMustSucceedSession,
    DontUseThisTypeSession,
    NonPagedPoolCacheAlignedSession,
    PagedPoolCacheAlignedSession,
    NonPagedPoolCacheAlignedMustSSession
} POOL_TYPE;
```

Tag
> The tag identifying allocations from the lookaside list

Size
> The size of the blocks on the lookaside list.

Remarks

An array of structures are returned, one per lookaside list. The number of structures can be obtained by dividing the ReturnLength by the size of the structure.

The lookaside lists reported on by this information class are only available to kernel mode code. Their purpose is to speed the allocation and deallocation of blocks of memory from paged and nonpaged pool. A nonpaged lookaside list is initialized by the routine ExInitializeNPagedLookasideList.

Lookaside lists are documented in the DDK.

SystemSetTimeSlipEvent

```
typedef struct _SYSTEM_SET_TIME_SLIP_EVENT { // Information Class 46
    HANDLE TimeSlipEvent;
} SYSTEM_SET_TIME_SLIP_EVENT, *PSYSTEM_SET_TIME_SLIP_EVENT;
```

Members

TimeSlipEvent
A handle to an event object. The handle must grant EVENT_MODIFY_STATE access.

Remarks

This information class can only be set. SeSystemtimePrivilege is required to set the value. The TimeSlipEvent will be signaled when the kernel debugger has caused time to slip by blocking the system clock interrupt.

SystemCreateSession

```
typedef struct _SYSTEM_CREATE_SESSION { // Information Class 47
    ULONG SessionId;
} SYSTEM_CREATE_SESSION, *PSYSTEM_CREATE_SESSION;
```

Members

SessionId
An identifier for the session. Valid on output.

Remarks

This information class can only be set. It creates a Windows Terminal Server session and assigns the session an identifier. This information class is valid only when Windows Terminal Server is running. In all other cases, the return status is STATUS_INVALID_SYSTEM_SERVICE.

SystemDeleteSession

```
typedef struct _SYSTEM_DELETE_SESSION { // Information Class 48
    ULONG SessionId;
} SYSTEM_DELETE_SESSION, *PSYSTEM_DELETE_SESSION;
```

Members

SessionId
An identifier for the session

Remarks

This information class can only be set. This information class is valid only when Windows Terminal Server is running. In all other cases the return status is STATUS_INVALID_SYSTEM_SERVICE.

SystemRangeStartInformation

```
typedef struct _SYSTEM_RANGE_START_INFORMATION { // Information Class 50
    PVOID SystemRangeStart;
} SYSTEM_RANGE_START_INFORMATION, *PSYSTEM_RANGE_START_INFORMATION;
```

Members

SystemRangeStart

The base address of the system (kernel) portion of the virtual address space.

Remarks

None.

SystemVerifierInformation

Format unknown.

Remarks

This information class can be both queried and set. `SeDebugPrivilege` is required to set the values.

This information class queries and sets information maintained by the device driver verifier. The "Driver Verifier" is described in the DDK documentation.

SystemAddVerifier

Format unknown.

Remarks

This information class is only valid when `ZwSetSystemInformation` is invoked from kernel mode.

This information class configures the device driver verifier. The "Driver Verifier" is described in the DDK documentation.

SystemSessionProcessesInformation

```
typedef struct _SYSTEM_SESSION_PROCESSES_INFORMATION { // Information Class 53
    ULONG SessionId;
    ULONG BufferSize;
    PVOID Buffer;
} SYSTEM_SESSION_PROCESSES_INFORMATION, *PSYSTEM_SESSION_PROCESSES_INFORMATION;
```

Members

SessionId
The SessionId for which to retrieve a list of processes and threads.

BufferSize
The size in bytes of the buffer in which to return the list of processes and threads.

Buffer
Points to a caller-allocated buffer or variable that receives the list of processes and threads.

Remarks

Unlike other information classes, this information class uses the `SystemInformation` argument of `ZwQuerySystemInformation` as an input buffer.

The information returned is in the same format as that returned by `SystemProcessesAndThreadsInformation`, but contains information only on the processes in the specified session.

The following information classes are only available in "checked" versions of the kernel.

SystemPoolBlocksInformation

```
typedef struct _SYSTEM_POOL_BLOCKS_INFORMATION { // Info Classes 14 and 15
    ULONG PoolSize;
    PVOID PoolBase;
    USHORT Unknown;
    ULONG NumberOfBlocks;
    SYSTEM_POOL_BLOCK PoolBlocks[1];
} SYSTEM_POOL_BLOCKS_INFORMATION, *PSYSTEM_POOL_BLOCKS_INFORMATION;

typedef struct _SYSTEM_POOL_BLOCK {
    BOOLEAN Allocated;
    USHORT Unknown;
    ULONG Size;
    CHAR Tag[4];
} SYSTEM_POOL_BLOCK, *PSYSTEM_POOL_BLOCK;
```

Members

PoolSize
The size in bytes of the pool.

PoolBase
The base address of the pool.

Unknown
The alignment of the pool; interpretation uncertain.

NumberOfBlocks
   The number of blocks in the pool.

PoolBlocks
   An array of SYSTEM_POOL_BLOCK structures describing the blocks in the pool. The number of elements in the array is available in the NumberOfBlocks member.

   The members of SYSTEM_POOL_BLOCK follow.

Allocated
   A boolean indicating whether this is an allocated or free block.

Unknown
   Interpretation unknown.

Size
   The size in bytes of the block.

Tag
   The four character tag string identifying the contents of the pool allocation.

Remarks

Information class 14 returns data on the paged pool and information class 15 returns data on the nonpaged pool.

The paged and nonpaged pools reported on by these information classes are only available to kernel mode code. Blocks are allocated from paged and nonpaged pool by the routines ExAllocatePoolXxx. The use of pool memory is documented in the DDK.

SystemMemoryUsageInformation

```
typedef struct _SYSTEM_MEMORY_USAGE_INFORMATION { // Info Classes 25 and 29
    ULONG Reserved;
    PVOID EndOfData;
    SYSTEM_MEMORY_USAGE MemoryUsage[1];
} SYSTEM_MEMORY_USAGE_INFORMATION, *PSYSTEM_MEMORY_USAGE_INFORMATION;

typedef struct _SYSTEM_MEMORY_USAGE {
    PVOID Name;
    USHORT Valid;
    USHORT Standby;
    USHORT Modified;
    USHORT PageTables;
} SYSTEM_MEMORY_USAGE, *PSYSTEM_MEMORY_USAGE;
```

Members

EndOfData
A pointer to the end of the valid data in the `SystemInformation` buffer.

MemoryUsage
An array of `SYSTEM_MEMORY_USAGE` structures describing the usage of physical memory. The number of elements in the array is deducible from the `EndOfData` member.

The members of `SYSTEM_MEMORY_USAGE` follow.

Name
The name of the object using the memory. This can be either a Unicode or ANSI string.

Valid
The number of valid pages used by the object. If the object is a process, this is the number of valid private pages.

Standby
The number of pages recently used by the object that are now on the Standby list.

Modified
The number of pages recently used by the object, which are now on the Modified list.

PageTables
The number of pagetable pages used by the object. The only objects that use pagetables are processes. On an Intel platform using large (4-MByte) pages, the pagetables are charged against nonpaged pool rather than processes.

Remarks

Information class 29 does not provide the information on the pages in the Standby and Modified lists.

There is no indication of whether the name is a Unicode or ANSI string other than the string data itself (for example, if every second byte is zero, the string must be Unicode).

Information class 25 is able to account for the use of almost all the physical memory in the system. The difference between sum of the `Valid`, `Standby` and `Modified` pages and the `NumberOfPhysicalPages` (returned by the `SystemBasicInformation` class) is normally close to the number of pages on the Free and Zeroed memory lists.

Example 1.1: A Partial ToolHelp Library Implementation

```
#include "ntdll.h"
#include <tlhelp32.h>
#include <stdio.h>

struct ENTRIES {
    ULONG Offset;
```

```
    ULONG Count;
    ULONG Index;
    ENTRIES() : Offset(0), Count(0), Index(0) {}
    ENTRIES(ULONG m, ULONG n) : Offset(m), Count(n), Index(0) {}
};

enum EntryType {
    ProcessType,
    ThreadType,
    MaxType
};


NT::PSYSTEM_PROCESSES GetProcessesAndThreads()
{
    ULONG n = 0x100;
    NT::PSYSTEM_PROCESSES sp = new NT::SYSTEM_PROCESSES[n];

    while (NT::ZwQuerySystemInformation(
                            NT::SystemProcessesAndThreadsInformation,
                            sp, n * sizeof *sp, 0)
            == STATUS_INFO_LENGTH_MISMATCH)
        delete [] sp, sp = new NT::SYSTEM_PROCESSES[n = n * 2];

    return sp;
}

ULONG ProcessCount(NT::PSYSTEM_PROCESSES sp)
{
    ULONG n = 0;

    bool done = false;

    for (NT::PSYSTEM_PROCESSES p = sp; !done;
        p = NT::PSYSTEM_PROCESSES(PCHAR(p) + p->NextEntryDelta))
        n++, done = p->NextEntryDelta == 0;

    return n;
}

ULONG ThreadCount(NT::PSYSTEM_PROCESSES sp)
{
    ULONG n = 0;

    bool done = false;

    for (NT::PSYSTEM_PROCESSES p = sp; !done;
        p = NT::PSYSTEM_PROCESSES(PCHAR(p) + p->NextEntryDelta))
        n += p->ThreadCount, done = p->NextEntryDelta == 0;

    return n;
}

VOID AddProcesses(PPROCESSENTRY32 pe, NT::PSYSTEM_PROCESSES sp)
{
    bool done = false;

    for (NT::PSYSTEM_PROCESSES p = sp; !done;
        p = NT::PSYSTEM_PROCESSES(PCHAR(p) + p->NextEntryDelta)) {

        pe->dwSize = sizeof *pe;
        pe->cntUsage = 0;
        pe->th32ProcessID = p->ProcessId;
```

```cpp
            pe->th32DefaultHeapID = 0;
            pe->th32ModuleID = 0;
            pe->cntThreads = p->ThreadCount;
            pe->th32ParentProcessID = p->InheritedFromProcessId;
            pe->pcPriClassBase = p->BasePriority;
            pe->dwFlags = 0;
            sprintf(pe->szExeFile, "%.*ls",
                    p->ProcessName.Length / 2, p->ProcessName.Buffer);

            pe++;

            done = p->NextEntryDelta == 0;
        }
    }

    VOID AddThreads(PTHREADENTRY32 te, NT::PSYSTEM_PROCESSES sp)
    {
        bool done = false;

        for (NT::PSYSTEM_PROCESSES p = sp; !done;
             p = NT::PSYSTEM_PROCESSES(PCHAR(p) + p->NextEntryDelta)) {

            for (ULONG i = 0; i < p->ThreadCount; i++) {

                te->dwSize = sizeof *te;
                te->cntUsage = 0;
                te->th32ThreadID = DWORD(p->Threads[i].ClientId.UniqueThread);
                te->th32OwnerProcessID = p->ProcessId;
                te->tpBasePri = p->Threads[i].BasePriority;
                te->tpDeltaPri = p->Threads[i].Priority
                                 - p->Threads[i].BasePriority;
                te->dwFlags = 0;

                te++;
            }

            done = p->NextEntryDelta == 0;
        }
    }

    template<class T>
    BOOL GetEntry(HANDLE hSnapshot, T entry, bool first, EntryType type)
    {
        ENTRIES *entries = (ENTRIES*)MapViewOfFile(hSnapshot, FILE_MAP_WRITE,
                                                   0, 0, 0);
        if (entries == 0) return FALSE;

        BOOL rv = TRUE;

        entries[type].Index = first ? 0 : entries[type].Index + 1;

        if (entries[type].Index >= entries[type].Count)
            SetLastError(ERROR_NO_MORE_FILES), rv = FALSE;

        if (entry->dwSize < sizeof *entry)
            SetLastError(ERROR_INSUFFICIENT_BUFFER), rv = FALSE;

        if (rv)
            *entry = T(PCHAR(entries)+entries[type].Offset)[entries[type].Index];

        UnmapViewOfFile(entries);

        return rv;
    }
```

```
HANDLE
WINAPI
CreateToolhelp32Snapshot(DWORD flags, DWORD)
{
    NT::PSYSTEM_PROCESSES sp =
        (flags & (TH32CS_SNAPPROCESS | TH32CS_SNAPTHREAD))
            ? GetProcessesAndThreads() : 0;

    ENTRIES entries[MaxType];
    ULONG n = sizeof entries;

    if (flags & TH32CS_SNAPPROCESS) {
        entries[ProcessType] = ENTRIES(n, ProcessCount(sp));
        n += entries[ProcessType].Count * sizeof (PROCESSENTRY32);
    }
    if (flags & TH32CS_SNAPTHREAD) {
        entries[ThreadType] = ENTRIES(n, ThreadCount(sp));
        n += entries[ThreadType].Count * sizeof (THREADENTRY32);
    }

    SECURITY_ATTRIBUTES sa = {sizeof sa, 0, (flags & TH32CS_INHERIT) != 0};

    HANDLE hMap = CreateFileMapping(HANDLE(0xFFFFFFFF), &sa,
                                    PAGE_READWRITE | SEC_COMMIT, 0, n, 0);

    ENTRIES *p = (ENTRIES*)MapViewOfFile(hMap, FILE_MAP_WRITE, 0, 0, 0);

    for (int i = 0; i < MaxType; i++) p[i] = entries[i];

    if (flags & TH32CS_SNAPPROCESS)
        AddProcesses(PPROCESSENTRY32(PCHAR(p) + entries[ProcessType].Offset),
                     sp);
    if (flags & TH32CS_SNAPTHREAD)
        AddThreads(PTHREADENTRY32(PCHAR(p) + entries[ThreadType].Offset),
                   sp);

    UnmapViewOfFile(p);

    if (sp) delete [] sp;

    return hMap;
}

BOOL
WINAPI
Thread32First(HANDLE hSnapshot, PTHREADENTRY32 te)
{
    return GetEntry(hSnapshot, te, true, ThreadType);
}

BOOL
WINAPI
Thread32Next(HANDLE hSnapshot, PTHREADENTRY32 te)
{
    return GetEntry(hSnapshot, te, false, ThreadType);
}

BOOL
WINAPI
Process32First(HANDLE hSnapshot, PPROCESSENTRY32 pe)
{
    return GetEntry(hSnapshot, pe, true, ProcessType);
}
```

```
BOOL
WINAPI
Process32Next(HANDLE hSnapshot, PPROCESSENTRY32 pe)
{
    return GetEntry(hSnapshot, pe, false, ProcessType);
}
```

ZwQuerySystemInformation with an information class of
SystemProcessesAndThreadsInformation returns a superset of the information
concerning processes and threads that is available via the ToolHelp library (if it were
implemented in Windows NT 4.0). Example 1.1 uses this information class to implement a subset of the ToolHelp library; the remaining functions of the ToolHelp library
are addressed in later chapters.

The Win32 function CreateToolhelp32Snapshot returns a handle to a snapshot of the
processes and threads (and modules and heaps) in the system. The Win32 documentation states that this handle (and the snapshot itself) is freed by calling CloseHandle.
ZwQuerySystemInformation also returns a "snapshot," but this snapshot is just data in a
caller-supplied buffer. To implement the documented behavior of
CreateToolhelp32Snapshot, it is necessary to encapsulate the information returned by
ZwQuerySystemInformation in a kernel object so that CloseHandle can free it.

The only suitable kernel object is a section object (known as a file mapping object by
Win32). The idea is to create a paging-file backed section object and then map a view
of this section into the address space so that the information returned from
ZwQuerySystemInformation can be copied to it. The view is then unmapped so that
closing the section handle will free the snapshot (mapped views prevent the section
object from being deleted).

The routines that return information from the snapshot must then just map the section, copy the relevant data to the caller-supplied buffer, and unmap the section.

Example 1.2: Listing Open Handles of a Process

```
#include "ntdll.h"
#include <stdlib.h>
#include <stdio.h>
#include <vector>
#include <map>

#pragma warning(disable:4786) // identifier was truncated in the debug info

struct OBJECTS_AND_TYPES {
    std::map<ULONG, NT::PSYSTEM_OBJECT_TYPE_INFORMATION, std::less<ULONG> >
        types;
    std::map<PVOID, NT::PSYSTEM_OBJECT_INFORMATION, std::less<PVOID> >
        objects;
};

std::vector<NT::SYSTEM_HANDLE_INFORMATION> GetHandles()
{
    ULONG n;
    PULONG p = new ULONG[n = 0x100];

    while (NT::ZwQuerySystemInformation(NT::SystemHandleInformation,
                                        p, n * sizeof *p, 0)
```

```
                == STATUS_INFO_LENGTH_MISMATCH)

        delete [] p, p = new ULONG[n *= 2];

    NT::PSYSTEM_HANDLE_INFORMATION h = NT::PSYSTEM_HANDLE_INFORMATION(p + 1);

    return std::vector<NT::SYSTEM_HANDLE_INFORMATION>(h, h + *p);
}

OBJECTS_AND_TYPES GetObjectsAndTypes()
{
    ULONG n;
    PCHAR p = new CHAR[n = 0x1000];

    while (NT::ZwQuerySystemInformation(NT::SystemObjectInformation,
                                        p, n * sizeof *p, 0)
            == STATUS_INFO_LENGTH_MISMATCH)

        delete [] p, p = new CHAR[n *= 2];

    OBJECTS_AND_TYPES oats;

    for (NT::PSYSTEM_OBJECT_TYPE_INFORMATION
         t = NT::PSYSTEM_OBJECT_TYPE_INFORMATION(p); ;
         t = NT::PSYSTEM_OBJECT_TYPE_INFORMATION(p + t->NextEntryOffset)) {

        oats.types[t->TypeNumber] = t;

        for (NT::PSYSTEM_OBJECT_INFORMATION
             o = NT::PSYSTEM_OBJECT_INFORMATION(PCHAR(t->Name.Buffer)
                                        + t->Name.MaximumLength); ;
             o = NT::PSYSTEM_OBJECT_INFORMATION(p + o->NextEntryOffset)) {

            oats.objects[o->Object] = o;

            if (o->NextEntryOffset == 0) break;
        }
        if (t->NextEntryOffset == 0) break;
    }

    return oats;
}

int main(int argc, char *argv[])
{
    if (argc == 1) return 0;

    ULONG pid = strtoul(argv[1], 0, 0);

    OBJECTS_AND_TYPES oats = GetObjectsAndTypes();

    std::vector<NT::SYSTEM_HANDLE_INFORMATION> handles = GetHandles();

    NT::SYSTEM_OBJECT_INFORMATION defobj = {0};

    printf("Object   Hnd  Access Fl Atr  #H   #P Type         Name\n");

    for (std::vector<NT::SYSTEM_HANDLE_INFORMATION>::iterator
         h = handles.begin(); h != handles.end(); h++) {

        if (h->ProcessId == pid) {

            NT::PSYSTEM_OBJECT_TYPE_INFORMATION
```

```
                t = oats.types[h->ObjectTypeNumber];
        NT::PSYSTEM_OBJECT_INFORMATION
                o = oats.objects[h->Object];

        if (o == 0) o = &defobj;

        printf("%p %04hx %6lx %2x %3hx %3ld %4ld %-14.*S %.*S\n",
                h->Object, h->Handle, h->GrantedAccess, int(h->Flags),
                o->Flags, o->HandleCount, o->PointerCount,
                t->Name.Length, t->Name.Buffer,
                o->Name.Length, o->Name.Buffer);
        }
    }
    return 0;
}
```

Example 1.2 assumes that the `NtGlobalFlag` `FLG_MAINTAIN_OBJECT_TYPELIST` was set at boot time. An alternative method of obtaining a list of open handles using a combination of `ZwQuerySystemInformation` and `ZwQueryObject` appears in Chapter 2, "Objects, Object Directories, and Symbolic Links," in Example 2.1.

The program uses the address of the kernel object to which a handle refers to correlate the information returned by the information classes `SystemHandleInformation` and `SystemObjectInformation`; a Standard Template Library (STL) map is used for this purpose.

The list of handles in the system is scanned for handles owned by a particular process identifier, and then information about the handle and the object to which it refers is displayed.

ZwQuerySystemEnvironmentValue

`ZwQuerySystemEnvironmentValue` queries the value of a system environment variable stored in the non-volatile (CMOS) memory of the system.

```
NTSYSAPI
NTSTATUS
NTAPI
ZwQuerySystemEnvironmentValue(
    IN PUNICODE_STRING Name,
    OUT PVOID Value,
    IN ULONG ValueLength,
    OUT PULONG ReturnLength OPTIONAL
    );
```

Parameters

Name
   The name of system environment value to be queried.

Value
   Points to a caller-allocated buffer or variable that receives the requested system environment value.

ValueLength
   The size in bytes of `Value`.

ReturnLength
Optionally points to a variable that receives the number of bytes actually returned to Value. If ValueLength is too small to contain the available data, the variable is set to the number of bytes required for the available data. If this information is not needed by the caller, ReturnLength may be specified as a null pointer.

Return Value

Returns STATUS_SUCCESS or an error status, such as STATUS_PRIVILEGE_NOT_HELD, STATUS_BUFFER_OVERFLOW, or STATUS_UNSUCCESSFUL.

Related Win32 Functions

None.

Remarks

SeSystemEnvironmentPrivilege is required to query system environment values.

The information returned in Buffer is an array of WCHAR. The ReturnLength value contains the length of the string in bytes.

ZwQuerySystemEnvironmentValue queries environment values stored in CMOS. The standard Hardware Abstraction Layer (HAL) for the Intel platform only supports one environment value, "LastKnownGood," which takes the values "TRUE" and "FALSE." It is queried by writing 0xb to port 0x70 and reading from port 0x71. A value of zero is interpreted as "FALSE," other values as "TRUE."

ZwSetSystemEnvironmentValue

ZwSetSystemEnvironmentValue sets the value of a system environment variable stored in the non-volatile (CMOS) memory of the system.

```
NTSYSAPI
NTSTATUS
NTAPI
ZwSetSystemEnvironmentValue(
    IN PUNICODE_STRING Name,
    IN PUNICODE_STRING Value
    );
```

Parameters

Name
The name of system environment value to be set.

Value
The value to be set.

Return Value

Returns STATUS_SUCCESS or an error status, such as STATUS_PRIVILEGE_NOT_HELD or STATUS_UNSUCCESSFUL.

Related Win32 Functions

None.

Remarks

SeSystemEnvironmentPrivilege is required to set system environment values.

ZwSetSystemEnvironmentValue sets environment values stored in CMOS. The standard HAL for the Intel platform only supports one environment value, "LastKnownGood," which takes the values "TRUE" and "FALSE." It is set by writing 0xb to port 0x70 and writing 0 (for "FALSE") or 1 (for "TRUE") to port 0x71.

ZwShutdownSystem

ZwShutdownSystem shuts down the system.

```
NTSYSAPI
NTSTATUS
NTAPI
ZwShutdownSystem(
    IN SHUTDOWN_ACTION Action
    );
```

Parameters

Action

The action to be performed after shutdown. Permitted values are drawn from the enumeration SHUTDOWN_ACTION.

```
typedef enum _SHUTDOWN_ACTION {
    ShutdownNoReboot,
    ShutdownReboot,
    ShutdownPowerOff
} SHUTDOWN_ACTION;
```

Return Value

Returns STATUS_SUCCESS or an error status, such as STATUS_PRIVILEGE_NOT_HELD.

Related Win32 Functions

ExitWindows(Ex), InitiateSystemShutdown.

Remarks

SeShutdownPrivilege is required to shut down the system.

User-mode applications and services are not informed of the shutdown (drivers of devices that have registered for shutdown notification by calling IoRegisterShutdownNotification are informed).

The system must have hardware support for power-off if the power-off action is to be used successfully.

ZwSystemDebugControl

ZwSystemDebugControl performs a subset of the operations available to a kernel mode debugger.

```
NTSYSAPI
NTSTATUS
NTAPI
ZwSystemDebugControl(
    IN DEBUG_CONTROL_CODE ControlCode,
    IN PVOID InputBuffer OPTIONAL,
    IN ULONG InputBufferLength,
    OUT PVOID OutputBuffer OPTIONAL,
    IN ULONG OutputBufferLength,
    OUT PULONG ReturnLength OPTIONAL
    );
```

Parameters

ControlCode

The control code for operation to be performed. Permitted values are drawn from the enumeration DEBUG_CONTROL_CODE.

```
typedef enum _DEBUG_CONTROL_CODE {
    DebugGetTraceInformation = 1,
    DebugSetInternalBreakpoint,
    DebugSetSpecialCall,
    DebugClearSpecialCalls,
    DebugQuerySpecialCalls,
    DebugDbgBreakPoint
} DEBUG_CONTROL_CODE;
```

InputBuffer

Points to a caller-allocated buffer or variable that contains the data required to perform the operation. This parameter can be null if the ControlCode parameter specifies an operation that does not require input data.

InputBufferLength

The size in bytes of InputBuffer.

OutputBuffer

Points to a caller-allocated buffer or variable that receives the operation's output data. This parameter can be null if the ControlCode parameter specifies an operation that does not produce output data.

OutputBufferLength

The size in bytes of OutputBuffer.

ReturnLength

Optionally points to a variable that receives the number of bytes actually returned to OutputBuffer. If this information is not needed, ReturnLength may be a null pointer.

Return Value

Returns STATUS_SUCCESS or an error status, such as STATUS_PRIVILEGE_NOT_HELD, STATUS_INVALID_INFO_CLASS or STATUS_INFO_LENGTH_MISMATCH.

Related Win32 Functions

None.

Remarks

SeDebugPrivilege is required to use **ZwSystemDebugControl** in Windows 2000.

ZwSystemDebugControl allows a process to perform a subset of the functions available to a kernel mode debugger.

The system should be booted from a configuration that has the boot.ini "/DEBUG" (or equivalent) option enabled; otherwise a kernel debugger variable needed for the correct operation of internal breakpoints is not initialized.

The data structures used by **ZwSystemDebugControl** are defined in windbgkd.h (included with the Platform SDK). An up-to-date copy of this file is needed to compile the code in Examples 1.3 and 1.4. One of the structures used by **ZwSystemDebugControl** includes a union that has grown over time, and **ZwSystemDebugControl** checks that the input/output buffers are large enough to hold the largest member of the union.

DebugGetTraceInformation

```
typedef struct _DBGKD_GET_INTERNAL_BREAKPOINT { // DebugGetTraceInformation
    DWORD_PTR BreakpointAddress;
    DWORD Flags;
    DWORD Calls;
    DWORD MaxCallsPerPeriod;
    DWORD MinInstructions;
    DWORD MaxInstructions;
    DWORD TotalInstructions;
} DBGKD_GET_INTERNAL_BREAKPOINT, *PDBGKD_GET_INTERNAL_BREAKPOINT;

#define DBGKD_INTERNAL_BP_FLAG_COUNTONLY 0x01 // don't count instructions
#define DBGKD_INTERNAL_BP_FLAG_INVALID   0x02 // disabled BP
#define DBGKD_INTERNAL_BP_FLAG_SUSPENDED 0x04 // temporarily suspended
#define DBGKD_INTERNAL_BP_FLAG_DYING     0x08 // kill on exit
```

DebugGetTraceInformation does not require an InputBuffer and returns an array of DBGKD_GET_INTERNAL_BREAKPOINT structures in the output buffer, one for each of the internal breakpoints set.

Instruction counting counts the instructions from the breakpoint until the return from the routine containing the breakpoint. Ideally, the breakpoint should be placed at the beginning of a routine. The user mode debugger (windbg, cdb, ntsd) command "wt" performs user mode instruction counting.

If instruction counting is enabled, MinInstructions contains the minimum number of instructions encountered when executing the routine, MaxInstructions contains the maximum, and TotalInstructions contains the total number of instructions executed by all invocations of the routine (since the breakpoint was inserted).

Calls is the number of times the breakpoint has been encountered.

Flags indicates whether instruction counting is enabled and whether the breakpoint has been suspended.

DebugSetInternalBreakpoint

```
typedef struct _DBGKD_MANIPULATE_STATE {
    DWORD ApiNumber;
    WORD  ProcessorLevel;
    WORD  Processor;
    DWORD ReturnStatus;
    union {
        DBGKD_READ_MEMORY ReadMemory;
        DBGKD_WRITE_MEMORY WriteMemory;
        DBGKD_READ_MEMORY64 ReadMemory64;
        DBGKD_WRITE_MEMORY64 WriteMemory64;
        DBGKD_GET_CONTEXT GetContext;
        DBGKD_SET_CONTEXT SetContext;
        DBGKD_WRITE_BREAKPOINT WriteBreakPoint;
        DBGKD_RESTORE_BREAKPOINT RestoreBreakPoint;
        DBGKD_CONTINUE Continue;
        DBGKD_CONTINUE2 Continue2;
        DBGKD_READ_WRITE_IO ReadWriteIo;
        DBGKD_READ_WRITE_IO_EXTENDED ReadWriteIoExtended;
        DBGKD_QUERY_SPECIAL_CALLS QuerySpecialCalls;
        DBGKD_SET_SPECIAL_CALL SetSpecialCall;
        DBGKD_SET_INTERNAL_BREAKPOINT SetInternalBreakpoint;
        DBGKD_GET_INTERNAL_BREAKPOINT GetInternalBreakpoint;
        DBGKD_GET_VERSION GetVersion;
        DBGKD_BREAKPOINTEX BreakPointEx;
        DBGKD_PAGEIN PageIn;
        DBGKD_READ_WRITE_MSR ReadWriteMsr;
    } u;
} DBGKD_MANIPULATE_STATE, *PDBGKD_MANIPULATE_STATE;

typedef struct _DBGKD_SET_INTERNAL_BREAKPOINT { // DebugSetInternalBreakpoint
    DWORD_PTR BreakpointAddress;
    DWORD Flags;
} DBGKD_SET_INTERNAL_BREAKPOINT, *PDBGKD_SET_INTERNAL_BREAKPOINT;
```

DebugSetInternalBreakpoint does not require an OutputBuffer and expects the InputBuffer to point to a DBGKD_MANIPULATE_STATE structure. The only values in this structure that are required are the two values in the DBGKD_SET_INTERNAL_BREAKPOINT structure. InputBufferLength is the size of the DBGKD_MANIPULATE_STATE structure.

BreakpointAddress is the address of the breakpoint. If a breakpoint already exists at this address, the Flags are used to manipulate the breakpoint, otherwise a new breakpoint is established. Breakpoints are deleted by setting the DBGKD_INTERNAL_BP_FLAG_INVALID flag and are temporarily suspended by setting the DBGKD_INTERNAL_BP_FLAG_SUSPENDED flag. The counting or non-counting nature of the breakpoint can be controlled by setting or clearing the DBGKD_INTERNAL_BP_FLAG_COUNTONLY flag.

Breakpoints can be set at any address, but if the address is not at the start of an instruction then an STATUS_ILLEGAL_INSTRUCTION exception may be raised resulting in a system crash. The intention is that breakpoints should be set at the start of routines but, particularly if instruction counting is disabled, this is not essential.

DebugSetSpecialCall

```
typedef struct _DBGKD_SET_SPECIAL_CALL { // DebugSetSpecialCall
    DWORD SpecialCall;
} DBGKD_SET_SPECIAL_CALL, *PDBGKD_SET_SPECIAL_CALL;
```

`DebugSetSpecialCall` does not require an OutputBuffer and expects the `InputBuffer` to point to a `DBGKD_MANIPULATE_STATE` structure. The only value in this structure that is required is the value in the `DBGKD_SET_SPECIAL_CALL` structure. `InputBufferLength` must be four rather than the size of the `DBGKD_MANIPULATE_STATE` structure—this is a bug.

"Special Calls" are routines that should be treated specially when counting the instructions executed by some routine. The special calls set by the kernel debugger are:

```
HAL!@KfLowerIrql@4
HAL!@KfReleaseSpinLock@8
HAL!@HalRequestSoftwareInterrupt@4
NTOSKRNL!SwapContext
NTOSKRNL!@KiUnlockDispatcherDatabase@4
```

Whether the members of this list are necessary or sufficient to ensure correct operation of the instruction counting feature is difficult to say.

DebugClearSpecialCalls

`DebugClearSpecialCalls` requires neither an `InputBuffer` nor an `OutputBuffer`. It clears the list of special calls.

DebugQuerySpecialCalls

```
typedef struct _DBGKD_QUERY_SPECIAL_CALLS { // DebugQuerySpecialCalls
    DWORD NumberOfSpecialCalls;
    // DWORD SpecialCalls[];
} DBGKD_QUERY_SPECIAL_CALLS, *PDBGKD_QUERY_SPECIAL_CALLS;
```

`DebugQuerySpecialCalls` does not require an `InputBuffer` and expects the `OutputBuffer` to point to a buffer large enough to hold a `DBGKD_MANIPULATE_STATE` structure and an array of `DWORD`s, one per special call. It returns a list of the special calls.

DebugDbgBreakPoint

`DebugDbgBreakPoint` requires neither an `InputBuffer` nor an `OutputBuffer`. If the kernel debugger is enabled it causes a kernel mode debug break point to be executed. This debug control code is only valid in Windows 2000.

The code in Examples 1.3 and 1.4 demonstrates how to set internal breakpoints and get trace information.

Example 1.3: Setting an Internal Breakpoint

```
#include "ntdll.h"
#include "windbgkd.h"
#include <imagehlp.h>
#include <stdlib.h>

void LoadModules()
{
    ULONG n;
    NT::ZwQuerySystemInformation(NT::SystemModuleInformation,
                                 &n, 0, &n);
```

```
    PULONG p = new ULONG[n];
    NT::ZwQuerySystemInformation(NT::SystemModuleInformation,
                                 p, n * sizeof *p, 0);

    NT::PSYSTEM_MODULE_INFORMATION module
        = NT::PSYSTEM_MODULE_INFORMATION(p + 1);

    for (ULONG i = 0; i < *p; i++)
        SymLoadModule(0, 0, module[i].ImageName,
                      module[i].ImageName + module[i].ModuleNameOffset,
                      ULONG(module[i].Base), module[i].Size);

    delete [] p;
}

DWORD GetAddress(PSTR expr)
{
    PCHAR s;
    ULONG n = strtoul(expr, &s, 16);

    if (*s == 0) return n;

    IMAGEHLP_SYMBOL symbol;

    symbol.SizeOfStruct = sizeof symbol;
    symbol.MaxNameLength = sizeof symbol.Name;

    return SymGetSymFromName(0, expr, &symbol) == TRUE ? symbol.Address : 0;
}

void SetSpecialCall(DWORD addr)
{
    DBGKD_MANIPULATE_STATE op = {0};
    op.u.SetSpecialCall.SpecialCall = addr;

    NT::ZwSystemDebugControl(NT::DebugSetSpecialCall, &op, 4, 0, 0, 0);
}

void SetSpecialCalls()
{
    DBGKD_MANIPULATE_STATE op[4];

    NT::ZwSystemDebugControl(NT::DebugQuerySpecialCalls,
                             0, 0, op, sizeof op, 0);

    if (op[0].u.QuerySpecialCalls.NumberOfSpecialCalls == 0) {
        SetSpecialCall(GetAddress("HAL!KfLowerIrql"));
        SetSpecialCall(GetAddress("HAL!KfReleaseSpinLock"));
        SetSpecialCall(GetAddress("HAL!HalRequestSoftwareInterrupt"));
        SetSpecialCall(GetAddress("NTOSKRNL!SwapContext"));
        SetSpecialCall(GetAddress("NTOSKRNL!KiUnlockDispatcherDatabase"));
    }
}

int main(int argc, char *argv[])
{
    if (argc < 2) return 0;

    NT:: SYSTEM_KERNEL_DEBUGGER_INFORMATION kd;

    NT::ZwQuerySystemInformation(NT::SystemKernelDebuggerInformation,
                                 &kd, sizeof kd, 0);
    if (kd.DebuggerEnabled == FALSE) return 0;
```

```
EnablePrivilege(SE_DEBUG_NAME);

SymInitialize(0, 0, FALSE);
SymSetOptions(SymGetOptions() ¦ SYMOPT_DEFERRED_LOADS);

LoadModules();

SetSpecialCalls();

DBGKD_MANIPULATE_STATE op = {0};
op.u.SetInternalBreakpoint.BreakpointAddress = GetAddress(argv[1]);
op.u.SetInternalBreakpoint.Flags = argc < 3 ? 0 : strtoul(argv[2], 0, 16);

NT::ZwSystemDebugControl(NT::DebugSetInternalBreakpoint,
                         &op, sizeof op, 0, 0, 0);

return 0;
}
```

If the kernel debugger is not enabled, an important debugger variable is not initialized. Therefore, Example 1.3 first uses `ZwQuerySystemInformation` to check the debugger status and if it is enabled, the program then sets the special calls and creates or updates a breakpoint.

The program also demonstrates how to obtain a list of the kernel modules and their base addresses. This information is needed by the Imagehlp API routines, which are used to translate symbolic names into addresses.

The program assumes that `SymLoadModule` will find the correct symbol files; if this routine finds the wrong symbol files (for example, symbols for a checked rather than free build), a system crash is almost guaranteed.

Example 1.4: Getting Trace Information

```
#include "ntdll.h"
#include "windbgkd.h"
#include <stdio.h>

int main()
{
    DBGKD_GET_INTERNAL_BREAKPOINT bp[20];
    ULONG n;

    EnablePrivilege(SE_DEBUG_NAME);

    NT::ZwSystemDebugControl(NT::DebugGetTraceInformation,
                             0, 0, bp, sizeof bp, &n);

    for (int i = 0; i * sizeof (DBGKD_GET_INTERNAL_BREAKPOINT) < n; i++)

        printf("%lx %lx %ld %ld %ld %ld %ld\n",
               bp[i].BreakpointAddress, bp[i].Flags,
               bp[i].Calls, bp[i].MaxCallsPerPeriod,
               bp[i].MinInstructions, bp[i].MaxInstructions,
               bp[i].TotalInstructions);

    return 0;
}
```

The output produced by Example 1.4 after an internal breakpoint had been set at
`NTOSKRNL!NtCreateProcess` was:

`80193206 0 6 0 19700 21010 121149`

Therefore, the minimum number of instructions executed by `NtCreateProcess` was
19,700, the maximum number was 21,010, and the average number was about 20,191.

2

Objects, Object Directories, and Symbolic Links

The system services described in this chapter either operate on objects without regard to their type or manage the object namespace.

OBJECT_ATTRIBUTES

Almost all of the **ZwCreateXxx** and **ZwOpenXxx** routines require a pointer to an OBJECT_ATTRIBUTES structure as one of their parameters.

```
typedef struct _OBJECT_ATTRIBUTES {
    ULONG Length;
    HANDLE RootDirectory;
    PUNICODE_STRING ObjectName;
    ULONG Attributes;
    PSECURITY_DESCRIPTOR SecurityDescriptor;
    PSECURITY_QUALITY_OF_SERVICE SecurityQualityOfService;
} OBJECT_ATTRIBUTES, *POBJECT_ATTRIBUTES;
```

Members

Length

The size in bytes of the OBJECT_ATTRIBUTES structure.

RootDirectory

Optionally specifies a handle to a "container" object. The ObjectName will be interpreted as a name relative to this container. Possible "container" object types include Object Directories, File Directories, and Registry Keys.

ObjectName

Optionally specifies a name for the object to be created or opened.

Attributes

A bit mask specifying attributes. This member can be zero, or a combination of the following flags:

```
OBJ_INHERIT              0x00000002
OBJ_PERMANENT            0x00000010
OBJ_EXCLUSIVE            0x00000020
OBJ_CASE_INSENSITIVE     0x00000040
OBJ_OPENIF               0x00000080
OBJ_OPENLINK             0x00000100
OBJ_KERNEL_HANDLE        0x00000200
```

The meanings of the individual flags are discussed in "Remarks." Depending on the type of object to be created or opened, some of the flags are not valid and their presence will result in the routine returning STATUS_INVALID_PARAMETER.

SecurityDescriptor

Optionally specifies a security descriptor to be applied to the object. Only meaningful when creating a new object.

SecurityQualityOfService

Optionally specifies a security Quality of Service (QoS) to be applied to the object. Only meaningful when creating new Token or inter-process communication objects (such as named pipes).

Remarks

The kernel does not maintain information about the current directory of a process. (This information is maintained in user mode by ntdll.dll.). Therefore, when the Win32 function CreateFile is called to open a file with a relative (to the current directory) pathname, the RootDirectory member is used to convey the current directory information to the kernel. The Win32 registry functions always create or open subkeys of existing key objects; when these functions call the appropriate native system service, they store the existing key in the RootDirectory member and the subkey name in the ObjectName member.

The OBJ_INHERIT flag specifies whether the handle can be inherited. Even if the handle can be inherited, whether it is actually inherited depends on the arguments to the **ZwCreateProcess** routine.

If an object has a name and is created with OBJ_PERMANENT, it will continue to exist, even after the last handle reference to it has been closed. SeCreatePermanentPrivilege is needed when specifying OBJ_PERMANENT. To delete a permanent object, it is necessary to first obtain a handle to the object and then to make the object temporary by calling **ZwMakeTemporaryObject**.

Directory and SymbolicLink objects are normally created as permanent objects, but other objects such as Sections and Events can also be made permanent. ("Permanent" means until next reboot.)

The OBJ_EXCLUSIVE flag specifies whether an object is exclusive to one process. If an object is created with this flag, then attempts by other processes to access the object (by opening it by name or duplicating its handle) will fail with STATUS_ACCESS_DENIED.

The OBJ_CASE_INSENSITIVE flag controls how names are compared. If OBJ_CASE_INSENSITIVE is set, subsequent name-lookup requests will ignore the case of **ObjectName** rather than performing an exact-match search.

The OBJ_OPENIF flag specifies how the **ZwCreateXxx** routines should behave if an object with the specified name already exists. If OBJ_OPENIF is set, the routines return the information status STATUS_OBJECT_NAME_EXISTS and also return a handle to the existing object. If OBJ_OPENIF is clear, the routines return the error status STATUS_OBJECT_NAME_COLLISION and do not return a valid handle.

The OBJ_OPENLINK flag specifies whether the object itself or the object to which it is linked should be opened. This flag is normally only used with Registry Keys. For example, "\Registry\Machine\Security\Sam" is a registry link to "\Registry\Machine\Sam," and if it is opened with OBJ_OPENLINK then the returned handle will refer to "\Registry\Machine\Sam." These links are distinct from the Symbolic Link objects created by **ZwCreateSymbolicLinkObject**.

The OBJ_KERNEL_HANDLE flag is only valid in Windows 2000. If a handle to an object is created in kernel mode and OBJ_KERNEL_HANDLE is specified, the handle is created in the "System" process rather than the current process.

ZwQueryObject

ZwQueryObject queries generic information about any object.

```
NTSYSAPI
NTSTATUS
NTAPI
ZwQueryObject(
    IN HANDLE ObjectHandle,
    IN OBJECT_INFORMATION_CLASS ObjectInformationClass,
    OUT PVOID ObjectInformation,
    IN ULONG ObjectInformationLength,
    OUT PULONG ReturnLength OPTIONAL
    );
```

Parameters

ObjectHandle

A handle to an object. The handle need not grant any specific access. If the information class requested does not return information which is specific to a particular object or handle, this parameter may be zero.

ObjectInformationClass

The type of object information to be queried. The permitted values are drawn from the enumeration OBJECT_INFORMATION_CLASS, described in the following section.

ObjectInformation

Points to a caller-allocated buffer or variable that receives the requested object information.

ObjectInformationLength
> Specifies the size in bytes of `ObjectInformation` that the caller should set according to the given `ObjectInformationClass`.

ReturnLength
> Optionally points to a variable that receives the number of bytes actually returned to `ObjectInformation`. If `ObjectInformationLength` is too small to contain the available data, the variable is set to the number of bytes required for the available data. If this information is not needed, `ReturnLength` may be a null pointer.

Return Value

Returns `STATUS_SUCCESS` or an error status, such as `STATUS_INVALID_HANDLE`, `STATUS_INVALID_INFO_CLASS`, or `STATUS_INFO_LENGTH_MISMATCH`.

Related Win32 Functions

`GetHandleInformation`.

Remarks

ZwQueryObject returns generic information about objects. For most object types there is a native API routine that returns object type specific information. For example, **ZwQueryInformationProcess** returns information specific to process objects.

ZwSetInformationObject

ZwSetInformationObject sets attributes on a handle to an object.

```
NTSYSAPI
NTSTATUS
NTAPI
ZwSetInformationObject(
    IN HANDLE ObjectHandle,
    IN OBJECT_INFORMATION_CLASS ObjectInformationClass,
    IN PVOID ObjectInformation,
    IN ULONG ObjectInformationLength
    );
```

Parameters

ObjectHandle
> A handle to an object. The handle need not grant any specific access.

ObjectInformationClass
> The type of object information to be set. The permitted values are a subset of the enumeration `OBJECT_INFORMATION_CLASS`, described in the following section.

ObjectInformation
> Points to a caller-allocated buffer or variable that contains the object information to be set.

ObjectInformationLength
Specifies the size in bytes of ObjectInformation that the caller should set according to the given ObjectInformationClass.

Return Value

Returns STATUS_SUCCESS or an error status, such as STATUS_INVALID_HANDLE, STATUS_INVALID_INFO_CLASS, or STATUS_INFO_LENGTH_MISMATCH.

Related Win32 Functions

SetHandleInformation.

Remarks

The Win32 function SetHandleInformation exposes the full functionality of **ZwSetInformationObject**.

OBJECT_INFORMATION_CLASS

```
                                          Query   Set
typedef enum _OBJECT_INFORMATION_CLASS {
    ObjectBasicInformation,        // 0     Y      N
    ObjectNameInformation,         // 1     Y      N
    ObjectTypeInformation,         // 2     Y      N
    ObjectAllTypesInformation,     // 3     Y      N
    ObjectHandleInformation        // 4     Y      Y
} OBJECT_INFORMATION_CLASS;
```

ObjectBasicInformation

```
typedef struct _OBJECT_BASIC_INFORMATION { // Information Class 0
    ULONG Attributes;
    ACCESS_MASK GrantedAccess;
    ULONG HandleCount;
    ULONG PointerCount;
    ULONG PagedPoolUsage;
    ULONG NonPagedPoolUsage;
    ULONG Reserved[3];
    ULONG NameInformationLength;
    ULONG TypeInformationLength;
    ULONG SecurityDescriptorLength;
    LARGE_INTEGER CreateTime;
} OBJECT_BASIC_INFORMATION, *POBJECT_BASIC_INFORMATION;
```

Members

Attributes
A bit array of flags that specify properties of the object and the handle referring to it that was used in the call to **ZwQueryObject**. Observed values include:

```
        HANDLE_FLAG_INHERIT              0x01
        HANDLE_FLAG_PROTECT_FROM_CLOSE   0x02
        PERMANENT                        0x10
        EXCLUSIVE                        0x20 (different encoding than in
                                              SYSTEM_OBJECT_INFORMATION)
```

GrantedAccess

The access to the object granted when the handle was created.

HandleCount

The number of handle references to the object.

PointerCount

The number of pointer references to the object.

PagedPoolUsage

The amount of paged pool used by the object if different from the default for the object type.

NonPagedPoolUsage

The amount of nonpaged pool used by the object if different from the default for the object type.

NameInformationLength

The size in bytes of the buffer that would be needed to hold the information returned by the `ObjectNameInformation` class for the handle if this information is available. For object types that manage their own namespace, such as Files and Keys, this value is normally zero, meaning just that the value is unknown.

TypeInformationLength

The size in bytes of the buffer that would theoretically be needed to hold the information returned by the `ObjectTypeInformation` class for the handle. In practice, if this length is not a multiple of four, the required length is the lowest multiple of four that is greater than `TypeInformationLength`.

SecurityDescriptorLength

The size in bytes of the buffer that would be needed to hold the information returned by a call to `ZwQuerySecurityObject` for the handle. This information is only available if the `ObjectHandle` parameter grants `READ_CONTROL` access, otherwise zero is returned.

CreateTime

If the object is a Symbolic Link, the creation time of the object in the standard time format (that is, the number of 100-nanosecond intervals since January 1, 1601), otherwise zero.

Remarks

The code in Example 2.1 uses this information class.

ObjectNameInformation

```
typedef struct _OBJECT_NAME_INFORMATION { // Information Class 1
    UNICODE_STRING Name;
} OBJECT_NAME_INFORMATION, *POBJECT_NAME_INFORMATION;
```

Members

Name
  The name of the object.

Remarks

The `ObjectInformation` buffer should be large enough to hold a `UNICODE_STRING` structure and the associated Buffer, which holds the characters of the string.

If the object to which the handle refers is a file object and the handle was opened for synchronous access (by specifying `FILE_SYNCHRONOUS_IO_ALERT` or `FILE_SYNCHRONOUS_IO_NONALERT` as `CreateOptions`), queries of this information class will be synchronized with other file operations on the handle.

The code in Example 2.1 uses this information class.

ObjectTypeInformation

```
typedef struct _OBJECT_TYPE_INFORMATION { // Information Class 2
    UNICODE_STRING Name;
    ULONG ObjectCount;
    ULONG HandleCount;
    ULONG Reserved1[4];
    ULONG PeakObjectCount;
    ULONG PeakHandleCount;
    ULONG Reserved2[4];
    ULONG InvalidAttributes;
    GENERIC_MAPPING GenericMapping;
    ULONG ValidAccess;
    UCHAR Unknown;
    BOOLEAN MaintainHandleDatabase;
    POOL_TYPE PoolType;
    ULONG PagedPoolUsage;
    ULONG NonPagedPoolUsage;
} OBJECT_TYPE_INFORMATION, *POBJECT_TYPE_INFORMATION;
```

Members

Name
  A name that identifies this object type.

ObjectCount
  The number of objects of this type in the system.

HandleCount
  The number of handles to objects of this type in the system.

PeakObjectCount
The peak number of objects of this type in the system.

PeakHandleCount
The peak number of handles to objects of this type in the system.

InvalidAttributes
A bit mask of the OBJ_Xxx attributes that are not valid for objects of this type.

GenericMapping
The mapping of generic access rights to specific access rights for this object type.

ValidAccessMask
The valid specific access rights for this object type.

Unknown
Interpretation unknown. Same as SYSTEM_OBJECT_TYPE_INFORMATION.Unknown.

MaintainHandleDatabase
Specifies whether the handles to objects of this type should be recorded in the objects to which they refer.

PoolType
The type of pool from which this object type is allocated (paged or nonpaged).

PagedPoolUsage
The amount of paged pool used by objects of this type.

NonPagedPoolUsage
The amount of nonpaged pool used by objects of this type.

Remarks

The ObjectInformation buffer should be large enough to hold the Buffer associated with the Name UNICODE_STRING.

This information is similar to that returned by **ZwQuerySystemInformation** with an information class of SystemObjectInformation (17).

The code in Example 2.1 uses this information class.

ObjectAllTypesInformation

```
typedef struct _OBJECT_ALL_TYPES_INFORMATION { // Information Class 3
    ULONG NumberOfTypes;
    OBJECT_TYPE_INFORMATION TypeInformation;
} OBJECT_ALL_TYPES_INFORMATION, *POBJECT_ALL_TYPES_INFORMATION;
```

Members

NumberOfTypes
The number of types known to the object manager.

TypeInformation
A sequence of OBJECT_TYPE_INFORMATION structures, one per type.

Remarks

The ObjectHandle parameter need not contain a valid handle to query this information class.

The Buffer associated with the type name immediately follows each OBJECT_TYPE_INFORMATION structure. The next OBJECT_TYPE_INFORMATION structure follows this Buffer, starting on the first four-byte boundary.

This information is similar to that returned by **ZwQuerySystemInformation** with an information class of SystemObjectInformation (17).

ObjectHandleInformation

```
typedef struct _OBJECT_HANDLE_ATTRIBUTE_INFORMATION { // Information Class 4
    BOOLEAN Inherit;
    BOOLEAN ProtectFromClose;
} OBJECT_HANDLE_ATTRIBUTE_INFORMATION, *POBJECT_HANDLE_ATTRIBUTE_INFORMATION;
```

Members

Inherit
Specifies whether the handle should be inherited by child processes.

ProtectFromClose
Specifies whether the handle should be protected from being closed.

Remarks

This information class can be both queried and set.

The Win32 functions GetHandleInformation and SetHandleInformation query and set this information.

ZwDuplicateObject

ZwDuplicateObject duplicates the handle to an object.

```
NTSYSAPI
NTSTATUS
NTAPI
ZwDuplicateObject(
    IN HANDLE SourceProcessHandle,
    IN HANDLE SourceHandle,
```

```
IN HANDLE TargetProcessHandle,
OUT PHANDLE TargetHandle OPTIONAL,
IN ACCESS_MASK DesiredAccess,
IN ULONG Attributes,
IN ULONG Options
);
```

Parameters

SourceProcessHandle
Identifies the process containing the handle to duplicate. The handle must grant
PROCESS_DUP_HANDLE access.

SourceHandle
Identifies the handle to duplicate. The handle need not grant any specific access.

TargetProcessHandle
Identifies the process that is to receive the duplicated handle. The handle must grant
PROCESS_DUP_HANDLE access.

TargetHandle
Points to a caller-allocated buffer or variable that receives the value of the duplicate
handle. If TargetHandle is a null pointer, the handle is duplicated, but its value is not
returned to the caller.

DesiredAccess
Specifies the access requested for the new handle. This parameter is ignored if the
Options parameter specifies the DUPLICATE_SAME_ACCESS flag.

Attributes
Specifies the set of attributes for the new handle. The valid values include
HANDLE_FLAG_INHERIT and HANDLE_FLAG_PROTECT_FROM_CLOSE. This parameter is
ignored if the Options parameter specifies the DUPLICATE_SAME_ATTRIBUTES flag.

Options
Specifies optional actions. This parameter can be zero, or any combination of the
following flags:

DUPLICATE_CLOSE_SOURCE	Closes the source handle. This occurs regardless of any error status returned.
DUPLICATE_SAME_ACCESS	Ignores the DesiredAccess parameter. The duplicate handle has the same access as the source handle.
DUPLICATE_SAME_ATTRIBUTES	Ignores the Attributes parameter. The duplicate handle has the same attributes as the source handle.

Return Value

Returns STATUS_SUCCESS or an error status, such as STATUS_INVALID_HANDLE,
STATUS_ACCESS_DENIED, or STATUS_PROCESS_IS_TERMINATING.

Related Win32 Functions

DuplicateHandle.

Remarks

The Win32 function DuplicateHandle exposes the full functionality of
ZwDuplicateObject.

ZwMakeTemporaryObject

ZwMakeTemporaryObject removes the permanent attribute of an object if it was
present.

```
NTSYSAPI
NTSTATUS
NTAPI
ZwMakeTemporaryObject(
    IN HANDLE Handle
    );
```

Parameters

Handle
A handle to an object. The handle need not grant any specific access.

Return Value

Returns STATUS_SUCCESS or an error status, such as STATUS_INVALID_HANDLE or
STATUS_ACCESS_DENIED.

Related Win32 Functions

None.

Remarks

ZwMakeTemporaryObject is documented in the DDK.

ZwClose

ZwClose closes a handle to an object.

```
NTSYSAPI
NTSTATUS
NTAPI
ZwClose(
    IN HANDLE Handle
    );
```

Parameters

Handle
A handle to an object. The handle need not grant any specific access.

Return Value

Returns STATUS_SUCCESS or an error status, such as STATUS_INVALID_HANDLE, or STATUS_HANDLE_NOT_CLOSABLE.

Related Win32 Functions

CloseHandle.

Remarks

ZwClose is documented in the DDK.

Example 2.1: Listing Open Handles of a Process

```
#include "ntdll.h"
#include <stdlib.h>
#include <stdio.h>

int main(int argc, char *argv[])
{
    if (argc == 1) return 0;

    ULONG pid = strtoul(argv[1], 0, 0);

    EnablePrivilege(SE_DEBUG_NAME);

    HANDLE hProcess = OpenProcess(PROCESS_DUP_HANDLE, FALSE, pid);

    ULONG n = 0x1000;
    PULONG p = new ULONG[n];

    while (NT::ZwQuerySystemInformation(NT::SystemHandleInformation,
                                       p, n * sizeof *p, 0)
           == STATUS_INFO_LENGTH_MISMATCH)

        delete [] p, p = new ULONG[n *= 2];

    NT::PSYSTEM_HANDLE_INFORMATION h = NT::PSYSTEM_HANDLE_INFORMATION(p + 1);

    for (ULONG i = 0; i < *p; i++) {

        if (h[i].ProcessId == pid) {
            HANDLE hObject;

            if (NT::ZwDuplicateObject(hProcess, HANDLE(h[i].Handle),
                                      NtCurrentProcess(), &hObject,
                                      0, 0, DUPLICATE_SAME_ATTRIBUTES)
                != STATUS_SUCCESS) continue;

            NT::OBJECT_BASIC_INFORMATION obi;
```

```
        NT::ZwQueryObject(hObject, NT::ObjectBasicInformation,
                          &obi, sizeof obi, &n);

        printf("%p %04hx %6lx %2x %3lx %3ld %4ld ",
               h[i].Object, h[i].Handle, h[i].GrantedAccess,
               int(h[i].Flags), obi.Attributes,
               obi.HandleCount - 1, obi.PointerCount - 2);

        n = obi.TypeInformationLength + 2;

        NT::POBJECT_TYPE_INFORMATION oti
            = NT::POBJECT_TYPE_INFORMATION(new CHAR[n]);

        NT::ZwQueryObject(hObject, NT::ObjectTypeInformation,
                          oti, n, &n);

        printf("%-14.*ws ", oti[0].Name.Length / 2, oti[0].Name.Buffer);

        n = obi.NameInformationLength == 0
            ? MAX_PATH * sizeof (WCHAR) : obi.NameInformationLength;

        NT::POBJECT_NAME_INFORMATION oni
            = NT::POBJECT_NAME_INFORMATION(new CHAR[n]);

        NTSTATUS rv = NT::ZwQueryObject(hObject,
                                        NT::ObjectNameInformation,
                                        oni, n, &n);
        if (NT_SUCCESS(rv))
            printf("%.*ws", oni[0].Name.Length / 2, oni[0].Name.Buffer);

        printf("\n");

        CloseHandle(hObject);
    }
  }
  delete [] p;

  CloseHandle(hProcess);

  return 0;
}
```

Unlike Example 1.2, Example 2.1 does not require any particular setting of
NtGlobalFlag. However, it has the drawback of hanging when querying the names
of pipes that have been opened for synchronous access and that have a pending read or
write operation. All services have such a handle (used for communication with the
Service Control Manager).

When displaying the HandleCount and PointerCount values, Example 1.2 subtracts the
contribution to the counts arising from its own references to the object.

ZwQuerySecurityObject

```
ZwQuerySecurityObject retrieves a copy of the security descriptor protecting an
object.
NTSYSAPI
NTSTATUS
NTAPI
ZwQuerySecurityObject(
```

```
IN HANDLE Handle,
IN SECURITY_INFORMATION SecurityInformation,
OUT PSECURITY_DESCRIPTOR SecurityDescriptor,
IN ULONG SecurityDescriptorLength,
OUT PULONG ReturnLength
);
```

Parameters

Handle

A handle to an object. The handle must either grant READ_CONTROL access to the object or the caller must be the owner of the object. To access the system ACL of the object, the handle must grant ACCESS_SYSTEM_SECURITY.

SecurityInformation

A bit mask specifying the type of information being requested. The defined values are:

OWNER_SECURITY_INFORMATION	0x01
GROUP_SECURITY_INFORMATION	0x02
DACL_SECURITY_INFORMATION	0x04
SACL_SECURITY_INFORMATION	0x08

SecurityDescriptor

Points to a caller-allocated buffer or variable that receives the requested security information in the form of a SECURITY_DESCRIPTOR. The SECURITY_DESCRIPTOR structure is returned in self-relative format.

SecurityDescriptorLength

The size in bytes of SecurityDescriptor.

ReturnLength

Points to a variable that receives the number of bytes actually returned to SecurityDescriptor. If SecurityDescriptorLength is too small to contain the available data, the variable is set to the number of bytes required for the available data.

Return Value

Returns STATUS_SUCCESS or an error status, such as STATUS_ACCESS_DENIED or STATUS_BUFFER_TOO_SMALL.

Related Win32 Functions

GetKernelObjectSecurity, GetUserObjectSecurity.

Remarks

GetKernelObjectSecurity and GetUserObjectSecurity both expose the full functionality of **ZwQuerySecurityObject**.

SeSecurityPrivilege is needed to open an object for ACCESS_SYSTEM_SECURITY access. This privilege need not be enabled at the time of calling **ZwQuerySecurityObject**.

ZwSetSecurityObject

ZwSetSecurityObject sets the security descriptor protecting an object.

```
NTSYSAPI
NTSTATUS
NTAPI
ZwSetSecurityObject(
    IN HANDLE Handle,
    IN SECURITY_INFORMATION SecurityInformation,
    IN PSECURITY_DESCRIPTOR SecurityDescriptor
    );
```

Parameters

Handle

A handle to an object. The handle must either grant WRITE_OWNER and/or WRITE_DAC access to the object as appropriate, or the caller must be the owner of the object. To access the system ACL of the object, the handle must grant ACCESS_SYSTEM_SECURITY.

SecurityInformation

A bit mask specifying the type of information being set. The defined values are:

```
OWNER_SECURITY_INFORMATION      0x01
GROUP_SECURITY_INFORMATION      0x02
DACL_SECURITY_INFORMATION       0x04
SACL_SECURITY_INFORMATION       0x08
```

SecurityDescriptor

Points to a SECURITY_DESCRIPTOR structure containing the new security information. The SECURITY_DESCRIPTOR structure must be in self-relative format.

Return Value

Returns STATUS_SUCCESS or an error status, such as STATUS_ACCESS_DENIED.

Related Win32 Functions

SetKernelObjectSecurity, SetUserObjectSecurity.

Remarks

SetKernelObjectSecurity and SetUserObjectSecurity both expose the full functionality of **ZwSetSecurityObject**.

SeSecurityPrivilege is needed to open an object for ACCESS_SYSTEM_SECURITY access. This privilege need not be enabled at the time of calling **ZwSetSecurityObject**.

ZwCreateDirectoryObject

ZwCreateDirectoryObject creates or opens an object directory.

```
NTSYSAPI
NTSTATUS
NTAPI
```

```
ZwCreateDirectoryObject(
    OUT PHANDLE DirectoryHandle,
    IN ACCESS_MASK DesiredAccess,
    IN POBJECT_ATTRIBUTES ObjectAttributes
    );
```

Parameters

DirectoryHandle

Points to a caller-allocated buffer or variable that receives the value of the directory object handle if the call is successful.

DesiredAccess

The type of access that the caller requires to the directory object. This parameter can be zero, or any combination of the following flags:

DIRECTORY_QUERY	Query access
DIRECTORY_TRAVERSE	Name lookup access
DIRECTORY_CREATE_OBJECT	Name creation access
DIRECTORY_CREATE_SUBDIRECTORY	Subdirectory creation access
DIRECTORY_ALL_ACCESS	All of the preceding + STANDARD_RIGHTS_REQUIRED

ObjectAttributes

Points to a structure that specifies the object's attributes, including the name for the new directory object. OBJ_OPENLINK is not a valid attribute for a directory object.

Return Value

Returns STATUS_SUCCESS or an error status, such as STATUS_ACCESS_DENIED, STATUS_OBJECT_NAME_EXISTS, or STATUS_OBJECT_NAME_COLLISION.

Related Win32 Functions

None.

Remarks

ZwCreateDirectoryObject is documented in the DDK.

ZwOpenDirectoryObject

ZwOpenDirectoryObject opens an object directory.

```
NTSYSAPI
NTSTATUS
NTAPI
ZwOpenDirectoryObject(
    OUT PHANDLE DirectoryHandle,
    IN ACCESS_MASK DesiredAccess,
    IN POBJECT_ATTRIBUTES ObjectAttributes
    );
```

Parameters

DirectoryHandle

Points to a caller-allocated buffer or variable that receives the value of the directory object handle if the call is successful.

DesiredAccess

Specifies the type of access that the caller requires to the directory object. This parameter can be zero, or any combination of the following flags:

```
DIRECTORY_QUERY                 Query access
DIRECTORY_TRAVERSE              Name lookup access
DIRECTORY_CREATE_OBJECT        Name creation access
DIRECTORY_CREATE_SUBDIRECTORY  Subdirectory creation access
DIRECTORY_ALL_ACCESS           All of the preceding +
                               STANDARD_RIGHTS_REQUIRED
```

ObjectAttributes

Points to a structure that specifies the object's attributes, including the name of the directory object. OBJ_OPENLINK is not a valid attribute for a directory object.

Return Value

Returns STATUS_SUCCESS or an error status, such as STATUS_ACCESS_DENIED, or STATUS_OBJECT_NAME_NOT_FOUND.

Related Win32 Functions

None.

Remarks

None.

ZwQueryDirectoryObject

ZwQueryDirectoryObject retrieves information about the contents of an object directory.

```
NTSYSAPI
NTSTATUS
NTAPI
ZwQueryDirectoryObject(
    IN HANDLE DirectoryHandle,
    OUT PVOID Buffer,
    IN ULONG BufferLength,
    IN BOOLEAN ReturnSingleEntry,
    IN BOOLEAN RestartScan,
    IN OUT PULONG Context,
    OUT PULONG ReturnLength OPTIONAL
    );
```

Parameters

DirectoryHandle
A handle to a directory object. The handle must grant `DIRECTORY_QUERY` access.

Buffer
Points to a caller-allocated buffer or variable that receives the names of entries in the directory.

BufferLength
Specifies the size in bytes of `Buffer`.

ReturnSingleEntry
Specifies whether a single entry should be returned; if false, as many entries as will fit in the buffer are returned.

RestartScan
Specifies whether the scan of the directory should be restarted; if true, the input value of the `Context` parameter is ignored.

Context
Points to a caller-allocated buffer or variable that maintains the position of a directory scan.

ReturnLength
Optionally points to number of bytes actually returned to Buffer. If this information is not needed, `ReturnLength` may be a null pointer.

Return Value

Returns `STATUS_SUCCESS` or an error status, such as `STATUS_ACCESS_DENIED`, `STATUS_MORE_ENTRIES`, `STATUS_NO_MORE_ENTRIES`, or `STATUS_BUFFER_TOO_SMALL`.

Related Win32 Functions

`QueryDosDevice`.

Remarks

The information returned to `Buffer` is an array of `DIRECTORY_BASIC_INFORMATION` structures, terminated by a `DIRECTORY_BASIC_INFORMATION` structure containing all zeroes. The strings pointed to by the `UNICODE_STRING` members follow this data, and the `Buffer` must be large enough to contain them.

```
typedef struct _DIRECTORY_BASIC_INFORMATION {
    UNICODE_STRING ObjectName;
    UNICODE_STRING ObjectTypeName;
} DIRECTORY_BASIC_INFORMATION, *PDIRECTORY_BASIC_INFORMATION;
```

`QueryDosDevice` can only scan one fixed directory, namely "\??" (ignoring complications arising from multi-user support under Windows Terminal Server). This directory was formerly named "\DosDevices" and is conventionally used to store symbolic links to device objects.

ZwCreateSymbolicLinkObject

ZwCreateSymbolicLinkObject creates or opens a symbolic link object.

```
NTSYSAPI
NTSTATUS
NTAPI
ZwCreateSymbolicLinkObject(
    OUT PHANDLE SymbolicLinkHandle,
    IN ACCESS_MASK DesiredAccess,
    IN POBJECT_ATTRIBUTES ObjectAttributes,
    IN PUNICODE_STRING TargetName
    );
```

Parameters

SymbolicLinkHandle
    Points to a caller-allocated buffer or variable that receives the value of the symbolic
    link object handle if the call is successful.

DesiredAccess
    Specifies the type of access that the caller requires to the symbolic link object. This
    parameter can be zero, or any combination of the following flags:

SYMBOLIC_LINK_QUERY	Query access
SYMBOLIC_LINK_ALL_ACCESS	All of the preceding +
	STANDARD_RIGHTS_REQUIRED

ObjectAttributes
    Points to a structure that specifies the object's attributes, including the name of the
    symbolic link object. **OBJ_OPENLINK** is not a valid attribute for a symbolic link object.

TargetName
    Specifies the name of the object for which the symbolic link will be an alias.

Return Value

Returns STATUS_SUCCESS or an error status, such as STATUS_ACCESS_DENIED,
STATUS_OBJECT_NAME_EXISTS, or STATUS_OBJECT_NAME_COLLISION.

Related Win32 Functions

DefineDosDevice.

Remarks

DefineDosDevice can only create symbolic links in one fixed directory, namely "\??"
(ignoring complications arising from multi-user support under Windows Terminal
Server).

ZwOpenSymbolicLinkObject

ZwOpenSymbolicLinkObject opens a symbolic link object.

```
NTSYSAPI
NTSTATUS
NTAPI
ZwOpenSymbolicLinkObject(
    OUT PHANDLE SymbolicLinkHandle,
    IN ACCESS_MASK DesiredAccess,
    IN POBJECT_ATTRIBUTES ObjectAttributes
    );
```

Parameters

SymbolicLinkHandle

Points to a caller-allocated buffer or variable that receives the value of the symbolic link object handle if the call is successful.

DesiredAccess

Specifies the type of access that the caller requires to the symbolic link object. This parameter can be zero, or any combination of the following flags:

```
        SYMBOLIC_LINK_QUERY          Query access
        SYMBOLIC_LINK_ALL_ACCESS     All of the preceding +
                                     STANDARD_RIGHTS_REQUIRED
```

ObjectAttributes

Points to a structure that specifies the object's attributes, including the name of the symbolic link object. OBJ_OPENLINK is not a valid attribute for a symbolic link object.

Return Value

Returns STATUS_SUCCESS or an error status, such as STATUS_ACCESS_DENIED, or STATUS_OBJECT_NAME_NOT_FOUND.

Related Win32 Functions

None.

Remarks

None.

ZwQuerySymbolicLinkObject

ZwQuerySymbolicLinkObject retrieves the name of the target of a symbolic link.

```
NTSYSAPI
NTSTATUS
NTAPI
ZwQuerySymbolicLinkObject(
    IN HANDLE SymbolicLinkHandle,
    IN OUT PUNICODE_STRING TargetName,
    OUT PULONG ReturnLength OPTIONAL
    );
```

Parameters

SymbolicLinkHandle
> A handle to a symbolic link object. The handle must grant SYMBOLIC_LINK_QUERY access.

TargetName
> Points to a caller-allocated buffer or variable containing an initialised UNICODE_STRING with valid Buffer and MaximumLength members. If the call is successful, the Length member is updated.

ReturnLength
> Optionally points to number of bytes actually returned to TargetName.Buffer. If this information is not needed, ReturnLength may be a null pointer. This length includes the trailing UNICODE null character.

Return Value

Returns STATUS_SUCCESS or an error status, such as STATUS_ACCESS_DENIED or STATUS_BUFFER_TOO_SMALL.

Related Win32 Functions

QueryDosDevice.

Remarks

QueryDosDevice can only query symbolic links in one fixed directory, namely "\??"(ignoring complications arising from multi-user support under Windows Terminal Server).

3
Virtual Memory

The system services described in this chapter manipulate virtual memory.

ZwAllocateVirtualMemory

ZwAllocateVirtualMemory allocates virtual memory in the user mode address range.

```
NTSYSAPI
NTSTATUS
NTAPI
ZwAllocateVirtualMemory(
    IN HANDLE ProcessHandle,
    IN OUT PVOID *BaseAddress,
    IN ULONG ZeroBits,
    IN OUT PULONG AllocationSize,
    IN ULONG AllocationType,
    IN ULONG Protect
    );
```

Parameters

ProcessHandle

A handle of a process object, representing the process for which the virtual memory should be allocated. The handle must grant PROCESS_VM_OPERATION access.

BaseAddress

Points to a variable that will receive the base address of the allocated virtual memory. If the initial value of this variable is not null, the virtual memory is allocated starting at the specified address and rounded down to the nearest allocation granularity boundary if necessary.

ZeroBits

Specifies the number of high-order address bits that must be zero in the base address of the virtual memory. The value of this parameter must be less than 21; it is used only when the operating system determines where to allocate the virtual memory, such as when BaseAddress is null.

AllocationSize

It points to a variable that specifies the size, in bytes, of the virtual memory to allocate, and receives the size of virtual memory actually allocated. If `BaseAddress` is null, this value is rounded up to the next page size boundary; otherwise, it is adjusted to the size of all the pages that contain one or more bytes in the range from `BaseAddress` to (`BaseAddress+AllocationSize`).

AllocationType

A set of flags that describes the type of allocation to be performed for the specified region of pages. The permitted values are selected combinations of the flags:

```
MEM_COMMIT          0x001000 Commit memory
MEM_RESERVE         0x002000 Reserve but do not commit memory
MEM_RESET           0x080000 Mark data in memory as obsolete
MEM_TOP_DOWN        0x100000 Allocate at highest possible address
MEM_WRITE_WATCH     0x200000 Track writes to memory
MEM_PHYSICAL        0x400000 Create a physical view
```

Protect

Specifies the protection for the pages in the region. Permitted values are drawn from the following list, possibly combined with `PAGE_GUARD` or `PAGE_NOCACHE`:

```
PAGE_NOACCESS
PAGE_READONLY
PAGE_READWRITE
PAGE_EXECUTE
PAGE_EXECUTE_READ
PAGE_EXECUTE_READWRITE
```

Return Value

Returns `STATUS_SUCCESS` or an error status, such as `STATUS_NO_MEMORY`, `STATUS_CONFLICTING_ADDRESSES`, `STATUS_ALREADY_COMMITTED`, `STATUS_INVALID_PAGE_PROTECTION`, or `STATUS_PROCESS_IS_TERMINATING`.

Related Win32 Functions

`VirtualAlloc`, `VirtualAllocEx`.

Remarks

`VirtualAllocEx` exposes almost all of the functionality of **ZwAllocateVirtualMemory**.

To commit virtual memory, it must either first be reserved, or both `MEM_COMMIT` and `MEM_RESERVE` must be specified as the `AllocationType` (optionally combined with `MEM_TOP_DOWN`).

The flag `MEM_RESET` is documented in the Knowledge Base article Q162104 and in newer versions of the Platform SDK.

The flag `MEM_WRITE_WATCH` is only valid in Windows 2000. If the system does not support write watching and this flag is specified, **ZwAllocateVirtualMemory** fails with status `STATUS_NOT_SUPPORTED`.

The flag MEM_PHYSICAL is only valid in Windows 2000; it can only and must be combined with the flag MEM_RESERVE. It reserves a range of virtual addresses to be used to map views of physical memory allocated with **ZwAllocateUserPhysicalPages**.

ZwFreeVirtualMemory

ZwFreeVirtualMemory frees virtual memory in the user mode address range.

```
NTSYSAPI
NTSTATUS
NTAPI
ZwFreeVirtualMemory(
    IN HANDLE ProcessHandle,
    IN OUT PVOID *BaseAddress,
    IN OUT PULONG FreeSize,
    IN ULONG FreeType
    );
```

Parameters

ProcessHandle
A handle of a process object, representing the process from which the virtual memory should be freed. The handle must grant PROCESS_VM_OPERATION access.

BaseAddress
Points to a variable that specifies the base address of the virtual memory to be freed.

FreeSize
Points to a variable that specifies the size, in bytes, of the virtual memory to free and receives the size of virtual memory actually freed. If FreeType is MEM_RELEASE, this value must be zero.

FreeType
A set of flags that describes the type of de-allocation to be performed for the specified region of pages. The permitted values are:

MEM_DECOMMIT	Decommit but maintain reservation
MEM_RELEASE	Decommit and free reservation

Return Value

Returns STATUS_SUCCESS or an error status, such as STATUS_UNABLE_TO_FREE_VM, STATUS_UNABLE_TO_DELETE_SECTION, STATUS_FREE_VM_NOT_AT_BASE, STATUS_MEMORY_NOT_ALLOCATED, or STATUS_PROCESS_IS_TERMINATING.

Related Win32 Functions

VirtualFree, VirtualFreeEx.

Remarks

VirtualFreeEx exposes almost all of the functionality of **ZwFreeVirtualMemory**.

ZwQueryVirtualMemory

ZwQueryVirtualMemory retrieves information about virtual memory in the user mode address range.

```
NTSYSAPI
NTSTATUS
NTAPI
ZwQueryVirtualMemory(
    IN HANDLE ProcessHandle,
    IN PVOID BaseAddress,
    IN MEMORY_INFORMATION_CLASS MemoryInformationClass,
    OUT PVOID MemoryInformation,
    IN ULONG MemoryInformationLength,
    OUT PULONG ReturnLength OPTIONAL
    );
```

Parameters

ProcessHandle

A handle of a process object, representing the process whose virtual memory information is queried. The handle must grant PROCESS_QUERY_INFORMATION access.

BaseAddress

The base address of the region of pages to be queried. This value is rounded down to the next page boundary. If the information class requested does not return information that is specific to a particular address, this parameter may be zero.

MemoryInformationClass

The type of virtual memory information to be queried. The permitted values are drawn from the enumeration MEMORY_INFORMATION_CLASS, described in the following section.

MemoryInformation

Points to a caller-allocated buffer or variable that receives the requested virtual memory information.

MemoryInformationLength

Specifies the size in bytes of MemoryInformation, which the caller should set according to the given MemoryInformationClass.

ReturnLength

Optionally points to a variable that receives the number of bytes actually returned to MemoryInformation if the call was successful. If this information is not needed, ReturnLength may be a null pointer.

Return Value

Returns STATUS_SUCCESS or an error status, such as STATUS_INVALID_INFO_CLASS, STATUS_INFO_LENGTH_MISMATCH, STATUS_INVALID_ADDRESS, STATUS_FILE_INVALID, or STATUS_PROCESS_IS_TERMINATING.

Related Win32 Functions

VirtualQuery, VirtualQueryEx.

Remarks

None.

MEMORY_INFORMATION_CLASS

```
typedef enum _MEMORY_INFORMATION_CLASS {
    MemoryBasicInformation,
    MemoryWorkingSetList,
    MemorySectionName,
    MemoryBasicVlmInformation
} MEMORY_INFORMATION_CLASS;
```

MemoryBasicInformation

```
typedef struct _MEMORY_BASIC_INFORMATION { // Information Class 0
    PVOID BaseAddress;
    PVOID AllocationBase;
    ULONG AllocationProtect;
    ULONG RegionSize;
    ULONG State;
    ULONG Protect;
    ULONG Type;
} MEMORY_BASIC_INFORMATION, *PMEMORY_BASIC_INFORMATION;
```

Members

BaseAddress
The virtual base address of the region of pages.

AllocationBase
The virtual base address of the initial allocation region that contains this region.

AllocationProtect
The access protection of the pages specified when the region was initially allocated.
Possible values are drawn from the following list, possibly combined with PAGE_GUARD
or PAGE_NOCACHE:

```
PAGE_NOACCESS
PAGE_READONLY
PAGE_READWRITE
PAGE_EXECUTE
PAGE_EXECUTE_READ
PAGE_EXECUTE_READWRITE
```

RegionSize
The size, in bytes, of the region beginning at the base address in which all pages
belong to the same initial allocation region and have identical protection and state
attributes.

State

The state of the pages in the region. Possible values include:

```
MEM_COMMIT      Memory is reserved and committed
MEM_RESERVE     Memory is reserved but not committed
MEM_FREE        Memory is free
```

Protect

The current access protection of the pages in the region.

Type

The type of the pages in the region. Possible values include zero if the state is
MEM_FREE, or:

```
MEM_PRIVATE     Memory is private
MEM_MAPPED      Memory is shareable and mapped from a data section
MEM_IMAGE       Memory is shareable and mapped from an image section
```

Remarks

MEMORY_BASIC_INFORMATION is identical to the structure of the same name returned by
the Win32 function VirtualQueryEx.

MemoryWorkingSetList

```
typedef struct _MEMORY_WORKING_SET_LIST { // Information Class 1
    ULONG NumberOfPages;
    ULONG WorkingSetList[1];
} MEMORY_WORKING_SET_LIST, *PMEMORY_WORKING_SET_LIST;
```

Members

NumberOfPages

The number of pages in the working set list.

WorkingSetList

An array of working set list entries. The high 20 bits of an entry represent the high 20
bits of the virtual address of the working set list entry, and the low 12 bits are a bit
array of flags. The following flag interpretations are defined:

```
WSLE_PAGE_READONLY            0x001  // Page is read only
WSLE_PAGE_EXECUTE             0x002  // Page is executable
WSLE_PAGE_READWRITE           0x004  // Page is writeable
WSLE_PAGE_EXECUTE_READ        0x003
WSLE_PAGE_WRITECOPY           0x005  // Page should be copied on write
WSLE_PAGE_EXECUTE_READWRITE   0x006
WSLE_PAGE_EXECUTE_WRITECOPY   0x007  // Page should be copied on write
WSLE_PAGE_SHARE_COUNT_MASK    0x0E0
WSLE_PAGE_SHAREABLE           0x100  // Page is shareable
```

Remarks

ZwQueryVirtualMemory with an information class of MemoryWorkingSetList always
returns STATUS_SUCCESS. To test for success, verify that MemoryInformationLength is
greater than the ReturnLength.

Flag bits that are not defined are neither set nor cleared, and so it is advisable to zero the `MemoryInformation` buffer before calling `ZwQueryVirtualMemory`.

An indication of whether a page is locked (in memory or in the working set) is not returned although this information is stored in the working set list of the process.

The PSAPI function `QueryWorkingSet` uses this information class.

The share count for shareable pages is only available in Windows 2000. A share count of seven means that at least seven processes are sharing the page.

MemorySectionName

```
typedef struct _MEMORY_SECTION_NAME { // Information Class 2
    UNICODE_STRING SectionFileName;
} MEMORY_SECTION_NAME, *PMEMORY_SECTION_NAME;
```

Members

SectionFileName
The name of the file backing the section.

Remarks

The `BaseAddress` parameter must point to the base address of a mapped data section; the name of the file backing an image section is not returned (this seems to be an arbitrary restriction in the implementation of **ZwQueryVirtualMemory**).

`MemoryInformationLength` must be large enough to accommodate the `UNICODE_STRING` structure and the actual Unicode string name itself.

The PSAPI function `GetMappedFileName` uses this information class.

ZwLockVirtualMemory

ZwLockVirtualMemory locks virtual memory in the user mode address range, ensuring that subsequent accesses to the locked region of virtual memory will not incur page faults.

```
NTSYSAPI
NTSTATUS
NTAPI
ZwLockVirtualMemory(
    IN HANDLE ProcessHandle,
    IN OUT PVOID *BaseAddress,
    IN OUT PULONG LockSize,
    IN ULONG LockType
    );
```

Parameters

ProcessHandle
A handle of a process object, representing the process for which the virtual memory should be locked. The handle must grant `PROCESS_VM_OPERATION` access.

BaseAddress
Points to a variable that specifies the base address of the virtual memory to be locked, and receives the base address of the virtual memory actually locked.

LockSize
Points to a variable that specifies the size, in bytes, of the virtual memory to lock, and receives the size of virtual memory actually locked.

LockType
A set of flags that describes the type of locking to be performed for the specified region of pages. The permitted values are combinations of the flags:

```
LOCK_VM_IN_WSL  0x01    // Lock page in working set list
LOCK_VM_IN_RAM  0x02    // Lock page in physical memory
```

Return Value

Returns STATUS_SUCCESS, STATUS_WAS_LOCKED or an error status, such as STATUS_PRIVILEGE_NOT_HELD, STATUS_WORKING_SET_QUOTA, or STATUS_PROCESS_IS_TERMINATING.

Related Win32 Functions

VirtualLock.

Remarks

SeLockMemoryPrivilege is required to lock pages in physical memory.

All of the pages that contain one or more bytes in the range from BaseAddress to (BaseAddress+LockSize) are locked.

ZwUnlockVirtualMemory

ZwUnlockVirtualMemory unlocks virtual memory in the user mode address range.

```
NTSYSAPI
NTSTATUS
NTAPI
ZwUnlockVirtualMemory(
    IN HANDLE ProcessHandle,
    IN OUT PVOID *BaseAddress,
    IN OUT PULONG LockSize,
    IN ULONG LockType
    );
```

Parameters

ProcessHandle
A handle of a process object, representing the process for which the virtual memory should be unlocked. The handle must grant PROCESS_VM_OPERATION access.

BaseAddress
Points to a variable that specifies the base address of the virtual memory to be unlocked, and receives the size of virtual memory actually unlocked.

LockSize
Points to a variable that specifies the size, in bytes, of the virtual memory to unlock, and receives the size of virtual memory actually unlocked.

LockType
A set of flags that describes the type of unlocking to be performed for the specified region of pages. The permitted values are combinations of the flags:

```
LOCK_VM_IN_WSL  0x01    // Unlock page from working set list
LOCK_VM_IN_RAM  0x02    // Unlock page from physical memory
```

Return Value

Returns STATUS_SUCCESS or an error status, such as STATUS_PRIVILEGE_NOT_HELD, STATUS_NOT_LOCKED, or STATUS_PROCESS_IS_TERMINATING.

Related Win32 Functions

VirtualUnlock.

Remarks

SeLockMemoryPrivilege is required to unlock pages from physical memory.

All of the pages that contain one or more bytes in the range from BaseAddress to (BaseAddress+LockSize) are unlocked. They must all have been previously locked.

ZwReadVirtualMemory

ZwReadVirtualMemory reads virtual memory in the user mode address range of another process.

```
NTSYSAPI
NTSTATUS
NTAPI
ZwReadVirtualMemory(
    IN HANDLE ProcessHandle,
    IN PVOID BaseAddress,
    OUT PVOID Buffer,
    IN ULONG BufferLength,
    OUT PULONG ReturnLength OPTIONAL
    );
```

Parameters

ProcessHandle
A handle of a process object, representing the process from which the virtual memory should be read. The handle must grant PROCESS_VM_READ access.

BaseAddress
The base address of the virtual memory to read.

Buffer
Points to a caller-allocated buffer or variable that receives the contents of the virtual memory.

BufferLength
Specifies the size in bytes of Buffer and the number of bytes of virtual memory to read.

ReturnLength
Optionally points to a variable that receives the number of bytes actually returned to Buffer if the call was successful. If this information is not needed, ReturnLength may be a null pointer.

Return Value

Returns STATUS_SUCCESS or an error status, such as STATUS_ACCESS_VIOLATION or STATUS_PROCESS_IS_TERMINATING.

Related Win32 Functions

ReadProcessMemory.

Remarks

ReadProcessMemory exposes the full functionality of **ZwReadVirtualMemory**.

ZwWriteVirtualMemory

ZwWriteVirtualMemory writes virtual memory in the user mode address range of another process.

```
NTSYSAPI
NTSTATUS
NTAPI
ZwWriteVirtualMemory(
    IN HANDLE ProcessHandle,
    IN PVOID BaseAddress,
    IN PVOID Buffer,
    IN ULONG BufferLength,
    OUT PULONG ReturnLength OPTIONAL
    );
```

Parameters

ProcessHandle
A handle of a process object, representing the process to which the virtual memory should be written. The handle must grant PROCESS_VM_WRITE access.

BaseAddress
The base address of the virtual memory to write.

Buffer

Points to a caller-allocated buffer or variable that specifies the contents of the virtual memory.

BufferLength

Specifies the size in bytes of Buffer and the number of bytes of virtual memory to write.

ReturnLength

Optionally points to a variable that receives the number of bytes actually read from Buffer if the call was successful. If this information is not needed, ReturnLength may be a null pointer.

Return Value

Returns STATUS_SUCCESS or an error status, such as STATUS_ACCESS_VIOLATION or STATUS_PROCESS_IS_TERMINATING.

Related Win32 Functions

WriteProcessMemory.

Remarks

WriteProcessMemory exposes the full functionality of **ZwWriteVirtualMemory**. WriteProcessMemory tries to modify the protection on the virtual memory to ensure that write access is granted and flushes the instruction cache after the write (by calling **ZwFlushInstructionCache**).

ZwProtectVirtualMemory

ZwProtectVirtualMemory changes the protection on virtual memory in the user mode address range.

```
NTSYSAPI
NTSTATUS
NTAPI
ZwProtectVirtualMemory(
    IN HANDLE ProcessHandle,
    IN OUT PVOID *BaseAddress,
    IN OUT PULONG ProtectSize,
    IN ULONG NewProtect,
    OUT PULONG OldProtect
    );
```

Parameters

ProcessHandle

A handle of a process object, representing the process for which the virtual memory protection is to be changed. The handle must grant PROCESS_VM_OPERATION access.

BaseAddress

Points to a variable that specifies the base address of the virtual memory to protect, and receives the size of virtual memory actually protected.

ProtectSize

Points to a variable that specifies the size, in bytes, of the virtual memory to protect, and receives the size of virtual memory actually protected.

NewProtect

The new access protection. Permitted values are drawn from the following list, possibly combined with `PAGE_GUARD` or `PAGE_NOCACHE`.

```
PAGE_NOACCESS
PAGE_READONLY
PAGE_READWRITE
PAGE_WRITECOPY
PAGE_EXECUTE
PAGE_EXECUTE_READ
PAGE_EXECUTE_READWRITE
PAGE_EXECUTE_WRITECOPY
```

OldProtect

Points to a variable that receives the previous access protection of the first page in the specified region of pages.

Return Value

Returns `STATUS_SUCCESS` or an error status, such as `STATUS_NOT_COMMITTED` or `STATUS_PROCESS_IS_TERMINATING`.

Related Win32 Functions

`VirtualProtect`, `VirtualProtectEx`.

Remarks

`VirtualProtectEx` exposes almost all of the functionality of **ZwProtectVirtualMemory**.

ZwFlushVirtualMemory

ZwFlushVirtualMemory flushes virtual memory in the user mode address range that is mapped to a file.

```
NTSYSAPI
NTSTATUS
NTAPI
ZwFlushVirtualMemory(
    IN HANDLE ProcessHandle,
    IN OUT PVOID *BaseAddress,
    IN OUT PULONG FlushSize,
    OUT PIO_STATUS_BLOCK IoStatusBlock
    );
```

Parameters

ProcessHandle
  A handle of a process object, representing the process for which the virtual memory should be flushed. The handle must grant PROCESS_VM_OPERATION access.

BaseAddress
  Points to a variable that specifies the base address of the virtual memory to flush, and receives the size of virtual memory actually flushed. The address should refer to a region backed by a file data section.

FlushSize
  Points to a variable that specifies the size, in bytes, of the virtual memory to flush, and receives the size of virtual memory actually flushed. If the initial value of FlushSize is zero, the virtual memory is flushed from the BaseAddress to the end of the section.

IoStatusBlock
  Points to a variable that receives the status of the I/O operation (if any) needed to flush the virtual memory to its backing file.

Return Value

Returns STATUS_SUCCESS or an error status, such as STATUS_NOT_MAPPED_DATA or STATUS_PROCESS_IS_TERMINATING.

Related Win32 Functions

FlushViewOfFile.

Remarks

None.

ZwAllocateUserPhysicalPages

ZwAllocateUserPhysicalPages allocates pages of physical memory.

```
NTSYSAPI
NTSTATUS
NTAPI
ZwAllocateUserPhysicalPages(
    IN HANDLE ProcessHandle,
    IN PULONG NumberOfPages,
    OUT PULONG PageFrameNumbers
    );
```

Parameters

ProcessHandle
  A handle of a process object, representing the process for which the pages of physical memory should be allocated. The handle must grant PROCESS_VM_OPERATION access.

NumberOfPages
> Points to a variable that specifies the number of pages of physical memory to allocate.

PageFrameNumbers
> Points to a caller-allocated buffer or variable that receives the page frame numbers of the allocated pages.

Return Value

Returns STATUS_SUCCESS or an error status, such as STATUS_PRIVILEGE_NOT_HELD or STATUS_PROCESS_IS_TERMINATING.

Related Win32 Functions

AllocateUserPhysicalPages.

Remarks

SeLockMemoryPrivilege is required to allocate pages of physical memory.

AllocateUserPhysicalPages exposes the full functionality of **ZwAllocateUserPhysicalPages**.

AllocateUserPhysicalPages is part of the "Address Windowing Extensions" (AWE) API, which allows applications to use up to 64GB of physical non-paged memory in a 32-bit virtual address space. On the Intel platform, the Physical Address Extension (PAE) flag in the CR4 register is set (at boot time) to enable 36-bit physical addressing if the system has more than 4GB of physical memory.

The routine **ZwAllocateUserPhysicalPages** is only present in Windows 2000.

ZwFreeUserPhysicalPages

ZwFreeUserPhysicalPages frees pages of physical memory.

```
NTSYSAPI
NTSTATUS
NTAPI
ZwFreeUserPhysicalPages(
    IN HANDLE ProcessHandle,
    IN OUT PULONG NumberOfPages,
    IN PULONG PageFrameNumbers
    );
```

Parameters

ProcessHandle
> A handle of a process object, representing the process for which the pages of physical memory should be freed. The handle must grant PROCESS_VM_OPERATION access.

NumberOfPages
> Points to a variable that specifies the number of pages of physical memory to free, and receives the number of pages actually freed.

PageFrameNumbers
   Points to a caller-allocated buffer or variable that contains the page frame numbers of
   the pages to be freed.

Return Value

Returns STATUS_SUCCESS or an error status, such as STATUS_CONFLICTING_ADDRESSES
or STATUS_PROCESS_IS_TERMINATING.

Related Win32 Functions

FreeUserPhysicalPages.

Remarks

FreeUserPhysicalPages exposes the full functionality of **ZwFreeUserPhysicalPages**.

The routine **ZwFreeUserPhysicalPages** is only present in Windows 2000.

ZwMapUserPhysicalPages

ZwMapUserPhysicalPages maps pages of physical memory into a physical memory
view.

```
NTSYSAPI
NTSTATUS
NTAPI
ZwMapUserPhysicalPages(
    IN PVOID BaseAddress,
    IN PULONG NumberOfPages,
    IN PULONG PageFrameNumbers
    );
```

Parameters

BaseAddress
   The address within a physical memory view at which to map the physical memory. The address is rounded down to the nearest page boundary if necessary. A physical
   memory view is created by calling **ZwAllocateVirtualMemory** with an
   AllocationType of MEM_PHYSICAL | MEM_RESERVE.

NumberOfPages
   Points to a variable that specifies the number of pages of physical memory to map.

PageFrameNumbers
   Points to a caller-allocated buffer or variable that contains the page frame numbers of
   the pages to be mapped. If PageFrameNumbers is a null pointer, the physical memory
   mapped at BaseAddresses is unmapped.

Return Value

Returns STATUS_SUCCESS or an error status, such as STATUS_CONFLICTING_ADDRESSES
or STATUS_PROCESS_IS_TERMINATING.

Related Win32 Functions

MapUserPhysicalPages.

Remarks

MapUserPhysicalPages exposes the full functionality of **ZwMapUserPhysicalPages**.

The routine **ZwMapUserPhysicalPages** is only present in Windows 2000.

The physical pages must have been previously allocated by **ZwAllocateUserPhysicalPages.**

For unknown reasons, **ZwMapUserPhysicalPages** does not provide for specifying the process for which the mapping is to be performed; this is in contrast to all the other related routines, which do allow a process to be specified.

ZwMapUserPhysicalPagesScatter

ZwMapUserPhysicalPagesScatter maps pages of physical memory into a physical memory view.

```
NTSYSAPI
NTSTATUS
NTAPI
ZwMapUserPhysicalPagesScatter(
    IN PVOID *BaseAddresses,
    IN PULONG NumberOfPages,
    IN PULONG PageFrameNumbers
    );
```

Parameters

BaseAddress

Points to a caller-allocated buffer or variable that contains an array of the virtual addresses (within a physical memory view) at which to map the physical memory. The virtual addresses are rounded down to the nearest page boundary if necessary. A physical memory view is created by calling **ZwAllocateVirtualMemory** with an AllocationType of MEM_PHYSICAL | MEM_RESERVE.

NumberOfPages

Points to a variable that specifies the number of pages of physical memory to map.

PageFrameNumbers

Points to a caller-allocated buffer or variable that contains the page frame numbers of the pages to be mapped. If PageFrameNumbers is a null pointer, the physical memory mapped at BaseAddresses is unmapped.

Return Value

Returns STATUS_SUCCESS or an error status, such as STATUS_CONFLICTING_ADDRESSES or STATUS_PROCESS_IS_TERMINATING.

Related Win32 Functions

MapUserPhysicalPagesScatter.

Remarks

MapUserPhysicalPagesScatter exposes the full functionality of
ZwMapUserPhysicalPagesScatter.

The routine **ZwMapUserPhysicalPagesScatter** is only present in Windows 2000.

The physical pages must have been previously allocated by
ZwAllocateUserPhysicalPages.

ZwGetWriteWatch

ZwGetWriteWatch retrieves the addresses of pages that have been written to in a region
of virtual memory.

```
NTSYSAPI
NTSTATUS
NTAPI
ZwGetWriteWatch(
    IN HANDLE ProcessHandle,
    IN ULONG Flags,
    IN PVOID BaseAddress,
    IN ULONG RegionSize,
    OUT PULONG Buffer,
    IN OUT PULONG BufferEntries,
    OUT PULONG Granularity
    );
```

Parameters

ProcessHandle
A handle of a process object, representing the process from which the virtual memory
write watch information should be retrieved. The handle must grant
PROCESS_VM_OPERATION access.

Flags
A bit array of flags. The defined values include:

```
WRITE_WATCH_RESET_FLAG  0x01 // Reset the write watch information
```

BaseAddress
The base address of the region of memory for which the write watch information is
to be retrieved.

RegionSize
The size, in bytes, of the region of memory for which the write watch information is
to be retrieved.

Buffer

Points to a caller-allocated buffer or variable that receives an array of page addresses in the region of memory that have been written to since the region was allocated or the write watch information was reset.

BufferEntries

Points to a variable that specifies the maximum number of page addresses to return and receives the actual number of page addresses returned.

Granularity

Points to a variable that receives the granularity, in bytes, of the write detection. This is normally the size of a physical page.

Return Value

Returns STATUS_SUCCESS or an error status, such as STATUS_PROCESS_IS_TERMINATING, STATUS_INVALID_PARAMETER_1, STATUS_INVALID_PARAMETER_2, STATUS_INVALID_PARAMETER_3, or STATUS_INVALID_PARAMETER_5.

Related Win32 Functions

GetWriteWatch.

Remarks

GetWriteWatch most of the functionality of **ZwGetWriteWatch**.

The routine **ZwGetWriteWatch** is only present in Windows 2000.

ZwResetWriteWatch

ZwResetWriteWatch resets the virtual memory write watch information for a region of virtual memory.

```
NTSYSAPI
NTSTATUS
NTAPI
ZwResetWriteWatch(
    IN HANDLE ProcessHandle,
    IN PVOID BaseAddress,
    IN ULONG RegionSize
    );
```

Parameters

ProcessHandle

A handle of a process object, representing the process for which the virtual memory write watch information should be reset. The handle must grant PROCESS_VM_OPERATION access.

BaseAddress

The base address of the region of memory for which the write watch information is to be reset.

RegionSize
    The size, in bytes, of the region of memory for which the write watch information is
    to be reset.

Return Value

Returns STATUS_SUCCESS or an error status, such as
STATUS_PROCESS_IS_TERMINATING, STATUS_INVALID_PARAMETER_1,
STATUS_INVALID_PARAMETER_2, or STATUS_INVALID_PARAMETER_3.

Related Win32 Functions

ResetWriteWatch.

Remarks

ResetWriteWatch most of the functionality of **ZwResetWriteWatch**.

The routine **ZwResetWriteWatch** is only present in Windows 2000.

4
Sections

The system services described in this chapter create and manipulate section objects.
Section objects are objects that can be mapped into the virtual address space of a process.
The Win32 API refers to section objects as file-mapping objects.

ZwCreateSection

ZwCreateSection creates a section object.

```
NTSYSAPI
NTSTATUS
NTAPI
ZwCreateSection(
    OUT PHANDLE SectionHandle,
    IN ACCESS_MASK DesiredAccess,
    IN POBJECT_ATTRIBUTES ObjectAttributes,
    IN PLARGE_INTEGER SectionSize OPTIONAL,
    IN ULONG Protect,
    IN ULONG Attributes,
    IN HANDLE FileHandle
    );
```

Parameters

SectionHandle
Points to a variable that will receive the section object handle if the call is successful.

DesiredAccess
Specifies the type of access that the caller requires to the section object. This parameter can be zero, or any combination of the following flags:

```
SECTION_QUERY          Query access
SECTION_MAP_WRITE      Can be written when mapped
SECTION_MAP_READ       Can be read when mapped
SECTION_MAP_EXECUTE    Can be executed when mapped
SECTION_EXTEND_SIZE    Extend access
SECTION_ALL_ACCESS     All of the preceding +
                       STANDARD_RIGHTS_REQUIRED
```

ObjectAttributes

Points to a structure that specifies the object's attributes. OBJ_OPENLINK is not a valid attribute for a section object.

SectionSize

Optionally points to a variable that specifies the size, in bytes, of the section. If FileHandle is zero, the size must be specified; otherwise, it can be defaulted from the size of the file referred to by FileHandle.

Protect

The protection desired for the pages of the section when the section is mapped. This parameter can take one of the following values:

```
PAGE_READONLY
PAGE_READWRITE
PAGE_WRITECOPY
PAGE_EXECUTE
PAGE_EXECUTE_READ
PAGE_EXECUTE_READWRITE
PAGE_EXECUTE_WRITECOPY
```

Attributes

The attributes for the section. This parameter be a combination of the following values:

```
SEC_BASED     0x00200000 // Map section at same address in each process
SEC_NO_CHANGE 0x00400000 // Disable changes to protection of pages
SEC_IMAGE     0x01000000 // Map section as an image
SEC_VLM       0x02000000 // Map section in VLM region
SEC_RESERVE   0x04000000 // Reserve without allocating pagefile storage
SEC_COMMIT    0x08000000 // Commit pages; the default behavior
SEC_NOCACHE   0x10000000 // Mark pages as non-cacheable
```

FileHandle

Identifies the file from which to create the section object. The file must be opened with an access mode compatible with the protection flags specified by the Protect parameter. If FileHandle is zero, the function creates a section object of the specified size backed by the paging file rather than by a named file in the file system.

Return Value

Returns STATUS_SUCCESS or an error status, such as STATUS_ACCESS_DENIED, STATUS_INVALID_FILE_FOR_SECTION, STATUS_FILE_LOCK_CONFLICT, STATUS_MAPPED_FILE_SIZE_ZERO, STATUS_INVALID_PAGE_PROTECTION, STATUS_INVALID_IMAGE_FORMAT, STATUS_INCOMPATIBLE_FILE_MAP, STATUS_OBJECT_NAME_EXISTS, or STATUS_OBJECT_NAME_COLLISION.

Related Win32 Functions

CreateFileMapping.

Remarks

CreateFileMapping exposes almost all of the functionality of **ZwCreateSection**. The main missing features are the ability to specify the attributes SEC_BASED and SEC_NO_CHANGE, and the access SECTION_EXTEND. It is also not possible to specify the access SECTION_EXECUTE and the related PAGE_EXECUTE_Xxx protections.

SEC_VLM is only valid in Windows 2000 and is not implemented on the Intel platform.

ZwOpenSection

ZwOpenSection opens a section object.

```
NTSYSAPI
NTSTATUS
NTAPI
ZwOpenSection(
    OUT PHANDLE SectionHandle,
    IN ACCESS_MASK DesiredAccess,
    IN POBJECT_ATTRIBUTES ObjectAttributes
    );
```

Parameters

SectionHandle
  Points to a variable that will receive the section object handle if the call is successful.

DesiredAccess
  The type of access that the caller requires to the section object. This parameter can be zero, or any combination of the following flags:

SECTION_QUERY	Query access
SECTION_MAP_WRITE	Can be written when mapped
SECTION_MAP_READ	Can be read when mapped
SECTION_MAP_EXECUTE	Can be executed when mapped
SECTION_EXTEND_SIZE	Extend access
SECTION_ALL_ACCESS	All of the preceding + STANDARD_RIGHTS_REQUIRED

ObjectAttributes
  Points to a structure that specifies the object's attributes. OBJ_OPENLINK is not a valid attribute for a section object.

Return Value

Returns STATUS_SUCCESS or an error status, such as STATUS_ACCESS_DENIED or STATUS_OBJECT_NAME_NOT_FOUND.

Related Win32 Functions

OpenFileMapping.

Remarks

ZwOpenSection is documented in the DDK.

The DDK does not define all the access types listed above.

OpenFileMapping exposes almost all of the functionality of **ZwOpenSection**.

In addition to opening sections created by **ZwCreateSection**, **ZwOpenSection** can also open the section named "\Device\PhysicalMemory," which is backed by the physical memory of the system.

ZwQuerySection

ZwQuerySection retrieves information about a section object.

```
NTSYSAPI
NTSTATUS
NTAPI
ZwQuerySection(
    IN HANDLE SectionHandle,
    IN SECTION_INFORMATION_CLASS SectionInformationClass,
    OUT PVOID SectionInformation,
    IN ULONG SectionInformationLength,
    OUT PULONG ResultLength OPTIONAL
    );
```

Parameters

SectionHandle
A handle to a section object. The handle must grant SECTION_QUERY access.

SectionInformationClass
Specifies the type of section object information to be queried. The permitted values are drawn from the enumeration SECTION_INFORMATION_CLASS, described in the following section.

SectionInformation
Points to a caller-allocated buffer or variable that receives the requested section object information.

SectionInformationLength
Specifies the size in bytes of SectionInformation, which the caller should set according to the given SectionInformationClass.

ReturnLength
Optionally points to a variable that receives the number of bytes actually returned to SectionInformation if the call was successful. If this information is not needed, ReturnLength may be a null pointer.

Return Value

Returns STATUS_SUCCESS or an error status, such as STATUS_ACCESS_DENIED, STATUS_INVALID_HANDLE, STATUS_INVALID_INFO_CLASS, STATUS_INFO_LENGTH_MISMATCH, or STATUS_SECTION_NOT_IMAGE.

Related Win32 Functions

None.

Remarks

None.

SECTION_INFORMATION_CLASS

```
typedef enum _SECTION_INFORMATION_CLASS {
    SectionBasicInformation,
    SectionImageInformation
} SECTION_INFORMATION_CLASS;
```

SectionBasicInformation

```
typedef struct _SECTION_BASIC_INFORMATION { // Information Class 0
    PVOID BaseAddress;
    ULONG Attributes;
    LARGE_INTEGER Size;
} SECTION_BASIC_INFORMATION, *PSECTION_BASIC_INFORMATION;
```

Members

BaseAddress

If the section is a based section, BaseAddress contains the base address of the section; otherwise, it contains zero.

Attributes

A bit array of flags that specify properties of the section object. The possible flags are

```
SEC_BASED       0x00200000 // Section should be mapped at same address in each
                              process
SEC_NO_CHANGE   0x00400000 // Changes to protection of section pages are
                              disabled
SEC_FILE        0x00800000 // Section is backed by a file
SEC_IMAGE       0x01000000 // Section is mapped as an image
SEC_VLM         0x02000000 // Section maps VLM
SEC_RESERVE     0x04000000 // Section pages are reserved
SEC_COMMIT      0x08000000 // Section pages are committed
SEC_NOCACHE     0x10000000 // Section pages are non-cacheable
```

Size

The size in bytes of the section.

Remarks

None.

SectionImageInformation

```
typedef struct _SECTION_IMAGE_INFORMATION { // Information Class 1
    PVOID EntryPoint;
    ULONG Unknown1;
    ULONG StackReserve;
    ULONG StackCommit;
    ULONG Subsystem;
    USHORT MinorSubsystemVersion;
    USHORT MajorSubsystemVersion;
    ULONG Unknown2;
    ULONG Characteristics;
    USHORT ImageNumber;
    BOOLEAN Executable;
    UCHAR Unknown3;
    ULONG Unknown4[3];
} SECTION_IMAGE_INFORMATION, *PSECTION_IMAGE_INFORMATION;
```

Members

EntryPoint

The entry point of the image.

Unknown1

Normally contains zero; interpretation unknown.

StackReserve

The default amount of stack to reserve when creating the initial thread to execute this image section. The value is copied from the image header (`IMAGE_OPTIONAL_HEADER.SizeOfStackReserve`).

StackCommit

The default amount of stack to commit when creating the initial thread to execute this image section. The value is copied from the image header (`IMAGE_OPTIONAL_HEADER.SizeOfStackCommit`).

Subsystem

The subsystem under which the process created from this image section should run. The value is copied from the image header (`IMAGE_OPTIONAL_HEADER.Subsystem`).

MinorSubsystemVersion

The minor version number of the subsystem for which the image was built. The value is copied from the image header (`IMAGE_OPTIONAL_HEADER.MinorSubsystemVersion`).

MajorSubsystemVersion

The major version number of the subsystem for which the image was built. The value is copied from the image header (`IMAGE_OPTIONAL_HEADER.MinorSubsystemVersion`).

Unknown2

Normally contains zero; interpretation unknown.

Characteristics

A bit array of flags that specify properties of the image file. The value is copied from the image header (`IMAGE_FILE_HEADER.Characteristics`).

ImageNumber

The type of target machine on which the image will run. The value is copied from the image header (`IMAGE_FILE_HEADER.Machine`).

Executable

A boolean indicating whether the image file contains any executable code. The value is derived from the image header (`IMAGE_OPTIONAL_HEADER.SizeOfCode != 0`).

Unknown3

Normally contains zero; interpretation unknown.

Unknown4

Normally contains zero; interpretation unknown.

Remarks

The information class `SectionImageInformation` is valid only for image sections (sections for which `SEC_IMAGE` was specified as an attribute to **ZwCreateSection**).

ZwExtendSection

```
ZwExtendSection extends a file backed data section.
NTSYSAPI
NTSTATUS
NTAPI
ZwExtendSection(
    IN HANDLE SectionHandle,
    IN PLARGE_INTEGER SectionSize
    );
```

Parameters

SectionHandle

A handle to a section object. The handle must grant `SECTION_EXTEND_SIZE` access.

SectionSize

Points to a variable that contains the new size, in bytes, of the section.

Return Value

Returns `STATUS_SUCCESS` or an error status, such as `STATUS_INVALID_HANDLE`, `STATUS_ACCESS_DENIED`, or `STATUS_SECTION_NOT_EXTENDED`.

Related Win32 Functions

None.

Remarks

ZwExtendSection only extends data sections backed by a file.

ZwMapViewOfSection

ZwMapViewOfSection maps a view of a section to a range of virtual addresses.

```
NTSYSAPI
NTSTATUS
NTAPI
ZwMapViewOfSection(
    IN HANDLE SectionHandle,
    IN HANDLE ProcessHandle,
    IN OUT PVOID *BaseAddress,
    IN ULONG ZeroBits,
    IN ULONG CommitSize,
    IN OUT PLARGE_INTEGER SectionOffset OPTIONAL,
    IN OUT PULONG ViewSize,
    IN SECTION_INHERIT InheritDisposition,
    IN ULONG AllocationType,
    IN ULONG Protect
    );
```

Parameters

SectionHandle

A handle to the section object that is to be mapped. The handle must grant access compatible with the **Protect** parameter, which specifies the protection on the pages that map the section.

ProcessHandle

A handle of an process object, representing the process for which the view should be mapped. The handle must grant **PROCESS_VM_OPERATION** access.

BaseAddress

Points to a variable that will receive the base address of the view. If the initial value of this variable is not null, the view is allocated starting at the specified address, possibly rounded down.

ZeroBits

Specifies the number of high-order address bits that must be zero in the base address of the section view. The value of this parameter must be less than 21 and is used only when the operating system determines where to allocate the view, such as when **BaseAddress** is null.

CommitSize

Specifies the size, in bytes, of the initially committed region of the view. **CommitSize** is only meaningful for page-file backed sections; file backed sections, both data and image, are effectively committed at section creation time. This value is rounded up to the next page size boundary.

SectionOffset

Optionally points to a variable that contains the offset, in bytes, from the beginning of the section to the view, possibly rounded down.

ViewSize

Points to a variable that will receive the actual size, in bytes, of the view. If the initial value of this variable is zero, a view of the section will be mapped starting at the specified section offset and continuing to the end of the section. Otherwise, the initial value of this parameter specifies the size of the view, in bytes, and is rounded up to the next page size boundary.

InheritDispostion

Specifies how the view is to be shared by a child process created with a create process operation. Permitted values are drawn from the enumeration SECTION_INHERIT.

```
typedef enum _SECTION_INHERIT {
    ViewShare = 1,
    ViewUnmap = 2
} SECTION_INHERIT;
```

AllocationType

A set of flags that describes the type of allocation to be performed for the specified region of pages. The permitted values include:

```
AT_EXTENDABLE_FILE 0x00002000 // Allow view to exceed section size
MEM_TOP_DOWN       0x00100000 // Allocate at highest possible address
SEC_NO_CHANGE      0x00400000 // Disable changes to protection of pages
AT_RESERVED        0x20000000 // Valid but ignored
AT_ROUND_TO_PAGE   0x40000000 // Adjust address and size if necessary
```

Protect

Specifies the protection for the region of initially committed pages. The protection must be compatible with the protection specified when the section was created. (The protection can be more but not less restrictive.)

Return Value

Returns STATUS_SUCCESS, STATUS_IMAGE_NOT_AT_BASE, STATUS_IMAGE_MACHINE_TYPE_MISMATCH, or an error status, such as STATUS_INVALID_HANDLE, STATUS_ACCESS_DENIED, STATUS_CONFLICTING_ADDRESSES, STATUS_INVALID_VIEW_SIZE, STATUS_MAPPED_ALIGNMENT, or STATUS_PROCESS_IS_TERMINATING.

Related Win32 Functions

MapViewOfFile, MapViewOfFileEx.

Remarks

ZwMapViewOfSection is documented in the DDK.

When mapping "\Device\PhysicalMemory," the BaseAddress and SectionOffset are rounded down to the next page boundary. When mapping pagefile and data sections, BaseAddress and SectionOffset must be aligned with the system's allocation granularity unless the AllocationType flags include AT_ROUND_TO_PAGE; in which case, they are rounded down to the next page boundary.

The AllocationType flag AT_EXTENDABLE_FILE is only present in Windows 2000 and is only valid for data sections backed by a file mapped with PAGE_READWRITE or PAGE_EXECUTE_READWRITE protection. Changes to data within the view but beyond the size of the backing file are not permanently stored unless the section (and implicitly the backing file) is extended with **ZwExtendSection** to encompass the changes.

ZwUnmapViewOf Section

ZwUnmapViewOfSection unmaps a view of a section.

```
NTSYSAPI
NTSTATUS
NTAPI
ZwUnmapViewOfSection(
    IN HANDLE ProcessHandle,
    IN PVOID BaseAddress
    );
```

Parameters

ProcessHandle
A handle of an process object, representing the process for which the view should be unmapped. The handle must grant PROCESS_VM_OPERATION access.

BaseAddress
The base address of the view that is to be unmapped.

Return Value

Returns STATUS_SUCCESS or an error status, such as STATUS_NOT_MAPPED_VIEW, or STATUS_PROCESS_IS_TERMINATING.

Related Win32 Functions

UnmapViewOfFile.

Remarks

ZwUnmapViewOfSection is documented in the DDK.

ZwAreMappedFilesTheSame

ZwAreMappedFilesTheSame tests whether two pointers refer to image sections backed by the same file.

```
NTSYSAPI
NTSTATUS
NTAPI
ZwAreMappedFilesTheSame(
    IN PVOID Address1,
    IN PVOID Address2
    );
```

Parameters

Address1
A virtual address mapped to an image section.

Address2
A virtual address mapped to an image section.

Return Value

Returns STATUS_SUCCESS or an error status, such as STATUS_INVALID_ADDRESS, STATUS_CONFLICTING_ADDRESSES, or STATUS_NOT_SAME_DEVICE.

Related Win32 Functions

None.

Remarks

The routine **ZwAreMappedFilesTheSame** is only present in Windows 2000.

If the two pointers refer to image sections backed by the same file, **ZwAreMappedFilesTheSame** returns STATUS_SUCCESS; otherwise, it returns an error status.

5
Threads

The system services described in this chapter create and manipulate thread objects.

ZwCreateThread

ZwCreateThread creates a thread in a process.

```
NTSYSAPI
NTSTATUS
NTAPI
ZwCreateThread(
    OUT PHANDLE ThreadHandle,
    IN ACCESS_MASK DesiredAccess,
    IN POBJECT_ATTRIBUTES ObjectAttributes,
    IN HANDLE ProcessHandle,
    OUT PCLIENT_ID ClientId,
    IN PCONTEXT ThreadContext,
    IN PUSER_STACK UserStack,
    IN BOOLEAN CreateSuspended
    );
```

Parameters

ThreadHandle
Points to a variable that will receive the thread object handle if the call is successful.

DesiredAccess
Specifies the type of access that the caller requires to the thread object. This parameter can be zero or any combination of the following flags:

```
THREAD_TERMINATE               Terminate thread
THREAD_SUSPEND_RESUME          Suspend or resume thread
THREAD_ALERT                   Alert thread
THREAD_GET_CONTEXT             Get thread context
THREAD_SET_CONTEXT             Set thread context
THREAD_SET_INFORMATION         Set thread information
THREAD_QUERY_INFORMATION       Get thread information
THREAD_SET_THREAD_TOKEN        Set thread token
THREAD_IMPERSONATE             Allow thread to impersonate
THREAD_DIRECT_IMPERSONATION    Allow thread token to be impersonated
THREAD_ALL_ACCESS              All of the preceding +
                               STANDARD_RIGHTS_ALL
```

ObjectAttributes

Points to a structure that specifies the object's attributes. OBJ_PERMANENT, OBJ_EXCLUSIVE and OBJ_OPENIF are not valid attributes for a thread object.

ProcessHandle

A handle to the process in which the thread is to be created. The handle must grant PROCESS_CREATE_THREAD access.

ClientId

Points to a variable that will receive the thread and process identifiers if the call is successful.

ThreadContext

Points to a structure that specifies the initial values of the processor registers for the thread.

UserStack

Points to a structure that specifies the user mode stack of the thread.

CreateSuspended

A boolean specifying whether the thread should be created suspended or should be immediately allowed to begin execution.

Return Value

Returns STATUS_SUCCESS or an error status, such as STATUS_ACCESS_DENIED, STATUS_INVALID_HANDLE, or STATUS_PROCESS_IS_TERMINATING.

Related Win32 Functions

CreateThread, CreateRemoteThread.

Remarks

Practical examples of creating a thread using **ZwCreateThread** appear in Chapter 6, "Processes," in Examples 6.1 and 6.2.

The USER_STACK structure is defined as follows:

```
typedef struct _USER_STACK {
    PVOID FixedStackBase;
    PVOID FixedStackLimit;
    PVOID ExpandableStackBase;
    PVOID ExpandableStackLimit;
    PVOID ExpandableStackBottom;
} USER_STACK, *PUSER_STACK;
```

Members

FixedStackBase

A pointer to the base of a fixed-size stack.

FixedStackLimit
   A pointer to the limit (that is, top) of a fixed-size stack.

ExpandableStackBase
   A pointer to the base of the committed memory of an expandable stack.

ExpandableStackLimit
   A pointer to the limit (that is, top) of the committed memory of an expandable stack.

ExpandableStackBottom
   A pointer to the bottom of the reserved memory of an expandable stack.

Remarks

If `FixedStackBase` or `FixedStackLimit` are not null, they are used to delimit the initial stack of the thread; otherwise `ExpandableStackBase` and `ExpandableStackLimit` are used. Example 6.2 in Chapter 6 demonstrates how to initialize this structure.

ZwOpenThread

`ZwOpenThread` opens a thread object.

```
NTSYSAPI
NTSTATUS
NTAPI
ZwOpenThread(
    OUT PHANDLE ThreadHandle,
    IN ACCESS_MASK DesiredAccess,
    IN POBJECT_ATTRIBUTES ObjectAttributes,
    IN PCLIENT_ID ClientId
    );
```

Parameters

ThreadHandle
   Points to a variable that will receive the thread object handle if the call is successful.

DesiredAccess
   Specifies the type of access that the caller requires to the thread object. This parameter can be zero, or any combination of the following flags:

THREAD_TERMINATE	Terminate thread
THREAD_SUSPEND_RESUME	Suspend or resume thread
THREAD_ALERT	Alert thread
THREAD_GET_CONTEXT	Get thread context
THREAD_SET_CONTEXT	Set thread context
THREAD_SET_INFORMATION	Set thread information
THREAD_QUERY_INFORMATION	Get thread information
THREAD_SET_THREAD_TOKEN	Set thread token
THREAD_IMPERSONATE	Allow thread to impersonate
THREAD_DIRECT_IMPERSONATION	Allow thread token to be impersonated
THREAD_ALL_ACCESS	All of the preceding + STANDARD_RIGHTS_ALL

ObjectAttributes
Points to a structure that specifies the object's attributes. OBJ_PERMANENT, OBJ_EXCLUSIVE, and OBJ_OPENIF are not valid attributes for a thread object.

ClientId
Optionally points to a structure that contains optionally the process identifier (UniqueProcess) and the identifier of a thread in the process (UniqueThread).

Return Value

Returns STATUS_SUCCESS or an error status, such as STATUS_ACCESS_DENIED, STATUS_OBJECT_NAME_NOT_FOUND, STATUS_INVALID_PARAMETER_MIX, or STATUS_INVALID_PARAMETER.

Related Win32 Functions

OpenThread.

Remarks

Thread objects can be given names in the same way as other objects.

The thread to be opened is identified either by ObjectAttributes.ObjectName, or ClientId; it is an error to specify both.

If ClientId.UniqueProcess is not zero, it must be the identifier of the process in which the thread resides.

If the caller has SeDebugPrivilege, the check of whether the caller is granted access to the thread by its ACL is bypassed. (This behavior can be disabled under Windows NT 4.0 by setting the NtGlobalFlag FLG_IGNORE_DEBUG_PRIV.)

ZwTerminateThread

ZwTerminateThread terminates a thread.

```
NTSYSAPI
NTSTATUS
NTAPI
ZwTerminateThread(
    IN HANDLE ThreadHandle OPTIONAL,
    IN NTSTATUS ExitStatus
    );
```

Parameters

ThreadHandle
A handle to a thread object. The handle must grant THREAD_TERMINATE access. If this value is zero, the current thread is terminated.

ExitStatus
Specifies the exit status for the thread.

Return Value

Returns STATUS_SUCCESS or an error status, such as STATUS_ACCESS_DENIED or STATUS_CANT_TERMINATE_SELF.

Related Win32 Functions

TerminateThread, ExitThread.

Remarks

TerminateThread exposes the full functionality of **ZwTerminateThread**.

The current thread can be terminated by calling **ZwTerminateThread** with a thread handle of either zero or NtCurrentThread(). If the thread is the last thread in the process and ThreadHandle is zero, the error status STATUS_CANT_TERMINATE_SELF is returned.

ZwTerminateThread does not deallocate the initial stack of the thread because **ZwCreateThread** did not allocate it. The initial stack can be explicitly de-allocated (by calling **ZwFreeVirtualMemory**) after the thread has been terminated (when the thread object becomes signaled).

ZwQueryInformationThread

ZwQueryInformationThread retrieves information about a thread object.

```
NTSYSAPI
NTSTATUS
NTAPI
ZwQueryInformationThread(
    IN HANDLE ThreadHandle,
    IN THREADINFOCLASS ThreadInformationClass,
    OUT PVOID ThreadInformation,
    IN ULONG ThreadInformationLength,
    OUT PULONG ReturnLength OPTIONAL
    );
```

Parameters

ThreadHandle
A handle to a thread object. The handle must grant THREAD_QUERY_INFORMATION access.

ThreadInformationClass
Specifies the type of thread information to be queried. The permitted values are drawn from the enumeration THREADINFOCLASS, described in the following section.

ThreadInformation
Points to a caller-allocated buffer or variable that receives the requested thread information.

ThreadInformationLength
Specifies the size in bytes of ThreadInformation, which the caller should set according to the given ThreadInformationClass.

ReturnLength
Optionally points to a variable, which receives the number of bytes actually returned to ThreadInformation if the call was successful. If this information is not needed, ReturnLength may be a null pointer.

Return Value

Returns STATUS_SUCCESS or an error status, such as STATUS_ACCESS_DENIED, STATUS_INVALID_HANDLE, STATUS_INVALID_INFO_CLASS, or STATUS_INFO_LENGTH_MISMATCH.

Related Win32 Functions

GetThreadPriority, GetThreadPriorityBoost, GetThreadTimes, GetExitCodeThread, and GetThreadSelectorEntry.

Remarks

None.

ZwSetInformationThread

ZwSetInformationThread sets information affecting a thread object.

```
NTSYSAPI
NTSTATUS
NTAPI
ZwSetInformationThread(
    IN HANDLE ThreadHandle,
    IN THREADINFOCLASS ThreadInformationClass,
    IN PVOID ThreadInformation,
    IN ULONG ThreadInformationLength
    );
```

Parameters

ThreadHandle
A handle to a thread object. The handle must grant THREAD_QUERY_INFORMATION access. Some information classes also require THREAD_SET_THREAD_TOKEN access.

ThreadInformationClass
Specifies the type of thread information to be set. The permitted values are drawn from the enumeration THREADINFOCLASS, described in the following section.

ThreadInformation
Points to a caller-allocated buffer or variable that contains the thread information to be set.

ThreadInformationLength
> Specifies the size in bytes of ThreadInformation, which the caller should set according to the given ThreadInformationClass.

Return Value

Returns STATUS_SUCCESS or an error status, such as STATUS_ACCESS_DENIED, STATUS_INVALID_HANDLE, STATUS_INVALID_INFO_CLASS, STATUS_INFO_LENGTH_MISMATCH, or STATUS_PROCESS_IS_TERMINATING.

Related Win32 Functions

SetThreadAffinityMask, SetThreadIdealProcessor, SetThreadPriority, and SetThreadPriorityBoost.

Remarks

None.

THREADINFOCLASS

		Query	Set
typedef enum _THREADINFOCLASS {			
ThreadBasicInformation,	// 0	Y	N
ThreadTimes,	// 1	Y	N
ThreadPriority,	// 2	N	Y
ThreadBasePriority,	// 3	N	Y
ThreadAffinityMask,	// 4	N	Y
ThreadImpersonationToken,	// 5	N	Y
ThreadDescriptorTableEntry,	// 6	Y	N
ThreadEnableAlignmentFaultFixup,	// 7	N	Y
ThreadEventPair,	// 8	N	Y
ThreadQuerySetWin32StartAddress,	// 9	Y	Y
ThreadZeroTlsCell,	// 10	N	Y
ThreadPerformanceCount,	// 11	Y	N
ThreadAmILastThread,	// 12	Y	N
ThreadIdealProcessor,	// 13	N	Y
ThreadPriorityBoost,	// 14	Y	Y
ThreadSetTlsArrayAddress,	// 15	N	Y
ThreadIsIoPending,	// 16	Y	N
ThreadHideFromDebugger	// 17	N	Y
} THREADINFOCLASS;			

ThreadBasicInformation

```
typedef struct _THREAD_BASIC_INFORMATION { // Information Class 0
    NTSTATUS ExitStatus;
    PNT_TIB TebBaseAddress;
    CLIENT_ID ClientId;
    KAFFINITY AffinityMask;
    KPRIORITY Priority;
    KPRIORITY BasePriority;
} THREAD_BASIC_INFORMATION, *PTHREAD_BASIC_INFORMATION;
```

Members

ExitStatus

The exit status of the thread. If the process has not exited, this member normally contains STATUS_SUCCESS.

TebBaseAddress

The base address of the Thread Environment Block.

ClientId

The thread identifier and the identifier of the process in which the thread resides.

AffinityMask

The processor affinity mask of the thread.

Priority

The current priority of the thread.

BasePriority

The base priority of the thread.

Remarks

None.

ThreadTimes

```
typedef struct _KERNEL_USER_TIMES { // Information Class 1
    LARGE_INTEGER CreateTime;
    LARGE_INTEGER ExitTime;
    LARGE_INTEGER KernelTime;
    LARGE_INTEGER UserTime;
} KERNEL_USER_TIMES, *PKERNEL_USER_TIMES;
```

Members

CreateTime

The creation time of the thread in the standard time format (that is, the number of 100-nanosecond intervals since January 1, 1601).

ExitTime

The exit time of the thread in the standard time format (that is, the number of 100-nanosecond intervals since January 1, 1601). For threads which have not exited, this value is zero.

KernelTime

The time spent executing in kernel mode by the thread, measured in units of 100-nanoseconds.

UserTime

The time spent executing in user mode by the thread, measured in units of 100-nanoseconds.

Remarks

None.

ThreadPriority

```
KPRIORITY Priority;   // Information Class 2
```

This information class can only be set. It sets the priority of the thread. Priority should be a valid priority value (that is, a value in the range 1 to 31).

ThreadBasePriority

```
LONG BasePriority;   // Information Class 3
```

This information class can only be set. It sets the base priority of the thread. BasePriority is interpreted as a delta with respect to the current base priority; it can be positive or negative.

ThreadAffinityMask

```
KAFFINITY AffinityMask;   // Information Class 4
```

This information class can only be set. It sets the processor affinity mask for the thread.

ThreadImpersonationToken

```
HANDLE ImpersonationToken;   // Information Class 5
```

This information class can only be set. It sets the impersonation token of the thread. ImpersonationToken should either be a handle to an impersonation token granting TOKEN_IMPERSONATE access, or zero to terminate the impersonation.

ThreadEnableAlignmentFaultFixup

```
BOOLEAN EnableAlignmentFaultFixup;   // Information Class 7
```

This information class can only be set. It sets a flag in the thread indicating whether alignment faults should be fixed up. An alignment fault occurs, for example, when a word is loaded from an odd byte address and is fixed up by reading the word as two separate bytes. Alignment faults are only enabled on Intel processors when the AM flag is set in the Cr0 register, the AC flag is set in the EFlags register, and the current privilege level is three (user mode).

ThreadEventPair

`HANDLE EventPair;  // Information Class 8`

This information class can only be set. It sets the event pair of the thread. Event pair should be a handle to an event pair granting `STANDARD_RIGHTS_ALL` access. If the thread already has an event pair, the existing event pair is first dereferenced.

The thread `EventPair` is used by the routines **ZwSetLowWaitHighThread** and **ZwSetHighWaitLowThread**.

In Windows 2000, this information class has been removed and `STATUS_INVALID_INFO_CLASS` is returned.

ThreadQuerySetWin32StartAddress

`PVOID Win32StartAddress;  // Information Class 9`

This information class can be both queried and set.

For the Intel platform, the initial value of this variable is the value of the Eax register in the `CONTEXT` structure passed to **ZwCreateThread**. If the thread is started using the thread start thunk in kernel32.dll, Eax contains the "Win32 start address."

The field in the `ETHREAD` structure that is queried and set by this information class is also used to hold the "LpcReceivedMessageId." Any thread that has called **ZwReplyWaitReplyPort** or **ZwReplyWaitReceivePort** will have modified this field.

In David Solomon's *Inside Windows NT* (second edition, Microsoft Press, 1998) the output of the resource kit utility "`tlist`" is included to illustrate the difference between the actual start address and the Win32 start address; one of the Win32 start addresses in the `tlist` output is less than 0x10000 (normally a reserved region of the address space)—this thread has called **ZwReplyWaitReceivePort**.

ThreadZeroTlsCell

`ULONG ZeroTlsCell;  // Information Class 10`

This information class can only be set. It zeroes the Thread Local Storage cell identified by ZeroTlsCell (ZeroTlsCell is a TLS index).

ThreadPerformanceCount

`LARGE_INTEGER PerformanceCount;  // Information Class 11`

The performance count is always zero.

ThreadAmILastThread

`ULONG AmILastThread;  // Information Class 12`

AmILastThread is interpreted as a boolean and indicates whether the thread is the only one in the process.

ThreadIdealProcessor

ULONG IdealProcessor; // Information Class 13

This information class can only be set. It specifies the number of the preferred processor for the thread. A value of MAXIMUM_PROCESSORS tells the system that the thread has no preferred processor.

ThreadPriorityBoost

ULONG PriorityBoost; // Information Class 14

This information class can be both queried and set. PriorityBoost is interpreted as a boolean and specifies whether priority boosting is enabled or disabled.

ThreadSetTlsArrayAddress

PVOID SetTlsArrayAddress; // Information Class 15

This information class can only be set. It sets the address of the Thread Local Storage array.

ThreadIsIoPending

ULONG IsIoPending; // Information Class 16

IsIoPending is interpreted as a boolean and indicates whether the thread has any outstanding IRPs (I/O Request Packets).

ThreadHideFromDebugger

This information class can only be set. It disables the generation of debug events for the thread. This information class requires no data, and so ThreadInformation may be a null pointer. ThreadInformationLength should be zero.

ZwSuspendThread

ZwSuspendThread suspends the execution of a thread.

```
NTSYSAPI
NTSTATUS
NTAPI
ZwSuspendThread(
    IN HANDLE ThreadHandle,
    OUT PULONG PreviousSuspendCount OPTIONAL
    );
```

Parameters

ThreadHandle
> A handle to a thread object. The handle must grant THREAD_SUSPEND_RESUME access.

PreviousSuspendCount
> Optionally points to a variable that receives the previous suspend count of the thread.

Return Value

> Returns STATUS_SUCCESS or an error status, such as STATUS_ACCESS_DENIED, STATUS_INVALID_HANDLE, STATUS_SUSPEND_COUNT_EXCEEDED, or STATUS_THREAD_IS_TERMINATING.

Related Win32 Functions

> SuspendThread.

Remarks

> SuspendThread exposes the full functionality of **ZwSuspendThread**.

ZwResumeThread

ZwResumeThread decrements the suspend count of a thread and resumes the execution of the thread if the suspend count reaches zero.

```
NTSYSAPI
NTSTATUS
NTAPI
ZwResumeThread(
    IN HANDLE ThreadHandle,
    OUT PULONG PreviousSuspendCount OPTIONAL
    );
```

Parameters

ThreadHandle
> A handle to a thread object. The handle must grant THREAD_SUSPEND_RESUME access.

PreviousSuspendCount
> Optionally points to a variable that receives the previous suspend count of the thread.

Return Value

> Returns STATUS_SUCCESS or an error status, such as STATUS_ACCESS_DENIED, or STATUS_INVALID_HANDLE.

Related Win32 Functions

ResumeThread.

Remarks

ResumeThread exposes the full functionality of **ZwResumeThread**.

ZwGetContextThread

ZwGetContextThread retrieves the execution context of a thread.

```
NTSYSAPI
NTSTATUS
NTAPI
ZwGetContextThread(
    IN HANDLE ThreadHandle,
    OUT PCONTEXT Context
    );
```

Parameters

ThreadHandle
A handle to a thread object. The handle must grant THREAD_GET_CONTEXT access.

Context
Points to a caller-allocated buffer or variable that receives the thread context information.

Return Value

Returns STATUS_SUCCESS or an error status, such as STATUS_ACCESS_DENIED, or STATUS_INVALID_HANDLE.

Related Win32 Functions

GetThreadContext.

Remarks

GetThreadContext exposes the full functionality of **ZwGetContextThread**.

The ContextFlags member of the CONTEXT structure specifies which aspects of the thread's context should be retrieved.

For the Intel family of processors, the debug registers are only valid if at least one of Dr0-3 is enabled in Dr7—regardless of whether CONTEXT_DEBUG_REGISTERS is set. This means that Dr6 cannot reliably be used to detect the difference between a single step and a debug register breakpoint.

ZwSetContextThread

ZwSetContext sets the execution context of a thread.

```
NTSYSAPI
NTSTATUS
NTAPI
ZwSetContextThread(
    IN HANDLE ThreadHandle,
    IN PCONTEXT Context
    );
```

ThreadHandle
A handle to a thread object. The handle must grant THREAD_SET_CONTEXT access.

Context
Points to a caller-allocated buffer or variable that contains the thread context information.

Return Value

Returns STATUS_SUCCESS or an error status, such as STATUS_ACCESS_DENIED, or STATUS_INVALID_HANDLE.

Related Win32 Functions

SetThreadContext.

Remarks

SetThreadContext exposes the full functionality of **ZwSetContextThread**.

The ContextFlags member of the CONTEXT structure specifies which aspects of the thread's context should be set.

Some values in the CONTEXT structure that cannot be specified are silently set to the correct value. This includes bits in the CPU status register that specify the privileged processor mode, global enabling bits in the debugging register, and other states that must be controlled by the operating system.

For the Intel family of processors, the sanitization of the EFlags register disables the seemingly harmless Resume Flag (RF). This is a nuisance when developing a user mode debugger that implements some breakpoints with the debug registers; because to continue from a breakpoint, the breakpoint must first be removed, then the thread must be single stepped, and finally the breakpoint must be restored. To ensure that no other thread passes through the breakpoint while it is temporarily removed, all other threads should be suspended until the breakpoint is restored.

ZwQueueApcThread

ZwQueueApcThread queues a user APC request to the APC queue of a thread.

```
NTSYSAPI
NTSTATUS
NTAPI
```

```
ZwQueueApcThread(
    IN HANDLE ThreadHandle,
    IN PKNORMAL_ROUTINE ApcRoutine,
    IN PVOID ApcContext OPTIONAL,
    IN PVOID Argument1 OPTIONAL,
    IN PVOID Argument2 OPTIONAL
    );
```

Parameters

ThreadHandle

A handle to a thread object. The handle must grant THREAD_SET_CONTEXT access.

ApcRoutine

A pointer to the routine to execute. The signature of the routine is:

```
VOID (NTAPI *PKNORMAL_ROUTINE)(PVOID ApcContext,
                               PVOID Argument1, PVOID Argument2);
```

ApcContext

A void pointer that can be used to provide the ApcRoutine with contextual information.

Argument1

A void pointer that can be used to provide the ApcRoutine with additional information.

Argument2

A void pointer that can be used to provide the ApcRoutine with additional information.

Return Value

Returns STATUS_SUCCESS or an error status, such as STATUS_ACCESS_DENIED, or STATUS_INVALID_HANDLE.

Related Win32 Functions

QueueUserApc.

Remarks

The APCs created by **ZwQueueApcThread** are termed "User APCs" and are only called at well-defined points in the execution of thread to which they are queued. Specifically, the thread must either call a wait service specifying that alerts are enabled, or it must call **ZwTestAlert**.

If a wait service detects that there are queued user APCs for the thread, it returns with status STATUS_USER_APC.

ZwTestAlert

ZwTestAlert tests whether a thread has been alerted.

```
NTSYSAPI
NTSTATUS
NTAPI
ZwTestAlert(
    VOID
    );
```

Parameters

None.

Return Value

Returns STATUS_SUCCESS or STATUS_ALERTED.

Related Win32 Functions

None.

Remarks

ZwTestAlert tests whether the current thread has been alerted (and clears the alerted flag). It also enables the delivery of queued user APCs.

ZwAlertThread

ZwAlertThread wakes a thread from an alertable wait.

```
NTSYSAPI
NTSTATUS
NTAPI
ZwAlertThread(
    IN HANDLE ThreadHandle
    );
```

Parameters

ThreadHandle
A handle to a thread object. The handle must grant THREAD_ALERT access.

Return Value

Returns STATUS_SUCCESS or an error status, such as STATUS_ACCESS_DENIED, or STATUS_INVALID_HANDLE.

Related Win32 Functions

None.

Remarks

An alert is similar to a user APC without the procedure call. It has the same effect on wait services and is only distinguishable by the return status (STATUS_ALERTED rather than STATUS_USER_APC).

The Win32 wrappers around the alertable system services check for a return status of STATUS_ALERTED and restart the alertable wait if this value is returned. Thus, **ZwAlertThread** cannot be used to wake a thread that is sleeping as a result of a call to SleepEx, for example.

ZwAlertResumeThread

ZwAlertResumeThread wakes a thread from a possibly suspended alertable wait.

```
NTSYSAPI
NTSTATUS
NTAPI
ZwAlertResumeThread(
    IN HANDLE ThreadHandle,
    OUT PULONG PreviousSuspendCount OPTIONAL
    );
```

Parameters

ThreadHandle
A handle to a thread object. The handle must grant THREAD_SUSPEND_RESUME access.

PreviousSuspendCount
Optionally points to a variable that will receive the previous suspend count of the thread.

Return Value

Returns STATUS_SUCCESS or an error status, such as STATUS_ACCESS_DENIED or STATUS_INVALID_HANDLE.

Related Win32 Functions

None.

Remarks

If the thread was in an alertable wait state when it was suspended, **ZwAlertResumeThread** resumes the thread and alerts it so that it returns immediately from the wait with status STATUS_ALERTED.

ZwRegisterThreadTerminatePort

ZwRegisterThreadTerminatePort registers an LPC port that should be sent a message when the thread terminates.

```
NTSYSAPI
NTSTATUS
NTAPI
ZwRegisterThreadTerminatePort(
    IN HANDLE PortHandle
    );
```

Parameters

PortHandle
A handle to a port object. The handle need not grant any specific access.

Return Value

Returns STATUS_SUCCESS or an error status, such as STATUS_INVALID_HANDLE.

Related Win32 Functions

None.

ZwRegisterThreadTerminatePort adds the port to the list of ports that will receive an LPC message when the current thread terminates.

The message has a MessageType of LPC_CLIENT_DIED and contains 8 bytes of data, specifically the creation time of the thread in the standard time format (that is, the number of 100-nanosecond intervals since January 1, 1601).

ZwImpersonateThread

ZwImpersonateThread enables one thread to impersonate the security context of another.

```
NTSYSAPI
NTSTATUS
NTAPI
ZwImpersonateThread(
    IN HANDLE ThreadHandle,
    IN HANDLE TargetThreadHandle,
    IN PSECURITY_QUALITY_OF_SERVICE SecurityQos
    );
```

Parameters

ThreadHandle
A handle to the thread which is to impersonate another thread. The handle must grant THREAD_IMPERSONATION access.

TargetThreadHandle
A handle to the thread which is to be impersonated. The handle must grant THREAD_DIRECT_IMPERSONATE access.

SecurityQoS
Points to a structure that specifies the security Quality of Service (QoS).

Return Value

Returns STATUS_SUCCESS or an error status, such as STATUS_ACCESS_DENIED or
STATUS_INVALID_HANDLE.

Related Win32 Functions

None.

Remarks

The impersonation is ended by calling **ZwSetInformationThread** with an information class of ThreadImpersonationToken, specifying an ImpersonationToken handle of
zero.

ZwImpersonateAnonymousToken

ZwImpersonateAnonymousToken sets the impersonation token of a thread to the
anonymous token (a token with no privileges and "Everyone" as the sole group
membership).

```
NTSYSAPI
NTSTATUS
NTAPI
ZwImpersonateAnonymousToken(
    IN HANDLE ThreadHandle
    );
```

Parameters

ThreadHandle
A handle to a thread object. The handle must grant THREAD_IMPERSONATION access.

Return Value

Returns STATUS_SUCCESS or an error status, such as STATUS_ACCESS_DENIED or
STATUS_INVALID_HANDLE.

Related Win32 Functions

None.

Remarks

The routine **ZwImpersonateAnonymousToken** is only present in Windows 2000.

The impersonation is ended by calling **ZwSetInformationThread** with an information
class of ThreadImpersonationToken, specifying an ImpersonationToken handle of
zero.

6
Processes

The system services described in this chapter create and manipulate process objects.

ZwCreateProcess

ZwCreateProcess creates a process object.

```
NTSYSAPI
NTSTATUS
NTAPI
ZwCreateProcess(
    OUT PHANDLE ProcessHandle,
    IN ACCESS_MASK DesiredAccess,
    IN POBJECT_ATTRIBUTES ObjectAttributes,
    IN HANDLE InheritFromProcessHandle,
    IN BOOLEAN InheritHandles,
    IN HANDLE SectionHandle OPTIONAL,
    IN HANDLE DebugPort OPTIONAL,
    IN HANDLE ExceptionPort OPTIONAL
    );
```

Parameters

ProcessHandle
  Points to a variable that will receive the process object handle if the call is successful.

DesiredAccess
  Specifies the type of access that the caller requires to the process object. This parameter can be zero, or any combination of the following flags:

```
PROCESS_TERMINATE            Terminate process
PROCESS_CREATE_THREAD        Create threads in process
PROCESS_SET_SESSIONID        Set process session id
PROCESS_VM_OPERATION         Protect and lock memory of process
PROCESS_VM_READ              Read memory of process
PROCESS_VM_WRITE             Write memory of process
PROCESS_DUP_HANDLE           Duplicate handles of process
PROCESS_CREATE_PROCESS       Bequeath address space and handles to
                             new process
```

```
PROCESS_SET_QUOTA              Set process quotas
PROCESS_SET_INFORMATION        Set information about process
PROCESS_QUERY_INFORMATION      Query information about process
PROCESS_SET_PORT               Set process exception or debug port
PROCESS_ALL_ACCESS             All of the preceding +
                               STANDARD_RIGHTS_ALL
```

ObjectAttributes

Points to a structure that specifies the object's attributes. OBJ_PERMANENT, OBJ_EXCLUSIVE, and OBJ_OPENIF are not valid attributes for a process object.

InheritFromProcessHandle

A handle to the process object from which access token, virtual address space, and handles can be inherited. The handle must grant PROCESS_CREATE_PROCESS access.

InheritHandles

Specifies whether open inheritable handles should be inherited from the process referred to by InheritFromProcessHandle.

SectionHandle

Optionally specifies a handle to an image section that grants SECTION_MAP_EXECUTE access. If this value is zero, the new process inherits the address space from the process referred to by InheritFromProcessHandle. In Windows 2000 the lowest bit specifies (when set) that the process should not be associated with the job of the InheritFromProcessHandle process.

DebugPort

Optionally specifies a handle to a port that will receive debug messages. If this value is zero, no debug messages are sent. The handle need not grant any particular access. The circumstances under which messages are sent to the debug port and their content are described in Appendix C, "Exceptions and Debugging."

ExceptionPort

Optionally specifies a handle to a port that will receive exception messages. If this value is zero, no exception messages are sent. The handle need not grant any particular access. The circumstances under which messages are sent are sent to the exception port and their content is described in Appendix C.

Return Value

Returns STATUS_SUCCESS or an error status, such as STATUS_ACCESS_DENIED or STATUS_INVALID_HANDLE.

Related Win32 Functions

CreateProcess, CreateProcessAsUser.

Remarks

The process created does not contain any threads.

The include file ntdef.h contains the following comments and definition:

```
// Low order two bits of a handle are ignored by the system and available
// for use by application code as tag bits.  The remaining bits are opaque
// and [...]

#define OBJ_HANDLE_TAGBITS  0x00000003L
```

This property of handles allows the lowest order bit of SectionHandle to be used to specify whether the created process should belong to the job of the process from which it inherits. If the job limits do not allow a new process to break away from the job, ZwCreateProcess fails with STATUS_ACCESS_DENIED.

Because Win32 programs do not normally inherit an address space and only occasionally make use of the ability to inherit handles, another way of creating a process which does not belong to the job (if any) of its creator is to specify some other process (that is not part of the job) as the "inherit from process."

Practical examples of creating a process and thread from an image section and by inheriting address space (forking) appear in Examples 6.1 and 6.2, after the necessary ancillary routines have been introduced.

The InheritedFromUniqueProcessId member of the PROCESS_BASIC_INFORMATION structure is often interpreted as being the identifier of the parent process, and in a sense this is correct. However, it is not necessarily the identifier of the process that called ZwCreateProcess, but rather the identifier of the process whose handle is passed as the InheritFromProcessHandle parameter; most of the time, these are one and the same process.

ZwOpenProcess

ZwOpenProcess opens a process object.

```
NTSYSAPI
NTSTATUS
NTAPI
ZwOpenProcess(
    OUT PHANDLE ProcessHandle,
    IN ACCESS_MASK DesiredAccess,
    IN POBJECT_ATTRIBUTES ObjectAttributes,
    IN PCLIENT_ID ClientId OPTIONAL
    );
```

Parameters

ProcessHandle
Points to a variable that will receive the process object handle if the call is successful.

DesiredAccess

Specifies the type of access that the caller requires to the process object. This parameter can be zero, or any combination of the following flags:

PROCESS_TERMINATE	Terminate process
PROCESS_CREATE_THREAD	Create threads in process
PROCESS_SET_SESSIONID	Set process session id
PROCESS_VM_OPERATION	Protect and lock memory of process
PROCESS_VM_READ	Read memory of process
PROCESS_VM_WRITE	Write memory of process
PROCESS_DUP_HANDLE	Duplicate handles of process
PROCESS_CREATE_PROCESS	Bequeath address space and handles to new process
PROCESS_SET_QUOTA	Set process quotas
PROCESS_SET_INFORMATION	Set information about process
PROCESS_QUERY_INFORMATION	Query information about process
PROCESS_SET_PORT	Set process exception or debug port
PROCESS_ALL_ACCESS	All of the preceding + STANDARD_RIGHTS_ALL

ObjectAttributes

Points to a structure that specifies the object's attributes. OBJ_PERMANENT, OBJ_EXCLUSIVE, and OBJ_OPENIF are not valid attributes for a process object.

ClientId

Optionally points to a structure that contains the process identifier (UniqueProcess) and optionally the identifier of a thread in the process (UniqueThread).

Return Value

Returns STATUS_SUCCESS or an error status, such as STATUS_ACCESS_DENIED, STATUS_OBJECT_NAME_NOT_FOUND, STATUS_INVALID_PARAMETER_MIX, or STATUS_INVALID_PARAMETER.

Related Win32 Functions

OpenProcess.

Remarks

Process objects can be given names in the same way as other objects. This name is different from what is commonly referred to as the process name, which is actually the name of the executable file from which the initial section object of the process was created.

The process to be opened is identified either by ObjectAttributes.ObjectName or ClientId; it is an error to specify both.

If ClientId.UniqueThread is not zero, it must be the identifier of a thread in the process identified by ClientId.UniqueProcess.

If the caller has SeDebugPrivilege, the check of whether the caller is granted access to the process by its ACL is bypassed. (This behavior can be disabled under Windows NT 4.0 by setting the NtGlobalFlag FLG_IGNORE_DEBUG_PRIV.)

ZwTerminateProcess

ZwTerminateProcess terminates a process and the threads that it contains.

```
NTSYSAPI
NTSTATUS
NTAPI
ZwTerminateProcess(
    IN HANDLE ProcessHandle OPTIONAL,
    IN NTSTATUS ExitStatus
    );
```

Parameters

ProcessHandle
A handle to a process object. The handle must grant PROCESS_TERMINATE access. If this value is zero, the current process is terminated.

ExitStatus
Specifies the exit status for the process and for all threads terminated as a result of this call.

Return Value

Returns STATUS_SUCCESS or an error status, such as STATUS_ACCESS_DENIED or STATUS_PROCESS_IS_TERMINATING.

Related Win32 Functions

TerminateProcess, ExitProcess.

Remarks

TerminateProcess exposes the full functionality of **ZwTerminateProcess**.

ZwQueryInformationProcess

ZwQueryInformationProcess retrieves information about a process object.

```
NTSYSAPI
NTSTATUS
NTAPI
ZwQueryInformationProcess(
    IN HANDLE ProcessHandle,
    IN PROCESSINFOCLASS ProcessInformationClass,
    OUT PVOID ProcessInformation,
    IN ULONG ProcessInformationLength,
    OUT PULONG ReturnLength OPTIONAL
    );
```

Parameters

ProcessHandle
A handle to a process object. The handle must grant PROCESS_QUERY_INFORMATION access. Some information classes also require PROCESS_VM_READ access.

ProcessInformationClass

Specifies the type of process information to be queried. The permitted values are drawn from the enumeration PROCESSINFOCLASS, described in the following section.

ProcessInformation

Points to a caller-allocated buffer or variable that receives the requested process information.

ProcessInformationLength

Specifies the size in bytes of ProcessInformation, which the caller should set according to the given ProcessInformationClass.

ReturnLength

Optionally points to a variable that receives the number of bytes actually returned to ProcessInformation if the call was successful. If this information is not needed, ReturnLength may be a null pointer.

Return Value

Returns STATUS_SUCCESS or an error status, such as STATUS_ACCESS_DENIED, STATUS_INVALID_HANDLE, STATUS_INVALID_INFO_CLASS, STATUS_INFO_LENGTH_MISMATCH, or STATUS_NOT_SUPPORTED.

Related Win32 Functions

GetProcessAffinityMask, GetProcessPriorityBoost, GetProcessWorkingSetSize, GetProcessTimes, GetExitCodeProcess, SetErrorMode.

Remarks

None.

ZwSetInformationProcess

ZwSetInformationProcess sets information affecting a process object.

```
NTSYSAPI
NTSTATUS
NTAPI
ZwSetInformationProcess(
    IN HANDLE ProcessHandle,
    IN PROCESSINFOCLASS ProcessInformationClass,
    IN PVOID ProcessInformation,
    IN ULONG ProcessInformationLength
    );
```

Parameters

ProcessHandle

A handle to a process object. The handle should normally grant PROCESS_SET_INFORMATION access. Some information classes require PROCESS_VM_WRITE, PROCESS_SET_PORT, PROCESS_SET_QUOTA or PROCESS_SET_SESSIONID access in addition or instead.

ProcessInformationClass
Specifies the type of process information to be set. The permitted values are drawn from the enumeration PROCESSINFOCLASS, described in the following section.

ProcessInformation
Points to a caller-allocated buffer or variable that contains the process information to be set.

ProcessInformationLength
Specifies the size in bytes of ProcessInformation, which the caller should set according to the given ProcessInformationClass.

Return Value

Returns STATUS_SUCCESS or an error status, such as STATUS_ACCESS_DENIED, STATUS_INVALID_HANDLE, STATUS_INVALID_INFO_CLASS, STATUS_INFO_LENGTH_MISMATCH, STATUS_PORT_ALREADY_SET, STATUS_PRIVILEGE_NOT_HELD, or STATUS_PROCESS_IS_TERMINATING.

Related Win32 Functions

SetProcessAffinityMask, SetProcessPriorityBoost, SetProcessWorkingSetSize, SetErrorMode.

Remarks

None.

PROCESSINFOCLASS

		Query	Set
typedef enum _PROCESSINFOCLASS {			
ProcessBasicInformation,	// 0	Y	N
ProcessQuotaLimits,	// 1	Y	Y
ProcessIoCounters,	// 2	Y	N
ProcessVmCounters,	// 3	Y	N
ProcessTimes,	// 4	Y	N
ProcessBasePriority,	// 5	N	Y
ProcessRaisePriority,	// 6	N	Y
ProcessDebugPort,	// 7	Y	Y
ProcessExceptionPort,	// 8	N	Y
ProcessAccessToken,	// 9	N	Y
ProcessLdtInformation,	// 10	Y	Y
ProcessLdtSize,	// 11	N	Y
ProcessDefaultHardErrorMode,	// 12	Y	Y
ProcessIoPortHandlers,	// 13	N	Y
ProcessPooledUsageAndLimits,	// 14	Y	N
ProcessWorkingSetWatch,	// 15	Y	Y
ProcessUserModeIOPL,	// 16	N	Y
ProcessEnableAlignmentFaultFixup,	// 17	N	Y
ProcessPriorityClass,	// 18	N	Y
ProcessWx86Information,	// 19	Y	N
ProcessHandleCount,	// 20	Y	N
ProcessAffinityMask,	// 21	N	Y
ProcessPriorityBoost,	// 22	Y	Y
ProcessDeviceMap,	// 23	Y	Y

```
    ProcessSessionInformation,          // 24   Y        Y
    ProcessForegroundInformation,       // 25   N        Y
    ProcessWow64Information             // 26   Y        N
} PROCESSINFOCLASS;
```

ProcessBasicInformation

```
typedef struct _PROCESS_BASIC_INFORMATION { // Information Class 0
    NTSTATUS ExitStatus;
    PPEB PebBaseAddress;
    KAFFINITY AffinityMask;
    KPRIORITY BasePriority;
    ULONG UniqueProcessId;
    ULONG InheritedFromUniqueProcessId;
} PROCESS_BASIC_INFORMATION, *PPROCESS_BASIC_INFORMATION;
```

Members

ExitStatus
The exit status of the process. If the process has not exited, this member normally contains STATUS_PENDING.

PebBaseAddress
The base address of the Process Environment Block (PEB).

AffinityMask
The processor affinity mask of the process.

BasePriority
The base priority of the process.

UniqueProcessId
The process identifier of the process.

InheritedFromUniqueProcessId
The process identifier of the process from which inheritable handles and address space may have been inherited.

Remarks

None.

ProcessQuotaLimits

```
typedef struct _QUOTA_LIMITS { // Information Class 1
    ULONG PagedPoolLimit;
    ULONG NonPagedPoolLimit;
    ULONG MinimumWorkingSetSize;
    ULONG MaximumWorkingSetSize;
    ULONG PagefileLimit;
    LARGE_INTEGER TimeLimit;
} QUOTA_LIMITS, *PQUOTA_LIMITS;
```

Members

PagedPoolLimit
The size in bytes of the paged pool quota of the processes sharing the quota block.

NonPagedPoolLimit
The size in bytes of the nonpaged pool quota of the processes sharing the quota block.

MinimumWorkingSetSize
The size in bytes of the minimum working set size of the process.

MaximumWorkingSetSize
The size in bytes of the maximum working set size of the process.

PagefileLimit
The size in pages of the pagefile quota of the processes sharing the quota block.

TimeLimit
The execution time limit of the processes sharing the quota block measured in units of 100-nanoseconds. Execution time limits are not supported.

Remarks

This information class can be both queried and set.

When setting quota limits, if MinimumWorkingSetSize and MaximumWorkingSetSize are both non-zero, the working set size is adjusted and the other values are ignored. Otherwise, the working set size is not adjusted, and if the process is still using the default quota block and SeIncreaseQuotaPrivilege is enabled, the other quota values are updated.

ProcessIoCounters

```
typedef struct _IO_COUNTERS { // Information Class 2
    LARGE_INTEGER ReadOperationCount;
    LARGE_INTEGER WriteOperationCount;
    LARGE_INTEGER OtherOperationCount;
    LARGE_INTEGER ReadTransferCount;
    LARGE_INTEGER WriteTransferCount;
    LARGE_INTEGER OtherTransferCount;
} IO_COUNTERS, *PIO_COUNTERS;
```

Members

ReadOperationCount
The number of calls to **ZwReadFile** by the process.

WriteOperationCount
The number of calls to **ZwWriteFile** by the process.

OtherOperationCount

The number of calls to all other I/O system services such as `ZwDeviceIoControlFile` by the process.

ReadTransferCount

The number of bytes read by all calls to `ZwReadFile` by the process.

WriteTransferCount

The number of bytes written by all calls to `ZwWriteFile` by the process.

OtherTransferCount

The number of bytes transferred to satisfy all other I/O operations such as `ZwDeviceIoControlFile` by the process.

Remarks

Windows NT 4.0 does not support the accounting of I/O operations on a per-process basis, and `ZwQuerySystemInformation` returns STATUS_NOT_SUPPORTED if this information class is queried. Windows 2000 supports this information class.

ProcessVmCounters

```
typedef struct _VM_COUNTERS { // Information Class 3
    ULONG PeakVirtualSize;
    ULONG VirtualSize;
    ULONG PageFaultCount;
    ULONG PeakWorkingSetSize;
    ULONG WorkingSetSize;
    ULONG QuotaPeakPagedPoolUsage;
    ULONG QuotaPagedPoolUsage;
    ULONG QuotaPeakNonPagedPoolUsage;
    ULONG QuotaNonPagedPoolUsage;
    ULONG PagefileUsage;
    ULONG PeakPagefileUsage;
} VM_COUNTERS, *PVM_COUNTERS;
```

Members

PeakVirtualSize

The peak size in bytes of the virtual address space of the process.

VirtualSize

The size in bytes of the virtual address space of the process.

PageFaultCount

The number of page faults incurred by the process.

PeakWorkingSetSize

The peak size in bytes of the working set list of the process.

WorkingSetSize
> The size in bytes of the working set list of the process.

QuotaPeakPagedPoolUsage
> The peak size in bytes of paged pool charged to the process.

QuotaPagedPoolUsage
> The size in bytes of paged pool charged to the process.

QuotaPeakNonPagedPoolUsage
> The peak size in bytes of nonpaged pool charged to the process.

QuotaNonPagedPoolUsage
> The size in bytes of nonpaged pool charged to the process.

PagefileUsage
> The size in bytes of pagefile pages used by the process.

PeakPagefileUsage
> The peak size in bytes of pagefile pages used by the process.

Remarks

> None.

ProcessTimes

```
typedef struct _KERNEL_USER_TIMES { // Information Class 4
    LARGE_INTEGER CreateTime;
    LARGE_INTEGER ExitTime;
    LARGE_INTEGER KernelTime;
    LARGE_INTEGER UserTime;
} KERNEL_USER_TIMES, *PKERNEL_USER_TIMES;
```

Members

CreateTime
> The creation time of the process in the standard time format (that is, the number of 100-nanosecond intervals since January 1, 1601).

ExitTime
> The exit time of the process in the standard time format (that is, the number of 100-nanosecond intervals since January 1, 1601). For processes which have not exited, this value is zero.

KernelTime
> The sum of the time spent executing in kernel mode by the threads of the process, which is measured in units of 100-nanoseconds.

UserTime
> The sum of the time spent executing in user mode by the threads of the process, which is measured in units of 100-nanoseconds.

Remarks

None.

ProcessBasePriority

```
KPRIORITY BasePriority;  // Information Class 5
```

This information class can only be set. It sets the base priority of the process and iterates over the threads of the process, setting their base priorities. SeIncreaseBasePriorityPrivilege is needed to increase the base priority. The memory priority of the process is also set, based on the result of masking BasePriority with 0x80000000.

ProcessRaisePriority

```
ULONG RaisePriority;  // Information Class 6
```

This information class can only be set. It iterates over the threads of the process, increasing their priority by RaisePriority (up to a maximum of the highest non-realtime priority).

ProcessDebugPort

```
HANDLE DebugPort;  // Information Class 7
```

When querying this information class, the value is interpreted as a boolean indicating whether a debug port has been set or not. The debug port can be set only if it was previously zero (in Windows NT 4.0, once set the port can also be reset to zero). The handle which is set must be a handle to a port object. (Zero is also allowed in Windows NT 4.0.)

ProcessExceptionPort

```
HANDLE ExceptionPort;  // Information Class 8
```

This information class can only be set. The exception port can be set only if it was previously zero. The handle must be a handle to a port object.

ProcessAccessToken

```
typedef struct _PROCESS_ACCESS_TOKEN { // Information Class 9
    HANDLE Token;
    HANDLE Thread;
} PROCESS_ACCESS_TOKEN, *PPROCESS_ACCESS_TOKEN;
```

Members

Token

A handle to a primary token to assign to the process. The handle must grant `TOKEN_ASSIGN_PRIMARY` access.

Thread

Not used.

Remarks

This information class can only be set. `SeAssignPrimaryTokenPrivilege` is required unless the token is a Windows 2000 filtered copy of the token of the current process. If the token is inappropriate, **ZwSetInformationProcess** may return `STATUS_BAD_TOKEN_TYPE` or `STATUS_TOKEN_ALREADY_IN_USE`.

ProcessDefaultHardErrorMode

```
ULONG DefaultHardErrorMode;   // Information Class 12
```

This information can be both queried and set. The hard error mode is a bit array of flags that correspond to the flags used by the Win32 function `SetErrorMode`, with the exception that the meaning of the lowest bit is inverted. The Win32 flags are:

```
SEM_FAILCRITICALERRORS       0x0001
SEM_NOGPFAULTERRORBOX        0x0002
SEM_NOALIGNMENTFAULTEXCEPT   0x0004
SEM_NOOPENFILEERRORBOX       0x8000
```

So, setting a hard error mode of one means do not fail critical errors.

ProcessPooledUsageAndLimits

```
typedef struct _POOLED_USAGE_AND_LIMITS { // Information Class 14
    ULONG PeakPagedPoolUsage;
    ULONG PagedPoolUsage;
    ULONG PagedPoolLimit;
    ULONG PeakNonPagedPoolUsage;
    ULONG NonPagedPoolUsage;
    ULONG NonPagedPoolLimit;
    ULONG PeakPagefileUsage;
    ULONG PagefileUsage;
    ULONG PagefileLimit;
} POOLED_USAGE_AND_LIMITS, *PPOOLED_USAGE_AND_LIMITS;
```

Members

PeakPagedPoolUsage

The peak size in bytes of the paged pool charged to the processes sharing the quota block.

PagedPoolUsage

The size in bytes of the paged pool charged to the processes sharing the quota block.

PagedPoolLimit
> The size in bytes of the paged pool quota of the processes sharing the quota block.

PeakNonPagedPoolUsage
> The peak size in bytes of the nonpaged pool charged to the processes sharing the quota block.

NonPagedPoolUsage
> The size in bytes of the nonpaged pool charged to the processes sharing the quota block.

NonPagedPoolLimit
> The size in bytes of the nonpaged pool quota of the processes sharing the quota block.

PeakPagefileUsage
> The peak size in pages of the pagefile used by the processes sharing the quota block.

PagefileUsage
> The size in pages of the pagefile used by the processes sharing the quota block.

PagefileLimit
> The size in pages of the pagefile quota of the processes sharing the quota block.

Remarks

None.

ProcessWorkingSetWatch

```
typedef struct _PROCESS_WS_WATCH_INFORMATION { // Information Class 15
    PVOID FaultingPc;
    PVOID FaultingVa;
} PROCESS_WS_WATCH_INFORMATION, *PPROCESS_WS_WATCH_INFORMATION;
```

Members

FaultingPc
> Pointer to the instruction that caused the page fault.

FaultingVa
> The virtual address referenced by the instruction. The low bit indicates whether the fault was soft (if set) or hard (if clear).

Remarks

When setting this information class, no information is required, and so `ProcessInformation` may be null and `ProcessInformationLength` should be zero.

When querying this information class, an array of PROCESS_WS_WATCH_INFORMATION structures are returned; the end of the array is marked by an element with a FaultingPc value of zero.

The system records the first 1020 page faults that occur either after working set watching is enabled, or after the working set watch information is queried.

ProcessUserModeIOPL

```
UserModeIOPL;  // Information Class 16
```

This information class can only be set and no information is required. Therefore, ProcessInformation may be null and ProcessInformationLength should be zero.

SeTcbPrivilege is required to set this information class.

This information class is only meaningful for Intel processors; it modifies the I/O Privilege Level for the process so that the process may directly access the I/O ports and execute other instructions that are sensitive to IOPL.

ProcessEnableAlignmentFaultFixup

```
BOOLEAN EnableAlignmentFaultFixup;  // Information Class 17
```

This information class only can be set and is equivalent to calling ZwSystemInformationProcess with an information class of ProcessDefaultHardErrorMode and a value of SEM_NOALIGNMENTFAULTEXCEPT.

ProcessPriorityClass

```
typedef struct _PROCESS_PRIORITY_CLASS { // Information Class 18
    BOOLEAN Foreground;
    UCHAR PriorityClass;
} PROCESS_PRIORITY_CLASS, *PPROCESS_PRIORITY_CLASS;
```

Members

Foreground
   Specifies whether the process is running in the foreground. Performance factors affected include scheduling quantum and working set trimming and growth.

PriorityClass
   The scheduling priority class of the process. Permitted values are zero to four (for Windows NT 4.0) or six (for Windows 2000). SeIncreaseBasePriorityPrivilege is required to set PriorityClass to four. The defined values include:

```
PC_IDLE            1
PC_NORMAL          2
PC_HIGH            3
PC_REALTIME        4
PC_BELOW_NORMAL    5
PC_ABOVE_NORMAL    6
```

Remarks

This information class can only be set.

Scheduling priority parameter changes are propagated to all the threads of the process.

ProcessWx86Information

```
ULONG Wx86Information;  // Information Class 19
```

Wx86Information always contains zero.

ProcessHandleCount

```
ULONG HandleCount;  // Information Class 20
```

HandleCount receives a count of the number of open handles of the process.

ProcessAffinityMask

```
KAFFINITY AffinityMask;  // Information Class 21
```

This information class only can be set. The specified processor affinity mask is propagated to all the threads of the process.

ProcessPriorityBoost

```
ULONG PriorityBoost;  // Information Class 22
```

This information can be both queried and set. PriorityBoost is interpreted as a boolean and specifies whether priority boosting is enabled or disabled. Changes to PriorityBoost are propagated to all the threads of the process.

ProcessDeviceMap

```
typedef struct _PROCESS_DEVICEMAP_INFORMATION { // Information Class 23
    union {
        struct {
            HANDLE DirectoryHandle;
        } Set;
        struct {
            ULONG DriveMap;
            UCHAR DriveType[32];
        } Query;
    };
} PROCESS_DEVICEMAP_INFORMATION, *PPROCESS_DEVICEMAP_INFORMATION;
```

Members

DirectoryHandle
A handle to an object directory granting DIRECTORY_TRAVERSE access.

DriveMap
   A bit array representing the disk drives available to the process.

DriveType
   An array of values representing the types of disk drives. The defined types include:

```
DRIVE_UNKNOWN     0
DRIVE_NO_ROOT_DIR 1
DRIVE_REMOVABLE   2
DRIVE_FIXED       3
DRIVE_REMOTE      4
DRIVE_CDROM       5
DRIVE_RAMDISK     6
```

Remarks

When a symbolic link with a name conforming to the DOS drive letter format (an alphabetic character followed by a colon) is created in an object directory, the device map of the directory is updated to reflect the presence of a new disk drive. When a process sets its device map to an object directory handle, it references the device map of the directory, giving the process access to all the disk drives symbolically linked to the directory with DOS format names. By default, the device map of a process refers to the device map associated with the object directory named "\??".

ProcessSessionInformation

```
typedef struct _PROCESS_SESSION_INFORMATION { // Information Class 24
    ULONG SessionId;
} PROCESS_SESSION_INFORMATION, *PPROCESS_SESSION_INFORMATION;
```

Members

SessionId
   A numeric identifier for a session.

Remarks

`SeTcbPrivilege` is required to set this information class.

Session identifiers are used by Windows Terminal Server to distinguish between client sessions.

The session identifier is stored in the EPROCESS structure, the process token, and in the Process Environment Block (PEB) of the target process.

ProcessForegroundInformation

```
BOOLEAN Foreground;  // Information Class 25
```

Specifies whether the process is running in the foreground. The performance factors that are affected include scheduling quantum and working set trimming and growth.

This information class sets one of the parameters that also can be set using the information class, `ProcessPriorityClass`.

ProcessWow64Information

```
ULONG Wow64Information;  // Information Class 26
```

Wow64Information normally contains zero on the Intel platform.

The following routines are not part of the Native API, but they perform the useful task of building a complex data structure in self-relative (normalized) form. The routines are part of the Run-Time Library (RTL) included in ntdll.dll.

RtlCreateProcessParameters

RtlCreateProcessParameters creates and populates the data structure used to hold the user mode process parameters.

```
NTSTATUS
NTAPI
RtlCreateProcessParameters(
    OUT PPROCESS_PARAMETERS *ProcessParameters,
    IN PUNICODE_STRING ImageFile,
    IN PUNICODE_STRING DllPath OPTIONAL,
    IN PUNICODE_STRING CurrentDirectory OPTIONAL,
    IN PUNICODE_STRING CommandLine OPTIONAL,
    IN ULONG CreationFlags,
    IN PUNICODE_STRING WindowTitle OPTIONAL,
    IN PUNICODE_STRING Desktop OPTIONAL,
    IN PUNICODE_STRING Reserved OPTIONAL,
    IN PUNICODE_STRING Reserved2 OPTIONAL
    );
```

Parameters

ProcessParameters
Points to a variable that will receive a pointer to the process parameters if the call is successful.

ImageFile
Optionally points to the image file name from which the process was created.

DllPath
Optionally points to the search path that was used to search for the image file and its referenced DLLs.

CurrentDirectory
Optionally points to the current directory name of the process.

CommandLine
Optionally points to the command line used to start the process.

CreationFlags
A bit array of flags.

WindowTitle
Optionally points to a window title for the process.

Desktop
Optionally points to the name of the desktop used by the process.

Reserved
Related to STARTUPINFO.lpReserved. It is not used by Win32 subsystem.

Reserved2
Related to STARTUPINFO.cbReserved2 and STARTUPINFO.lpReserved2. It is not used by
Win32 subsystem.

Return Value

Returns STATUS_SUCCESS or an error status.

Related Win32 Functions

None.

Remarks

The process parameters are created by the caller of **ZwCreateProcess** and copied to
the new process. The process parameters contain pointers to strings, and to facilitate
copying of the data to a different virtual address (in another process), these pointers
are initially stored in normalized form (relative to the start of the structure). They are
converted to normal pointers after the copy is complete.

If an optional parameter is omitted, by specifying a null pointer, the parameter value is
copied from the process parameters of the current process, except for CommandLine,
which is copied from ImageFile.

The process parameters are pointed to by the PEB of a process.

RtlDestroyProcessParameters

RtlDestroyProcessParameters deallocates the data structure used to hold the user
mode process parameters.

```
NTSTATUS
NTAPI
RtlDestroyProcessParameters(
    IN PPROCESS_PARAMETERS ProcessParameters
    );
```

Parameters

ProcessParameters
Points to the process parameters to be deallocated.

Return Value

Returns STATUS_SUCCESS or an error status.

Related Win32 Functions

None.

Remarks

None.

PROCESS_PARAMETERS

```
typedef struct _PROCESS_PARAMETERS {
    ULONG AllocationSize;
    ULONG Size;
    ULONG Flags;
    ULONG Reserved;
    LONG Console;
    ULONG ProcessGroup;
    HANDLE hStdInput;
    HANDLE hStdOutput;
    HANDLE hStdError;
    UNICODE_STRING CurrentDirectoryName;
    HANDLE CurrentDirectoryHandle;
    UNICODE_STRING DllPath;
    UNICODE_STRING ImageFile;
    UNICODE_STRING CommandLine;
    PWSTR Environment;
    ULONG dwX;
    ULONG dwY;
    ULONG dwXSize;
    ULONG dwYSize;
    ULONG dwXCountChars;
    ULONG dwYCountChars;
    ULONG dwFillAttribute;
    ULONG dwFlags;
    ULONG wShowWindow;
    UNICODE_STRING WindowTitle;
    UNICODE_STRING Desktop;
    UNICODE_STRING Reserved;
    UNICODE_STRING Reserved2;
} PROCESS_PARAMETERS, *PPROCESS_PARAMETERS;
```

Members

AllocationSize

The size in bytes of virtual memory allocated to hold the process parameters.

Size

The size in bytes of virtual memory used to hold the process parameters.

Flags

A bit array of flags.

Reserved
> Reserved; always contains zero.

Console
> The numeric identifier of the console to be used by the new process. A value of -1 indicates that the process does not have access to a console, and a value of -2 indicates that the process should be given access to a new console.

ProcessGroup
> The numeric identifier of the process group of the process.

hStdInput
> The handle that will be used as the standard input handle for the new process if STARTF_USESTDHANDLES is specified in dwFlags.

hStdOutput
> The handle that will be used as the standard output handle for the new process if STARTF_USESTDHANDLES is specified in dwFlags.

hStdError
> The handle that will be used as the standard error handle for the new process if STARTF_USESTDHANDLES is specified in dwFlags.

CurrentDirectoryName
> The name of the current directory of the process.

CurrentDirectoryHandle
> The handle to the current directory of the process.

DllPath
> The search path that was used to search for the image file of the process and its referenced DLLs.

ImageFile
> The image file name from which the process was created.

CommandLine
> The command line used to start the process.

Environment
> A pointer to the environment block of the process that contains the environment variable strings.

dwX
> The x offset, in pixels, of the upper left corner of a window if a new window is created, and STARTF_USEPOSITION is specified in dwFlags.

dwY

The y offset, in pixels, of the upper left corner of a window if a new window is created, and STARTF_USEPOSITION is specified in dwFlags.

dwXSize

The width, in pixels, of a window if a new window is created, and STARTF_USESIZE is specified in dwFlags.

dwYSize

The height, in pixels, of a window if a new window is created, and STARTF_USESIZE is specified in dwFlags.

dwXCountChars

The width, in characters, of a screen buffer if a new console window is created, and STARTF_USECOUNTCHARS is specified in dwFlags.

dwYCountChars

The height, in characters, of a screen buffer if a new console window is created, and STARTF_USECOUNTCHARS is specified in dwFlags.

dwFillAttribute

The initial text and background colors if a new console window is created, and STARTF_USEFILLATTRIBUTE is specified in dwFlags.

dwFlags

The bit field that determines whether certain PROCESS_PARAMETERS members are used when the process creates a window.

wShowWindow

The show state if a new window is created, and STARTF_USESHOWWINDOW is specified in dwFlags.

WindowTitle

The window title for the process.

Desktop

The name of the desktop used by the process.

Remarks

When using the Win32 function CreateProcess to create a process, many of the fields of the PROCESS_PARAMETERS structure are initialized based on information in the STARTUPINFO structure passed as argument to CreateProcess.

The following routines are not part of the Native API, but they gather information about processes which is useful to debuggers and other clients of the ToolHelp library.

The routines are part of the RTL included in ntdll.dll.

RtlCreateQueryDebugBuffer

`RtlCreateQueryDebugBuffer` creates the data structure required by
`RtlQueryProcessDebugInformation`.

```
PDEBUG_BUFFER
NTAPI
RtlCreateQueryDebugBuffer(
    IN ULONG Size,
    IN BOOLEAN EventPair
    );
```

Parameters

Size

Optionally specifies the size of the debug buffer. If `Size` is zero, a default size is used.

EventPair

Specifies whether an event pair should be used to synchronize the retrieval of debug
information. If true, a thread will be created in the target process that will be used to
service each request for information. If false, a thread is created and destroyed in the
target process for each request.

Return Value

Returns a pointer to a `DEBUG_BUFFER` or a null pointer.

Related Win32 Functions

None.

Remarks

None.

RtlQueryProcessDebugInformation

`RtlQueryProcessDebugInformation` queries information about a process that is maintained in user mode.

```
NTSTATUS
NTAPI
RtlQueryProcessDebugInformation(
    IN ULONG ProcessId,
    IN ULONG DebugInfoClassMask,
    IN OUT PDEBUG_BUFFER DebugBuffer
    );
```

Parameters

ProcessId

Specifies the identifier of the process that is to be queried.

DebugInfoClassMask

A bit array specifying which type of information is to be queried. Multiple types of information can be retrieved in a single call. This parameter can be any combination of the following flags:

```
PDI_MODULES       0x01  // The loaded modules of the process
PDI_BACKTRACE     0x02  // The heap stack back traces
PDI_HEAPS         0x04  // The heaps of the process
PDI_HEAP_TAGS     0x08  // The heap tags
PDI_HEAP_BLOCKS   0x10  // The heap blocks
PDI_LOCKS         0x20  // The locks created by the process
```

DebugBuffer

Points to an initialized DEBUG_BUFFER that will be updated to contain the requested information.

Return Value

Returns STATUS_SUCCESS or an error status.

Related Win32 Functions

None.

Remarks

There are parallels between this information about processes and the information returned by **ZwQuerySystemInformation** about the system. For example, heaps are a process equivalent of system pools, and locks are a process equivalent of system resources.

The reason that this information is retrieved with an RTL routine rather than a system service is that the information is created and maintained entirely in user mode by ntdll.dll—the kernel is unaware of its existence.

The information about modules and heaps can be used to implement the ToolHelp functions that report on modules and heaps. Example 6.3 builds upon an earlier example to add this functionality.

PSAPI does not use **RtlQueryProcessDebugInformation** to retrieve process module information. It directly reads and interprets the virtual memory used by ntdll.dll to store the information.

RtlDestroyQueryDebugBuffer

RtlDestroyQueryDebugBuffer deallocates the data structure used by **RtlQueryProcessDebugInformation**.

```
NTSTATUS
NTAPI
RtlDestroyQueryDebugBuffer(
    IN PDEBUG_BUFFER DebugBuffer
    );
```

Parameters

DebugBuffer
Points to the debug buffer to be deallocated.

Return Value

Returns STATUS_SUCCESS.

Related Win32 Functions

None.

Remarks

If there is a thread in a target process still waiting to service query requests, it is first
terminated, and its stack deallocated.

DEBUG_BUFFER

```
typedef struct _DEBUG_BUFFER {
    HANDLE SectionHandle;
    PVOID SectionBase;
    PVOID RemoteSectionBase;
    ULONG SectionBaseDelta;
    HANDLE EventPairHandle;
    ULONG Unknown[2];
    HANDLE RemoteThreadHandle;
    ULONG InfoClassMask;
    ULONG SizeOfInfo;
    ULONG AllocatedSize;
    ULONG SectionSize;
    PVOID ModuleInformation;
    PVOID BackTraceInformation;
    PVOID HeapInformation;
    PVOID LockInformation;
    PVOID Reserved[8];
} DEBUG_BUFFER, *PDEBUG_BUFFER;
```

Members

ModuleInformation
A pointer to the module information if this was requested. The data pointed to by
ModuleInformation is a ULONG count of the number of modules followed immediately
by an array of DEBUG_MODULE_INFORMATION.

BackTraceInformation
A pointer to the heap stack back-trace information if this was requested.

HeapInformation
A pointer to the heap information if this was requested. The data pointed to by
HeapInformation is a ULONG count of the number of heaps followed immediately by an
array of DEBUG_HEAP_INFORMATION.

LockInformation

A pointer to the lock information if this was requested. The data pointed to by LockInformation is a ULONG count of the number of locks followed immediately by an array of DEBUG_LOCK_INFORMATION.

Remarks

The other members of DEBUG_BUFFER are opaque.

DEBUG_MODULE_INFORMATION

```
typedef struct _DEBUG_MODULE_INFORMATION { // c.f. SYSTEM_MODULE_INFORMATION
    ULONG Reserved[2];
    ULONG Base;
    ULONG Size;
    ULONG Flags;
    USHORT Index;
    USHORT Unknown;
    USHORT LoadCount;
    USHORT ModuleNameOffset;
    CHAR ImageName[256];
} DEBUG_MODULE_INFORMATION, *PDEBUG_MODULE_INFORMATION;
```

Members

Base

The base address of the module.

Size

The size of the module.

Flags

A bit array of flags describing the state of the module. Observed values include:

```
LDRP_STATIC_LINK             0x00000002
LDRP_IMAGE_DLL               0x00000004
LDRP_LOAD_IN_PROGRESS        0x00001000
LDRP_UNLOAD_IN_PROGRESS      0x00002000
LDRP_ENTRY_PROCESSED         0x00004000
LDRP_ENTRY_INSERTED          0x00008000
LDRP_CURRENT_LOAD            0x00010000
LDRP_FAILED_BUILTIN_LOAD     0x00020000
LDRP_DONT_CALL_FOR_THREADS   0x00040000
LDRP_PROCESS_ATTACH_CALLED   0x00080000
LDRP_DEBUG_SYMBOLS_LOADED    0x00100000
LDRP_IMAGE_NOT_AT_BASE       0x00200000
LDRP_WX86_IGNORE_MACHINETYPE 0x00400000
```

Index

The index of the module in the array of modules.

Unknown

Interpretation unknown.

LoadCount

The number of references to the module.

ModuleNameOffset
The offset to the final filename component of the image name.

ImageName
The filepath of the module.

Remarks

None.

DEBUG_HEAP_INFORMATION

```
typedef struct _DEBUG_HEAP_INFORMATION {
    ULONG Base;
    ULONG Flags;
    USHORT Granularity;
    USHORT Unknown;
    ULONG Allocated;
    ULONG Committed;
    ULONG TagCount;
    ULONG BlockCount;
    ULONG Reserved[7];
    PVOID Tags;
    PVOID Blocks;
} DEBUG_HEAP_INFORMATION, *PDEBUG_HEAP_INFORMATION;
```

Members

Base
The base address of the heap.

Flags
A bit array of flags describing heap options.

Granularity
The granularity of allocation from the heap.

Unknown
Interpretation unknown.

Allocated
The size in bytes of memory allocated from the heap.

Committed
The size in bytes of the memory committed to the heap.

TagCount
The number of tags pointed to by Tags.

BlockCount
The number of blocks pointed to by Blocks.

Tags

A pointer to an array of tag information. Heap tags are used to track the usage of heap blocks.

Blocks

A pointer to an array of block information.

Remarks

The flags PDI_HEAP_TAGS and PDI_HEAP_BLOCKS must be specified in addition to PDI_HEAPS if information on heap tags or blocks is required.

DEBUG_LOCK_INFORMATION

```
typedef struct _DEBUG_LOCK_INFORMATION { // c.f. SYSTEM_LOCK_INFORMATION
    PVOID Address;
    USHORT Type;
    USHORT CreatorBackTraceIndex;
    ULONG OwnerThreadId;
    ULONG ActiveCount;
    ULONG ContentionCount;
    ULONG EntryCount;
    ULONG RecursionCount;
    ULONG NumberOfSharedWaiters;
    ULONG NumberOfExclusiveWaiters;
} DEBUG_LOCK_INFORMATION, *PDEBUG_LOCK_INFORMATION;
```

Members

Address

The address of the lock structure.

Type

The type of the lock. This is either RTL_CRITSECT_TYPE (0) or RTL_RESOURCE_TYPE (1).

CreatorBackTraceIndex

Normally contains zero.

OwnerThreadId

The thread identifier of the owner of the lock (the exclusive owner if the lock is a resource).

ActiveCount

The number of threads granted access to the lock. Critical sections count from -1, and resources count from 0.

ContentionCount

The number of times a thread had to wait for the lock.

EntryCount

The number of times a critical section has been entered. This does not include the number of times that the critical section was entered without waiting.

RecursionCount

The number of times a thread has recursively entered a critical section.

NumberOfSharedWaiters

The number of threads waiting for shared access to the resource.

NumberOfExclusiveWaiters

The number of threads waiting for exclusive access to the resource.

Remarks

There are two types of user mode locks: critical sections and resources. The resource lock is similar in functionality to the kernel mode resource lock and provides multiple reader, single writer functionality.

Example 6.1: Forking a Win32 Process

```c
#include "ntdll.h"
#include <stdio.h>

namespace NT {
    extern "C" {

NTSTATUS
NTAPI
CsrClientCallServer(
    IN PVOID Message,
    IN PVOID,
    IN ULONG Opcode,
    IN ULONG Size
    );

    }
}

VOID InheritAll()
{
    ULONG n = 0x1000;
    PULONG p = new ULONG[n];

    while (NT::ZwQuerySystemInformation(NT::SystemHandleInformation,
                                        p, n * sizeof *p, 0)
           == STATUS_INFO_LENGTH_MISMATCH)
        delete [] p, p = new ULONG[n *= 2];

    NT::PSYSTEM_HANDLE_INFORMATION h = NT::PSYSTEM_HANDLE_INFORMATION(p + 1);

    ULONG pid = GetCurrentProcessId();

    for (ULONG i = 0; i < *p; i++)
        if (h[i].ProcessId == pid)
            SetHandleInformation(HANDLE(h[i].Handle),
                                 HANDLE_FLAG_INHERIT, HANDLE_FLAG_INHERIT);
    delete [] p;
}

VOID InformCsrss(HANDLE hProcess, HANDLE hThread, ULONG pid, ULONG tid)
{
    struct CSRSS_MESSAGE {
```

```
            ULONG Unknown1;
            ULONG Opcode;
            ULONG Status;
            ULONG Unknown2;
        };

        struct {
            NT::PORT_MESSAGE PortMessage;
            CSRSS_MESSAGE CsrssMessage;
            PROCESS_INFORMATION ProcessInformation;
            NT::CLIENT_ID Debugger;
            ULONG CreationFlags;
            ULONG VdmInfo[2];
        } csrmsg = {{0}, {0}, {hProcess, hThread, pid, tid}, {0}, 0, {0}};

        NT::CsrClientCallServer(&csrmsg, 0, 0x10000, 0x24);
    }


    __declspec(naked) int child()
    {
        typedef BOOL (WINAPI *CsrpConnectToServer)(PWSTR);

        CsrpConnectToServer(0x77F8F65D)(L"\\Windows");
        __asm mov    eax, 0
        __asm mov    esp, ebp
        __asm pop    ebp
        __asm ret
    }


    #pragma optimize("y", off)  // disable frame pointer omission

    int fork()
    {
        HANDLE hProcess, hThread;

        InheritAll();

        NT::OBJECT_ATTRIBUTES oa = {sizeof oa};

        NT::ZwCreateProcess(&hProcess, PROCESS_ALL_ACCESS, &oa,
                            NtCurrentProcess(), TRUE, 0, 0, 0);

        NT::CONTEXT context = {CONTEXT_FULL
                               | CONTEXT_DEBUG_REGISTERS
                               | CONTEXT_FLOATING_POINT};

        NT::ZwGetContextThread(NtCurrentThread(), &context);

        context.Eip = ULONG(child);

        MEMORY_BASIC_INFORMATION mbi;

        NT::ZwQueryVirtualMemory(NtCurrentProcess(), PVOID(context.Esp),
                                 NT::MemoryBasicInformation, &mbi, sizeof mbi, 0);

        NT::USER_STACK stack = {0, 0, PCHAR(mbi.BaseAddress) + mbi.RegionSize,
                                mbi.BaseAddress, mbi.AllocationBase};

        NT::CLIENT_ID cid;

        NT::ZwCreateThread(&hThread, THREAD_ALL_ACCESS, &oa,
```

```
                    hProcess, &cid, &context, &stack, TRUE);

    NT::THREAD_BASIC_INFORMATION tbi;

    NT::ZwQueryInformationThread(NtCurrentThread(),
                                 NT::ThreadBasicInformation,
                                 &tbi, sizeof tbi, 0);

    NT::PNT_TIB tib = tbi.TebBaseAddress;

    NT::ZwQueryInformationThread(hThread, NT::ThreadBasicInformation,
                                 &tbi, sizeof tbi, 0);

    NT::ZwWriteVirtualMemory(hProcess, tbi.TebBaseAddress,
                             &tib->ExceptionList, sizeof tib->ExceptionList,
                             0);

    InformCsrss(hProcess, hThread,
                ULONG(cid.UniqueProcess), ULONG(cid.UniqueThread));

    NT::ZwResumeThread(hThread, 0);

    NT::ZwClose(hThread);
    NT::ZwClose(hProcess);

    return int(cid.UniqueProcess);
}

#pragma optimize("", on)


int main()
{
    int n = fork();
    Sleep(n * 10);
    Beep(100, 100);
    printf("%d\n", n);
    return 0;
}
```

There is much about Example 6.1 that needs explaining. The main part of the example implements a fork library routine that is exercised by the function main.

main first tries to report the success or failure of the fork using the minimum of functionality by beeping the system beeper; if the fork is successful, two beeps should be heard. main then tries to print the return value of fork on its standard output, which requires communication with the Win32 subsystem process (csrss.exe) if the standard output is a console.

The following steps are taken by the fork routine to make a copy of the current process:

- Mark all the open handles of the process as inheritable. Typically, neither the handles created explicitly by a Win32 program, nor the handles created implicitly by Win32 DLLs such as kernel32.dll are marked as inheritable.

- Call **ZwCreateProcess** to create the process. If this call returns successfully, a new process has been created that shares a copy of the address space of the current process.

- Gather the information needed by `ZwCreateThread` to create the initial thread in the process: an execution context and a stack. The execution context is obtained by calling `ZwGetContextThread` for the current thread. Although the Platform SDK documentation for `GetThreadContext` states that it is not possible to get a valid context for a running thread, the returned context is a good starting point and the most volatile members of the context are explicitly set later. The dimensions of the stack of the current thread are obtained by calling `ZwQueryVirtualMemory`.

- Update the Eip (instruction pointer) member of the context to point to the thunk (a routine named `child`) at which the initial thread will start running and then create the thread in a suspended state by calling `ZwCreateThread`.

- The calling thread may have established some frame-based exception handlers and the next step is to enable these in the new thread by copying the `ExceptionList` pointer from the Thread Environment Block (TEB) of the current thread to the TEB of new thread.

- `InformCsrss` informs the Win32 subsystem that a Win32 client process is about to start; this gives the subsystem the opportunity to modify some settings of the process, such as setting process debug and exception ports.

- Resume the initial thread in the forked process by calling `ZwResumeThread`, and return the process identifier of the new process to the caller.

`InformCsrss` just initializes a data structure and calls the routine `CsrClientCallServer` (exported by ntdll.dll) to forward the data to csrss.exe. Internally `CsrClientCallServer` uses the native LPC mechanism to convey the data.

The initial thread in the new process starts execution at the start of the `child` routine. This `__declspec(naked)` routine expects that a standard call frame has been established by fork (hence, the `"#pragma optimize("y", off)"` to disable frame pointer omission for the routine fork) that enables the Esp and Ebp registers to be set with some simple assembly code. A zero is stored in Eax so that when the child process checks the return value of fork, it will find that it is zero.

When kernel32.dll is initialized in the new process, it calls a `CsrXxx` routine that checks whether the process is connected to a subsystem and if not connects it. Unfortunately, the check just examines the value of a global variable and because this variable was copied from the parent (along with the rest of the parent's address space), it appears that the new process is already connected.

There is no good solution to this problem, and the example calls a hexadecimal address (which varies from service pack to service pack) that is the start of the private routine `CsrpConnectToServer`; this routine connects unconditionally to the subsystem and updates the global variable.

ntdll.dll exports a number of routines whose names start with `Csr`; the function of these routines is to support interaction between clients and subsystems. It is difficult to decide whether these routines are specific to communication with the Win32 subsystem or are intended to be used more widely. They are not used by the Posix or OS/2 subsystems, but they are parameterized in a way that suggests generality (for example, the `"\Windows"` argument to `CsrpConnectToServer`, which is used to identify a named LPC port to which the subsystem is listening).

When Example 6.1 is compiled and linked, its executable file contains imports from two or three DLLs: ntdll.dll, kernel32.dll and possibly a C run-time library DLL. Some versions of msvcrt.dll (a C run-time library DLL) also have problems arising from global variables already having been initialized (by the parent process) before their DllEntryPoint routine is first invoked. Statically linking to the C run-time library often solves this problem, but it bodes ill for the suitability of many other common DLLs for forking.

Example 6.2: Creating a Win32 Process

```
#include "ntdll.h"
#include <stdio.h>

namespace NT {
    extern "C" {

NTSTATUS
NTAPI
CsrClientCallServer(
    IN PVOID Message,
    IN PVOID,
    IN ULONG Opcode,
    IN ULONG Size
    );

    }
}

VOID InformCsrss(HANDLE hProcess, HANDLE hThread, ULONG pid, ULONG tid)
{
    struct CSRSS_MESSAGE {
        ULONG Unknown1;
        ULONG Opcode;
        ULONG Status;
        ULONG Unknown2;
    };

    struct {
        NT::PORT_MESSAGE PortMessage;
        CSRSS_MESSAGE CsrssMessage;
        PROCESS_INFORMATION ProcessInformation;
        NT::CLIENT_ID Debugger;
        ULONG CreationFlags;
        ULONG VdmInfo[2];
    } csrmsg = {{0}, {0}, {hProcess, hThread, pid, tid}, {0}, 0, {0}};

    NT::CsrClientCallServer(&csrmsg, 0, 0x10000, 0x24);
}

PWSTR CopyEnvironment(HANDLE hProcess)
{
    PWSTR env = GetEnvironmentStringsW();

    ULONG n;
    for (n = 0; env[n] != 0; n += wcslen(env + n) + 1) ; n *= sizeof *env;

    ULONG m = n;
    PVOID p = 0;
    NT::ZwAllocateVirtualMemory(hProcess, &p, 0, &m,
                                MEM_COMMIT, PAGE_READWRITE);
```

```
    NT::ZwWriteVirtualMemory(hProcess, p, env, n, 0);

    return PWSTR(p);
}

VOID CreateProcessParameters(HANDLE hProcess, NT::PPEB Peb,
                             NT::PUNICODE_STRING ImageFile)
{
    NT::PPROCESS_PARAMETERS pp;

    NT::RtlCreateProcessParameters(&pp, ImageFile, 0, 0, 0, 0, 0, 0, 0, 0);

    pp->Environment = CopyEnvironment(hProcess);

    ULONG n = pp->Size;
    PVOID p = 0;
    NT::ZwAllocateVirtualMemory(hProcess, &p, 0, &n,
                                MEM_COMMIT, PAGE_READWRITE);

    NT::ZwWriteVirtualMemory(hProcess, p, pp, pp->Size, 0);

    NT::ZwWriteVirtualMemory(hProcess, PCHAR(Peb) + 0x10, &p, sizeof p, 0);

    NT::RtlDestroyProcessParameters(pp);
}

int exec(NT::PUNICODE_STRING name)
{
    HANDLE hProcess, hThread, hSection, hFile;

    NT::OBJECT_ATTRIBUTES oa = {sizeof oa, 0, name, OBJ_CASE_INSENSITIVE};
    NT::IO_STATUS_BLOCK iosb;
    NT::ZwOpenFile(&hFile, FILE_EXECUTE | SYNCHRONIZE, &oa, &iosb,
                   FILE_SHARE_READ, FILE_SYNCHRONOUS_IO_NONALERT);

    oa.ObjectName = 0;

    NT::ZwCreateSection(&hSection, SECTION_ALL_ACCESS, &oa, 0,
                        PAGE_EXECUTE, SEC_IMAGE, hFile);

    NT::ZwClose(hFile);

    NT::ZwCreateProcess(&hProcess, PROCESS_ALL_ACCESS, &oa,
                        NtCurrentProcess(), TRUE, hSection, 0, 0);

    NT::SECTION_IMAGE_INFORMATION sii;
    NT::ZwQuerySection(hSection, NT::SectionImageInformation,
                       &sii, sizeof sii, 0);

    NT::ZwClose(hSection);

    NT::USER_STACK stack = {0};

    ULONG n = sii.StackReserve;
    NT::ZwAllocateVirtualMemory(hProcess, &stack.ExpandableStackBottom, 0, &n,
                                MEM_RESERVE, PAGE_READWRITE);

    stack.ExpandableStackBase = PCHAR(stack.ExpandableStackBottom)
                                + sii.StackReserve;
    stack.ExpandableStackLimit = PCHAR(stack.ExpandableStackBase)
                                 - sii.StackCommit;
```

```
        n = sii.StackCommit + PAGE_SIZE;
        PVOID p = PCHAR(stack.ExpandableStackBase) - n;
        NT::ZwAllocateVirtualMemory(hProcess, &p, 0, &n,
                                    MEM_COMMIT, PAGE_READWRITE);

        ULONG x; n = PAGE_SIZE;
        NT::ZwProtectVirtualMemory(hProcess, &p, &n,
                                    PAGE_READWRITE | PAGE_GUARD, &x);

        NT::CONTEXT context = {CONTEXT_FULL};
        context.SegGs = 0;
        context.SegFs = 0x38;
        context.SegEs = 0x20;
        context.SegDs = 0x20;
        context.SegSs = 0x20;
        context.SegCs = 0x18;
        context.EFlags = 0x3000;
        context.Esp = ULONG(stack.ExpandableStackBase) - 4;
        context.Eip = ULONG(sii.EntryPoint);

        NT::CLIENT_ID cid;

        NT::ZwCreateThread(&hThread, THREAD_ALL_ACCESS, &oa,
                           hProcess, &cid, &context, &stack, TRUE);

        NT::PROCESS_BASIC_INFORMATION pbi;
        NT::ZwQueryInformationProcess(hProcess, NT::ProcessBasicInformation,
                                      &pbi, sizeof pbi, 0);

        CreateProcessParameters(hProcess, pbi.PebBaseAddress, name);

        InformCsrss(hProcess, hThread,
                    ULONG(cid.UniqueProcess), ULONG(cid.UniqueThread));

        NT::ZwResumeThread(hThread, 0);

        NT::ZwClose(hProcess);
        NT::ZwClose(hThread);

        return int(cid.UniqueProcess);
}

#pragma comment(linker, "-entry:wmainCRTStartup")
extern "C"
int wmain(int argc, wchar_t *argv[])
{
        NT::UNICODE_STRING ImageFile;
        NT::RtlInitUnicodeString(&ImageFile, argv[1]);

        exec(&ImageFile);

        return 0;
}
```

Example 6.2 demonstrates how to create a process from an executable PE format file.
The argument to the program is the full path in the native NT format of the executable
file. To start notepad the argument could be "\SystemRoot\System32\notepad.exe."

The following steps are taken by the `exec` routine to create a new process running a specific image file:

- Open the executable file, and create an image section from it by calling **ZwCreateSection** with an argument of SEC_IMAGE. Once the section has been created, the file can be closed.

- Call **ZwCreateProcess** to create the process. If this call returns successfully, a new process has been created that has the image section and ntdll.dll mapped into its address space.

- Call **ZwQuerySection** to obtain information about the image, such as its entry point and suggested stack size. Once this information has been obtained, the section handle can be closed because the section is now referenced by the new process.

- Create the user mode stack. **ZwAllocateVirtualMemory** is used to perform the allocations, and **ZwProtectVirtualMemory** is used to establish a guard page at the end of the committed region of the stack.

- Establish the execution context of the initial thread by storing fixed values into the CONTEXT structure and updating the stack pointer (Esp) to point to the new stack and the instruction pointer (Eip) to point to the entry point of the image. The Win32 functions CreateProcess and CreateThread set Eip to the address of a thunk in kernel32.dll that establishes a frame-based exception handler before calling the image entry point, but this example does not bother with that refinement.

- Create the initial thread in a suspended state by calling **ZwCreateThread**.

- Create and copy the process parameters (including process environment) to the new process and update the PEB of the new process to point to them.

- **InformCsrss** informs the Win32 subsystem that a Win32 client process is about to start; this gives the subsystem the opportunity to modify some settings of the process, such as setting process debug and exception ports.

- Resume the initial thread in the new process by calling **ZwResumeThread**.

At any time after the creation of the process and before resuming the initial thread, the process parameters can be created. The process parameters contain process information that is maintained and manipulated in user mode such as the current directory, the command line, the environment, and so on. Most values can be copied from the current process.

First the environment is copied to the new process, then the process parameters themselves (which contain a pointer to the environment), and finally the PEB of the new process is patched to point to the process parameters.

Example 6.3: Using RtlQueryProcessDebugInformation to Extend ToolHelp Library Implementation

```cpp
#include "ntdll.h"
#include <tlhelp32.h>
#include <stdlib.h>
#include <stdio.h>

struct ENTRIES {
    ULONG Offset;
    ULONG Count;
    ULONG Index;
    ENTRIES() : Offset(0), Count(0), Index(0) {}
    ENTRIES(ULONG m, ULONG n) : Offset(m), Count(n), Index(0) {}
};

enum EntryType {
    ProcessType,
    ThreadType,
    ModuleType,
    HeapType,
    MaxType
};

NT::PSYSTEM_PROCESSES GetProcessesAndThreads()
{
    ULONG n = 0x100;
    NT::PSYSTEM_PROCESSES sp = new NT::SYSTEM_PROCESSES[n];

    while (NT::ZwQuerySystemInformation(
                            NT::SystemProcessesAndThreadsInformation,
                            sp, n * sizeof *sp, 0)
            == STATUS_INFO_LENGTH_MISMATCH)
        delete [] sp, sp = new NT::SYSTEM_PROCESSES[n = n * 2];
    return sp;
}

NT::PDEBUG_BUFFER GetModulesAndHeaps(ULONG pid, ULONG mask)
{
    NT::PDEBUG_BUFFER db = NT::RtlCreateQueryDebugBuffer(0, FALSE);
    NT::RtlQueryProcessDebugInformation(pid, mask, db);
    return db;
}

ULONG ProcessCount(NT::PSYSTEM_PROCESSES sp)
{
    ULONG n = 0;
    bool done = false;

    for (NT::PSYSTEM_PROCESSES p = sp; !done;
         p = NT::PSYSTEM_PROCESSES(PCHAR(p) + p->NextEntryDelta))
        n++, done = p->NextEntryDelta == 0;
    return n;
}

ULONG ThreadCount(NT::PSYSTEM_PROCESSES sp)
{
    ULONG n = 0;
    bool done = false;

    for (NT::PSYSTEM_PROCESSES p = sp; !done;
```

```
            p = NT::PSYSTEM_PROCESSES(PCHAR(p) + p->NextEntryDelta))
            n += p->ThreadCount, done = p->NextEntryDelta == 0;
    return n;
}

ULONG ModuleCount(NT::PDEBUG_BUFFER db)
{
    return db->ModuleInformation ? *PULONG(db->ModuleInformation) : 0;
}

ULONG HeapCount(NT::PDEBUG_BUFFER db)
{
    return db->HeapInformation ? *PULONG(db->HeapInformation) : 0;
}

VOID AddProcesses(PPROCESSENTRY32 pe, NT::PSYSTEM_PROCESSES sp)
{
    bool done = false;

    for (NT::PSYSTEM_PROCESSES p = sp; !done;
         p = NT::PSYSTEM_PROCESSES(PCHAR(p) + p->NextEntryDelta)) {

        pe->dwSize = sizeof *pe;
        pe->cntUsage = 0;
        pe->th32ProcessID = p->ProcessId;
        pe->th32DefaultHeapID = 0;
        pe->th32ModuleID = 0;
        pe->cntThreads = p->ThreadCount;
        pe->th32ParentProcessID = p->InheritedFromProcessId;
        pe->pcPriClassBase = p->BasePriority;
        pe->dwFlags = 0;
        sprintf(pe->szExeFile, "%.*ls",
                p->ProcessName.Length / 2, p->ProcessName.Buffer);

        pe++;

        done = p->NextEntryDelta == 0;
    }
}

VOID AddThreads(PTHREADENTRY32 te, NT::PSYSTEM_PROCESSES sp)
{
    bool done = false;

    for (NT::PSYSTEM_PROCESSES p = sp; !done;
         p = NT::PSYSTEM_PROCESSES(PCHAR(p) + p->NextEntryDelta)) {

        for (ULONG i = 0; i < p->ThreadCount; i++) {

            te->dwSize = sizeof *te;
            te->cntUsage = 0;
            te->th32ThreadID = DWORD(p->Threads[i].ClientId.UniqueThread);
            te->th32OwnerProcessID = p->ProcessId;
            te->tpBasePri = p->Threads[i].BasePriority;
            te->tpDeltaPri = p->Threads[i].Priority
                             - p->Threads[i].BasePriority;
            te->dwFlags = 0;

            te++;
        }

        done = p->NextEntryDelta == 0;
    }
```

```
}

VOID AddModules(PMODULEENTRY32 me, NT::PDEBUG_BUFFER db, ULONG pid)
{
    ULONG n = ModuleCount(db);
    NT::PDEBUG_MODULE_INFORMATION p
        = NT::PDEBUG_MODULE_INFORMATION(PULONG(db->ModuleInformation) + 1);

    for (ULONG i = 0; i < n; i++) {

        me->dwSize = sizeof *me;
        me->th32ModuleID = 0;
        me->th32ProcessID = pid;
        me->GlblcntUsage = p[i].LoadCount;
        me->ProccntUsage = p[i].LoadCount;
        me->modBaseAddr = PBYTE(p[i].Base);
        me->modBaseSize = p[i].Size;
        me->hModule = HMODULE(p[i].Base);
        sprintf(me->szModule,  "%s", p[i].ImageName + p[i].ModuleNameOffset);
        sprintf(me->szExePath, "%s", p[i].ImageName);

        me++;
    }
}

VOID AddHeaps(PHEAPLIST32 hl, NT::PDEBUG_BUFFER db, ULONG pid)
{
    ULONG n = HeapCount(db);
    NT::PDEBUG_HEAP_INFORMATION p
        = NT::PDEBUG_HEAP_INFORMATION(PULONG(db->HeapInformation) + 1);

    for (ULONG i = 0; i < n; i++) {

        hl->dwSize = sizeof *hl;
        hl->th32ProcessID = pid;
        hl->th32HeapID = p[i].Base;
        hl->dwFlags = p[i].Flags;

        hl++;
    }
}

template<class T>
BOOL GetEntry(HANDLE hSnapshot, T entry, bool first, EntryType type)
{
    ENTRIES *entries = (ENTRIES*)MapViewOfFile(hSnapshot, FILE_MAP_WRITE,
                                               0, 0, 0);
    if (entries == 0) return FALSE;

    BOOL rv = TRUE;

    entries[type].Index = first ? 0 : entries[type].Index + 1;

    if (entries[type].Index >= entries[type].Count)
        SetLastError(ERROR_NO_MORE_FILES), rv = FALSE;
    if (entry->dwSize < sizeof *entry)
        SetLastError(ERROR_INSUFFICIENT_BUFFER), rv = FALSE;
    if (rv)
        *entry = T(PCHAR(entries)
                    + entries[type].Offset)[entries[type].Index];
```

```
    UnmapViewOfFile(entries);
    return rv;
}

HANDLE
WINAPI
CreateToolhelp32Snapshot(DWORD flags, DWORD pid)
{
    if (pid == 0) pid = GetCurrentProcessId();

    ULONG mask = ((flags & TH32CS_SNAPMODULE) ? PDI_MODULES : 0) |
                 ((flags & TH32CS_SNAPHEAPLIST) ? PDI_HEAPS : 0);

    NT::PDEBUG_BUFFER db =
        (flags & (TH32CS_SNAPMODULE | TH32CS_SNAPHEAPLIST))
            ? GetModulesAndHeaps(pid, mask) : 0;

    NT::PSYSTEM_PROCESSES sp =
        (flags & (TH32CS_SNAPPROCESS | TH32CS_SNAPTHREAD))
            ? GetProcessesAndThreads() : 0;

    ENTRIES entries[MaxType];
    ULONG n = sizeof entries;

    if (flags & TH32CS_SNAPPROCESS) {
        entries[ProcessType] = ENTRIES(n, ProcessCount(sp));
        n += entries[ProcessType].Count * sizeof (PROCESSENTRY32);
    }
    if (flags & TH32CS_SNAPTHREAD) {
        entries[ThreadType] = ENTRIES(n, ThreadCount(sp));
        n += entries[ThreadType].Count * sizeof (THREADENTRY32);
    }
    if (flags & TH32CS_SNAPMODULE) {
        entries[ModuleType] = ENTRIES(n, ModuleCount(db));
        n += entries[ModuleType].Count * sizeof (MODULEENTRY32);
    }
    if (flags & TH32CS_SNAPHEAPLIST) {
        entries[HeapType] = ENTRIES(n, HeapCount(db));
        n += entries[HeapType].Count * sizeof (HEAPLIST32);
    }

    SECURITY_ATTRIBUTES sa = {sizeof sa, 0, (flags & TH32CS_INHERIT) != 0};

    HANDLE hMap = CreateFileMapping(HANDLE(0xFFFFFFFF), &sa,
                                    PAGE_READWRITE | SEC_COMMIT, 0, n, 0);

    ENTRIES *p = (ENTRIES*)MapViewOfFile(hMap, FILE_MAP_WRITE, 0, 0, 0);

    for (int i = 0; i < MaxType; i++) p[i] = entries[i];

    if (flags & TH32CS_SNAPPROCESS)
        AddProcesses(PPROCESSENTRY32(PCHAR(p) + entries[ProcessType].Offset),
                     sp);
    if (flags & TH32CS_SNAPTHREAD)
        AddThreads(PTHREADENTRY32(PCHAR(p) + entries[ThreadType].Offset),
                   sp);
    if (flags & TH32CS_SNAPMODULE)
        AddModules(PMODULEENTRY32(PCHAR(p) + entries[ModuleType].Offset),
                   db, pid);
    if (flags & TH32CS_SNAPHEAPLIST)
        AddHeaps(PHEAPLIST32(PCHAR(p) + entries[HeapType].Offset),
                 db, pid);
```

```
    UnmapViewOfFile(p);

    if (sp) delete [] sp;

    if (db) NT::RtlDestroyQueryDebugBuffer(db);

    return hMap;
}

BOOL
WINAPI
Process32First(HANDLE hSnapshot, PPROCESSENTRY32 pe)
{
    return GetEntry(hSnapshot, pe, true, ProcessType);
}

BOOL
WINAPI
Process32Next(HANDLE hSnapshot, PPROCESSENTRY32 pe)
{
    return GetEntry(hSnapshot, pe, false, ProcessType);
}

BOOL
WINAPI
Thread32First(HANDLE hSnapshot, PTHREADENTRY32 te)
{
    return GetEntry(hSnapshot, te, true, ThreadType);
}

BOOL
WINAPI
Thread32Next(HANDLE hSnapshot, PTHREADENTRY32 te)
{
    return GetEntry(hSnapshot, te, false, ThreadType);
}

BOOL
WINAPI
Module32First(HANDLE hSnapshot, PMODULEENTRY32 me)
{
    return GetEntry(hSnapshot, me, true, ModuleType);
}

BOOL
WINAPI
Module32Next(HANDLE hSnapshot, PMODULEENTRY32 me)
{
    return GetEntry(hSnapshot, me, false, ModuleType);
}

BOOL
WINAPI
Heap32ListFirst(HANDLE hSnapshot, PHEAPLIST32 hl)
{
    return GetEntry(hSnapshot, hl, true, HeapType);
}

BOOL
WINAPI
Heap32ListNext(HANDLE hSnapshot, PHEAPLIST32 hl)
{
    return GetEntry(hSnapshot, hl, false, HeapType);
```

}

Example 6.3 extends Example 1.1 in Chapter 1, "System Information and Control," to provide support for retrieving module and heap information. The code implements ANSI (rather than Unicode) versions of the routines and, apart from the routines to implement enumerating heap entries, is an almost complete implementation of the ToolHelp library.

7
Jobs

The system services described in this chapter create and manipulate job objects. Job objects are only available in Windows 2000.

ZwCreateJobObject

ZwCreateJobObject creates or opens a job object.

```
NTSYSAPI
NTSTATUS
NTAPI
ZwCreateJobObject(
    OUT PHANDLE JobHandle,
    IN ACCESS_MASK DesiredAccess,
    IN POBJECT_ATTRIBUTES ObjectAttributes
    );
```

Parameters

JobHandle
> Points to a variable that will receive the job object handle if the call is successful.

DesiredAccess
> Specifies the type of access that the caller requires to the job object. This parameter can be zero, or any combination of the following flags:

JOB_OBJECT_ASSIGN_PROCESS	Add process to job
JOB_OBJECT_SET_ATTRIBUTES	Set job attributes
JOB_OBJECT_QUERY	Query job attributes
JOB_OBJECT_TERMINATE	Terminate job
JOB_OBJECT_SET_SECURITY_ATTRIBUTES	Set job security attributes
JOB_OBJECT_ALL_ACCESS	All of the preceding + STANDARD_RIGHTS_ALL

ObjectAttributes
> Points to a structure that specifies the object's attributes.

Return Value

Returns STATUS_SUCCESS or an error status, such as STATUS_ACCESS_DENIED.

Related Win32 Functions

CreateJobObject.

Remarks

The routine **ZwCreateJobObject** is only present in Windows 2000.

ZwOpenJobObject

ZwOpenJobObject opens a job object.

```
NTSYSAPI
NTSTATUS
NTAPI
ZwOpenJobObject(
    OUT PHANDLE JobHandle,
    IN ACCESS_MASK DesiredAccess,
    IN POBJECT_ATTRIBUTES ObjectAttributes
    );
```

Parameters

JobHandle
Points to a variable that will receive the job object handle if the call is successful.

DesiredAccess
Specifies the type of access that the caller requires to the job object. This parameter can be zero, or any combination of the following flags:

```
JOB_OBJECT_ASSIGN_PROCESS            Add process to job
JOB_OBJECT_SET_ATTRIBUTES            Set job attributes
JOB_OBJECT_QUERY                     Query job attributes
JOB_OBJECT_TERMINATE                 Terminate job
JOB_OBJECT_SET_SECURITY_ATTRIBUTES   Set job security attributes
JOB_OBJECT_ALL_ACCESS                All of the preceding +
                                     STANDARD_RIGHTS_ALL
```

ObjectAttributes
Points to a structure that specifies the object's attributes.

Return Value

Returns STATUS_SUCCESS or an error status, such as STATUS_ACCESS_DENIED or STATUS_OBJECT_NAME_NOT_FOUND.

Related Win32 Functions

OpenJobObject.

Remarks

The routine **ZwOpenJobObject** is only present in Windows 2000.

ZwTerminateJobObject

ZwTerminateJobObject terminates a job and the processes and threads that it contains.

```
NTSYSAPI
NTSTATUS
NTAPI
ZwTerminateJobObject(
    IN HANDLE JobHandle,
    IN NTSTATUS ExitStatus
    );
```

Parameters

JobHandle
A handle to a job object. The handle must grant JOB_OBJECT_TERMINATE access.

ExitStatus
Specifies the exit status for all processes and threads terminated as a result of this call.

Return Value

Returns STATUS_SUCCESS or an error status, such as STATUS_ACCESS_DENIED.

Related Win32 Functions

TerminateJobObject.

Remarks

TerminateJobObject exposes the full functionality of **ZwTerminateJobObject.**

The routine **ZwTerminateJobObject** is only present in Windows 2000.

ZwAssignProcessToJobObject

ZwAssignProcessToJobObject associates a process with a job.

```
NTSYSAPI
NTSTATUS
NTAPI
ZwAssignProcessToJobObject(
    IN HANDLE JobHandle,
    IN HANDLE ProcessHandle
    );
```

Parameters

JobHandle
A handle to a job object. The handle must grant JOB_OBJECT_ASSIGN_PROCESS access.

ProcessHandle
A handle to a process object. The handle must grant PROCESS_SET_QUOTA and
PROCESS_TERMINATE access.

Return Value

Returns STATUS_SUCCESS or an error status, such as STATUS_ACCESS_DENIED or
STATUS_PROCESS_IS_TERMINATING.

Related Win32 Functions

AssignProcessToJobObject.

Remarks

AssignProcessToJobObject exposes the full functionality of
ZwAssignProcessToJobObject.

The routine **ZwAssignProcessToJobObject** is only present in Windows 2000.

ZwQueryInformationJobObject

ZwQueryInformationJobObject retrieves information about a job object.

```
NTSYSAPI
NTSTATUS
NTAPI
ZwQueryInformationJobObject(
    IN HANDLE JobHandle,
    IN JOBOBJECTINFOCLASS JobInformationClass,
    OUT PVOID JobInformation,
    IN ULONG JobInformationLength,
    OUT PULONG ReturnLength OPTIONAL
    );
```

Parameters

JobHandle
A handle to a job object. The handle must grant JOB_OBJECT_QUERY access.

JobInformationClass
Specifies the type of job information to be queried. The permitted values are drawn
from the enumeration JOBOBJECTINFOCLASS, described in the following section.

JobInformation
Points to a caller-allocated buffer or variable that receives the requested job
information.

JobInformationLength
Specifies the size in bytes of JobInformation, which the caller should set according to
the given JobInformationClass.

ReturnLength
Optionally points to a variable that receives the number of bytes actually returned to
JobInformation if the call was successful. If this information is not needed,
ReturnLength may be a null pointer.

Return Value

Returns STATUS_SUCCESS or an error status, such as STATUS_ACCESS_DENIED, STATUS_INVALID_HANDLE, STATUS_INVALID_INFO_CLASS, STATUS_INFO_LENGTH_MISMATCH, or STATUS_BUFFER_OVERFLOW.

Related Win32 Functions

QueryInformationJobObject.

Remarks

QueryInformationJobObject exposes the full functionality of **ZwQueryInformationJobObject.**

The routine **ZwQueryInformationJobObject** is only present in Windows 2000.

ZwSetInformationJobObject

ZwSetInformationJobObject sets information affecting a job object.

```
NTSYSAPI
NTSTATUS
NTAPI
ZwSetInformationJobObject(
    IN HANDLE JobHandle,
    IN JOBOBJECTINFOCLASS JobInformationClass,
    IN PVOID JobInformation,
    IN ULONG JobInformationLength
    );
```

Parameters

JobHandle
A handle to a job object. The handle must grant JOB_OBJECT_SET_ATTRIBUTES access. Some information classes also require JOB_OBJECT_SET_SECURITY_ATTRIBUTES access.

JobInformationClass
Specifies the type of job information to be set. The permitted values are drawn from the enumeration JOBOBJECTINFOCLASS, described in the following section.

JobInformation
Points to a caller-allocated buffer or variable that contains the job information to be set.

JobInformationLength
Specifies the size in bytes of JobInformation that the caller should set according to the given JobInformationClass.

Return Value

Returns STATUS_SUCCESS or an error status, such as STATUS_ACCESS_DENIED, STATUS_INVALID_HANDLE, STATUS_INVALID_INFO_CLASS, or STATUS_INFO_LENGTH_MISMATCH.

Related Win32 Functions

SetInformationJobObject.

Remarks

SetInformationJobObject exposes the full functionality of **ZwSetInformationJobObject**.

The routine **ZwSetInformationJobObject** is only present in Windows 2000.

JOBOBJECTINFOCLASS

```
                                                           Query   Set
typedef enum _JOBOBJECTINFOCLASS {
    JobObjectBasicAccountingInformation = 1,        // Y      N
    JobObjectBasicLimitInformation,                 // Y      Y
    JobObjectBasicProcessIdList,                    // Y      N
    JobObjectBasicUIRestrictions,                   // Y      Y
    JobObjectSecurityLimitInformation,              // Y      Y
    JobObjectEndOfJobTimeInformation,               // N      Y
    JobObjectAssociateCompletionPortInformation,    // N      Y
    JobObjectBasicAndIoAccountingInformation,       // Y      N
    JobObjectExtendedLimitInformation               // Y      Y
} JOBOBJECTINFOCLASS;
```

JobObjectBasicAccountingInformation

```
typedef struct _JOBOBJECT_BASIC_ACCOUNTING_INFORMATION {
    LARGE_INTEGER TotalUserTime;
    LARGE_INTEGER TotalKernelTime;
    LARGE_INTEGER ThisPeriodTotalUserTime;
    LARGE_INTEGER ThisPeriodTotalKernelTime;
    ULONG TotalPageFaultCount;
    ULONG TotalProcesses;
    ULONG ActiveProcesses;
    ULONG TotalTerminatedProcesses;
} JOBOBJECT_BASIC_ACCOUNTING_INFORMATION,
  *PJOBOBJECT_BASIC_ACCOUNTING_INFORMATION;
```

Members

TotalUserTime
  The total time spent executing in user mode, measured in units of 100-nanoseconds, of all the threads that ever belonged to the job.

TotalKernelTime
  The total time spent executing in kernel mode, measured in units of 100-nanoseconds, of all the threads that ever belonged to the job.

ThisPeriodTotalUserTime
  The total time spent executing in user mode, measured in units of 100-nanoseconds, of all the threads that ever belonged to the job since the user mode execution time limit was last set.

ThisPeriodTotalKernelTime
> The total time spent executing in kernel mode, measured in units of 100-nanoseconds, of all the threads that ever belonged to the job since the kernel mode execution time limit was last set.

TotalPageFaultCount
> The total number of page faults incurred by all processes that ever belonged to the job.

TotalProcesses
> The total number of processes that ever belonged to the job.

ActiveProcesses
> The number of processes that currently belong to the job.

TotalTerminatedProcesses
> The total number of processes that have been terminated because a job limit was exceeded.

Remarks

> JOBOBJECT_BASIC_ACCOUNTING_INFORMATION is identical to the structure of the same name used by the Win32 function, QueryInformationJobObject.

JobObjectBasicLimitInformation

```
typedef struct _JOBOBJECT_BASIC_LIMIT_INFORMATION {
    LARGE_INTEGER PerProcessUserTimeLimit;
    LARGE_INTEGER PerJobUserTimeLimit;
    ULONG LimitFlags;
    ULONG MinimumWorkingSetSize;
    ULONG MaximumWorkingSetSize;
    ULONG ActiveProcessLimit;
    ULONG Affinity;
    ULONG PriorityClass;
    ULONG SchedulingClass;
} JOBOBJECT_BASIC_LIMIT_INFORMATION, *PJOBOBJECT_BASIC_LIMIT_INFORMATION;
```

Members

PerProcessUserTimeLimit
> The limit on the time spent executing in user mode, measured in units of 100-nanoseconds, of all the threads in any one process belonging to the job. When setting limits, this member is ignored unless LimitFlags specifies JOB_OBJECT_LIMIT_PROCESS_TIME.

PerJobUserTimeLimit
> The limit on the time spent executing in user mode, measured in units of 100-nanoseconds, of the job. When setting limits, this member is ignored unless LimitFlags specifies JOB_OBJECT_LIMIT_JOB_TIME. When querying limits, the value is the total time allowed to all threads that ever belonged to the job; subtracting TotalUserTime (from

JOBOBJECT_BASIC_ACCOUNTING_INFORMATION) gives the remaining time. When setting limits, the value is the time remaining until the job user mode execution time limit is reached.

LimitFlags

Specifies which limits are in force. When setting limits, if a limit is not specified as being in force, the value of its member in the limit structure is ignored. Some limit flags are only valid when specified in conjunction with a JOBOBJECT_EXTENDED_LIMIT_INFORMATION structure.

```
JOB_OBJECT_LIMIT_WORKINGSET                     0x0001
JOB_OBJECT_LIMIT_PROCESS_TIME                   0x0002
JOB_OBJECT_LIMIT_JOB_TIME                       0x0004
JOB_OBJECT_LIMIT_ACTIVE_PROCESS                 0x0008
JOB_OBJECT_LIMIT_AFFINITY                       0x0010
JOB_OBJECT_LIMIT_PRIORITY_CLASS                 0x0020
JOB_OBJECT_LIMIT_PRESERVE_JOB_TIME              0x0040
JOB_OBJECT_LIMIT_SCHEDULING_CLASS               0x0080
JOB_OBJECT_LIMIT_PROCESS_MEMORY                 0x0100
JOB_OBJECT_LIMIT_JOB_MEMORY                     0x0200
JOB_OBJECT_LIMIT_DIE_ON_UNHANDLED_EXCEPTION     0x0400
JOB_OBJECT_BREAKAWAY_OK                         0x0800
JOB_OBJECT_SILENT_BREAKAWAY                     0x1000
```

Minimum WorkingSetSize

The minimum working set size, in bytes, for all processes belonging to the job. When setting limits, this member is ignored unless LimitFlags specifies JOB_OBJECT_LIMIT_WORKINGSET.

Maximum WorkingSetSize

The maximum working set size, in bytes, for all processes belonging to the job. When setting limits, this member is ignored unless LimitFlags specifies JOB_OBJECT_LIMIT_WORKINGSET.

Affinity

The processor affinity for all processes belonging to the job. When setting limits, this member is ignored unless LimitFlags specifies JOB_OBJECT_LIMIT_AFFINITY.

PriorityClass

The priority class for all processes belonging to the job. When setting limits, this member is ignored unless LimitFlags specifies JOB_OBJECT_LIMIT_PRIORITY_CLASS. The defined priority classes include:

```
PC_IDLE           1
PC_NORMAL         2
PC_HIGH           3
PC_REALTIME       4
PC_BELOW_NORMAL   5
PC_ABOVE_NORMAL   6
```

SeIncreaseBasePriorityPrivilege is required to set PriorityClass to PC_REALTIME.

SchedulingClass
> The scheduling class for all processes belonging to the job. When setting limits, this
> member is ignored unless `LimitFlags` specifies `JOB_OBJECT_LIMIT_SCHEDULING_CLASS`.
> The scheduling class affects the thread scheduling quantum: the higher the class the
> longer the quantum. The permitted values range from zero to nine;
> `SeIncreaseBasePriorityPrivilege` is required to set `SchedulingClass` to values greater
> than five.

Remarks

> `JOBOBJECT_BASIC_LIMIT_INFORMATION` is identical to the structure of the same name
> used by the Win32 functions `QueryInformationJobObject` and
> `SetInformationJobObject`. However the `PriorityClass` field is encoded differently: the
> Win32 functions use the `XXX_PRIORITY_CLASS` values defined in winbase.h.

> Although `JOB_OBJECT_LIMIT_DIE_ON_UNHANDLED_EXCEPTION`, `JOB_OBJECT_BREAKAWAY_OK`
> and `JOB_OBJECT_SILENT_BREAKAWAY` are not associated with any particular member of
> `JOBOBJECT_EXTENDED_LIMIT_INFORMATION`, they are only valid when specified with the
> information class `JobObjectExtendedLimitInformation`.

> The breakaway flags `JOB_OBJECT_BREAKAWAY_OK` and `JOB_OBJECT_SILENT_BREAKAWAY`
> determine whether new processes created by members of the job can be disassociated
> from the job. `JOB_OBJECT_SILENT_BREAKAWAY` means that the disassociation is automatic
> whilst `JOB_OBJECT_BREAKAWAY_OK` means that the creator of a new process can request
> that it be disassociated when calling **ZwCreateProcess**.

JobObjectBasicProcessIdList

```
typedef struct _JOBOBJECT_BASIC_PROCESS_ID_LIST {
    ULONG NumberOfAssignedProcesses;
    ULONG NumberOfProcessIdsInList;
    ULONG_PTR ProcessIdList[1];
} JOBOBJECT_BASIC_PROCESS_ID_LIST, *PJOBOBJECT_BASIC_PROCESS_ID_LIST;
```

Members

NumberOfAssignedProcesses
> The number of active processes belonging to the job.

NumberOfProcessIdsInList
> The number of process identifiers in the `ProcessIdList` array. If
> **ZwQueryInformationJobObject** fails with `STATUS_BUFFER_OVERFLOW`, `ProcessIdList` con-
> tains a subset of the process identifiers belonging to the job.

ProcessIdList
> An array of the process identifiers of the processes belonging to the job.

Remarks

> `JOBOBJECT_BASIC_PROCESS_ID_LIST` is identical to the structure of the same name used
> by the Win32 function `QueryInformationJobObject`.

JobObjectBasicUIRestrictions

```
typedef struct _JOBOBJECT_BASIC_UI_RESTRICTIONS {
    ULONG UIRestrictionsClass;
} JOBOBJECT_BASIC_UI_RESTRICTIONS, *PJOBOBJECT_BASIC_UI_RESTRICTIONS;
```

Members

UIRestrictionsClass

Specifies restrictions on the user interface behavior of processes belonging to the job. The following restrictions are defined:

```
JOB_OBJECT_UILIMIT_HANDLES           0x0001
JOB_OBJECT_UILIMIT_READCLIPBOARD     0x0002
JOB_OBJECT_UILIMIT_WRITECLIPBOARD    0x0004
JOB_OBJECT_UILIMIT_SYSTEMPARAMETERS  0x0008
JOB_OBJECT_UILIMIT_DISPLAYSETTINGS   0x0010
JOB_OBJECT_UILIMIT_GLOBALATOMS       0x0020
JOB_OBJECT_UILIMIT_DESKTOP           0x0040
JOB_OBJECT_UILIMIT_EXITWINDOWS       0x0080
```

Remarks

JOBOBJECT_BASIC_UI_RESTRICTIONS is identical to the structure of the same name used by the Win32 functions QueryInformationJobObject and SetInformationJobObject.

JobObjectSecurityLimitInformation

```
typedef struct _JOBOBJECT_SECURITY_LIMIT_INFORMATION {
    ULONG SecurityLimitFlags;
    HANDLE JobToken;
    PTOKEN_GROUPS SidsToDisable;
    PTOKEN_PRIVILEGES PrivilegesToDelete;
    PTOKEN_GROUPS RestrictedSids;
} JOBOBJECT_SECURITY_LIMIT_INFORMATION,
    *PJOBOBJECT_SECURITY_LIMIT_INFORMATION;
```

Members

SecurityLimitFlags

Specifies restrictions on the tokens of processes belonging to the job. The following restrictions are defined:

```
JOB_OBJECT_SECURITY_NO_ADMIN          0x0001
JOB_OBJECT_SECURITY_RESTRICTED_TOKEN  0x0002
JOB_OBJECT_SECURITY_ONLY_TOKEN        0x0004
JOB_OBJECT_SECURITY_FILTER_TOKENS     0x0008
```

JobToken

A handle to a token object. The handle must grant TOKEN_ASSIGN_PRIMARY, TOKEN_DUPLICATE, and TOKEN_IMPERSONATE access. SeAssignPrimaryTokenPrivilege is required unless the token is a filtered copy of the token of the current process. When setting limits, this member is ignored unless SecurityLimitFlags specifies JOB_OBJECT_SECURITY_ONLY_TOKEN.

Sids To Disable

A pointer to a `TOKEN_GROUPS` structure specifying the groups to be converted to deny-only groups in the tokens of processes added to the job. When setting limits, this member is ignored unless `SecurityLimitFlags` specifies `JOB_OBJECT_SECURITY_FILTER_TOKENS`.

Privileges To Delete

A pointer to a `TOKEN_PRIVILEGES` structure specifying the privileges to be deleted from the tokens of processes added to the job. When setting limits, this member is ignored unless `SecurityLimitFlags` specifies `JOB_OBJECT_SECURITY_FILTER_TOKENS`.

Restricted Sids

A pointer to a `TOKEN_GROUPS` structure that specifies the restricted groups to be added to the tokens of processes added to the job. When setting limits, this member is ignored unless `SecurityLimitFlags` specifies `JOB_OBJECT_SECURITY_FILTER_TOKENS`.

Remarks

`JOBOBJECT_SECURITY_LIMIT_INFORMATION` is identical to the structure of the same name used by the Win32 functions `QueryInformationJobObject` and `SetInformationJobObject`.

When querying `JobObjectSecurityLimitInformation`, enough space must be allocated to hold the `JOBOBJECT_SECURITY_LIMIT_INFORMATION` structure and the referenced privileges and groups. The `ReturnLength` information only indicates that the size of the `JOBOBJECT_SECURITY_LIMIT_INFORMATION` structure has been copied to the `JobInformation` buffer—this is a minor bug. If a job token is set, its value cannot be retrieved by querying this information class.

JobObjectEndOfJobTimeInformation

```
typedef struct _JOBOBJECT_END_OF_JOB_TIME_INFORMATION {
    ULONG EndOfJobTimeAction;
} JOBOBJECT_END_OF_JOB_TIME_INFORMATION,
  *PJOBOBJECT_END_OF_JOB_TIME_INFORMATION;
```

Members

End Of Job Time Action

Specifies the action to be taken when the `PerJobUserTimeLimit` is reached. The following actions are defined:

```
JOB_OBJECT_TERMINATE_AT_END_OF_JOB  0
JOB_OBJECT_POST_AT_END_OF_JOB       1
```

Remarks

`JOBOBJECT_END_OF_JOB_TIME_INFORMATION` is identical to the structure of the same name used by the Win32 functions `QueryInformationJobObject` and `SetInformationJobObject`.

JobObjectAssociateCompletionPortInformation

```
typedef struct _JOBOBJECT_ASSOCIATE_COMPLETION_PORT {
    PVOID CompletionKey;
    HANDLE CompletionPort;
} JOBOBJECT_ASSOCIATE_COMPLETION_PORT, *PJOBOBJECT_ASSOCIATE_COMPLETION_PORT;
```

Members

CompletionKey

The value to be used as the `CompletionKey` argument to **ZwSetIoCompletion** when messages are sent on behalf of the job.

CompletionPort

The handle to be used as the `IoCompletionHandle` argument to **ZwSetIoCompletion** when messages are sent on behalf of the job. The handle must grant `IO_COMPLETION_MODIFY_STATE` access.

Remarks

`JOBOBJECT_ASSOCIATE_COMPLETION_PORT` is identical to the structure of the same name used by the Win32 functions `QueryInformationJobObject` and `SetInformationJobObject`.

The job sends messages to the completion port when certain events occur. After calling **ZwRemoveIoCompletion** to retrieve a message, the type of event is available in the Information member of the `IO_STATUS_BLOCK` pointed to by the `IoStatusBlock` argument. The following types of events are defined:

```
JOB_OBJECT_MSG_END_OF_JOB_TIME          1
JOB_OBJECT_MSG_END_OF_PROCESS_TIME      2
JOB_OBJECT_MSG_ACTIVE_PROCESS_LIMIT     3
JOB_OBJECT_MSG_ACTIVE_PROCESS_ZERO      4
JOB_OBJECT_MSG_NEW_PROCESS              6
JOB_OBJECT_MSG_EXIT_PROCESS             7
JOB_OBJECT_MSG_ABNORMAL_EXIT_PROCESS    8
JOB_OBJECT_MSG_PROCESS_MEMORY_LIMIT     9
JOB_OBJECT_MSG_JOB_MEMORY_LIMIT        10
```

Depending upon the event type, the variable pointed to by the `CompletionValue` argument to **ZwRemoveIoCompletion** may contain the process identifier of the process within the job that caused the event.

JobObjectBasicAndIoAccountingInformation

```
typedef struct JOBOBJECT_BASIC_AND_IO_ACCOUNTING_INFORMATION {
    JOBOBJECT_BASIC_ACCOUNTING_INFORMATION BasicInfo;
    IO_COUNTERS IoInfo;
} JOBOBJECT_BASIC_AND_IO_ACCOUNTING_INFORMATION,
  *PJOBOBJECT_BASIC_AND_IO_ACCOUNTING_INFORMATION;
```

Members

BasicInfo

A JOBOBJECT_BASIC_ACCOUNTING_INFORMATION structure that contains the basic accounting information for the job.

IoInfo

An IO_COUNTERS structure that contains the I/O accounting information for the job

Remarks

JOBOBJECT_BASIC_AND_IO_ACCOUNTING_INFORMATION is identical to the structure of the same name used by the Win32 function QueryInformationJobObject.

JobObjectExtendedLimitInformation

```
typedef struct _JOBOBJECT_EXTENDED_LIMIT_INFORMATION {
    JOBOBJECT_BASIC_LIMIT_INFORMATION BasicLimitInformation;
    IO_COUNTERS IoInfo;
    ULONG ProcessMemoryLimit;
    ULONG JobMemoryLimit;
    ULONG PeakProcessMemoryUsed;
    ULONG PeakJobMemoryUsed;
} JOBOBJECT_EXTENDED_LIMIT_INFORMATION,
  *PJOBOBJECT_EXTENDED_LIMIT_INFORMATION;
```

Members

BasicLimitInformation

A JOBOBJECT_BASIC_LIMIT_INFORMATION structure that specifies the basic limits for the job.

IoInfo

An IO_COUNTERS structure. Not currently used.

ProcessMemoryLimit

The maximum amount of committed virtual memory, in bytes, for any processes belonging to the job. When setting limits, this member is ignored unless BasicLimitInformation.LimitFlags specifies JOB_OBJECT_LIMIT_PROCESS_MEMORY.

JobMemoryLimit

The maximum amount of committed virtual memory, in bytes, for all processes belonging to the job. When setting limits, this member is ignored unless BasicLimitInformation.LimitFlags specifies JOB_OBJECT_LIMIT_JOB_MEMORY.

PeakProcessMemoryUsed

The peak amount of virtual memory committed by any process that ever belonged to the job. This member cannot be set.

PeakJobMemoryUsed
> The peak amount of virtual memory committed by all process belonging to the job. This member cannot be set.

Remarks

JOBOBJECT_EXTENDED_LIMIT_INFORMATION is identical to the structure of the same name used by the Win32 functions QueryInformationJobObject and SetInformationJobObject.

8
Tokens

The system services described in this chapter create and manipulate token objects. Token objects are objects that encapsulate the privileges and access rights of an agent (a thread or process).

ZwCreateToken

ZwCreateToken creates a token object.

```
NTSYSAPI
NTSTATUS
NTAPI
ZwCreateToken(
    OUT PHANDLE TokenHandle,
    IN ACCESS_MASK DesiredAccess,
    IN POBJECT_ATTRIBUTES ObjectAttributes,
    IN TOKEN_TYPE Type,
    IN PLUID AuthenticationId,
    IN PLARGE_INTEGER ExpirationTime,
    IN PTOKEN_USER User,
    IN PTOKEN_GROUPS Groups,
    IN PTOKEN_PRIVILEGES Privileges,
    IN PTOKEN_OWNER Owner,
    IN PTOKEN_PRIMARY_GROUP PrimaryGroup,
    IN PTOKEN_DEFAULT_DACL DefaultDacl,
    IN PTOKEN_SOURCE Source
    );
```

Parameters

TokenHandle

Points to a variable that will receive the token object handle if the call is successful.

DesiredAccess

Specifies the type of access that the caller requires to the token object. This parameter can be zero, or any combination of the following flags:

```
TOKEN_ASSIGN_PRIMARY    Can be assigned as primary token
TOKEN_DUPLICATE         Can be duplicated
TOKEN_IMPERSONATE       Can be assigned as impersonation token
TOKEN_QUERY             Can be queried
```

```
TOKEN_QUERY_SOURCE            Can be queried for source
TOKEN_ADJUST_PRIVILEGES       Token privileges can be adjusted
TOKEN_ADJUST_GROUPS           Token groups can be adjusted
TOKEN_ADJUST_DEFAULT          Token default ACL and owner can be adjusted
TOKEN_ADJUST_SESSIONID        Token session id can be adjusted
TOKEN_ALL_ACCESS              All of the preceding +
                              STANDARD_RIGHTS_REQUIRED
```

ObjectAttributes

Points to a structure that specifies the object's attributes. OBJ_OPENLINK is not a valid attribute for a token object.

Token Type

Specifies the type of token object to be created. The permitted values are drawn from the enumeration TOKEN_TYPE:

```
typedef enum _TOKEN_TYPE {
    TokenPrimary = 1,
    TokenImpersonation
} TOKEN_TYPE, *PTOKEN_TYPE;
```

AuthenticationId

Points to a structure that specifies the value that is used to correlate the token with other authentication information.

Expiration Time

Points to a structure that specifies the time at which the token will expire in the standard time format (that is, the number of 100-nanosecond intervals since January 1, 1601). An expiration time value of -1 indicates that the token does not expire.

User

Points to a structure that specifies which user the token will represent.

Groups

Points to a structure that specifies to which groups the user represented by the token will belong.

Privileges

Points to a structure that specifies which privileges are granted to the user that the token will represent.

Owner

Points to a structure that specifies the default owner for objects created by the user which the token will represent.

PrimaryGroup

Points to a structure that specifies the default group for objects created by the user that the token will represent.

DefaultDacl
> Points to a structure that specifies the default ACL for objects created by the user that the token will represent.

Source
> Points to a structure that identifies the creator of the token.

Return Value

> Returns STATUS_SUCCESS or an error status, such as STATUS_INVALID_OWNER, STATUS_BAD_IMPERSONATION_LEVEL, STATUS_NO_SUCH_LOGON_SESSION, or STATUS_PRIVILEGE_NOT_HELD.

Related Win32 Functions

> None.

Remarks

> SeCreateTokenPrivilege is required to create a token.

> The AuthenticationId parameter should correspond to a Local Security Authority (LSA) "Logon Session" identifier. This provides the link to credential information. If the credentials for a user are not available or not required (as when the token will only be used to access resources local to the system), AuthenticationId could be specified as SYSTEM_LUID (defined in winnt.h) or copied from the process's current token. In Windows 2000, the AuthenticationId ANONYMOUS_LOGON_LUID could also be used.

> TOKEN_ADJUST_SESSIONID is only valid in Windows 2000.

> Example 8.1 creates a token that is used as an argument to CreateProcessAsUser.

ZwOpenProcessToken

ZwOpenProcessToken opens the token of a process.

```
NTSYSAPI
NTSTATUS
NTAPI
ZwOpenProcessToken(
    IN HANDLE ProcessHandle,
    IN ACCESS_MASK DesiredAccess,
    OUT PHANDLE TokenHandle
    );
```

Parameters

ProcessHandle
> A handle to a process object. The handle must grant PROCESS_QUERY_INFORMATION access.

DesiredAccess

Specifies the type of access that the caller requires to the token object. This parameter can be zero, or any combination of the following flags:

```
TOKEN_ASSIGN_PRIMARY        Can be assigned as primary token
TOKEN_DUPLICATE             Can be duplicated
TOKEN_IMPERSONATE           Can be assigned as impersonation token
TOKEN_QUERY                 Can be queried
TOKEN_QUERY_SOURCE          Can be queried for source
TOKEN_ADJUST_PRIVILEGES     Token privileges can be adjusted
TOKEN_ADJUST_GROUPS         Token groups can be adjusted
TOKEN_ADJUST_DEFAULT        Token default ACL and owner can be adjusted
TOKEN_ADJUST_SESSIONID      Token session id can be adjusted
TOKEN_ALL_ACCESS            All of the preceding +
                            STANDARD_RIGHTS_REQUIRED
```

TokenHandle

Points to a variable that will receive the token object handle if the call is successful.

Return Value

Returns STATUS_SUCCESS or an error status, such as STATUS_ACCESS_DENIED or STATUS_INVALID_HANDLE.

Related Win32 Functions

OpenProcessToken.

Remarks

OpenProcessToken exposes the full functionality of **ZwOpenProcessToken**.

TOKEN_ADJUST_SESSIONID is only valid in Windows 2000.

ZwOpenThreadToken

ZwOpenThreadToken opens the token of a thread.

```
NTSYSAPI
NTSTATUS
NTAPI
ZwOpenThreadToken(
    IN HANDLE ThreadHandle,
    IN ACCESS_MASK DesiredAccess,
    IN BOOLEAN OpenAsSelf,
    OUT PHANDLE TokenHandle
    );
```

Parameters

ThreadHandle

A handle to a thread. The handle must grant THREAD_QUERY_INFORMATION access.

DesiredAccess

Specifies the type of access that the caller requires to the token object. This parameter can be zero, or any combination of the following flags:

```
TOKEN_ASSIGN_PRIMARY        Can be assigned as primary token
TOKEN_DUPLICATE             Can be duplicated
TOKEN_IMPERSONATE           Can be assigned as impersonation token
TOKEN_QUERY                 Can be queried
TOKEN_QUERY_SOURCE          Can be queried for source
TOKEN_ADJUST_PRIVILEGES     Token privileges can be adjusted
TOKEN_ADJUST_GROUPS         Token groups can be adjusted
TOKEN_ADJUST_DEFAULT        Token default ACL and owner can be adjusted
TOKEN_ADJUST_SESSIONID      Token session id can be adjusted
TOKEN_ALL_ACCESS            All of the preceding +
                            STANDARD_RIGHTS_REQUIRED
```

OpenAsSelf

A boolean specifying whether the security context of the process should be used to check the access to the token object. If `OpenAsSelf` is false, the security context of the thread is used, which may be an impersonation context.

TokenHandle

Points to a variable that will receive the token object handle if the call is successful.

Return Value

Returns STATUS_SUCCESS or an error status, such as STATUS_ACCESS_DENIED, STATUS_INVALID_HANDLE, or STATUS_NO_TOKEN.

Related Win32 Functions

OpenThreadToken.

Remarks

OpenThreadToken exposes the full functionality of **ZwOpenThreadToken**.

TOKEN_ADJUST_SESSIONID is only valid in Windows 2000.

ZwDuplicateToken

ZwDuplicateToken makes a duplicate copy of a token.

```
NTSYSAPI
NTSTATUS
NTAPI
ZwDuplicateToken(
    IN HANDLE ExistingTokenHandle,
    IN ACCESS_MASK DesiredAccess,
    IN POBJECT_ATTRIBUTES ObjectAttributes,
    IN BOOLEAN EffectiveOnly,
    IN TOKEN_TYPE TokenType,
    OUT PHANDLE NewTokenHandle
    );
```

Parameters

ExistingTokenHandle
    A handle to a token object. The handle must grant `TOKEN_DUPLICATE` access.

DesiredAccess
    Specifies the type of access that the caller requires to the token object. This parameter can be zero, or any combination of the following flags:

```
TOKEN_ASSIGN_PRIMARY       Can be assigned as primary token
TOKEN_DUPLICATE            Can be duplicated
TOKEN_IMPERSONATE          Can be assigned as impersonation token
TOKEN_QUERY                Can be queried
TOKEN_QUERY_SOURCE         Can be queried for source
TOKEN_ADJUST_PRIVILEGES    Token privileges can be adjusted
TOKEN_ADJUST_GROUPS        Token groups can be adjusted
TOKEN_ADJUST_DEFAULT       Token default ACL and owner can be adjusted
TOKEN_ADJUST_SESSIONID     Token session id can be adjusted
TOKEN_ALL_ACCESS           All of the preceding +
                           STANDARD_RIGHTS_REQUIRED
```

ObjectAttributes
    Points to a structure that specifies the object's attributes. `OBJ_OPENLINK` is not a valid attribute for a token object.

EffectiveOnly
    A boolean specifying whether the privileges and groups present, but disabled, in the existing token may be enabled in the new token.

TokenType
    Specifies the type of token object to be created. The permitted values are drawn from the enumeration `TOKEN_TYPE`:

```
typedef enum _TOKEN_TYPE {
    TokenPrimary = 1,
    TokenImpersonation
} TOKEN_TYPE, *PTOKEN_TYPE;
```

NewTokenHandle
    Points to a variable that will receive the token object handle if the call is successful.

Return Value

Returns `STATUS_SUCCESS` or an error status, such as `STATUS_ACCESS_DENIED` or `STATUS_INVALID_HANDLE`.

Related Win32 Functions

`DuplicateToken, DuplicateTokenEx`.

Remarks

`DuplicateTokenEx` exposes most of the functionality of **ZwDuplicateToken**.

`TOKEN_ADJUST_SESSIONID` is only valid in Windows 2000.

ZwFilterToken

ZwFilterToken creates a child of an existing token and applies restrictions to the child token.

```
NTSYSAPI
NTSTATUS
NTAPI
ZwFilterToken(
    IN HANDLE ExistingTokenHandle,
    IN ULONG Flags,
    IN PTOKEN_GROUPS SidsToDisable,
    IN PTOKEN_PRIVILEGES PrivilegesToDelete,
    IN PTOKEN_GROUPS SidsToRestricted,
    OUT PHANDLE NewTokenHandle
    );
```

Parameters

ExistingTokenHandle

A handle to a token object. The handle must grant TOKEN_DUPLICATE access.

Flags

A bit array of flags that affect the filtering of the token. The following value is defined:

```
DELETE_MAX_PRIVILEGES  1  // Delete all privileges except
                          // SeChangeNotifyPrivilege
```

SidsToDisable

Points to a structure that specifies which SIDs are to be disabled in the new token (by adding the attribute SE_GROUP_USE_FOR_DENY_ONLY to the SID). SIDs present in SidsToDisable that are not present in the existing token are ignored, as are the Attributes members of the array SidsToDisable->Groups.

PrivilegesToDelete

Points to a structure that specifies which privileges present in the existing token are not to be copied to the new token. Privileges present in PrivilegesToDelete that are not present in the existing token are ignored, as are the Attributes members of the array PrivilegesToDelete->Privileges. If Flags specifies DELETE_MAX_PRIVILEGES and SeChangeNotifyPrivilege is present in PrivilegesToDelete, it is deleted along with all other privileges.

SidsToRestrict

Points to a structure that specifies which SIDs are to be added to the restricted SIDs of the token. SIDs present in SidsToRestrict that are already present in the restricted SIDs of the existing token are ignored. The Attributes members of SidsToRestrict->Groups must be zero.

NewTokenHandle

Points to a variable that will receive the token object handle if the call is successful.

Return Value

Returns STATUS_SUCCESS or an error status, such as STATUS_ACCESS_DENIED or STATUS_INVALID_HANDLE.

Related Win32 Functions

CreateRestrictedToken.

Remarks

CreateRestrictedToken exposes the full functionality of **ZwFilterToken**.

The routine **ZwFilterToken** is only present in Windows 2000.

ZwAdjustPrivilegesToken

ZwAdjustPrivilegesToken adjusts the attributes of the privileges in a token.

```
NTSYSAPI
NTSTATUS
NTAPI
ZwAdjustPrivilegesToken(
    IN HANDLE TokenHandle,
    IN BOOLEAN DisableAllPrivileges,
    IN PTOKEN_PRIVILEGES NewState,
    IN ULONG BufferLength,
    OUT PTOKEN_PRIVILEGES PreviousState OPTIONAL,
    OUT PULONG ReturnLength
    );
```

Parameters

TokenHandle

A handle to a token object. The handle must grant TOKEN_ADJUST_PRIVILEGES access.

DisableAllPrivileges

A boolean specifying whether all of the token's privileges should be disabled. If DisableAllPrivileges is true, the NewState parameter is ignored.

NewState

Points to a structure that specifies the new state of a set of privileges present in the token.

BufferLength

Specifies the size in bytes of the structure pointed to by PreviousState.

PreviousState

Points to a caller-allocated buffer or variable that receives the previous state of the privileges. If PreviousState is not a null pointer, TokenHandle must also grant TOKEN_QUERY access.

ReturnLength

Optionally points to a variable that receives the number of bytes actually returned to PreviousState if the call was successful. If PreviousState is not a null pointer, ReturnLength must be a valid pointer.

Return Value

Returns STATUS_SUCCESS, STATUS_NOT_ALL_ASSIGNED or an error status, such as STATUS_ACCESS_DENIED, STATUS_INVALID_HANDLE, or STATUS_BUFFER_TOO_SMALL.

Related Win32 Functions

AdjustTokenPrivileges.

Remarks

AdjustTokenPrivileges exposes the full functionality of **ZwAdjustTokenPrivileges**.

ZwAdjustGroupsToken

ZwAdjustGroupsToken adjusts the attributes of the groups in a token.

```
NTSYSAPI
NTSTATUS
NTAPI
ZwAdjustGroupsToken(
    IN HANDLE TokenHandle,
    IN BOOLEAN ResetToDefault,
    IN PTOKEN_GROUPS NewState,
    IN ULONG BufferLength,
    OUT PTOKEN_GROUPS PreviousState OPTIONAL,
    OUT PULONG ReturnLength
    );
```

Parameters

TokenHandle

A handle to a token object. The handle must grant TOKEN_ADJUST_GROUPS access.

ResetToDefault

A boolean specifying whether all of the token's groups should be reset to their default state. If ResetToDefault is true, the NewState parameter is ignored.

NewState

Points to a structure that specifies the new state of a set of groups present in the token.

BufferLength

Specifies the size in bytes of the structure pointed to by PreviousState.

PreviousState

Points to a caller-allocated buffer or variable that receives the previous state of the groups. If PreviousState is not a null pointer, TokenHandle must also grant TOKEN_QUERY access.

ReturnLength
> Optionally points to a variable that receives the number of bytes actually returned to PreviousState if the call was successful. If PreviousState is not a null pointer, ReturnLength must be a valid pointer.

Return Value

> Returns STATUS_SUCCESS, STATUS_NOT_ALL_ASSIGNED or an error status, such as STATUS_ACCESS_DENIED, STATUS_INVALID_HANDLE, or STATUS_BUFFER_TOO_SMALL.

Related Win32 Functions

> AdjustTokenGroups.

Remarks

> AdjustTokenGroups exposes the full functionality of ZwAdjustTokenGroups.

ZwQueryInformationToken

ZwQueryInformationToken retrieves information about a token object.

```
NTSYSAPI
NTSTATUS
NTAPI
ZwQueryInformationToken(
    IN HANDLE TokenHandle,
    IN TOKEN_INFORMATION_CLASS TokenInformationClass,
    OUT PVOID TokenInformation,
    IN ULONG TokenInformationLength,
    OUT PULONG ReturnLength
    );
```

Parameters

TokenHandle
> A handle to a token object. The handle must grant TOKEN_QUERY access for most information classes. To query the token source TOKEN_QUERY_SOURCE access must be granted.

TokenInformationClass
> Specifies the type of token information to be queried. The permitted values are drawn from the enumeration TOKEN_INFORMATION_CLASS, described in the following section.

TokenInformation
> Points to a caller-allocated buffer or variable that receives the requested token information.

TokenInformationLength
> Specifies the size in bytes of TokenInformation, which the caller should set according to the given TokenInformationClass.

ReturnLength
   Points to a variable that receives the number of bytes actually returned to
   TokenInformation; if TokenInformationLength is too small to contain the available
   data, ReturnLength points to the number of bytes required for the available data.

Return Value

Returns STATUS_SUCCESS or an error status, such as STATUS_ACCESS_DENIED,
STATUS_INVALID_HANDLE, STATUS_INVALID_INFO_CLASS, or STATUS_BUFFER_TOO_SMALL.

Related Win32 Functions

GetTokenInformation.

Remarks

GetTokenInformation exposes the full functionality of **ZwQueryInformationToken**.

ZwSetInformationToken

ZwSetInformationToken sets information affecting a token object.

```
NTSYSAPI
NTSTATUS
NTAPI
ZwSetInformationToken(
    IN HANDLE TokenHandle,
    IN TOKEN_INFORMATION_CLASS TokenInformationClass,
    IN PVOID TokenInformation,
    IN ULONG TokenInformationLength
    );
```

Parameters

TokenHandle
   A handle to a token object. The handle must grant TOKEN_ADJUST_DEFAULT access.
   Some information classes also require TOKEN_ADJUST_SESSIONID access.

TokenInformationClass
   Specifies the type of token information to be set. The permitted values are a subset of
   the enumeration TOKEN_INFORMATION_CLASS, described in the following section.

TokenInformation
   Points to a caller-allocated buffer or variable that contains the token information to
   be set.

TokenInformationLength
   Specifies the size in bytes of TokenInformation, which the caller should set according
   to the given TokenInformationClass.

Return Value

Returns STATUS_SUCCESS or an error status, such as STATUS_ACCESS_DENIED,
STATUS_INVALID_HANDLE, STATUS_INVALID_INFO_CLASS,
STATUS_INFO_LENGTH_MISMATCH, STATUS_INVALID_OWNER, or
STATUS_ALLOTTED_SPACE_EXCEEDED.

Related Win32 Functions

SetTokenInformation.

Remarks

SetTokenInformation exposes the full functionality of **ZwSetInformationToken**.

TOKEN_INFORMATION_CLASS

```
                                              Query   Set
typedef enum _TOKEN_INFORMATION_CLASS {
    TokenUser = 1,                      // 1    Y      N
    TokenGroups,                        // 2    Y      N
    TokenPrivileges,                    // 3    Y      N
    TokenOwner,                         // 4    Y      Y
    TokenPrimaryGroup,                  // 5    Y      Y
    TokenDefaultDacl,                   // 6    Y      Y
    TokenSource,                        // 7    Y      N
    TokenType,                          // 8    Y      N
    TokenImpersonationLevel,            // 9    Y      N
    TokenStatistics,                    // 10   Y      N
    TokenRestrictedSids,                // 11   Y      N
    TokenSessionId                      // 12   Y      Y
} TOKEN_INFORMATION_CLASS;
```

TokenUser

```
typedef struct _TOKEN_USER { // Information Class 1
    SID_AND_ATTRIBUTES User;
} TOKEN_USER, *PTOKEN_USER;
```

Members

User
    The SID of the user. No attributes are defined.

Remarks

None.

TokenGroups and TokenRestrictedSids

```
typedef struct _TOKEN_GROUPS { // Information Classes 2 and 11
    ULONG GroupCount;
    SID_AND_ATTRIBUTES Groups[ANYSIZE_ARRAY];
} TOKEN_GROUPS, *PTOKEN_GROUPS;
```

Members

GroupCount
   The numbers of groups in the array Groups.

Groups
   An array of SIDs of groups and their associated attributes. The following attributes are
   defined:

```
SE_GROUP_MANDATORY              0x00000001
SE_GROUP_ENABLED_BY_DEFAULT     0x00000002
SE_GROUP_ENABLED                0x00000004
SE_GROUP_OWNER                  0x00000008
SE_GROUP_USE_FOR_DENY_ONLY      0x00000010
SE_GROUP_RESOURCE               0x20000000
SE_GROUP_LOGON_ID               0xC0000000
```

Remarks

TokenRestrictedSids is only valid in Windows 2000.

TokenPrivileges

```
typedef struct _TOKEN_PRIVILEGES { // Information Class 3
    ULONG PrivilegeCount;
    LUID_AND_ATTRIBUTES Privileges[ANYSIZE_ARRAY];
} TOKEN_PRIVILEGES, *PTOKEN_PRIVILEGES;
```

Members

PrivilegeCount
   The numbers of privileges in the array Privileges.

Privileges
   An array of LUIDs identifying privileges and their associated attributes. The following
   attributes are defined:

```
SE_PRIVILEGE_ENABLED_BY_DEFAULT 0x00000001
SE_PRIVILEGE_ENABLED            0x00000002
```

Remarks

None.

TokenOwner

```
typedef struct _TOKEN_OWNER { // Information Class 4
    PSID Owner;
} TOKEN_OWNER, *PTOKEN_OWNER;
```

Members

Owner
> The SID that will be recorded as the owner of any objects created by a process using this access token.

Remarks

> None.

TokenPrimaryGroup

```
typedef struct _TOKEN_PRIMARY_GROUP { // Information Class 5
    PSID PrimaryGroup;
} TOKEN_PRIMARY_GROUP, *PTOKEN_PRIMARY_GROUP;
```

Members

PrimaryGroup
> The SID that will be recorded as the primary group of any objects created by a process using this access token.

Remarks

> None.

TokenDefaultDacl

```
typedef struct _TOKEN_DEFAULT_DACL { // Information Class 6
    PACL DefaultDacl;
} TOKEN_DEFAULT_DACL, *PTOKEN_DEFAULT_DACL;
```

Members

DefaultDacl
> The Discretionary ACL that will be assigned to any objects created by a process using this access token, unless an explicit ACL is specified.

Remarks

> None.

TokenSource

```
typedef struct _TOKEN_SOURCE { // Information Class 7
    CHAR SourceName[8];
    LUID SourceIdentifier;
} TOKEN_SOURCE, *PTOKEN_SOURCE;
```

Members

SourceName
A textual identifier of the creator of the token.

SourceIdentifier
A numeric identifier of the creator of the token.

Remarks

None.

TokenType

```
typedef enum _TOKEN_TYPE { // Information Class 8
    TokenPrimary = 1,
    TokenImpersonation
} TOKEN_TYPE, *PTOKEN_TYPE;
```

TokenImpersonationLevel

```
typedef enum _SECURITY_IMPERSONATION_LEVEL { // Information Class 9
    SecurityAnonymous,
    SecurityIdentification,
    SecurityImpersonation,
    SecurityDelegation
} SECURITY_IMPERSONATION_LEVEL, * PSECURITY_IMPERSONATION_LEVEL;
```

TokenStatistics

```
typedef struct _TOKEN_STATISTICS { // Information Class 10
    LUID TokenId;
    LUID AuthenticationId;
    LARGE_INTEGER ExpirationTime;
    TOKEN_TYPE TokenType;
    SECURITY_IMPERSONATION_LEVEL ImpersonationLevel;
    ULONG DynamicCharged;
    ULONG DynamicAvailable;
    ULONG GroupCount;
    ULONG PrivilegeCount;
    LUID ModifiedId;
} TOKEN_STATISTICS, *PTOKEN_STATISTICS;
```

Members

TokenId
A locally unique identifier (LUID) that identifies the instance of the token object.

AuthenticationId
A LUID assigned to the session the token represents. There can be many tokens representing a single logon session.

Expiration Time

The time at which the token expires in the standard time format (that is, the number of 100-nanosecond intervals since January 1, 1601). An expiration time value of −1 indicates that the token does not expire.

Token Type

Specifies the type of the token (primary or impersonation).

ImpersonationLevel

Specifies the impersonation level of the token. This member is valid only if the `TokenType` is `TokenImpersonation`.

DynamicCharged

The size, in bytes, of memory allocated for storing default protection and a primary group identifier.

DynamicAvailable

The size, in bytes, of memory allocated for storing default protection and a primary group identifier that has not been used.

GroupCount

The number of group SIDs included in the token.

PrivilegeCount

The number of privileges included in the token.

ModifiedId

A LUID that changes each time the token is modified. An application can use this value as a test of whether a security context has changed since it was last used.

Remarks

None.

TokenSessionId

```
ULONG SessionId; // Information Class 12
```

A numeric identifier for a session.

`TokenSessionId` is only valid in Windows 2000.

Although the session identifier can be set in any version of Windows 2000, it is only meaningful to Windows Terminal Server.

Example 8.1: Creating a Command Window for the SYSTEM User

```
#include "ntdll.h"

PVOID GetFromToken(HANDLE hToken, TOKEN_INFORMATION_CLASS tic)
{
    DWORD n;

    BOOL rv = GetTokenInformation(hToken, tic, 0, 0, &n);
    if (rv == FALSE && GetLastError() != ERROR_INSUFFICIENT_BUFFER) return 0;

    PBYTE p = new BYTE[n];

    return GetTokenInformation(hToken, tic, p, n, &n) == FALSE ? 0 : p;
}

HANDLE SystemToken()
{
    EnablePrivilege(SE_CREATE_TOKEN_NAME);

    HANDLE hToken;
    OpenProcessToken(GetCurrentProcess(), TOKEN_QUERY | TOKEN_QUERY_SOURCE,
                     &hToken);

    SID_IDENTIFIER_AUTHORITY nt = SECURITY_NT_AUTHORITY;

    PSID system;
    AllocateAndInitializeSid(&nt, 1, SECURITY_LOCAL_SYSTEM_RID,
                             0, 0, 0, 0, 0, 0, 0, &system);

    TOKEN_USER user = {{system, 0}};

    LUID luid;
    AllocateLocallyUniqueId(&luid);

    TOKEN_SOURCE source = {{'*', '*', 'A', 'N', 'O', 'N', '*', '*'},
                           {luid.LowPart, luid.HighPart}};

    LUID authid = SYSTEM_LUID;

    PTOKEN_STATISTICS stats
        = PTOKEN_STATISTICS(GetFromToken(hToken, TokenStatistics));

    NT::SECURITY_QUALITY_OF_SERVICE sqos
        = {sizeof sqos, NT::SecurityAnonymous,
           SECURITY_STATIC_TRACKING, FALSE};

    NT::OBJECT_ATTRIBUTES oa = {sizeof oa, 0, 0, 0, 0, &sqos};

    HANDLE hToken2 = 0;

    NT::ZwCreateToken(&hToken2, TOKEN_ALL_ACCESS, &oa, TokenPrimary,
                NT::PLUID(&authid), // NT::PLUID(&stats->AuthenticationId),
                NT::PLARGE_INTEGER(&stats->ExpirationTime),
                &user,
                PTOKEN_GROUPS(GetFromToken(hToken, TokenGroups)),
                PTOKEN_PRIVILEGES(GetFromToken(hToken, TokenPrivileges)),
                PTOKEN_OWNER(GetFromToken(hToken, TokenOwner)),
                PTOKEN_PRIMARY_GROUP(GetFromToken(hToken, TokenPrimaryGroup)),
                PTOKEN_DEFAULT_DACL(GetFromToken(hToken, TokenDefaultDacl)),
```

```
                    &source);

    CloseHandle(hToken);

    return hToken2;
}

int main()
{
    PROCESS_INFORMATION pi;
    STARTUPINFO si = {sizeof si};

    return CreateProcessAsUser(SystemToken(), 0, "cmd", 0, 0, FALSE,
                               CREATE_NEW_CONSOLE | CREATE_NEW_PROCESS_GROUP,
                               0, 0, &si, &pi);
}
```

Example 8.1 copies most of the information for the new token from the existing token, but changes the token user to be SYSTEM and changes the authentication identifier to be SYSTEM_LUID, breaking the link between the new token and the credentials of the current user.

If NT::PLUID(&stats->AuthenticationId) had been used as the authentication identifier rather than NT::PLUID(&authid), the token would represent SYSTEM on the local system and the logged on user on the network.

9
Synchronization

The system services described in this chapter create and manipulate objects that can be used to synchronize threads.

ZwWaitForSingleObject

ZwWaitForSingleObject waits for an object to become signaled.

```
NTSYSAPI
NTSTATUS
NTAPI
ZwWaitForSingleObject(
    IN HANDLE Handle,
    IN BOOLEAN Alertable,
    IN PLARGE_INTEGER Timeout OPTIONAL
    );
```

Parameters

Handle
A handle to an object. The handle must grant SYNCHRONIZE access.

Alertable
A boolean specifying whether the wait can be interrupted by the delivery of a user APC.

Timeout
Optionally points to a value that specifies the absolute or relative time at which the wait is to be timed out. A negative value specifies an interval relative to the current time. The value is expressed in units of 100 nanoseconds. Absolute times track any changes in the system time; relative times are not affected by system time changes. If Timeout is a null pointer, the wait will not timeout.

Return Value

Returns STATUS_SUCCESS, STATUS_ALERTED, STATUS_USER_APC, STATUS_TIMEOUT, STATUS_ABANDONED, or an error status, such as STATUS_ACCESS_DENIED or STATUS_INVALID_HANDLE.

Related Win32 Functions

WaitForSingleObject, WaitForSingleObjectEx.

Remarks

WaitForSingleObjectEx exposes most of the functionality of **ZwWaitForSingleObject**.

The Handle parameter can be a handle to any kernel object type. If the object is not waitable, it is considered to be always signaled.

ZwSignalAndWaitForSingleObject

ZwSignalAndWaitForSingleObject signals one object and waits for another to become signaled.

```
NTSYSAPI
NTSTATUS
NTAPI
ZwSignalAndWaitForSingleObject(
    IN HANDLE HandleToSignal,
    IN HANDLE HandleToWait,
    IN BOOLEAN Alertable,
    IN PLARGE_INTEGER Timeout OPTIONAL
    );
```

Parameters

HandleToSignal
A handle to the object that is to be signaled. This object can be a semaphore, a mutant, or an event. If the handle is a semaphore, SEMAPHORE_MODIFY_STATE access is required. If the handle is an event, EVENT_MODIFY_STATE access is required. If the handle is a mutant, SYNCHRONIZE access is assumed because only the owner of a mutant may release it.

HandleToWait
A handle to the object that is to be waited upon. The handle must grant SYNCHRONIZE access.

Alertable
A boolean specifying whether the wait can be interrupted by the delivery of a user APC.

Timeout
Optionally points to a value that specifies the absolute or relative time at which the wait is to be timed out. A negative value specifies an interval relative to the current time. The value is expressed in units of 100 nanoseconds. Absolute times track any changes in the system time; relative times are not affected by system time changes. If Timeout is a null pointer, the wait will not timeout.

Return Value

Returns STATUS_SUCCESS, STATUS_ALERTED, STATUS_USER_APC, STATUS_TIMEOUT, STATUS_ABANDONED, or an error status, such as STATUS_ACCESS_DENIED or STATUS_INVALID_HANDLE.

Related Win32 Functions

SignalObjectAndWait.

Remarks

SignalObjectAndWait exposes most of the functionality of **ZwSignalAndWaitForSingleObject**.

The HandleToWait parameter can be a handle to any kernel object type. If the object is not waitable, it is considered to be always signaled.

ZwWaitForMultipleObjects

ZwWaitForMultipleObjects waits for one or more objects to become signaled.

```
NTSYSAPI
NTSTATUS
NTAPI
ZwWaitForMultipleObjects(
    IN ULONG HandleCount,
    IN PHANDLE Handles,
    IN WAIT_TYPE WaitType,
    IN BOOLEAN Alertable,
    IN PLARGE_INTEGER Timeout OPTIONAL
    );
```

Parameters

HandleCount
The number of handles to objects to be waited on. This value must be at most MAXIMUM_WAIT_OBJECTS.

Handles
Points to a caller-allocated buffer or variable that contains the array of object handles to be waited upon. Each handle must grant SYNCHRONIZE access.

WaitType
Specifies the type of wait to be performed. The permitted values are drawn from the enumeration WAIT_TYPE:

```
typedef enum _WAIT_TYPE {
    WaitAll,                    // Wait for any handle to be signaled
    WaitAny                     // Wait for all handles to be signaled
} WAIT_TYPE, *PWAIT_TYPE;
```

Alertable
A boolean specifying whether the wait can be interrupted by the delivery of a user APC.

Timeout
    Optionally points to a value that specifies the absolute or relative time at which the wait is to be timed out. A negative value specifies an interval relative to the current time. The value is expressed in units of 100 nanoseconds. Absolute times track any changes in the system time; relative times are not affected by system time changes. If Timeout is a null pointer, the wait will not timeout.

Return Value

Returns STATUS_SUCCESS, STATUS_ALERTED, STATUS_USER_APC, STATUS_TIMEOUT, STATUS_ABANDONED, STATUS_ABANDONED_WAIT_0 to STATUS_ABANDONED_WAIT_63, STATUS_WAIT_0 to STATUS_WAIT_63, or an error status, such as STATUS_ACCESS_DENIED or STATUS_INVALID_HANDLE.

Related Win32 Functions

WaitForMultipleObjects, WaitForMultipleObjectsEx.

Remarks

WaitForMultipleObjectsEx exposes most of the functionality of **ZwWaitForMultipleObjects**.

The handles in the Handles parameter can be handles to any kernel object type. If the object is not waitable, it is considered to be always signaled.

ZwCreateTimer

ZwCreateTimer creates or opens a timer object.

```
NTSYSAPI
NTSTATUS
NTAPI
ZwCreateTimer(
    OUT PHANDLE TimerHandle,
    IN ACCESS_MASK DesiredAccess,
    IN POBJECT_ATTRIBUTES ObjectAttributes,
    IN TIMER_TYPE TimerType
    );
```

Parameters

TimerHandle
    Points to a variable that will receive the timer object handle if the call is successful.

DesiredAccess
    Specifies the type of access that the caller requires to the timer object. This parameter can be zero, or any combination of the following flags:

```
TIMER_QUERY_STATE      Query access
TIMER_MODIFY_STATE     Modify access
TIMER_ALL_ACCESS       All of the preceding + STANDARD_RIGHTS_ALL
```

ObjectAttributes

Points to a structure that specifies the object's attributes. OBJ_OPENLINK is not a valid attribute for a timer object.

TimerType

Specifies the type of the timer. The permitted values are drawn from the enumeration TIMER_TYPE:

```
typedef enum _TIMER_TYPE {
    NotificationTimer,         // A manual-reset timer
    SynchronizationTimer       // An auto-reset timer
} TIMER_TYPE;
```

Return Value

Returns STATUS_SUCCESS or an error status, such as STATUS_ACCESS_DENIED.

Related Win32 Functions

CreateWaitableTimer.

Remarks

CreateWaitableTimer exposes most of the functionality of **ZwCreateTimer**.

ZwOpenTimer

ZwOpenTimer opens a timer object.

```
NTSYSAPI
NTSTATUS
NTAPI
ZwOpenTimer(
    OUT PHANDLE TimerHandle,
    IN ACCESS_MASK DesiredAccess,
    IN POBJECT_ATTRIBUTES ObjectAttributes
    );
```

Parameters

TimerHandle

Points to a variable that will receive the timer object handle if the call is successful.

DesiredAccess

Specifies the type of access that the caller requires to the timer object. This parameter can be zero, or any combination of the following flags:

```
TIMER_QUERY_STATE      Query access
TIMER_MODIFY_STATE     Modify access
TIMER_ALL_ACCESS       All of the preceding + STANDARD_RIGHTS_ALL
```

ObjectAttributes

Points to a structure that specifies the object's attributes. OBJ_OPENLINK is not a valid attribute for a timer object.

Return Value

Returns STATUS_SUCCESS or an error status, such as STATUS_ACCESS_DENIED or STATUS_OBJECT_NAME_NOT_FOUND.

Related Win32 Functions

OpenWaitableTimer.

Remarks

OpenWaitableTimer exposes most of the functionality of **ZwOpenTimer**.

ZwCancelTimer

ZwCancelTimer deactivates a timer.

```
NTSYSAPI
NTSTATUS
NTAPI
ZwCancelTimer(
    IN HANDLE TimerHandle,
    OUT PBOOLEAN PreviousState OPTIONAL
    );
```

Parameters

TimerHandle
A handle to a timer object. The handle must grant TIMER_MODIFY_STATE access.

PreviousState
Optionally points to a variable that receives the signal state of the timer. A value of true means that the timer is signaled.

Return Value

Returns STATUS_SUCCESS or an error status, such as STATUS_ACCESS_DENIED or STATUS_INVALID_HANDLE.

Related Win32 Functions

CancelWaitableTimer.

Remarks

CancelWaitableTimer exposes most of the functionality of **ZwCancelTimer**.

If the timer is not signaled when **ZwCancelTimer** is invoked, any waiting threads continue to wait until either they timeout the wait, or the timer is reactivated (by **ZwSetTimer**) and eventually signaled.

ZwSetTimer

ZwSetTimer sets properties of and activates a timer.

```
NTSYSAPI
NTSTATUS
NTAPI
ZwSetTimer(
    IN HANDLE TimerHandle,
    IN PLARGE_INTEGER DueTime,
    IN PTIMER_APC_ROUTINE TimerApcRoutine OPTIONAL,
    IN PVOID TimerContext,
    IN BOOLEAN Resume,
    IN LONG Period,
    OUT PBOOLEAN PreviousState OPTIONAL
    );
```

Parameters

TimerHandle

A handle to a timer object. The handle must grant TIMER_MODIFY_STATE access.

DueTime

Points to a value that specifies the absolute or relative time at which the timer is to be signaled. A negative value specifies an interval relative to the current time. The value is expressed in units of 100 nanoseconds. Absolute times track any changes in the system time; relative times are not affected by system time changes.

TimerApcRoutine

Specifies an optional timer APC routine. The timer APC routine has the following prototype:

```
VOID (APIENTRY *PTIMER_APC_ROUTINE)(PVOID TimerContext,
                                    ULONG TimerLowValue,
                                    ULONG TimerHighValue);
```

TimerContext

A void pointer that will be passed as argument to the timer APC routine.

Resume

Specifies whether to restore a system in suspended power conservation mode when the timer state is set to signaled.

Period

The period of the timer, in milliseconds. If **Period** is zero, the timer is signaled once. If **Period** is greater than zero, the timer is periodic.

PreviousState

Optionally points to a variable that receives the signal state of the timer. A value of true means that the timer is signaled.

Return Value

Returns STATUS_SUCCESS, STATUS_TIMER_RESUME_IGNORED or an error status, such as STATUS_ACCESS_DENIED or STATUS_INVALID_HANDLE.

Related Win32 Functions

SetWaitableTimer.

Remarks

SetWaitableTimer exposes most of the functionality of **ZwSetTimer**.

ZwQueryTimer

ZwQueryTimer retrieves information about a timer object.

```
NTSYSAPI
NTSTATUS
NTAPI
ZwQueryTimer(
    IN HANDLE TimerHandle,
    IN TIMER_INFORMATION_CLASS TimerInformationClass,
    OUT PVOID TimerInformation,
    IN ULONG TimerInformationLength,
    OUT PULONG ResultLength OPTIONAL
    );
```

Parameters

TimerHandle
A handle to a timer object. The handle must grant TIMER_QUERY_STATE access.

TimerInformationClass
Specifies the type of timer object information to be queried. The permitted values are drawn from the enumeration TIMER_INFORMATION_CLASS, described in the following section.

TimerInformation
Points to a caller-allocated buffer or variable that receives the requested timer object information.

TimerInformationLength
The size in bytes of TimerInformation, which the caller should set according to the given TimerInformationClass.

ReturnLength
Optionally points to a variable that receives the number of bytes actually returned to TimerInformation if the call was successful. If this information is not needed, ReturnLength may be a null pointer.

Return Value

Returns STATUS_SUCCESS or an error status, such as STATUS_ACCESS_DENIED,
STATUS_INVALID_HANDLE, STATUS_INVALID_INFO_CLASS, or STATUS_INFO_LENGTH_MISMATCH.

Related Win32 Functions

None.

Remarks

None.

TIMER_INFORMATION_CLASS

```
typedef enum _TIMER_INFORMATION_CLASS {
    TimerBasicInformation
} TIMER_INFORMATION_CLASS;
```

TimerBasicInformation

```
typedef struct _TIMER_BASIC_INFORMATION {
    LARGE_INTEGER TimeRemaining;
    BOOLEAN SignalState;
} TIMER_BASIC_INFORMATION, *PTIMER_BASIC_INFORMATION;
```

Members

TimeRemaining

The number of 100-nanosecond units remaining before the timer is next signaled.

SignalState

A boolean indicating whether the timer is signaled.

Remarks

None.

ZwCreateEvent

ZwCreateEvent creates or opens an event object.

```
NTSYSAPI
NTSTATUS
NTAPI
ZwCreateEvent(
    OUT PHANDLE EventHandle,
    IN ACCESS_MASK DesiredAccess,
    IN POBJECT_ATTRIBUTES ObjectAttributes,
    IN EVENT_TYPE EventType,
    IN BOOLEAN InitialState
    );
```

Parameters

EventHandle

Points to a variable that will receive the event object handle if the call is successful.

DesiredAccess

Specifies the type of access that the caller requires to the event object. This parameter can be zero, or any combination of the following flags:

```
EVENT_QUERY_STATE       Query access
EVENT_MODIFY_STATE      Modify access
EVENT_ALL_ACCESS        All of the preceding + STANDARD_RIGHTS_ALL
```

ObjectAttributes

Points to a structure that specifies the object's attributes. OBJ_OPENLINK is not a valid attribute for an event object.

EventType

Specifies the type of the event. The permitted values are drawn from the enumeration EVENT_TYPE:

```
typedef enum _EVENT_TYPE {
    NotificationEvent,          // A manual-reset event
    SynchronizationEvent        // An auto-reset event
} EVENT_TYPE;
```

InitialState

Specifies the initial state of the event. TRUE indicates signaled.

Return Value

Returns STATUS_SUCCESS or an error status, such as STATUS_ACCESS_DENIED.

Related Win32 Functions

CreateEvent.

Remarks

CreateEvent exposes most of the functionality of **ZwCreateEvent**.

ZwOpenEvent

ZwOpenEvent opens an event object.

```
NTSYSAPI
NTSTATUS
NTAPI
ZwOpenEvent(
    OUT PHANDLE EventHandle,
    IN ACCESS_MASK DesiredAccess,
    IN POBJECT_ATTRIBUTES ObjectAttributes
    );
```

Parameters

EventHandle
Points to a variable that will receive the event object handle if the call is successful.

DesiredAccess
Specifies the type of access that the caller requires to the event object. This parameter can be zero, or any combination of the following flags:

```
EVENT_QUERY_STATE      Query access
EVENT_MODIFY_STATE     Modify access
EVENT_ALL_ACCESS       All of the preceding + STANDARD_RIGHTS_ALL
```

ObjectAttributes
Points to a structure that specifies the object's attributes. OBJ_OPENLINK is not a valid attribute for an event object.

Return Value

Returns STATUS_SUCCESS or an error status, such as STATUS_ACCESS_DENIED or STATUS_OBJECT_NAME_NOT_FOUND.

Related Win32 Functions

OpenEvent.

Remarks

OpenEvent exposes most of the functionality of **ZwOpenEvent**.

ZwSetEvent

ZwSetEvent sets an event object to the signaled state.

```
NTSYSAPI
NTSTATUS
NTAPI
ZwSetEvent(
    IN HANDLE EventHandle,
    OUT PULONG PreviousState OPTIONAL
    );
```

Parameters

EventHandle
A handle to an event object. The handle must grant EVENT_MODIFY_STATE access.

PreviousState
Optionally points to a variable that receives the previous signal state of the event. A non-zero value means that the event was signaled.

Return Value

Returns STATUS_SUCCESS or an error status, such as STATUS_ACCESS_DENIED or
STATUS_INVALID_HANDLE.

Related Win32 Functions

SetEvent.

Remarks

SetEvent exposes most of the functionality of **ZwSetEvent**.

ZwPulseEvent

ZwPulseEvent sets an event object to the signaled state releasing all or one waiting
thread (depending upon the event type) and then resets the event to the unsignaled
state.

```
NTSYSAPI
NTSTATUS
NTAPI
ZwPulseEvent(
    IN HANDLE EventHandle,
    OUT PULONG PreviousState OPTIONAL
    );
```

Parameters

EventHandle
  A handle to an event object. The handle must grant EVENT_MODIFY_STATE access.

PreviousState
  Optionally points to a variable that receives the previous signal state of the event. A
  non-zero value means that the event was signaled.

Return Value

Returns STATUS_SUCCESS or an error status, such as STATUS_ACCESS_DENIED or
STATUS_INVALID_HANDLE.

Related Win32 Functions

PulseEvent.

Remarks

PulseEvent exposes most of the functionality of **ZwPulseEvent**.

ZwResetEvent

ZwResetEvent resets an event object to the unsignaled state.

```
NTSYSAPI
NTSTATUS
NTAPI
ZwResetEvent(
    IN HANDLE EventHandle,
    OUT PULONG PreviousState OPTIONAL
    );
```

Parameters

EventHandle
A handle to an event object. The handle must grant EVENT_MODIFY_STATE access.

PreviousState
Optionally points to a variable that receives the previous signal state of the event. A non-zero value means that the event was signaled.

Return Value

Returns STATUS_SUCCESS or an error status, such as STATUS_ACCESS_DENIED or STATUS_INVALID_HANDLE.

Related Win32 Functions

None.

Remarks

The Win32 function ResetEvent uses the native function **ZwClearEvent**, which differs from **ZwResetEvent** by not returning the previous state of the event.

ZwClearEvent

ZwClearEvent resets an event object to the unsignaled state.

```
NTSYSAPI
NTSTATUS
NTAPI
ZwClearEvent(
    IN HANDLE EventHandle
    );
```

Parameters

EventHandle
A handle to an event object. The handle must grant EVENT_MODIFY_STATE access.

Return Value

Returns STATUS_SUCCESS or an error status, such as STATUS_ACCESS_DENIED or STATUS_INVALID_HANDLE.

Related Win32 Functions

ResetEvent.

Remarks

ResetEvent exposes the full functionality of **ZwClearEvent**.

ZwQueryEvent

ZwQueryEvent retrieves information about an event object.

```
NTSYSAPI
NTSTATUS
NTAPI
ZwQueryEvent(
    IN HANDLE EventHandle,
    IN EVENT_INFORMATION_CLASS EventInformationClass,
    OUT PVOID EventInformation,
    IN ULONG EventInformationLength,
    OUT PULONG ResultLength OPTIONAL
    );
```

Parameters

EventHandle
A handle to an event object. The handle must grant EVENT_QUERY_STATE access.

EventInformationClass
Specifies the type of event object information to be queried. The permitted values are drawn from the enumeration EVENT_INFORMATION_CLASS, described in the following section.

EventInformation
Points to a caller-allocated buffer or variable that receives the requested event object information.

EventInformationLength
The size in bytes of EventInformation, which the caller should set according to the given EventInformationClass.

ReturnLength
Optionally points to a variable that receives the number of bytes actually returned to EventInformation if the call was successful. If this information is not needed, ReturnLength may be a null pointer.

Return Value

Returns STATUS_SUCCESS or an error status, such as STATUS_ACCESS_DENIED, STATUS_INVALID_HANDLE, STATUS_INVALID_INFO_CLASS, or STATUS_INFO_LENGTH_MISMATCH.

Related Win32 Functions

None.

Remarks

None.

EVENT_INFORMATION_CLASS

```
typedef enum _EVENT_INFORMATION_CLASS {
    EventBasicInformation
} EVENT_INFORMATION_CLASS;
```

EventBasicInformation

```
typedef struct _EVENT_BASIC_INFORMATION {
    EVENT_TYPE EventType;
    LONG SignalState;
} EVENT_BASIC_INFORMATION, *PEVENT_BASIC_INFORMATION;
```

Members

EventType

The type of the event. The permitted values are drawn from the enumeration
EVENT_TYPE:

```
typedef enum _EVENT_TYPE {
        NotificationEvent,        // A manual-reset event
        SynchronizationEvent      // An auto-reset event
    } EVENT_TYPE;
```

SignalState

Indicates whether the event is signaled. A non-zero value means that the event is
signaled.

Remarks

None.

ZwCreateSemaphore

ZwCreateSemaphore creates or opens a semaphore object.

```
NTSYSAPI
NTSTATUS
NTAPI
ZwCreateSemaphore(
    OUT PHANDLE SemaphoreHandle,
    IN ACCESS_MASK DesiredAccess,
    IN POBJECT_ATTRIBUTES ObjectAttributes,
    IN LONG InitialCount,
    IN LONG MaximumCount
    );
```

Parameters

SemaphoreHandle
Points to a variable that will receive the semaphore object handle if the call is successful.

DesiredAccess
Specifies the type of access that the caller requires to the semaphore object. This parameter can be zero, or any combination of the following flags:

```
SEMAPHORE_QUERY_STATE   Query access
SEMAPHORE_MODIFY_STATE  Modify access
SEMAPHORE_ALL_ACCESS    All of the preceding + STANDARD_RIGHTS_ALL
```

ObjectAttributes
Points to a structure that specifies the object's attributes. OBJ_OPENLINK is not a valid attribute for a semaphore object.

InitialCount
Specifies the initial count for the semaphore object.

MaximumCount
Specifies the maximum count for the semaphore object.

Return Value

Returns STATUS_SUCCESS or an error status, such as STATUS_ACCESS_DENIED.

Related Win32 Functions

CreateSemaphore.

Remarks

CreateSemaphore exposes most of the functionality of **ZwCreateSemaphore**.

ZwOpenSemaphore

ZwOpenSemaphore opens a semaphore object.

```
NTSYSAPI
NTSTATUS
NTAPI
ZwOpenSemaphore(
    OUT PHANDLE SemaphoreHandle,
    IN ACCESS_MASK DesiredAccess,
    IN POBJECT_ATTRIBUTES ObjectAttributes
    );
```

Parameters

SemaphoreHandle
  Points to a variable that will receive the semaphore object handle if the call is successful.

DesiredAccess
  Specifies the type of access that the caller requires to the semaphore object. This parameter can be zero, or any combination of the following flags:

```
SEMAPHORE_QUERY_STATE    Query access
SEMAPHORE_MODIFY_STATE   Modify access
SEMAPHORE_ALL_ACCESS     All of the preceding + STANDARD_RIGHTS_ALL
```

ObjectAttributes
  Points to a structure that specifies the object's attributes. OBJ_OPENLINK is not a valid attribute for a semaphore object.

Return Value

  Returns STATUS_SUCCESS or an error status, such as STATUS_ACCESS_DENIED or STATUS_OBJECT_NAME_NOT_FOUND.

Related Win32 Functions

  OpenSemaphore.

Remarks

  OpenSemaphore exposes most of the functionality of **ZwOpenSemaphore**.

ZwReleaseSemaphore

ZwReleaseSemaphore increases the count of a semaphore by a given amount.

```
NTSYSAPI
NTSTATUS
NTAPI
ZwReleaseSemaphore(
    IN HANDLE SemaphoreHandle,
    IN LONG ReleaseCount,
    OUT PLONG PreviousCount OPTIONAL
    );
```

Parameters

SemaphoreHandle
  A handle to a semaphore object. The handle must grant SEMAPHORE_MODIFY_STATE access.

ReleaseCount
  Specifies the amount by which the semaphore object's current count is to be increased.

PreviousCount
Optionally points to a variable that receives the previous count for the semaphore.

Return Value

Returns STATUS_SUCCESS or an error status, such as STATUS_ACCESS_DENIED or
STATUS_INVALID_HANDLE.

Related Win32 Functions

ReleaseSemaphore.

Remarks

ReleaseSemaphore exposes the full functionality of **ZwReleaseSemaphore**.

ZwQuerySemaphore

ZwQuerySemaphore retrieves information about a semaphore object.

```
NTSYSAPI
NTSTATUS
NTAPI
ZwQuerySemaphore(
    IN HANDLE SemaphoreHandle,
    IN SEMAPHORE_INFORMATION_CLASS SemaphoreInformationClass,
    OUT PVOID SemaphoreInformation,
    IN ULONG SemaphoreInformationLength,
    OUT PULONG ResultLength OPTIONAL
    );
```

Parameters

SemaphoreHandle
A handle to a semaphore object. The handle must grant SEMAPHORE_QUERY_STATE access.

SemaphoreInformationClass
Specifies the type of semaphore object information to be queried. The permitted values are drawn from the enumeration SEMAPHORE_INFORMATION_CLASS, described in the following section.

SemaphoreInformation
Points to a caller-allocated buffer or variable that receives the requested semaphore object information.

SemaphoreInformationLength
Specifies the size in bytes of SemaphoreInformation, which the caller should set according to the given SemaphoreInformationClass.

ReturnLength
Optionally points to a variable that receives the number of bytes actually returned to SemaphoreInformation if the call was successful. If this information is not needed, ReturnLength may be a null pointer.

Return Value

Returns STATUS_SUCCESS or an error status, such as STATUS_ACCESS_DENIED, STATUS_INVALID_HANDLE, STATUS_INVALID_INFO_CLASS, or STATUS_INFO_LENGTH_MISMATCH.

Related Win32 Functions

None.

Remarks

None.

SEMAPHORE_INFORMATION_CLASS

```
typedef enum _SEMAPHORE_INFORMATION_CLASS {
    SemaphoreBasicInformation
} SEMAPHORE_INFORMATION_CLASS;
```

SemaphoreBasicInformation

```
typedef struct _SEMAPHORE_BASIC_INFORMATION {
    LONG CurrentCount;
    LONG MaximumCount;
} SEMAPHORE_BASIC_INFORMATION, *PSEMAPHORE_BASIC_INFORMATION;
```

Members

CurrentCount
Specifies the current count for the semaphore object.

MaximumCount
Specifies the maximum count for the semaphore object.

Remarks

None.

ZwCreateMutant

ZwCreateMutant creates or opens a mutant object.

```
NTSYSAPI
NTSTATUS
NTAPI
ZwCreateMutant(
    OUT PHANDLE MutantHandle,
    IN ACCESS_MASK DesiredAccess,
    IN POBJECT_ATTRIBUTES ObjectAttributes,
    IN BOOLEAN InitialOwner
    );
```

Parameters

MutantHandle
Points to a variable that will receive the mutant object handle if the call is successful.

DesiredAccess
Specifies the type of access that the caller requires to the mutant object. This parameter can be zero, or any combination of the following flags:

```
MUTANT_QUERY_STATE      Query access
MUTANT_ALL_ACCESS       All of the preceding + STANDARD_RIGHTS_ALL
```

ObjectAttributes
Points to a structure that specifies the object's attributes. OBJ_OPENLINK is not a valid attribute for a mutant object.

InitialOwner
Specifies whether the calling thread should be the initial owner of the mutant.

Return Value

Returns STATUS_SUCCESS or an error status, such as STATUS_ACCESS_DENIED.

Related Win32 Functions

CreateMutex.

Remarks

CreateMutex exposes most of the functionality of **ZwCreateMutant**.

ZwOpenMutant

ZwOpenMutant opens a mutant object.

```
NTSYSAPI
NTSTATUS
NTAPI
ZwOpenMutant(
    OUT PHANDLE MutantHandle,
    IN ACCESS_MASK DesiredAccess,
    IN POBJECT_ATTRIBUTES ObjectAttributes
    );
```

Parameters

MutantHandle
Points to a variable that will receive the mutant object handle if the call is successful.

DesiredAccess

Specifies the type of access that the caller requires to the mutant object. This parameter can be zero, or any combination of the following flags:

```
MUTANT_QUERY_STATE      Query access
MUTANT_ALL_ACCESS       All of the preceding + STANDARD_RIGHTS_ALL
```

ObjectAttributes

Points to a structure that specifies the object's attributes. OBJ_OPENLINK is not a valid attribute for a mutant object.

Return Value

Returns STATUS_SUCCESS or an error status, such as STATUS_ACCESS_DENIED or STATUS_OBJECT_NAME_NOT_FOUND.

Related Win32 Functions

OpenMutex.

Remarks

OpenMutex exposes most of the functionality of **ZwOpenMutant**.

ZwReleaseMutant

ZwReleaseMutant releases ownership of a mutant object.

```
NTSYSAPI
NTSTATUS
NTAPI
ZwReleaseMutant(
    IN HANDLE MutantHandle,
    OUT PULONG PreviousState
    );
```

Parameters

MutantHandle

A handle to a mutant object. The handle need not grant any specific access.

PreviousState

Optionally points to a variable which receives the previous state of the semaphore.

Return Value

Returns STATUS_SUCCESS or an error status, such as STATUS_ACCESS_DENIED or STATUS_INVALID_HANDLE.

Related Win32 Functions

ReleaseMutex.

Remarks

ReleaseMutex exposes most of the functionality of **ZwReleaseMutant**.

ZwQueryMutant

ZwQueryMutant retrieves information about a mutant object.

```
NTSYSAPI
NTSTATUS
NTAPI
ZwQueryMutant(
    IN HANDLE MutantHandle,
    IN MUTANT_INFORMATION_CLASS MutantInformationClass,
    OUT PVOID MutantInformation,
    IN ULONG MutantInformationLength,
    OUT PULONG ResultLength OPTIONAL
    );
```

Parameters

MutantHandle
A handle to a mutant object. The handle must grant MUTANT_QUERY_STATE access.

MutantInformationClass
Specifies the type of mutant object information to be queried. The permitted values
are drawn from the enumeration MUTANT_INFORMATION_CLASS, described in the following
section.

MutantInformation
Points to a caller-allocated buffer or variable that receives the requested mutant object
information.

MutantInformationLength
Specifies the size in bytes of MutantInformation, which the caller should set according
to the given MutantInformationClass.

ReturnLength
Optionally points to a variable that receives the number of bytes actually returned to
MutantInformation if the call was successful. If this information is not needed,
ReturnLength may be a null pointer.

Return Value

Returns STATUS_SUCCESS or an error status, such as STATUS_ACCESS_DENIED,
STATUS_INVALID_HANDLE, STATUS_INVALID_INFO_CLASS, or STATUS_INFO_LENGTH_MISMATCH.

Related Win32 Functions

None.

Remarks

None.

MUTANT_INFORMATION_CLASS

```
typedef enum _MUTANT_INFORMATION_CLASS {
    MutantBasicInformation
} MUTANT_INFORMATION_CLASS;
```

MutantBasicInformation

```
typedef struct _MUTANT_BASIC_INFORMATION {
    LONG SignalState;
    BOOLEAN Owned;
    BOOLEAN Abandoned;
} MUTANT_BASIC_INFORMATION, *PMUTANT_BASIC_INFORMATION;
```

Members

SignalState

The signal state of the mutant. A positive value indicates that the mutant is signaled.
A non-positive value indicates that a thread has recursively acquired the mutant
(1 - SignalState) times.

Owned

A boolean indicating whether the mutant is owned by the current thread.

Abandoned

A boolean indicating whether the mutant has been abandoned (that is, a thread owned
the mutant when it terminated).

Remarks

None.

ZwCreateIoCompletion

ZwCreateIoCompletion creates or opens an I/O completion object.

```
NTSYSAPI
NTSTATUS
NTAPI
ZwCreateIoCompletion(
    OUT PHANDLE IoCompletionHandle,
    IN ACCESS_MASK DesiredAccess,
    IN POBJECT_ATTRIBUTES ObjectAttributes,
    IN ULONG NumberOfConcurrentThreads
    );
```

Parameters

IoCompletionHandle

Points to a variable that will receive the I/O completion object handle if the call is
successful.

DesiredAccess

    Specifies the type of access that the caller requires to the I/O completion object. This parameter can be zero, or any combination of the following flags:

```
IO_COMPLETION_QUERY_STATE    Query access
IO_COMPLETION_MODIFY_STATE   Modify access
IO_COMPLETION_ALL_ACCESS     All of the preceding + STANDARD_RIGHTS_ALL
```

ObjectAttributes

    Points to a structure that specifies the object's attributes. OBJ_OPENLINK and OBJ_PERMANENT are not valid attributes for an I/O completion object.

NumberOfConcurrentThreads

    Specifies the number of threads that are allowed to execute concurrently.

Return Value

Returns STATUS_SUCCESS or an error status, such as STATUS_ACCESS_DENIED.

Related Win32 Functions

CreateIoCompletionPort.

Remarks

The Win32 function CreateIoCompletionPort creates an I/O completion object by calling **ZwCreateIoCompletion** and then optionally associates the I/O completion object handle and a completion key with a file handle by calling **ZwSetInformationFile** with a FileInformationClass of FileCompletionInformation.

ZwOpenIoCompletion

ZwOpenIoCompletion opens an I/O completion object.

```
NTSYSAPI
NTSTATUS
NTAPI
ZwOpenIoCompletion(
    OUT PHANDLE IoCompletionHandle,
    IN ACCESS_MASK DesiredAccess,
    IN POBJECT_ATTRIBUTES ObjectAttributes
    );
```

Parameters

IoCompletionHandle

    Points to a variable that will receive the I/O completion object handle if the call is successful.

DesiredAccess
> Specifies the type of access that the caller requires to the I/O completion object. This
> parameter can be zero, or any combination of the following flags:

```
IO_COMPLETION_QUERY_STATE    Query access
IO_COMPLETION_MODIFY_STATE   Modify access
IO_COMPLETION_ALL_ACCESS     All of the preceding + STANDARD_RIGHTS_ALL
```

ObjectAttributes
> Points to a structure that specifies the object's attributes. OBJ_OPENLINK and
> OBJ_PERMANENT are not valid attributes for an I/O completion object.

Return Value

> Returns STATUS_SUCCESS or an error status, such as STATUS_ACCESS_DENIED or
> STATUS_OBJECT_NAME_NOT_FOUND.

Related Win32 Functions

> None.

Remarks

> None.

ZwSetIoCompletion

ZwSetIoCompletion queues an I/O completion message to an I/O completion object.

```
NTSYSAPI
NTSTATUS
NTAPI
ZwSetIoCompletion(
    IN HANDLE IoCompletionHandle,
    IN ULONG CompletionKey,
    IN ULONG CompletionValue,
    IN NTSTATUS Status,
    IN ULONG Information
    );
```

Parameters

IoCompletionHandle
> A handle to an I/O completion object. The handle must grant
> IO_COMPLETION_MODIFY_STATE access.

CompletionKey
> Specifies a value to be returned to a caller of **ZwRemoveIoCompletion** via the
> CompletionKey parameter of that routine.

CompletionValue
> Specifies a value to be returned to a caller of **ZwRemoveIoCompletion** via the
> CompletionValue parameter of that routine.

Status

Specifies a value to be returned to a caller of `ZwRemoveIoCompletion` via the parameter `IoStatusBlock->Status`.

Information

Specifies a value to be returned to a caller of `ZwRemoveIoCompletion` via the parameter `IoStatusBlock->Information`.

Return Value

Returns STATUS_SUCCESS or an error status, such as STATUS_ACCESS_DENIED or STATUS_INVALID_HANDLE.

Related Win32 Functions

PostQueuedCompletionStatus.

Remarks

PostQueuedCompletionStatus exposes most of the functionality of `ZwSetIoCompletion`.

ZwRemoveIoCompletion

`ZwRemoveIoCompletion` dequeues an I/O completion message from an I/O completion object.

```
NTSYSAPI
NTSTATUS
NTAPI
ZwRemoveIoCompletion(
    IN HANDLE IoCompletionHandle,
    OUT PULONG CompletionKey,
    OUT PULONG CompletionValue,
    OUT PIO_STATUS_BLOCK IoStatusBlock,
    IN PLARGE_INTEGER Timeout OPTIONAL
    );
```

Parameters

IoCompletionHandle

A handle to an I/O completion object. The handle must grant IO_COMPLETION_MODIFY_STATE access.

CompletionKey

Points to a variable that receives the value of the CompletionKey.

CompletionValue

Points to a variable that receives the value of the CompletionValue.

IoStatusBlock

Points to a caller-allocated buffer or variable that receives the IO_STATUS_BLOCK of the completed I/O operation.

Timeout

Optionally points to a value that specifies the absolute or relative time at which the wait is to be timed out. A negative value specifies an interval relative to the current time. The value is expressed in units of 100 nanoseconds. Absolute times track any changes in the system time; relative times are not affected by system time changes. If Timeout is a null pointer, the wait will not timeout.

Return Value

Returns STATUS_SUCCESS, STATUS_TIMEOUT or an error status, such as STATUS_ACCESS_DENIED or STATUS_INVALID_HANDLE.

Related Win32 Functions

GetQueuedCompletionStatus.

Remarks

GetQueuedCompletionStatus exposes most of the functionality of **ZwRemoveIoCompletion**.

ZwQueryIoCompletion

ZwQueryIoCompletion retrieves information about an I/O completion object.

```
NTSYSAPI
NTSTATUS
NTAPI
ZwQueryIoCompletion(
    IN HANDLE IoCompletionHandle,
    IN IO_COMPLETION_INFORMATION_CLASS IoCompletionInformationClass,
    OUT PVOID IoCompletionInformation,
    IN ULONG IoCompletionInformationLength,
    OUT PULONG ResultLength OPTIONAL
    );
```

Parameters

IoCompletionHandle

A handle to an I/O completion object. The handle must grant IO_COMPLETION_QUERY_STATE access.

IoCompletionInformationClass

Specifies the type of I/O completion object information to be queried. The permitted values are drawn from the enumeration IO_COMPLETION_INFORMATION_CLASS, described in the following section.

IoCompletionInformation

Points to a caller-allocated buffer or variable that receives the requested I/O completion object information.

IoCompletionInformationLength

Specifies the size in bytes of `IoCompletionInformation`, which the caller should set according to the given `IoCompletionInformationClass`.

ReturnLength

Optionally points to a variable that receives the number of bytes actually returned to `IoCompletionInformation` if the call was successful. If this information is not needed, `ReturnLength` may be a null pointer.

Return Value

Returns `STATUS_SUCCESS` or an error status, such as `STATUS_ACCESS_DENIED`, `STATUS_INVALID_HANDLE`, `STATUS_INVALID_INFO_CLASS`, or `STATUS_INFO_LENGTH_MISMATCH`.

Related Win32 Functions

None.

Remarks

None.

IO_COMPLETION_INFORMATION_CLASS

```
typedef enum _IO_COMPLETION_INFORMATION_CLASS {
    IoCompletionBasicInformation
} IO_COMPLETION_INFORMATION_CLASS;
```

IoCompletionBasicInformation

```
typedef struct _IO_COMPLETION_BASIC_INFORMATION {
    LONG SignalState;
} IO_COMPLETION_BASIC_INFORMATION, *PIO_COMPLETION_BASIC_INFORMATION;
```

Members

SignalState

The signal state of the I/O completion object. A positive value indicates that the I/O completion object is signaled.

Remarks

None.

ZwCreateEventPair

`ZwCreateEventPair` creates or opens an event pair object.

```
NTSYSAPI
NTSTATUS
NTAPI
ZwCreateEventPair(
```

```
OUT PHANDLE EventPairHandle,
IN ACCESS_MASK DesiredAccess,
IN POBJECT_ATTRIBUTES ObjectAttributes
);
```

Parameters

EventPairHandle

Points to a variable that will receive the event pair object handle if the call is successful.

DesiredAccess

Specifies the type of access that the caller requires to the event pair object. This parameter can be zero or STANDARD_RIGHTS_ALL.

ObjectAttributes

Points to a structure that specifies the object's attributes. OBJ_OPENLINK is not a valid attribute for an event pair object.

Return Value

Returns STATUS_SUCCESS or an error status, such as STATUS_ACCESS_DENIED.

Related Win32 Functions

None.

Remarks

An event pair object is an object constructed from two KEVENT structures which are conventionally named "High" and "Low." They are optimized for fast client server interactions and are not often used by the operating system, having been superseded by the LPC port mechanism.

pstat.exe and kdextx86.dll report some threads as having a wait reason of "EventPairLow," but this is misleading. The numeric value of the wait reason for these threads is 0xF, and newer versions of ntddk.h translate this as "WrQueue" (0xE is "WrEventPair")—which better reflects the true reason for the wait. pstat and kdextx86 translate 0xE as "WrEventPairHigh" and 0xF as "WrEventPairLow."

ZwOpenEventPair

ZwOpenEventPair opens an event pair object.

```
NTSYSAPI
NTSTATUS
NTAPI
ZwOpenEventPair(
    OUT PHANDLE EventPairHandle,
    IN ACCESS_MASK DesiredAccess,
    IN POBJECT_ATTRIBUTES ObjectAttributes
    );
```

Parameters

EventPairHandle
Points to a variable that will receive the event pair object handle if the call is successful.

DesiredAccess
Specifies the type of access that the caller requires to the event pair object. This parameter can be zero or STANDARD_RIGHTS_ALL.

ObjectAttributes
Points to a structure that specifies the object's attributes. OBJ_OPENLINK is not a valid attribute for an event pair object.

Return Value

Returns STATUS_SUCCESS or an error status, such as STATUS_ACCESS_DENIED or STATUS_OBJECT_NAME_NOT_FOUND.

Related Win32 Functions

None.

Remarks

None.

ZwWaitLowEventPair

ZwWaitLowEventPair waits for the low event of an event pair to become signaled.

```
NTSYSAPI
NTSTATUS
NTAPI
ZwWaitLowEventPair(
    IN HANDLE EventPairHandle
    );
```

Parameters

EventPairHandle
A handle to an event pair object. The handle must grant SYNCHRONIZE access.

Return Value

Returns STATUS_SUCCESS or an error status, such as STATUS_ACCESS_DENIED or STATUS_INVALID_HANDLE.

Related Win32 Functions

None.

Remarks

The two events in an event pair are named "Low" and "High." **ZwWaitLowEventPair**
waits for the Low event to be set. The EventPairHandle itself is not directly waitable.

ZwWaitHighEventPair

ZwWaitHighEventPair waits for the high event of an event pair to become signaled.

```
NTSYSAPI
NTSTATUS
NTAPI
ZwWaitHighEventPair(
    IN HANDLE EventPairHandle
    );
```

Parameters

EventPairHandle
 A handle to an event pair object. The handle must grant SYNCHRONIZE access.

Return Value

Returns STATUS_SUCCESS or an error status, such as STATUS_ACCESS_DENIED or
STATUS_INVALID_HANDLE.

Related Win32 Functions

None.

Remarks

The two events in an event pair are named "Low" and "High." **ZwWaitHighEventPair**
waits for the High event to be set. The EventPairHandle itself is not directly waitable.

ZwSetLowWaitHighEventPair

ZwSetLowWaitHighEventPair signals the low event of an event pair and waits for the
high event to become signaled.

```
NTSYSAPI
NTSTATUS
NTAPI
ZwSetLowWaitHighEventPair(
    IN HANDLE EventPairHandle
    );
```

Parameters

EventPairHandle
 A handle to an event pair object. The handle must grant SYNCHRONIZE access.

Return Value

Returns STATUS_SUCCESS or an error status, such as STATUS_ACCESS_DENIED or STATUS_INVALID_HANDLE.

Related Win32 Functions

None.

Remarks

The two events in an event pair are named "Low" and "High."
ZwSetLowWaitHighEventPair signals the Low event and waits for the High event to be set. If a thread is waiting for the Low event, the system switches immediately to that thread rather choosing a thread to run based on scheduling priorities. This is the same mechanism that is used by LPC ports to improve the performance of client server interactions.

ZwSetHighWaitLowEventPair

ZwSetHighWaitLowEventPair signals the high event of an event pair and waits for the low event to become signaled.

```
NTSYSAPI
NTSTATUS
NTAPI
ZwSetHighWaitLowEventPair(
    IN HANDLE EventPairHandle
    );
```

Parameters

EventPairHandle
A handle to an event pair object. The handle must grant SYNCHRONIZE access.

Return Value

Returns STATUS_SUCCESS or an error status, such as STATUS_ACCESS_DENIED or STATUS_INVALID_HANDLE.

Related Win32 Functions

None.

Remarks

The two events in an event pair are named "Low" and "High."
ZwSetHighWaitLowEventPair signals the High event and waits for the Low event to be set. If a thread is waiting for the High event, the system switches immediately to that thread rather than choosing a thread to run based on scheduling priorities. This is the same mechanism that is used by LPC ports to improve the performance of client server interactions.

ZwSetLowEventPair

`ZwSetLowEventPair` signals the low event of an event pair object.

```
NTSYSAPI
NTSTATUS
NTAPI
ZwSetLowEventPair(
    IN HANDLE EventPairHandle
    );
```

Parameters

EventPairHandle

A handle to an event pair object. The handle must grant SYNCHRONIZE access.

Return Value

Returns STATUS_SUCCESS or an error status, such as STATUS_ACCESS_DENIED or STATUS_INVALID_HANDLE.

Related Win32 Functions

None.

Remarks

The two events in an event pair are named "Low" and "High." `ZwSetLowEventPair` signals the Low event.

ZwSetHighEventPair

`ZwSetHighEventPair` signals the high event of an event pair object.

```
NTSYSAPI
NTSTATUS
NTAPI
ZwSetHighEventPair(
    IN HANDLE EventPairHandle
    );
```

Parameters

EventPairHandle

A handle to an event pair object. The handle must grant SYNCHRONIZE access.

Return Value

Returns STATUS_SUCCESS or an error status, such as STATUS_ACCESS_DENIED or STATUS_INVALID_HANDLE.

Related Win32 Functions

None.

Remarks

The two events in an event pair are named "Low" and "High." **ZwSetHighEventPair** signals the High event.

10
Time

The system services described in this chapter are loosely concerned with time and timing.

ZwQuerySystemTime

`ZwQuerySystemTime` retrieves the system time.

```
NTSYSAPI
NTSTATUS
NTAPI
ZwQuerySystemTime(
    OUT PLARGE_INTEGER CurrentTime
    );
```

Parameters

CurrentTime
Points to a variable that receives the current time of day in the standard time format (that is, the number of 100-nanosecond intervals since January 1, 1601).

Return Value

Returns STATUS_SUCCESS or an error status.

Related Win32 Functions

None.

Remarks

GetSystemTime and GetSystemTimeAsFileTime read from the KUSER_SHARED_DATA page. This page is mapped read-only into the user mode range of the virtual address and read-write in the kernel range. The system clock tick updates the system time, which is stored in this page, directly. Reading the system time from this page is faster than calling **ZwQuerySystemTime**.

The KUSER_SHARED_DATA structure is defined in the Windows 2000 versions of ntddk.h.

ZwSetSystemTime

ZwSetSystemTime sets the system time.

```
NTSYSAPI
NTSTATUS
NTAPI
ZwSetSystemTime(
    IN PLARGE_INTEGER NewTime,
    OUT PLARGE_INTEGER OldTime OPTIONAL
    );
```

Parameters

NewTime
Points to a variable that specifies the new time of day in the standard time format (that is, the number of 100-nanosecond intervals since January 1, 1601).

OldTime
Optionally points to a variable that receives the old time of day in the standard time format (that is, the number of 100-nanosecond intervals since January 1, 1601).

Return Value

Returns STATUS_SUCCESS or an error status, such as STATUS_PRIVILEGE_NOT_HELD.

Related Win32 Functions

SetSystemTime.

Remarks

SeSystemtimePrivilege is required to set the system time.

ZwQueryPerformanceCounter

ZwQueryPerformanceCounter retrieves information from the high-resolution performance counter.

```
NTSYSAPI
NTSTATUS
NTAPI
ZwQueryPerformanceCounter(
    OUT PLARGE_INTEGER PerformanceCount,
    OUT PLARGE_INTEGER PerformanceFrequency OPTIONAL
    );
```

Parameters

PerformanceCount
Points to a variable that receives the current value of the performance counter.

PerformanceFrequency
Optionally points to a variable that receives the frequency of the performance counter
in units of counts per second.

Return Value

Returns STATUS_SUCCESS or an error status.

Related Win32 Functions

QueryPerformanceCounter, QueryPerformanceFrequency.

Remarks

Collectively QueryPerformanceCounter and QueryPerformanceFrequency expose the full
functionality of **ZwQueryPerformanceCounter**.

ZwSetTimerResolution

ZwSetTimerResolution sets the resolution of the system timer.

```
NTSYSAPI
NTSTATUS
NTAPI
ZwSetTimerResolution(
    IN ULONG RequestedResolution,
    IN BOOLEAN Set,
    OUT PULONG ActualResolution
    );
```

Parameters

RequestedResolution
The requested timer resolution in units of 100-nanoseconds.

Set
Specifies whether the requested resolution should be established or revoked.

ActualResolution
Points to a variable that receives the actual timer resolution in units of
100-nanoseconds.

Return Value

Returns STATUS_SUCCESS or an error status, such as STATUS_TIMER_RESOLUTION_NOT_SET.

Related Win32 Functions

timeBeginPeriod, timeEndPeriod.

Remarks

None.

ZwQueryTimerResolution

ZwQueryTimerResolution retrieves information about the resolution of the system timer.

```
NTSYSAPI
NTSTATUS
NTAPI
ZwQueryTimerResolution(
    OUT PULONG CoarsestResolution,
    OUT PULONG FinestResolution,
    OUT PULONG ActualResolution
    );
```

Parameters

CoarsestResolution

Points to a variable that receives the coarsest timer resolution that can be set in units of 100-nanoseconds.

FinestResolution

Points to a variable that receives the finest timer resolution, which can be set in units of 100-nanoseconds.

ActualResolution

Points to a variable that receives the actual timer resolution in units of 100-nanoseconds.

Related Win32 Functions

None.

Remarks

None.

ZwDelayExecution

ZwDelayExecution suspends the execution of the current thread for a specified interval.

```
NTSYSAPI
NTSTATUS
NTAPI
ZwDelayExecution(
    IN BOOLEAN Alertable,
    IN PLARGE_INTEGER Interval
    );
```

Parameters

Alertable

A boolean specifying whether the delay can be interrupted by the delivery of a user APC.

Interval

Points to a value that specifies the absolute or relative time at which the delay is to end. A negative value specifies an interval relative to the current time. The value is expressed in units of 100 nanoseconds. Absolute times track any changes in the system time; relative times are not affected by system time changes.

Return Value

Returns STATUS_SUCCESS, STATUS_ALERTED, STATUS_USER_APC, or an error status.

Related Win32 Functions

Sleep, SleepEx.

Remarks

SleepEx exposes most of the functionality of **ZwDelayExecution**.

ZwYieldExecution

ZwYieldExecution yields the use of the processor by the current thread to any other thread that is ready to use it.

```
NTSYSAPI
NTSTATUS
NTAPI
ZwYieldExecution(
    VOID
    );
```

Parameters

None

Return Value

Returns STATUS_SUCCESS or STATUS_NO_YIELD_PERFORMED.

Related Win32 Functions

SwitchToThread.

Remarks

SwitchToThread exposes the full functionality of **ZwYieldExecution**.

ZwGetTickCount

ZwGetTickCount retrieves the number of milliseconds that have elapsed since the system booted.

```
NTSYSAPI
ULONG
NTAPI
ZwGetTickCount(
    VOID
    );
```

Parameters

None.

Return Value

Returns the number of milliseconds that have elapsed since the system was booted.

Related Win32 Functions

None.

Remarks

GetTickCount reads from the KUSER_SHARED_DATA page. This page is mapped read-only into the user mode range of the virtual address and read-write in the kernel range. The system clock tick updates the system tick count, which is stored in this page, directly. Reading the tick count from this page is faster than calling ZwGetTickCount.

The KUSER_SHARED_DATA structure is defined in the Windows 2000 versions of ntddk.h.

11
Execution Profiling

The system services described in this chapter create and manipulate objects that gather execution profiling information.

KPROFILE_SOURCE

```
typedef enum _KPROFILE_SOURCE {
    ProfileTime
} KPROFILE_SOURCE;
```

Remarks

KPROFILE_SOURCE is defined in ntddk.h, and the definition there includes additional values. However only ProfileTime is implemented for the Intel family of processors by the standard Hardware Abstraction Layer (HAL) (named HAL.DLL on the installation CD).

ZwCreateProfile

ZwCreateProfile creates a profile object.

```
NTSYSAPI
NTSTATUS
NTAPI
ZwCreateProfile(
    OUT PHANDLE ProfileHandle,
    IN HANDLE ProcessHandle,
    IN PVOID Base,
    IN ULONG Size,
    IN ULONG BucketShift,
    IN PULONG Buffer,
    IN ULONG BufferLength,
    IN KPROFILE_SOURCE Source,
    IN ULONG ProcessorMask
    );
```

Parameters

ProfileHandle
   Points to a variable that will receive the profile object handle if the call is successful.

ProcessHandle
   A handle of a process object, representing the process for which profile data should be gathered. The handle must grant PROCESS_QUERY_INFORMATION access. If this handle is zero, profile data is gathered for the system.

Base
   The base address of a region of memory to profile.

Size
   The size, in bytes, of a region of memory to profile.

BucketShift
   Specifies the number of bits of right-shift to be applied to the instruction pointer when selecting the bucket to be incremented. Valid shift sizes are 0 to 31; if Size is greater than 0x10000, the shift size must be in the range 2 to 31.

Buffer
   Points to a caller-allocated buffer or variable that receives an array of ULONG values, one per bucket, representing the hit count for each bucket.

BufferLength
   The size, in bytes, of Buffer.

Source
   The source of the event that triggers sampling of the instruction pointer.

ProcessorMask
   A bit array of flags specifying whether profiling information should be gathered on the corresponding processor. If ProcessorMask is zero, profiling information is gathered on all active processors.

Return Value

Returns STATUS_SUCCESS or an error status, such as STATUS_INVALID_HANDLE, STATUS_ACCESS_DENIED, STATUS_PRIVILEGE_NOT_HELD, or STATUS_BUFFER_TOO_SMALL.

Related Win32 Functions

None.

Remarks

SeSystemProfilePrivilege is required to profile the system.

A profile source is a source of events. When an event from the source occurs, the *processor instruction pointer* (Eip) is sampled, and if it lies in the range Base to Base+Size of an active (started) profile object, the Buffer element at (Eip - Base) >> BucketShift is incremented.

Example 11.1 demonstrates the use of the profiling APIs to profile the kernel.

ZwSetIntervalProfile

ZwSetIntervalProfile sets the interval between profiling samples for the specified profiling source.

```
NTSYSAPI
NTSTATUS
NTAPI
ZwSetIntervalProfile(
    IN ULONG Interval,
    IN KPROFILE_SOURCE Source
    );
```

Parameters

Interval
Specifies the interval between profiling samples.

Source
Specifies the source of profiling events to be set.

Return Value

Returns STATUS_SUCCESS or an error status.

Related Win32 Functions

None.

Remarks

For the ProfileTime source, the interval unit is 100 nanoseconds; for other sources the interval might be the number of events from the event source to ignore between sampling.

ZwQueryIntervalProfile

ZwQueryIntervalProfile retrieves the interval between profiling samples for the specified profiling source.

```
NTSYSAPI
NTSTATUS
NTAPI
ZwQueryIntervalProfile(
```

```
    IN KPROFILE_SOURCE Source,
    OUT PULONG Interval
    );
```

Parameters

Source
Specifies the source of profiling events to be queried.

Interval
Points to a variable that receives the interval between profiling samples.

Return Value

Returns STATUS_SUCCESS or an error status.

Related Win32 Functions

None.

Remarks

None.

ZwStartProfile

ZwStartProfile starts the collection of profiling data.

```
NTSYSAPI
NTSTATUS
NTAPI
ZwStartProfile(
    IN HANDLE ProfileHandle
    );
```

Parameters

ProfileHandle
A handle to a profile object. The handle must grant PROFILE_START_STOP access.

Return Value

Returns STATUS_SUCCESS or an error status, such as STATUS_INVALID_HANDLE, STATUS_ACCESS_DENIED, STATUS_PROFILING_NOT_STOPPED, or STATUS_PROFILING_AT_LIMIT.

Related Win32 Functions

None.

Remarks

None.

ZwStopProfile

ZwStopProfile stops the collection of profiling data.

```
NTSYSAPI
NTSTATUS
NTAPI
ZwStopProfile(
    IN HANDLE ProfileHandle
    );
```

Parameters

ProfileHandle
   A handle to a profile object. The handle must grant PROFILE_START_STOP access.

Return Value

Returns STATUS_SUCCESS or an error status, such as STATUS_INVALID_HANDLE,
STATUS_ACCESS_DENIED, or STATUS_PROFILING_NOT_STARTED.

Related Win32 Functions

None.

Remarks

None.

Example 11.1: Profiling the Kernel

```c
#include "ntdll.h"
#include <stdio.h>
#include <imagehlp.h>

HANDLE hWakeup;

PULONG LoadDrivers()
{
    ULONG n = 0x1000;
    PULONG p = new ULONG[n];

    while (NT::ZwQuerySystemInformation(NT::SystemModuleInformation, p, n, 0)
            == STATUS_INFO_LENGTH_MISMATCH)
        delete [] p, p = new ULONG[n = n * 2];
    return p;
}

BOOL WINAPI ConsoleCtrlHandler(DWORD dwCtrlType)
{
    return dwCtrlType == CTRL_C_EVENT ? SetEvent(hWakeup) : FALSE;
}


int main()
{
    ULONG shift = 3;
```

```
EnablePrivilege(SE_SYSTEM_PROFILE_NAME);

PULONG modules = LoadDrivers();

NT::ZwSetIntervalProfile(10000, NT::ProfileTime);

NT::PSYSTEM_MODULE_INFORMATION m
    = NT::PSYSTEM_MODULE_INFORMATION(modules + 1);

PHANDLE h = new HANDLE[*modules];

PULONG* p = new PULONG[*modules];

for (ULONG i = 0; i < *modules; i++) {

    ULONG n = (m[i].Size >> (shift - 2)) + 1;

    p[i] = PULONG(VirtualAlloc(0, n, MEM_COMMIT, PAGE_READWRITE));

    NT::ZwCreateProfile(h + i, 0, m[i].Base, m[i].Size,
                        shift, p[i], n, NT::ProfileTime, 0);

    NT::ZwStartProfile(h[i]);
}

hWakeup = CreateEvent(0, FALSE, FALSE, 0);

SetConsoleCtrlHandler(ConsoleCtrlHandler, TRUE);

printf("collecting...\n");

WaitForSingleObject(hWakeup, INFINITE);

for (i = 0; i < *modules; i++) {

    NT::ZwStopProfile(h[i]);

    CloseHandle(h[i]);
}

SymInitialize(0, 0, FALSE);
SymSetOptions(SymGetOptions() | SYMOPT_DEFERRED_LOADS | SYMOPT_UNDNAME);

for (i = 0; i < *modules; i++) {

    SymLoadModule(0, 0, m[i].ImageName,
                  m[i].ImageName + m[i].ModuleNameOffset,
                  ULONG(m[i].Base), m[i].Size);

    printf("%s\n", m[i].ImageName + m[i].ModuleNameOffset);

    ULONG n = (m[i].Size >> shift) + 1;

    for (ULONG j = 0; j < n; j++) {

        if (p[i][j] != 0) {

            IMAGEHLP_SYMBOL symbol[10];

            symbol[0].SizeOfStruct = sizeof symbol[0];
            symbol[0].MaxNameLength = sizeof symbol - sizeof symbol[0];
```

```
            ULONG disp = 0;

            SymGetSymFromAddr(0, ULONG(m[i].Base) + (j << shift),
                              &disp, symbol);

            printf("%6ld %s+0x%lx\n", p[i][j], symbol[0].Name, disp);
        }
    }

    SymUnloadModule(0, ULONG(m[i].Base));

    VirtualFree(p[i], 0, MEM_RELEASE);
    }

    SymCleanup(0);

    delete [] m;
    delete [] h;
    delete [] p;

    return 0;
}
```

Example 11.1 implements broadly similar functionality to that found in the resource kit utility kernprof.exe. It uses **ZwQuerySystemInformation** to obtain the size and base address of the kernel modules and then creates and starts a profile object for each module. Data is gathered until interrupted by control-C and then the imagehlp library is used to help dump the collected data.

It is only useful for a profile to cover the code sections of a module, but it is harmless (if wasteful of buffer space) if the profile covers the whole module.

The rounding of the sampled instruction pointer that results from applying the BucketShift has the consequence that some samples are attributed to the wrong symbolic name. This problem is compounded in Windows 2000 because most of the executable modules have been through an optimization process that reorders the instructions of the executable to improve locality of reference; this means that the instructions that implement a routine are no longer contiguous in memory. Although the symbol files contain information about this reordering (the omap data), the incidence of false attribution is still quite high.

In the section of winbase.h that defines the values of the dwCreationFlag parameter of CreateProcess, the value PROFILE_USER also appears. If this value is specified when calling CreateProcess then, when kernel32.dll is initialized in the new process, psapi.dll is loaded and creates profiles for the user mode modules of the process, and when the process ends the collected data is written to the file "profile.out." Some parameters of the profiling performed by psapi.dll can be controlled by the resource kit utility profile.exe, which creates a named shared memory region to hold the parameters and then starts the program to be profiled with the PROFILE_USER flag; psapi.dll checks for the presence of this named shared memory region and, if found, customizes its behavior accordingly.

12

Ports (Local Procedure Calls)

The system services described in this chapter create and manipulate port objects. Port objects are used to implement the Local Procedure Call (LPC) mechanism.

Port objects are not directly exposed via the Win32 API, but they are used to implement the "ncalrpc" Remote Procedure Call (RPC) transport. The RPC run-time library greatly simplifies the use of port objects, but the library (rpcrt4.dll) imports functions from kernel32.dll, and so it can only be used by Win32 applications.

Port objects must be used explicitly to receive and process messages sent by the operating system, such as debug and exception messages. Example C.4 in Appendix C, "Exceptions and Debugging," demonstrates the use of some of the port functions to handle debug event messages.

PORT_MESSAGE

```
typedef struct _PORT_MESSAGE {
    USHORT DataSize;
    USHORT MessageSize;
    USHORT MessageType;
    USHORT VirtualRangesOffset;
    CLIENT_ID ClientId;
    ULONG MessageId;
    ULONG SectionSize;
    // UCHAR Data[];
} PORT_MESSAGE, *PPORT_MESSAGE;
```

Members

DataSize
The size in bytes of the data immediately following the PORT_MESSAGE structure.

MessageSize
The size in bytes of the message; this includes the size of the PORT_MESSAGE structure, the following data, and any additional trailing space that could be used to hold further data.

MessageType

Specifies the type of the message. The permitted values are drawn from the enumeration LPC_TYPE:

```
typedef enum _LPC_TYPE {
        LPC_NEW_MESSAGE,            // A new message
        LPC_REQUEST,               // A request message
        LPC_REPLY,                 // A reply to a request message
        LPC_DATAGRAM,              //
        LPC_LOST_REPLY,            //
        LPC_PORT_CLOSED,           // Sent when port is deleted
        LPC_CLIENT_DIED,           // Messages to thread termination ports
        LPC_EXCEPTION,             // Messages to thread exception port
        LPC_DEBUG_EVENT,           // Messages to thread debug port
        LPC_ERROR_EVENT,           // Used by ZwRaiseHardError
        LPC_CONNECTION_REQUEST     // Used by ZwConnectPort
        } LPC_TYPE;
```

VirtualRangesOffset

The offset, in bytes, from the start of the PORT_MESSAGE structure to an array of virtual address ranges. The format of the virtual address ranges is a ULONG count of the number of ranges immediately followed by an array of PVOID/ULONG address/length pairs.

ClientId

The client identifier (thread and process identifiers) of the sender of the message.

MessageId

A numeric identifier of the particular instance of the message.

SectionSize

The size, in bytes, of the section created by the sender of the message.

Data

The data of the message.

Remarks

All messages sent via ports begin with a PORT_MESSAGE header.

When initializing a PORT_MESSAGE structure, the MessageType should always be set to LPC_NEW_MESSAGE; when replying to a received message, the MessageType and MessageId of the received message should be copied to the reply message. The MessageType is updated by the system when the message is transferred.

The remaining message types can only be generated by kernel mode code calling LpcRequestPort or LpcRequestWaitReplyPort.

The amount of data that can be transferred with the PORT_MESSAGE is limited to about 300 bytes.

PORT_SECTION_WRITE

```
typedef struct _PORT_SECTION_WRITE {
    ULONG Length;
    HANDLE SectionHandle;
    ULONG SectionOffset;
    ULONG ViewSize;
    PVOID ViewBase;
    PVOID TargetViewBase;
} PORT_SECTION_WRITE, *PPORT_SECTION_WRITE;
```

Members

Length

The size, in bytes, of the PORT_SECTION_WRITE structure.

SectionHandle

A handle to a section object. The handle must grant SECTION_MAP_WRITE and SECTION_MAP_READ access.

SectionOffset

The offset in the section to map a view for the port data area. The offset must be aligned with the allocation granularity of the system.

ViewSize

The size, in bytes, of the view.

ViewBase

The base address of the view in the creator of the port section.

TargetViewBase

The base address of the view in the process connected to the port.

Remarks

The creator of the port section initializes the members Length, SectionHandle, SectionOffset and ViewSize; the other members are initialized by the system.

Port sections can be used to transfer data that is too large to fit in a port message. The system maps a view of the section in the peer process and makes the base address of the view available to the creator of the port section. The creator of the port section can then either write data to the view in self-relative format, or can fix up any pointers in the data so that they are valid in the context of the peer process.

PORT_SECTION_READ

```
typedef struct _PORT_SECTION_READ {
    ULONG Length;
    ULONG ViewSize;
    ULONG ViewBase;
} PORT_SECTION_READ, *PPORT_SECTION_READ;
```

Members

Length
> The size, in bytes, of the PORT_SECTION_READ structure.

ViewSize
> The size, in bytes, of the view.

ViewBase
> The base address of the view.

Remarks

> The peer of a process that creates a port section learns about the base address and view size of the section from the members of the PORT_SECTION_READ structure.

ZwCreatePort

ZwCreatePort creates a port object.

```
NTSYSAPI
NTSTATUS
NTAPI
ZwCreatePort(
    OUT PHANDLE PortHandle,
    IN POBJECT_ATTRIBUTES ObjectAttributes,
    IN ULONG MaxDataSize,
    IN ULONG MaxMessageSize,
    IN ULONG Reserved
    );
```

Parameters

PortHandle
> Points to a variable that will receive the port object handle if the call is successful.

ObjectAttributes
> Points to a structure that specifies the object's attributes. OBJ_KERNEL_HANDLE, OBJ_OPENLINK, OBJ_OPENIF, OBJ_EXCLUSIVE, OBJ_PERMANENT, and OBJ_INHERIT are not valid attributes for a port object.

MaxDataSize
> The maximum size, in bytes, of data that can be sent through the port.

MaxMessageSize
> The maximum size, in bytes, of a message that can be sent through the port.

Reserved
> Not used.

Return Value

Returns STATUS_SUCCESS or an error status.

Related Win32 Functions

None.

Remarks

ZwCreatePort verifies that (MaxDataSize <= 0x104) and
(MaxMessageSize <= 0x148).

ZwCreateWaitablePort

ZwCreateWaitablePort creates a waitable port object.

```
NTSYSAPI
NTSTATUS
NTAPI
ZwCreateWaitablePort(
    OUT PHANDLE PortHandle,
    IN POBJECT_ATTRIBUTES ObjectAttributes,
    IN ULONG MaxDataSize,
    IN ULONG MaxMessageSize,
    IN ULONG Reserved
    );
```

Parameters

PortHandle
Points to a variable that will receive the waitable port object handle if the call is
successful.

ObjectAttributes
Points to a structure that specifies the object's attributes. OBJ_KERNEL_HANDLE,
OBJ_OPENLINK, OBJ_OPENIF, OBJ_EXCLUSIVE, OBJ_PERMANENT, and OBJ_INHERIT are not
valid attributes for a waitable port object.

MaxDataSize
The maximum size, in bytes, of data that can be sent through the port.

MaxMessageSize
The maximum size, in bytes, of a message that can be sent through the port.

Reserved
Not used.

Return Value

Returns STATUS_SUCCESS or an error status.

Related Win32 Functions

None.

Remarks

ZwCreateWaitablePort verifies that (MaxDataSize <= 0x104) and (MaxMessageSize <= 0x148).

Waitable ports can be connected to with **ZwSecureConnectPort** and messages can be sent and received with **ZwReplyWaitReceivePort** or **ZwReplyWaitReceivePortEx**. The other port functions cannot be used with waitable ports. Requests can only be sent to waitable ports by kernel mode components calling the routines LpcRequestPort or LpcRequestWaitReplyPort.

The routine **ZwCreateWaitablePort** is only present in Windows 2000.

ZwConnectPort

ZwConnectPort creates a port connected to a named port.

```
NTSYSAPI
NTSTATUS
NTAPI
ZwConnectPort(
    OUT PHANDLE PortHandle,
    IN PUNICODE_STRING PortName,
    IN PSECURITY_QUALITY_OF_SERVICE SecurityQos,
    IN OUT PPORT_SECTION_WRITE WriteSection OPTIONAL,
    IN OUT PPORT_SECTION_READ ReadSection OPTIONAL,
    OUT PULONG MaxMessageSize OPTIONAL,
    IN OUT PVOID ConnectData OPTIONAL,
    IN OUT PULONG ConnectDataLength OPTIONAL
    );
```

Parameters

PortHandle
Points to a variable that will receive the port object handle if the call is successful.

PortName
Points to a structure that specifies the name of the port to connect to.

SecurityQos
Points to a structure that specifies the level of impersonation available to the port listener.

WriteSection
Optionally points to a structure describing the shared memory region used to send large amounts of data to the listener; if the call is successful, this will be updated.

ReadSection
> Optionally points to a caller-allocated buffer or variable that receives information on the shared memory region used by the listener to send large amounts of data to the caller.

MaxMessageSize
> Optionally points to a variable that receives the size, in bytes, of the largest message that can be sent through the port.

ConnectData
> Optionally points to a caller-allocated buffer or variable that specifies connect data to send to the listener, and receives connect data sent by the listener.

ConnectDataLength
> Optionally points to a variable that specifies the size, in bytes, of the connect data to send to the listener, and receives the size of the connect data sent by the listener.

Return Value

> Returns STATUS_SUCCESS or an error status, such as STATUS_ACCESS_DENIED, STATUS_OBJECT_NAME_NOT_FOUND, STATUS_PORT_CONNECTION_REFUSED, or STATUS_INVALID_PORT_HANDLE.

Related Win32 Functions

> Example 12.1 demonstrates the connection establishment process.

Remarks

> None.

ZwSecureConnectPort

ZwSecureConnectPort creates a port connected to a named port.

```
NTSYSAPI
NTSTATUS
NTAPI
ZwSecureConnectPort(
    OUT PHANDLE PortHandle,
    IN PUNICODE_STRING PortName,
    IN PSECURITY_QUALITY_OF_SERVICE SecurityQos,
    IN OUT PPORT_SECTION_WRITE WriteSection OPTIONAL,
    IN PSID ServerSid OPTIONAL
    IN OUT PPORT_SECTION_READ ReadSection OPTIONAL,
    OUT PULONG MaxMessageSize OPTIONAL,
    IN OUT PVOID ConnectData OPTIONAL,
    IN OUT PULONG ConnectDataLength OPTIONAL
    );
```

Parameters

PortHandle
Points to a variable that will receive the port object handle if the call is successful.

PortName
Points to a structure that specifies the name of the port to connect to.

SecurityQos
Points to a structure that specifies the level of impersonation available to the port listener.

WriteSection
Optionally points to a structure describing the shared memory region used to send large amounts of data to the listener; if the call is successful, this will be updated.

ServerSid
Optionally points to a structure that specifies the expected SID of the process listening for the connection.

ReadSection
Optionally points to a caller-allocated buffer or variable that receives information on the shared memory region used by the listener to send large amounts of data to the caller.

MaxMessageSize
Optionally points to a variable that receives the size, in bytes, of the largest message that can be sent through the port.

ConnectData
Optionally points to a caller-allocated buffer or variable that specifies connect data to send to the listener, and receives connect data sent by the listener.

ConnectDataLength
Optionally points to a variable that specifies the size, in bytes, of the connect data to send to the listener, and receives the size of the connect data sent by the listener.

Return Value

Returns STATUS_SUCCESS or an error status, such as STATUS_ACCESS_DENIED, STATUS_OBJECT_NAME_NOT_FOUND, STATUS_PORT_CONNECTION_REFUSED, STATUS_INVALID_PORT_HANDLE, or STATUS_SERVER_SID_MISMATCH.

Related Win32 Functions

None.

Remarks

The routine **ZwSecureConnectPort** is only present in Windows 2000.

The ServerSid parameter is used to ensure that the named port to which the connection will be made is being listened to by a process whose primary token identifies the TokenUser as ServerSid. This prevents messages containing sensitive data from being sent to an untrusted user who has managed somehow to usurp use of the port name.

ZwListenPort

ZwListenPort listens on a port for a connection request message.

```
NTSYSAPI
NTSTATUSNTAPI
ZwListenPort(
    IN HANDLE PortHandle,
    OUT PPORT_MESSAGE Message
    );
```

Parameters

PortHandle
A handle to a port object. The handle need not grant any specific access.

Message
Points to a caller-allocated buffer or variable that receives the connect message sent to the port.

Return Value

Returns STATUS_SUCCESS or an error status, such as STATUS_INVALID_HANDLE.

Related Win32 Functions

None.

Remarks

The message type of the received message is LPC_CONNECTION_REQUEST. The message data is the connect data specified in the call to **ZwConnectPort**.

ZwAcceptConnectPort

ZwAcceptConnectPort accepts or rejects a connection request.

```
NTSYSAPI
NTSTATUS
NTAPI
ZwAcceptConnectPort(
    OUT PHANDLE PortHandle,
    IN ULONG PortIdentifier,
    IN PPORT_MESSAGE Message,
    IN BOOLEAN Accept,
    IN OUT PPORT_SECTION_WRITE WriteSection OPTIONAL,
    IN OUT PPORT_SECTION_READ ReadSection OPTIONAL
    );
```

Parameters

PortHandle
Points to a variable that will receive the port object handle if the call is successful.

PortIdentifier
A numeric identifier to be associated with the port.

Message
Points to a caller-allocated buffer or variable that identifies the connection request and contains any connect data that should be returned to requestor of the connection.

Accept
Specifies whether the connection should be accepted or not.

WriteSection
Optionally points to a structure describing the shared memory region used to send large amounts of data to the requestor; if the call is successful, this will be updated.

ReadSection
Optionally points to a caller-allocated buffer or variable that receives information on the shared memory region used by the requestor to send large amounts of data to the caller.

Return Value

Returns STATUS_SUCCESS or an error status, such as STATUS_REPLY_MESSAGE_MISMATCH.

Related Win32 Functions

None.

Remarks

None.

ZwCompleteConnectPort

ZwCompleteConnectPort completes the port connection process.

```
NTSYSAPI
NTSTATUS
NTAPI
ZwCompleteConnectPort(
    IN HANDLE PortHandle
    );
```

Parameters

PortHandle
A handle to a port object. The handle need not grant any specific access.

Return Value

Returns STATUS_SUCCESS or an error status, such as STATUS_INVALID_HANDLE or STATUS_INVALID_PORT_HANDLE.

Related Win32 Functions

None.

Remarks

None.

ZwRequestPort

ZwRequestPort sends a request message to a port.

```
NTSYSAPI
NTSTATUS
NTAPI
ZwRequestPort(
    IN HANDLE PortHandle,
    IN PPORT_MESSAGE RequestMessage
    );
```

Parameters

PortHandle
A handle to a port object. The handle need not grant any specific access.

RequestMessage
Points to a caller-allocated buffer or variable that specifies the request message to send to the port.

Return Value

Returns STATUS_SUCCESS or an error status, such as STATUS_INVALID_HANDLE or STATUS_PORT_DISCONNECTED.

Related Win32 Functions

None.

Remarks

None.

ZwRequestWaitReplyPort

ZwRequestWaitReplyPort sends a request message to a port and waits for a reply message.

```
NTSYSAPI
NTSTATUS
NTAPI
ZwRequestWaitReplyPort(
    IN HANDLE PortHandle,
    IN PPORT_MESSAGE RequestMessage,
    OUT PPORT_MESSAGE ReplyMessage
    );
```

Parameters

PortHandle
   A handle to a port object. The handle need not grant any specific access.

RequestMessage
   Points to a caller-allocated buffer or variable that specifies the request message to send to the port.

ReplyMessage
   Points to a caller-allocated buffer or variable that receives the reply message sent to the port.

Return Value

Returns STATUS_SUCCESS or an error status, such as STATUS_INVALID_HANDLE, STATUS_PORT_DISCONNECTED, STATUS_THREAD_IS_TERMINATING, STATUS_REPLY_MESSAGE_MISMATCH or STATUS_LPC_REPLY_LOST.

Related Win32 Functions

None.

Remarks

None.

ZwReplyPort

ZwReplyPort sends a reply message to a port.

```
NTSYSAPI
NTSTATUS
NTAPI
ZwReplyPort(
    IN HANDLE PortHandle,
    IN PPORT_MESSAGE ReplyMessage
    );
```

Parameters

PortHandle

A handle to a port object. The handle need not grant any specific access.

ReplyMessage

Points to a caller-allocated buffer or variable that specifies the reply message to send to the port.

Return Value

Returns STATUS_SUCCESS or an error status, such as STATUS_INVALID_HANDLE or STATUS_REPLY_MESSAGE_MISMATCH.

Related Win32 Functions

None.

Remarks

None.

ZwReplyWaitReplyPort

ZwReplyWaitReplyPort sends a reply message to a port and waits for a reply message.

```
NTSYSAPI
NTSTATUS
NTAPI
ZwReplyWaitReplyPort(
    IN HANDLE PortHandle,
    IN OUT PPORT_MESSAGE ReplyMessage
    );
```

Parameters

PortHandle

A handle to a port object. The handle need not grant any specific access.

ReplyMessage

Points to a caller-allocated buffer or variable that specifies the reply message to send to the port and receives the reply message sent to the port.

Return Value

Returns STATUS_SUCCESS or an error status, such as STATUS_INVALID_HANDLE or STATUS_REPLY_MESSAGE_MISMATCH.

Related Win32 Functions

None.

Remarks

None.

ZwReplyWaitReceivePort

ZwReplyWaitReceivePort optionally sends a reply message to a port and waits for a message.

```
NTSYSAPI
NTSTATUS
NTAPI
ZwReplyWaitReceivePort(
    IN HANDLE PortHandle,
    OUT PULONG PortIdentifier OPTIONAL,
    IN PPORT_MESSAGE ReplyMessage OPTIONAL,
    OUT PPORT_MESSAGE Message
    );
```

Parameters

PortHandle
A handle to either a port object or a waitable port object. The handle need not grant any specific access.

PortIdentifier
Optionally points to a variable that receives a numeric identifier associated with the port.

ReplyMessage
Optionally points to a caller-allocated buffer or variable that specifies the reply message to send to the port.

Message
Points to a caller-allocated buffer or variable that receives the message sent to the port.

Return Value

Returns STATUS_SUCCESS or an error status, such as STATUS_INVALID_HANDLE or STATUS_REPLY_MESSAGE_MISMATCH.

Related Win32 Functions

None.

Remarks

None.

ZwReplyWaitReceivePortEx

ZwReplyWaitReceivePortEx optionally sends a reply message to a port and waits for a message.

```
NTSYSAPI
NTSTATUS
NTAPI
ZwReplyWaitReceivePortEx(
    IN HANDLE PortHandle,
    OUT PULONG PortIdentifier OPTIONAL,
    IN PPORT_MESSAGE ReplyMessage OPTIONAL,
    OUT PPORT_MESSAGE Message,
    IN PLARGE_INTEGER Timeout
    );
```

Parameters

PortHandle

A handle to either a port object or a waitable port object. The handle need not grant any specific access.

PortIdentifier

Optionally points to a variable that receives a numeric identifier associated with the port.

ReplyMessage

Optionally points to a caller-allocated buffer or variable that specifies the reply message to send to the port.

Message

Points to a caller-allocated buffer or variable that receives the message sent to the port.

Timeout

Optionally points to a value that specifies the absolute or relative time at which the wait is to be timed out. A negative value specifies an interval relative to the current time. The value is expressed in units of 100 nanoseconds. Absolute times track any changes in the system time; relative times are not affected by system time changes. If Timeout is a null pointer, the wait will not timeout.

Return Value

Returns STATUS_SUCCESS, STATUS_TIMEOUT or an error status, such as STATUS_INVALID_HANDLE or STATUS_REPLY_MESSAGE_MISMATCH.

Related Win32 Functions

None.

Remarks

The routine **ZwReplyWaitReceivePortEx** is only present in Windows 2000.

ZwReadRequestData

ZwReadRequestData reads the data from the process virtual address space referenced by a message.

```
NTSYSAPI
NTSTATUS
NTAPI
ZwReadRequestData(
    IN HANDLE PortHandle,
    IN PPORT_MESSAGE Message,
    IN ULONG Index,
    OUT PVOID Buffer,
    IN ULONG BufferLength,
    OUT PULONG ReturnLength OPTIONAL
    );
```

Parameters

PortHandle
    A handle to a port object. The handle need not grant any specific access.

Message
    Points to a caller-allocated buffer or variable that contains a message received from the port.

Index
    An index into the array of buffer address/length pairs in the Message.

Buffer
    Points to a caller-allocated buffer or variable that receives data transferred from the virtual address space of the sender of the Message.

BufferLength
    The size in bytes of Buffer.

ReturnLength
    Optionally points to a variable that receives the number of bytes actually transferred if the call was successful. If this information is not needed, ReturnLength may be a null pointer.

Return Value

Returns STATUS_SUCCESS or an error status, such as STATUS_INVALID_HANDLE.

Related Win32 Functions

None.

Remarks

The sender of the message should have initialized the VirtualRangesOffset member of the PORT_MESSAGE structure and stored valid virtual address range information in the data portion of the message.

ZwWriteRequestData

ZwWriteRequestData writes data to the process virtual address space referenced by a message.

```
NTSYSAPI
NTSTATUS
NTAPI
ZwWriteRequestData(
    IN HANDLE PortHandle,
    IN PPORT_MESSAGE Message,
    IN ULONG Index,
    IN PVOID Buffer,
    IN ULONG BufferLength,
    OUT PULONG ReturnLength OPTIONAL
    );
```

Parameters

PortHandle
   A handle to a port object. The handle need not grant any specific access.

Message
   Points to a caller-allocated buffer or variable that contains a message sent to the port.

Index
   An index into the array of buffer address/length pairs in the Message.

Buffer
   Points to a caller-allocated buffer or variable that contains data to be transferred to the virtual address space of the sender of the Message.

BufferLength
   The size in bytes of Buffer.

ReturnLength
   Optionally points to a variable that receives the number of bytes actually transferred if the call was successful. If this information is not needed, ReturnLength may be a null pointer.

Return Value

Returns STATUS_SUCCESS or an error status, such as STATUS_INVALID_HANDLE.

Related Win32 Functions

None.

Remarks

The sender of the message should have initialized the VirtualRangesOffset member of the PORT_MESSAGE structure and have stored valid virtual address range information in the data portion of the message.

ZwQueryInformationPort

ZwQueryInformationPort retrieves information about a port object.

```
NTSYSAPI
NTSTATUS
NTAPI
ZwQueryInformationPort(
    IN HANDLE PortHandle,
    IN PORT_INFORMATION_CLASS PortInformationClass,
    OUT PVOID PortInformation,
    IN ULONG PortInformationLength,
    OUT PULONG ReturnLength OPTIONAL
    );
```

Parameters

PortHandle

A handle to a port object. The handle must grant GENERIC_READ access.

PortInformationClass

Specifies the type of port object information to be queried. The permitted values are drawn from the enumeration PORT_INFORMATION_CLASS, described in the following section.

PortInformation

Points to a caller-allocated buffer or variable that receives the requested port object information.

PortInformationLength

Specifies the size in bytes of PortInformation, which the caller should set according to the given PortInformationClass.

ReturnLength

Optionally points to a variable that receives the number of bytes actually returned to PortInformation if the call was successful. If this information is not needed, ReturnLength may be a null pointer.

Return Value

Returns STATUS_SUCCESS or an error status, such as STATUS_INVALID_HANDLE or STATUS_INVALID_INFO_CLASS.

Related Win32 Functions

None.

Remarks

None.

PORT_INFORMATION_CLASS

```
typedef enum _PORT_INFORMATION_CLASS {
    PortBasicInformation
} PORT_INFORMATION_CLASS;
```

PortBasicInformation

```
typedef struct _PORT_BASIC_INFORMATION {
} PORT_BASIC_INFORMATION, *PPORT_BASIC_INFORMATION;
```

Remarks

PORT_BASIC_INFORMATION does not have any members.

ZwImpersonateClientOfPort

ZwImpersonateClientOfPort impersonates the security context of the client of a port.

```
NTSYSAPI
NTSTATUS
NTAPI
ZwImpersonateClientOfPort(
    IN HANDLE PortHandle,
    IN PPORT_MESSAGE Message
    );
```

Parameters

PortHandle
A handle to a port object. The handle need not grant any specific access.

Message
Points to a caller-allocated buffer or variable that contains a message sent by the client of the port.

Return Value

Returns STATUS_SUCCESS or an error status, such as STATUS_INVALID_HANDLE, STATUS_INVALID_PORT_HANDLE, or STATUS_PORT_DISCONNECTED.

Related Win32 Functions

None.

Remarks

None.

Example 12.1: Connecting to a Named Port

```
#include "ntdll.h"
#include <stdlib.h>
#include <stdio.h>

template <int i> struct PORT_MESSAGEX : NT::PORT_MESSAGE {
    UCHAR Data[i];
};

DWORD WINAPI client(PVOID)
{
    NT::UNICODE_STRING name;
    NT::RtlInitUnicodeString(&name, L"\\Test");

    HANDLE hSection = CreateFileMapping(HANDLE(0xFFFFFFFF), 0,
                                        PAGE_READWRITE, 0, 0x50000, 0);

    ULONG n, cd[] = {1, 2, 3, 4, 5}, cdn = sizeof cd;
    NT::SECURITY_QUALITY_OF_SERVICE sqos
        = {sizeof sqos, NT::SecurityImpersonation, TRUE, TRUE};
    NT::PORT_SECTION_WRITE psw = {sizeof psw, hSection, 0x20000, 0x30000};
    NT::PORT_SECTION_READ psr = {sizeof psr};
    HANDLE hPort;

    NT::ZwConnectPort(&hPort, &name, &sqos, &psw, &psr, &n, cd, &cdn);

    PORT_MESSAGEX<40> req, rep;
    CHAR txt[] = "Hello, World";

    memset(&req, 0xaa, sizeof req);
    memset(&rep, 0xcc, sizeof req);

    req.MessageType = NT::LPC_NEW_MESSAGE;
    req.MessageSize = sizeof req;
    req.VirtualRangesOffset = 0;
    req.DataSize = sizeof txt;
    strcpy(PSTR(req.Data), txt);

    while (true) {
        NT::ZwRequestWaitReplyPort(hPort, &req, &rep);

        printf("client(): type %hd, id %hu\n",
               rep.MessageType, rep.MessageId);

        Sleep(1000);
    }

    return 0;
}

int main()
{
    NT::UNICODE_STRING name;
    NT::RtlInitUnicodeString(&name, L"\\Test");

    NT::OBJECT_ATTRIBUTES oa = {sizeof oa, 0, &name};
    PORT_MESSAGEX<40> req;
    HANDLE hPort;

    memset(&req, 0xee, sizeof req);
```

```
NT::ZwCreatePort(&hPort, &oa, 0, sizeof req, 0);

ULONG tid;
HANDLE hThread = CreateThread(0, 0, client, 0, 0, &tid);

NT::ZwListenPort(hPort, &req);

ULONG n = 0x9000;
HANDLE hSection = CreateFileMapping(HANDLE(0xFFFFFFFF), 0,
                                    PAGE_READWRITE, 0, n, 0);
NT::PORT_SECTION_WRITE psw = {sizeof psw, hSection, 0, n};
NT::PORT_SECTION_READ psr = {sizeof psr};
HANDLE hPort2;

req.DataSize = 4; req.Data[0] = 0xfe;

NT::ZwAcceptConnectPort(&hPort2, 0xdeadbabe, &req, TRUE, &psw, &psr);

NT::ZwCompleteConnectPort(hPort2);

while (true) {
    ULONG portid;

    NT::ZwReplyWaitReceivePort(hPort2, &portid, 0, &req);

    printf("server(): type %hd, id %hu\n",
            req.MessageType, req.MessageId);

    req.DataSize = 1; req.Data[0] = 0xfd;

    NT::ZwReplyPort(hPort2, &req);
}

    return 0;
}
```

Example 12.1 is intended to be run under the control of a debugger so that the values of variables can be examined at each step of the program; it does not do anything useful and contains extraneous statements (such as the memset statements), which need not appear in production code.

The important steps taken by the function main are as follows:

1. Create a named port by calling **ZwCreatePort.** The MaxDataSize parameter is checked for consistency but is otherwise unused. Therefore a value of zero can be specified.

2. Listen on the port for connection requests. A connect message includes the connect data specified by the caller of **ZwConnectPort.** The connect data and the identity of the process making the request can be used to decide whether to accept or reject the connection request.

3. Update the data portion of the connection request message; these changes will be visible to the caller of **ZwConnectPort** upon return from that function.

4. In anticipation of the need to transfer large amounts of data, create a pagefile-backed section and associate with the port by calling **ZwAcceptConnectPort.**

5. Complete the connection by calling **ZwCompleteConnectPort.** This causes the client's call to **ZwConnectPort** to return.

6. Loop, receiving requests, acting upon the contained data and replying.

The important steps taken by the function **client** are as follows:

1. In anticipation of the need to transfer large amounts of data, create a pagefile-backed section.

2. Initialize the connect data, and connect to the named port by calling **ZwConnectPort.** This call also associates the section with the port.

3. Initialize the PORT_MESSAGE structure that will carry the requests to the server. The four fields that must be initialized are MessageType, MessageSize, DataSize, and VirtualRangesOffset.

4. Loop, sending requests and receiving replies.

13
Files

The system services described in this chapter create and manipulate file objects.

ZwCreateFile

ZwCreateFile creates or opens a file.

```
NTSYSAPI
NTSTATUS
NTAPI
ZwCreateFile(
    OUT PHANDLE FileHandle,
    IN ACCESS_MASK DesiredAccess,
    IN POBJECT_ATTRIBUTES ObjectAttributes,
    OUT PIO_STATUS_BLOCK IoStatusBlock,
    IN PLARGE_INTEGER AllocationSize OPTIONAL,
    IN ULONG FileAttributes,
    IN ULONG ShareAccess,
    IN ULONG CreateDisposition,
    IN ULONG CreateOptions,
    IN PVOID EaBuffer OPTIONAL,
    IN ULONG EaLength
    );
```

Parameters

FileHandle

Points to a variable that will receive the file object handle if the call is successful.

DesiredAccess

Specifies the type of access that the caller requires to the file object. This parameter can be zero, or any compatible combination of the following flags:

```
        FILE_ANY_ACCESS          0x0000    // any type

        FILE_READ_ACCESS         0x0001    // file & pipe
        FILE_READ_DATA           0x0001    // file & pipe
        FILE_LIST_DIRECTORY      0x0001    // directory

        FILE_WRITE_ACCESS        0x0002    // file & pipe
        FILE_WRITE_DATA          0x0002    // file & pipe
        FILE_ADD_FILE            0x0002    // directory
```

```
FILE_APPEND_DATA              0x0004    // file
FILE_ADD_SUBDIRECTORY         0x0004    // directory
FILE_CREATE_PIPE_INSTANCE     0x0004    // named pipe

FILE_READ_EA                  0x0008    // file & directory

FILE_WRITE_EA                 0x0010    // file & directory

FILE_EXECUTE                  0x0020    // file
FILE_TRAVERSE                 0x0020    // directory

FILE_DELETE_CHILD             0x0040    // directory

FILE_READ_ATTRIBUTES          0x0080    // all types

FILE_WRITE_ATTRIBUTES         0x0100    // all types

FILE_ALL_ACCESS                         // All of the preceding +
                                           STANDARD_RIGHTS_ALL
```

ObjectAttributes

Points to a structure that specifies the object's attributes. OBJ_PERMANENT, OBJ_EXCLUSIVE, and OBJ_OPENLINK are not valid attributes for a file object.

IoStatusBlock

Points to a variable that receives the final completion status and information about the requested operation. On return, the Information member contains create disposition, which will be one of the following values:

```
FILE_SUPERSEDED
FILE_OPENED
FILE_CREATED
FILE_OVERWRITTEN
FILE_EXISTS
FILE_DOES_NOT_EXIST
```

AllocationSize

Optionally specifies the initial allocation size in bytes for the file. A nonzero value has no effect unless the file is being created, overwritten, or superseded.

FileAttributes

Specifies file attributes to be applied if a new file is created. This parameter can be zero, or any compatible combination of the following flags:

```
FILE_ATTRIBUTE_READONLY
FILE_ATTRIBUTE_HIDDEN
FILE_ATTRIBUTE_SYSTEM
FILE_ATTRIBUTE_DIRECTORY
FILE_ATTRIBUTE_ARCHIVE
FILE_ATTRIBUTE_NORMAL
FILE_ATTRIBUTE_TEMPORARY
FILE_ATTRIBUTE_SPARSE_FILE
FILE_ATTRIBUTE_REPARSE_POINT
FILE_ATTRIBUTE_COMPRESSED
FILE_ATTRIBUTE_OFFLINE
FILE_ATTRIBUTE_NOT_CONTENT_INDEXED
FILE_ATTRIBUTE_ENCRYPTED
```

ShareAccess

Specifies the limitations on sharing of the file. This parameter can be zero, or any compatible combination of the following flags:

```
FILE_SHARE_READ
FILE_SHARE_WRITE
FILE_SHARE_DELETE
```

CreateDisposition

Specifies what to do, depending on whether the file already exists. This must be one of the following values:

```
FILE_SUPERSEDE
FILE_OPEN
FILE_CREATE
FILE_OPEN_IF
FILE_OVERWRITE
FILE_OVERWRITE_IF
```

CreateOptions

Specifies the options to be applied when creating or opening the file, as a compatible combination of the following flags:

```
FILE_DIRECTORY_FILE
FILE_WRITE_THROUGH
FILE_SEQUENTIAL_ONLY
FILE_NO_INTERMEDIATE_BUFFERING
FILE_SYNCHRONOUS_IO_ALERT
FILE_SYNCHRONOUS_IO_NONALERT
FILE_NON_DIRECTORY_FILE
FILE_CREATE_TREE_CONNECTION
FILE_COMPLETE_IF_OPLOCKED
FILE_NO_EA_KNOWLEDGE
FILE_OPEN_FOR_RECOVERY
FILE_RANDOM_ACCESS
FILE_DELETE_ON_CLOSE
FILE_OPEN_BY_FILE_ID
FILE_OPEN_FOR_BACKUP_INTENT
FILE_NO_COMPRESSION
FILE_RESERVE_OPFILTER
FILE_OPEN_REPARSE_POINT
FILE_OPEN_NO_RECALL
FILE_OPEN_FOR_FREE_SPACE_QUERY
```

EaBuffer

Points to a caller-allocated buffer or variable that contains Extended Attributes information.

EaLength

Specifies the size in bytes of EaBuffer.

Return Value

Returns STATUS_SUCCESS or an error status, such as STATUS_ACCESS_DENIED, STATUS_OBJECT_NAME_NOT_FOUND, STATUS_OBJECT_NAME_COLLISION, STATUS_OBJECT_NAME_INVALID, STATUS_SHARING_VIOLATION, STATUS_NOT_A_DIRECTORY, or STATUS_FILE_IS_A_DIRECTORY.

Related Win32 Functions

CreateFile.

Remarks

ZwCreateFile is documented in the DDK.

The kernel mode Transport Driver Interface (TDI) uses extended attributes extensively, and extended attributes can be stored and retrieved on NTFS files.

Example 13.1 demonstrates how to use FILE_OPEN_BY_FILE_ID.

ZwOpenFile

ZwOpenFile opens a file.

```
NTSYSAPI
NTSTATUS
NTAPI
ZwOpenFile(
    OUT PHANDLE FileHandle,
    IN ACCESS_MASK DesiredAccess,
    IN POBJECT_ATTRIBUTES ObjectAttributes,
    OUT PIO_STATUS_BLOCK IoStatusBlock,
    IN ULONG ShareAccess,
    IN ULONG OpenOptions
    );
```

Parameters

FileHandle
Points to a variable that will receive the file object handle if the call is successful.

DesiredAccess
Specifies the type of access that the caller requires to the file object. This parameter can be zero, or any compatible combination of the following flags:

```
FILE_ANY_ACCESS             0x0000    // any type

FILE_READ_ACCESS            0x0001    // file & pipe
FILE_READ_DATA              0x0001    // file & pipe
FILE_LIST_DIRECTORY         0x0001    // directory

FILE_WRITE_ACCESS           0x0002    // file & pipe
FILE_WRITE_DATA             0x0002    // file & pipe
FILE_ADD_FILE               0x0002    // directory

FILE_APPEND_DATA            0x0004    // file
FILE_ADD_SUBDIRECTORY       0x0004    // directory
FILE_CREATE_PIPE_INSTANCE   0x0004    // named pipe

FILE_READ_EA                0x0008    // file & directory

FILE_WRITE_EA               0x0010    // file & directory

FILE_EXECUTE                0x0020    // file
FILE_TRAVERSE               0x0020    // directory
```

```
FILE_DELETE_CHILD          0x0040    // directory

FILE_READ_ATTRIBUTES       0x0080    // all types

FILE_WRITE_ATTRIBUTES      0x0100    // all types

FILE_ALL_ACCESS            // All of the preceding + STANDARD_RIGHTS_ALL
```

ObjectAttributes

    Points to a structure that specifies the object's attributes. OBJ_PERMANENT, OBJ_EXCLUSIVE, and OBJ_OPENLINK are not valid attributes for a file object.

IoStatusBlock

    Points to a variable that receives the final completion status and information about the requested operation. If the call is successful, the Information member contains create disposition, which will be one of the following values:

```
FILE_OPENED
FILE_DOES_NOT_EXIST
```

ShareAccess

    Specifies the limitations on sharing of the file. This parameter can be zero, or any compatible combination of the following flags:

```
FILE_SHARE_READ
FILE_SHARE_WRITE
FILE_SHARE_DELETE
```

OpenOptions

    Specifies the options to be applied when opening the file as a compatible combination of the following flags:

```
FILE_DIRECTORY_FILE
FILE_WRITE_THROUGH
FILE_SEQUENTIAL_ONLY
FILE_NO_INTERMEDIATE_BUFFERING
FILE_SYNCHRONOUS_IO_ALERT
FILE_SYNCHRONOUS_IO_NONALERT
FILE_NON_DIRECTORY_FILE
FILE_CREATE_TREE_CONNECTION
FILE_COMPLETE_IF_OPLOCKED
FILE_NO_EA_KNOWLEDGE
FILE_OPEN_FOR_RECOVERY
FILE_RANDOM_ACCESS
FILE_DELETE_ON_CLOSE
FILE_OPEN_BY_FILE_ID
FILE_OPEN_FOR_BACKUP_INTENT
FILE_NO_COMPRESSION
FILE_RESERVE_OPFILTER
FILE_OPEN_REPARSE_POINT
FILE_OPEN_NO_RECALL
FILE_OPEN_FOR_FREE_SPACE_QUERY
```

Return Value

    Returns STATUS_SUCCESS or an error status, such as STATUS_ACCESS_DENIED, STATUS_OBJECT_NAME_NOT_FOUND, STATUS_OBJECT_NAME_INVALID, STATUS_SHARING_VIOLATION, STATUS_NOT_A_DIRECTORY, or STATUS_FILE_IS_A_DIRECTORY.

Related Win32 Functions

None.

Remarks

```
ZwOpenFile(FileHandle, DesiredAccess, ObjectAttributes, IoStatusBlock,
          ShareAccess, OpenOptions)
```

is equivalent to:

```
ZwCreateFile(FileHandle, DesiredAccess, ObjectAttributes, IoStatusBlock, 0, 0,
          ShareAccess, FILE_OPEN, OpenOptions, 0, 0)
```

ZwDeleteFile

ZwDeleteFile deletes a file.

```
NTSYSAPI
NTSTATUS
NTAPI
ZwDeleteFile(
    IN POBJECT_ATTRIBUTES ObjectAttributes
    );
```

Parameters

ObjectAttributes
Specifies the file to delete.

Return Value

Returns STATUS_SUCCESS or an error status, such as STATUS_ACCESS_DENIED or STATUS_OBJECT_NAME_NOT_FOUND.

Related Win32 Functions

None.

Remarks

There are alternative methods of deleting a file, and the Win32 DeleteFile function uses ZwSetInformationFile with a FileInformationClass of FileDispositionInformation.

ZwFlushBuffersFile

ZwFlushBuffersFile flushes any cached data to the storage medium or network.

```
NTSYSAPI
NTSTATUS
NTAPI
ZwFlushBuffersFile(
    IN HANDLE FileHandle,
    OUT PIO_STATUS_BLOCK IoStatusBlock
    );
```

Parameters

FileHandle
A handle to a file object. The handle need not grant any specific access.

IoStatusBlock
Points to a variable that receives the final completion status and information about the requested operation.

Return Value

Returns STATUS_SUCCESS or an error status, such as STATUS_ACCESS_DENIED or STATUS_INVALID_HANDLE.

Related Win32 Functions

FlushFileBuffers.

Remarks

If FileHandle refers to a file volume, all of the open files on the volume are flushed.

ZwCancelIoFile

ZwCancelIoFile cancels all pending I/O operations initiated by the current thread on the file object.

```
NTSYSAPI
NTSTATUS
NTAPI
ZwCancelIoFile(
    IN HANDLE FileHandle,
    OUT PIO_STATUS_BLOCK IoStatusBlock
    );
```

Parameters

FileHandle
A handle to a file object. The handle need not grant any specific access.

IoStatusBlock
Points to a variable that receives the final completion status and information about the requested operation.

Return Value

Returns STATUS_SUCCESS or an error status, such as STATUS_ACCESS_DENIED or STATUS_INVALID_HANDLE.

Related Win32 Functions

CancelIo.

Remarks

None.

ZwReadFile

ZwReadFile reads data from a file.

```
NTSYSAPI
NTSTATUS
NTAPI
ZwReadFile(
    IN HANDLE FileHandle,
    IN HANDLE Event OPTIONAL,
    IN PIO_APC_ROUTINE ApcRoutine OPTIONAL,
    IN PVOID ApcContext OPTIONAL,
    OUT PIO_STATUS_BLOCK IoStatusBlock,
    OUT PVOID Buffer,
    IN ULONG Length,
    IN PLARGE_INTEGER ByteOffset OPTIONAL,
    IN PULONG Key OPTIONAL
    );
```

Parameters

FileHandle

A handle to a file object. The handle must grant FILE_READ_DATA access.

Event

Optionally specifies a handle to an event object to signal when the operation completes. The handle must grant EVENT_MODIFY_STATE access.

ApcRoutine

Optionally points to a routine to execute when the operation completes. The signature of the routine is:

```
VOID (NTAPI *PIO_APC_ROUTINE)(PVOID ApcContext,
                              PIO_STATUS_BLOCK IoStatusBlock,
                              ULONG Reserved);
```

ApcContext

A void pointer that can be used to provide the ApcRoutine with contextual information.

IoStatusBlock

Points to a variable that receives the final completion status and information about the requested operation. On return, the Information member contains the number of bytes actually read.

Buffer
   Points to a caller-allocated buffer or variable that receives the data read from the file.

Length
   Specifies the size in bytes of Buffer and the number of bytes to read from the file.

ByteOffset
   Optionally points to a variable specifying the starting byte offset within the file at
   which to begin the read operation.

Key
   Optionally points to a variable that, if its value matches the key specified when the file
   byte range was locked, allows the lock to be ignored.

Return Value

Returns STATUS_SUCCESS, STATUS_PENDING or an error status, such as
STATUS_ACCESS_DENIED, STATUS_INVALID_HANDLE, STATUS_FILE_LOCK_CONFLICT, or
STATUS_END_OF_FILE.

Related Win32 Functions

ReadFile, ReadFileEx.

Remarks

ZwReadFile is documented in the DDK.

ZwWriteFile

ZwWriteFile writes data to a file.

```
NTSYSAPI
NTSTATUS
NTAPI
ZwWriteFile(
    IN HANDLE FileHandle,
    IN HANDLE Event OPTIONAL,
    IN PIO_APC_ROUTINE ApcRoutine OPTIONAL,
    IN PVOID ApcContext OPTIONAL,
    OUT PIO_STATUS_BLOCK IoStatusBlock,
    IN PVOID Buffer,
    IN ULONG Length,
    IN PLARGE_INTEGER ByteOffset OPTIONAL,
    IN PULONG Key OPTIONAL
    );
```

Parameters

FileHandle
   A handle to a file object. The handle must grant FILE_WRITE_DATA and/or
   FILE_APPEND_DATA access.

Event

Optionally specifies a handle to an event object to signal when the operation completes. The handle must grant EVENT_MODIFY_STATE access.

ApcRoutine

Optionally points to a routine to execute when the operation completes. The signature of the routine is:

```
VOID (NTAPI *PIO_APC_ROUTINE)(PVOID ApcContext,
                              PIO_STATUS_BLOCK IoStatusBlock,
                              ULONG Reserved);
```

ApcContext

A void pointer that can be used to provide the ApcRoutine with contextual information.

IoStatusBlock

Points to a variable that receives the final completion status and information about the requested operation. On return, the Information member contains the number of bytes actually written.

Buffer

Points to a caller-allocated buffer or variable that contains the data to write to the file.

Length

Specifies the size in bytes of Buffer and the number of bytes to write to the file.

ByteOffset

Optionally points to a variable specifying the starting byte offset within the file at which to begin the write operation.

Key

Optionally points to a variable that, if its value matches the key specified when the file byte range was locked, allows the lock to be ignored.

Return Value

Returns STATUS_SUCCESS, STATUS_PENDING or an error status, such as STATUS_ACCESS_DENIED, STATUS_INVALID_HANDLE, or STATUS_FILE_LOCK_CONFLICT.

Related Win32 Functions

WriteFile, WriteFileEx.

Remarks

ZwWriteFile is documented in the DDK.

ZwReadFileScatter

ZwReadFileScatter reads data from a file and stores it in a number of discontiguous buffers.

```
NTSYSAPI
NTSTATUS
NTAPI
ZwReadFileScatter(
    IN HANDLE FileHandle,
    IN HANDLE Event OPTIONAL,
    IN PIO_APC_ROUTINE ApcRoutine OPTIONAL,
    IN PVOID ApcContext OPTIONAL,
    OUT PIO_STATUS_BLOCK IoStatusBlock,
    IN PFILE_SEGMENT_ELEMENT Buffer,
    IN ULONG Length,
    IN PLARGE_INTEGER ByteOffset OPTIONAL,
    IN PULONG Key OPTIONAL
    );
```

Parameters

FileHandle

A handle to a file object. The handle must grant FILE_READ_DATA access.

Event

Optionally specifies a handle to an event object to signal when the operation completes. The handle must grant EVENT_MODIFY_STATE access.

ApcRoutine

Optionally points to a routine to execute when the operation completes. The signature of the routine is:

```
VOID (NTAPI *PIO_APC_ROUTINE)(PVOID ApcContext,
                              PIO_STATUS_BLOCK IoStatusBlock,
                              ULONG Reserved);
```

ApcContext

A void pointer that can be used to provide the ApcRoutine with contextual information.

IoStatusBlock

Points to a variable that receives the final completion status and information about the requested operation. On return, the Information member contains the number of bytes actually read.

Buffer

Points to a caller-allocated buffer or variable that contains an array of FILE_SEGMENT_ELEMENT pointers to buffers. Each buffer should be the size of a system memory page and should be aligned on a system memory page size boundary.

Length

Specifies the number of bytes to read from the file.

ByteOffset
> Optionally points to a variable specifying the starting byte offset within the file at
> which to begin the read operation.

Key
> Optionally points to a variable that, if its value matches the key specified when the file
> byte range was locked, allows the lock to be ignored.

Return Value

Returns STATUS_SUCCESS, STATUS_PENDING or an error status, such as
STATUS_ACCESS_DENIED, STATUS_INVALID_HANDLE, STATUS_FILE_LOCK_CONFLICT, or
STATUS_END_OF_FILE.

Related Win32 Functions

ReadFileScatter.

Remarks

None.

ZwWriteFileGather

ZwWriteFileGather retrieves data from a number of discontiguous buffers and writes it
to a file.

```
NTSYSAPI
NTSTATUS
NTAPI
ZwWriteFileGather(
    IN HANDLE FileHandle,
    IN HANDLE Event OPTIONAL,
    IN PIO_APC_ROUTINE ApcRoutine OPTIONAL,
    IN PVOID ApcContext OPTIONAL,
    OUT PIO_STATUS_BLOCK IoStatusBlock,
    IN PFILE_SEGMENT_ELEMENT Buffer,
    IN ULONG Length,
    IN PLARGE_INTEGER ByteOffset OPTIONAL,
    IN PULONG Key OPTIONAL
    );
```

Parameters

FileHandle
> A handle to a file object. The handle must grant FILE_WRITE_DATA and/or
> FILE_APPEND_DATA access.

Event
> Optionally specifies a handle to an event object to signal when the operation com-
> pletes. The handle must grant EVENT_MODIFY_STATE access.

ApcRoutine

Optionally points to a routine to execute when the operation completes. The signature of the routine is:

```
VOID (NTAPI *PIO_APC_ROUTINE)(PVOID ApcContext,
                              PIO_STATUS_BLOCK IoStatusBlock,
                              ULONG Reserved);
```

ApcContext

A void pointer that can be used to provide the ApcRoutine with contextual information.

IoStatusBlock

Points to a variable that receives the final completion status and information about the requested operation. On return, the **Information** member contains the number of bytes actually written.

Buffer

Points to a caller-allocated buffer or variable that contains an array of FILE_SEGMENT_ELEMENT pointers to buffers. Each buffer should be the size of a system memory page and should be aligned on a system memory page size boundary.

Length

Specifies the number of bytes to write to the file.

ByteOffset

Optionally points to a variable specifying the starting byte offset within the file at which to begin the write operation.

Key

Optionally points to a variable that, if its value matches the key specified when the file byte range was locked, allows the lock to be ignored.

Return Value

Returns STATUS_SUCCESS, STATUS_PENDING or an error status, such as STATUS_ACCESS_DENIED, STATUS_INVALID_HANDLE, or STATUS_FILE_LOCK_CONFLICT.

Related Win32 Functions

WriteFileGather.

Remarks

None.

ZwLockFile

ZwLockFile locks a region of a file.

```
NTSYSAPI
NTSTATUS
NTAPI
ZwLockFile(
    IN HANDLE FileHandle,
    IN HANDLE Event OPTIONAL,
    IN PIO_APC_ROUTINE ApcRoutine OPTIONAL,
    IN PVOID ApcContext OPTIONAL,
    OUT PIO_STATUS_BLOCK IoStatusBlock,
    IN PULARGE_INTEGER LockOffset,
    IN PULARGE_INTEGER LockLength,
    IN ULONG Key,
    IN BOOLEAN FailImmediately,
    IN BOOLEAN ExclusiveLock
    );
```

Parameters

FileHandle

A handle to a file object. The handle must grant FILE_READ_DATA and/or FILE_WRITE_DATA access.

Event

Optionally specifies a handle to an event object to signal when the operation completes. The handle must grant EVENT_MODIFY_STATE access.

ApcRoutine

Optionally points to a routine to execute when the operation completes. The signature of the routine is:

```
VOID (NTAPI *PIO_APC_ROUTINE)(PVOID ApcContext,
                              PIO_STATUS_BLOCK IoStatusBlock,
                              ULONG Reserved);
```

ApcContext

A void pointer that can be used to provide the ApcRoutine with contextual information.

IoStatusBlock

Points to a variable that receives the final completion status and information about the requested operation.

LockOffset

Points to a variable that specifies the offset, in bytes, to the byte range to lock.

LockLength

Points to a variable that specifies the length, in bytes, of the byte range to lock.

Key

Specifies a value that, if matched by the key specified in a call to **ZwReadFile** or **ZwWriteFile**, allows the lock to be ignored. Also used to group locks.

FailImmediately

Specifies whether the attempt to lock a byte range should return with an error status rather than wait if the lock cannot be acquired immediately.

ExclusiveLock

Specifies whether the lock should be exclusive or shared.

Return Value

Returns STATUS_SUCCESS, STATUS_PENDING or an error status, such as STATUS_ACCESS_DENIED, STATUS_INVALID_HANDLE, or STATUS_LOCK_NOT_GRANTED.

Related Win32 Functions

LockFile, LockFileEx.

Remarks

None.

ZwUnlockFile

ZwUnlockFile unlocks a locked region of a file.

```
NTSYSAPI
NTSTATUS
NTAPI
ZwUnlockFile(
    IN HANDLE FileHandle,
    OUT PIO_STATUS_BLOCK IoStatusBlock,
    IN PULARGE_INTEGER LockOffset,
    IN PULARGE_INTEGER LockLength,
    IN ULONG Key
    );
```

Parameters

FileHandle

A handle to a file object. The handle must grant FILE_READ_DATA and/or FILE_WRITE_DATA access.

IoStatusBlock

Points to a variable that receives the final completion status and information about the requested operation.

LockOffset

Points to a variable that specifies the offset, in bytes, to the byte range to unlock.

LockLength
Points to a variable that specifies the length, in bytes, of the byte range to unlock.

Key
Specifies a value that identifies the lock. This should match the value specified when the byte range was locked.

Return Value

Returns STATUS_SUCCESS, STATUS_PENDING or an error status, such as STATUS_ACCESS_DENIED, STATUS_INVALID_HANDLE or STATUS_RANGE_NOT_LOCKED.

Related Win32 Functions

UnlockFile, UnlockFileEx.

Remarks

None.

ZwDeviceIoControlFile

ZwDeviceIoControlFile performs an I/O control operation on a file object that represents a device.

```
NTSYSAPI
NTSTATUS
NTAPI
ZwDeviceIoControlFile(
    IN HANDLE FileHandle,
    IN HANDLE Event OPTIONAL,
    IN PIO_APC_ROUTINE ApcRoutine OPTIONAL,
    IN PVOID ApcContext OPTIONAL,
    OUT PIO_STATUS_BLOCK IoStatusBlock,
    IN ULONG IoControlCode,
    IN PVOID InputBuffer OPTIONAL,
    IN ULONG InputBufferLength,
    OUT PVOID OutputBuffer OPTIONAL,
    IN ULONG OutputBufferLength
    );
```

Parameters

FileHandle
A handle to a file object. The handle must grant access compatible with the access field of the IoControlCode.

Event
Optionally specifies a handle to an event object to signal when the operation completes. The handle must grant EVENT_MODIFY_STATE access.

ApcRoutine

Optionally points to a routine to execute when the operation completes. The signature of the routine is:

```
VOID (NTAPI *PIO_APC_ROUTINE)(PVOID ApcContext,
                              PIO_STATUS_BLOCK IoStatusBlock,
                              ULONG Reserved);
```

ApcContext

A void pointer that can be used to provide the ApcRoutine with contextual information.

IoStatusBlock

Points to a variable that receives the final completion status and information about the requested operation.

IoControlCode

Specifies the particular I/O control operation to perform.

InputBuffer

Optionally points to a caller-allocated buffer or variable that contains data specific to the IoControlCode.

InputBufferLength

The size, in bytes, of InputBuffer.

OutputBuffer

Optionally points to a caller-allocated buffer or variable that receives data specific to the IoControlCode.

OutputBufferLength

The size, in bytes, of OutputBuffer.

Return Value

Returns STATUS_SUCCESS, STATUS_PENDING or an error status, such as STATUS_ACCESS_DENIED, STATUS_INVALID_HANDLE, or STATUS_INVALID_DEVICE_REQUEST.

Related Win32 Functions

DeviceIoControl.

Remarks

None.

ZwFsControlFile

ZwFsControlFile performs a file system control operation on a file object that represents a file-structured device.

```
NTSYSAPI
NTSTATUS
NTAPI
ZwFsControlFile(
    IN HANDLE FileHandle,
    IN HANDLE Event OPTIONAL,
    IN PIO_APC_ROUTINE ApcRoutine OPTIONAL,
    IN PVOID ApcContext OPTIONAL,
    OUT PIO_STATUS_BLOCK IoStatusBlock,
    IN ULONG FsControlCode,
    IN PVOID InputBuffer OPTIONAL,
    IN ULONG InputBufferLength,
    OUT PVOID OutputBuffer OPTIONAL,
    IN ULONG OutputBufferLength
    );
```

Parameters

FileHandle

A handle to a file object. The handle must grant access compatible with the access field of the FsControlCode.

Event

Optionally specifies a handle to an event object to signal when the operation completes. The handle must grant EVENT_MODIFY_STATE access.

ApcRoutine

Optionally points to a routine to execute when the operation completes. The signature of the routine is:

```
VOID (NTAPI *PIO_APC_ROUTINE)(PVOID ApcContext,
                              PIO_STATUS_BLOCK IoStatusBlock,
                              ULONG Reserved);
```

ApcContext

A void pointer that can be used to provide the ApcRoutine with contextual information.

IoStatusBlock

Points to a variable that receives the final completion status and information about the requested operation.

FsControlCode

Specifies the particular file system control operation to perform.

InputBuffer

Optionally points to a caller-allocated buffer or variable that contains data specific to the FsControlCode.

InputBufferLength
   The size, in bytes, of `InputBuffer`.

OutputBuffer
   Optionally points to a caller-allocated buffer or variable that receives data specific to
   the `FsControlCode`.

OutputBufferLength
   The size, in bytes, of `OutputBuffer`.

Return Value

Returns STATUS_SUCCESS, STATUS_PENDING or an error status, such as
STATUS_ACCESS_DENIED, STATUS_INVALID_HANDLE, or STATUS_INVALID_DEVICE_REQUEST.

Related Win32 Functions

DeviceIoControl.

Remarks

The control codes and data structures for many interesting file system control operations are defined in winioctl.h.

ZwNotifyChangeDirectoryFile

ZwNotifyChangeDirectoryFile monitors a directory for changes.

```
ZwNotifyChangeDirectoryFile(
    IN HANDLE FileHandle,
    IN HANDLE Event OPTIONAL,
    IN PIO_APC_ROUTINE ApcRoutine OPTIONAL,
    IN PVOID ApcContext OPTIONAL,
    OUT PIO_STATUS_BLOCK IoStatusBlock,
    OUT PFILE_NOTIFY_INFORMATION Buffer,
    IN ULONG BufferLength,
    IN ULONG NotifyFilter,
    IN BOOLEAN WatchSubtree
    );
```

Parameters

FileHandle
   A handle to a file object. The handle must grant FILE_LIST_DIRECTORY access.

Event
   Optionally specifies a handle to an event object to signal when the operation completes. The handle must grant EVENT_MODIFY_STATE access.

ApcRoutine

Optionally points to a routine to execute when the operation completes. The signature of the routine is:

```
VOID (NTAPI *PIO_APC_ROUTINE)(PVOID ApcContext,
                              PIO_STATUS_BLOCK IoStatusBlock,
                              ULONG Reserved);
```

ApcContext

A void pointer that can be used to provide the ApcRoutine with contextual information.

IoStatusBlock

Points to a variable that receives the final completion status and information about the requested operation.

Buffer

Points to a caller-allocated buffer or variable that receives data describing the changes detected. The data is a sequence of FILE_NOTIFY_INFORMATION structures.

BufferLength

The size, in bytes, of Buffer.

NotifyFilter

Specifies the types of changes to be monitored. This parameter can be any combination of the following flags:

```
FILE_NOTIFY_CHANGE_FILE_NAME
FILE_NOTIFY_CHANGE_DIR_NAME
FILE_NOTIFY_CHANGE_ATTRIBUTES
FILE_NOTIFY_CHANGE_SIZE
FILE_NOTIFY_CHANGE_LAST_WRITE
FILE_NOTIFY_CHANGE_LAST_ACCESS
FILE_NOTIFY_CHANGE_CREATION
FILE_NOTIFY_CHANGE_EA
FILE_NOTIFY_CHANGE_SECURITY
FILE_NOTIFY_CHANGE_STREAM_NAME
FILE_NOTIFY_CHANGE_STREAM_SIZE
FILE_NOTIFY_CHANGE_STREAM_WRITE
```

WatchSubtree

Specifies whether changes to all the directories in the subtree below FileHandle should also be monitored.

Return Value

Returns STATUS_SUCCESS, STATUS_PENDING or an error status, such as STATUS_ACCESS_DENIED or STATUS_INVALID_HANDLE.

Related Win32 Functions

ReadDirectoryChangesW, FindFirstChangeNotification, FindNextChangeNotification.

Remarks

Although more FILTER_NOTIFY_XXX flags are defined than are listed in the Win32 documentation for ReadDirectoryChangesW, the supported file systems do not implement the corresponding functionality.

FILE_NOTIFY_INFORMATION

```
typedef struct _FILE_NOTIFY_INFORMATION {
    ULONG NextEntryOffset;
    ULONG Action;
    ULONG NameLength;
    ULONG Name[1];
} FILE_NOTIFY_INFORMATION, *PFILE_NOTIFY_INFORMATION;
```

Members

NextEntryOffset

The number of bytes that must be skipped to get to the next record. A value of zero indicates that this is the last record.

Action

The type of change that occurred. Possible values are:

```
FILE_ACTION_ADDED
FILE_ACTION_REMOVED
FILE_ACTION_MODIFIED
FILE_ACTION_RENAMED_OLD_NAME
FILE_ACTION_RENAMED_NEW_NAME
FILE_ACTION_ADDED_STREAM
FILE_ACTION_REMOVED_STREAM
FILE_ACTION_MODIFIED_STREAM
```

NameLength

Specifies the size, in bytes, of Name.

Name

Contains the name of the file or stream that changed.

Remarks

None.

ZwQueryEaFile

ZwQueryEaFile retrieves information about the extended attributes of a file.

```
NTSYSAPI
NTSTATUS
NTAPI
ZwQueryEaFile(
    IN HANDLE FileHandle,
    OUT PIO_STATUS_BLOCK IoStatusBlock,
    OUT PFILE_FULL_EA_INFORMATION Buffer,
    IN ULONG BufferLength,
    IN BOOLEAN ReturnSingleEntry,
    IN PFILE_GET_EA_INFORMATION EaList OPTIONAL,
    IN ULONG EaListLength,
    IN PULONG EaIndex OPTIONAL,
    IN BOOLEAN RestartScan
    );
```

Parameters

FileHandle
A handle to a file object. The handle must grant FILE_READ_EA access.

IoStatusBlock
Points to a variable that receives the final completion status and information about the requested operation.

Buffer
Points to a caller-allocated buffer or variable that receives the extended attributes. The data is a sequence of FILE_FULL_EA_INFORMATION structures.

BufferLength
The size, in bytes, of Buffer.

ReturnSingleEntry
Specifies whether a single entry should be returned. If false, as many entries as will fit in the buffer are returned.

EaList
Optionally points to a caller-allocated buffer or variable that contains a sequence of FILE_GET_EA_INFORMATION structures specifying the names of the extended attributes to query.

EaListLength
The size, in bytes, of EaList.

EaIndex
Optionally points to a variable that specifies the index of the extended attribute to query.

RestartScan
Specifies whether the scan of the extended attributes should be restarted.

Return Value

Returns STATUS_SUCCESS, STATUS_NO_MORE_ENTRIES or an error status, such as STATUS_ACCESS_DENIED, STATUS_INVALID_HANDLE, or STATUS_EA_LIST_INCONSISTENT.

Related Win32 Functions

None.

Remarks

NTFS supports extended attributes.

ZwSetEaFile

ZwSetEaFile sets the extended attributes of a file.

```
NTSYSAPI
NTSTATUS
NTAPI
ZwSetEaFile(
    IN HANDLE FileHandle,
    OUT PIO_STATUS_BLOCK IoStatusBlock,
    IN PFILE_FULL_EA_INFORMATION Buffer,
    IN ULONG BufferLength
    );
```

Parameters

FileHandle

A handle to a file object. The handle must grant FILE_WRITE_EA access.

IoStatusBlock

Points to a variable that receives the final completion status and information about the requested operation.

Buffer

Points to a caller-allocated buffer or variable that specifies the extended attributes. The data is a sequence of FILE_FULL_EA_INFORMATION structures.

BufferLength

The size, in bytes, of Buffer.

Return Value

Returns STATUS_SUCCESS or an error status, such as STATUS_ACCESS_DENIED, STATUS_INVALID_HANDLE, STATUS_INVALID_EA_NAME, or STATUS_INVALID_EA_FLAG.

Related Win32 Functions

None.

Remarks

None.

FILE_FULL_EA_INFORMATION

```
typedef struct _FILE_FULL_EA_INFORMATION {
    ULONG NextEntryOffset;
    UCHAR Flags;
    UCHAR EaNameLength;
    USHORT EaValueLength;
    CHAR EaName[1];
    // UCHAR EaData[];              // Variable length data not declared
} FILE_FULL_EA_INFORMATION, *PFILE_FULL_EA_INFORMATION;
```

Members

NextEntryOffset

The number of bytes that must be skipped to get to the next entry. A value of zero indicates that this is the last entry.

Flags

A bit array of flags qualifying the extended attribute.

EaNameLength

The size in bytes of the extended attribute name.

EaValueLength

The size in bytes of the extended attribute value.

EaName

The extended attribute name.

EaData

The extended attribute data. The data follows the variable length EaName and is located by adding EaNameLength + 1 to the address of the EaName member.

Remarks

FILE_FULL_EA_INFORMATION is documented in the DDK.

FILE_GET_EA_INFORMATION

```
typedef struct _FILE_GET_EA_INFORMATION {
    ULONG NextEntryOffset;
    UCHAR EaNameLength;
    CHAR EaName[1];
} FILE_GET_EA_INFORMATION, *PFILE_GET_EA_INFORMATION;
```

Members

NextEntryOffset

The number of bytes that must be skipped to get to the next entry. A value of zero indicates that this is the last entry.

EaNameLength
The size in bytes of the extended attribute name.

EaName
The extended attribute name.

Remarks

None.

ZwCreateNamedPipeFile

`ZwCreateNamedPipeFile` creates a named pipe.

```
NTSYSAPI
NTSTATUS
NTAPI
ZwCreateNamedPipeFile(
    OUT PHANDLE FileHandle,
    IN ACCESS_MASK DesiredAccess,
    IN POBJECT_ATTRIBUTES ObjectAttributes,
    OUT PIO_STATUS_BLOCK IoStatusBlock,
    IN ULONG ShareAccess,
    IN ULONG CreateDisposition,
    IN ULONG CreateOptions,
    IN BOOLEAN TypeMessage,
    IN BOOLEAN ReadmodeMessage,
    IN BOOLEAN Nonblocking,
    IN ULONG MaxInstances,
    IN ULONG InBufferSize,
    IN ULONG OutBufferSize,
    IN PLARGE_INTEGER DefaultTimeout OPTIONAL
    );
```

Parameters

FileHandle
Points to a variable that will receive the file object handle if the call is successful.

DesiredAccess
Specifies the type of access that the caller requires to the file object. This parameter can be zero, or any compatible combination of the following flags:

```
FILE_ANY_ACCESS           0x0000      // any type

FILE_READ_ACCESS          0x0001      // file & pipe
FILE_READ_DATA            0x0001      // file & pipe

FILE_WRITE_ACCESS         0x0002      // file & pipe
FILE_WRITE_DATA           0x0002      // file & pipe

FILE_CREATE_PIPE_INSTANCE 0x0004      // named pipe

FILE_READ_ATTRIBUTES      0x0080      // all types

FILE_WRITE_ATTRIBUTES     0x0100      // all types

FILE_ALL_ACCESS           // All of the preceding +
                             STANDARD_RIGHTS_ALL
```

ObjectAttributes

Points to a structure that specifies the object's attributes. OBJ_PERMANENT, OBJ_EXCLUSIVE, and OBJ_OPENLINK are not valid attributes for a file object.

IoStatusBlock

Points to a variable that receives the final completion status and information about the requested operation.

ShareAccess

Specifies the limitations on sharing of the file. This parameter can be zero, or any compatible combination of the following flags:

```
FILE_SHARE_READ
FILE_SHARE_WRITE
```

CreateDisposition

Specifies what to do, depending on whether the file already exists. This must be one of the following values:

```
FILE_OPEN
FILE_CREATE
FILE_OPEN_IF
```

CreateOptions

Specifies the options to be applied when creating or opening the file, as a compatible combination of the following flags:

```
FILE_WRITE_THROUGH
FILE_SYNCHRONOUS_IO_ALERT
FILE_SYNCHRONOUS_IO_NONALERT
```

TypeMessage

Specifies whether the data written to the pipe is interpreted as a sequence of messages or as a stream of bytes.

ReadmodeMessage

Specifies whether the data read from the pipe is interpreted as a sequence of messages or as a stream of bytes.

Nonblocking

Specifies whether non-blocking mode is enabled.

MaxInstances

Specifies the maximum number of instances that can be created for this pipe.

InBufferSize

Specifies the number of bytes to reserve for the input buffer. This value is advisory only.

OutBufferSize

Specifies the number of bytes to reserve for the output buffer. This value is advisory only.

DefaultTimeout
Optionally points to a variable that specifies the default timeout value in units of 100-nanoseconds.

Return Value

Returns STATUS_SUCCESS or an error status, such as STATUS_ACCESS_DENIED.

Related Win32 Functions

CreateNamedPipe.

Remarks

None.

ZwCreateMailslotFile

ZwCreateMailslotFile creates a mailslot.

```
NTSYSAPI
NTSTATUS
NTAPI
ZwCreateMailslotFile(
    OUT PHANDLE FileHandle,
    IN ACCESS_MASK DesiredAccess,
    IN POBJECT_ATTRIBUTES ObjectAttributes,
    OUT PIO_STATUS_BLOCK IoStatusBlock,
    IN ULONG CreateOptions,
    IN ULONG InBufferSize,
    IN ULONG MaxMessageSize,
    IN PLARGE_INTEGER ReadTimeout OPTIONAL
    );
```

Parameters

FileHandle
Points to a variable that will receive the file object handle if the call is successful.

DesiredAccess
Specifies the type of access that the caller requires to the file object. This parameter can be zero, or any compatible combination of the following flags:

```
FILE_ANY_ACCESS          0x0000      // any type

FILE_READ_ACCESS         0x0001      // file & pipe
FILE_READ_DATA           0x0001      // file & pipe

FILE_WRITE_ACCESS        0x0002      // file & pipe
FILE_WRITE_DATA          0x0002      // file & pipe

FILE_READ_ATTRIBUTES     0x0080      // all types

FILE_WRITE_ATTRIBUTES    0x0100      // all types

FILE_ALL_ACCESS                      // All of the preceding +
                                        STANDARD_RIGHTS_ALL
```

ObjectAttributes

Points to a structure that specifies the object's attributes. OBJ_PERMANENT, OBJ_EXCLUSIVE, and OBJ_OPENLINK are not valid attributes for a file object.

IoStatusBlock

Points to a variable that receives the final completion status and information about the requested operation.

CreateOptions

Specifies the options to be applied when creating or opening the file, as a compatible combination of the following flags:

```
FILE_SYNCHRONOUS_IO_ALERT
FILE_SYNCHRONOUS_IO_NONALERT
```

InBufferSize

Specifies the number of bytes to reserve for the input buffer. This value is advisory only.

MaxMessageSize

Specifies the maximum size, in bytes, of a single message that can be written to the mailslot.

ReadTimeout

Optionally points to a variable that specifies the read timeout value in units of 100-nanoseconds.

Return Value

Returns STATUS_SUCCESS or an error status, such as STATUS_ACCESS_DENIED.

Related Win32 Functions

CreateMailslot.

Remarks

None.

ZwQueryVolumeInformationFile

ZwQueryVolumeInformationFile retrieves information about a file system volume.

```
NTSYSAPI
NTSTATUS
NTAPI
ZwQueryVolumeInformationFile(
    IN HANDLE FileHandle,
    OUT PIO_STATUS_BLOCK IoStatusBlock,
    OUT PVOID VolumeInformation,
    IN ULONG VolumeInformationLength,
    IN FS_INFORMATION_CLASS VolumeInformationClass
    );
```

Parameters

FileHandle
A handle to a file object representing a volume. The handle must grant FILE_READ_DATA access for most information classes.

IoStatusBlock
Points to a variable that receives the final completion status and information about the requested operation.

VolumeInformation
Points to a caller-allocated buffer or variable that receives the requested volume information.

VolumeInformationLength
The size in bytes of VolumeInformation, which the caller should set according to the given VolumeInformationClass.

VolumeInformationClass
Specifies the type of volume information to be queried. The permitted values are a subset of the enumeration FS_INFORMATION_CLASS, described in the following section.

Return Value

Returns STATUS_SUCCESS or an error status, such as STATUS_ACCESS_DENIED, STATUS_INVALID_HANDLE, STATUS_INVALID_INFO_CLASS, or STATUS_INFO_LENGTH_MISMATCH.

Related Win32 Functions

GetVolumeInformation, GetDiskFreeSpace, GetDiskFreeSpaceEx, GetDriveType.

Remarks

None.

ZwSetVolumeInformationFile

ZwSetVolumeInformationFile sets information affecting a file system volume.

```
NTSYSAPI
NTSTATUS
NTAPI
ZwSetVolumeInformationFile(
    IN HANDLE FileHandle,
    OUT PIO_STATUS_BLOCK IoStatusBlock,
    IN PVOID Buffer,
    IN ULONG BufferLength,
    IN FS_INFORMATION_CLASS VolumeInformationClass
    );
```

Parameters

FileHandle
A handle to a file object representing a volume. The handle must grant FILE_WRITE_DATA access.

IoStatusBlock
Points to a variable that receives the final completion status and information about the requested operation.

VolumeInformation
Points to a caller-allocated buffer or variable that contains the volume information to be set.

VolumeInformationLength
Specifies the size in bytes of VolumeInformation, which the caller should set according to the given VolumeInformationClass.

VolumeInformationClass
Specifies the type of volume information to be set. The permitted values are a subset of the enumeration FS_INFORMATION_CLASS, described in the following section.

Return Value

Returns STATUS_SUCCESS or an error status, such as STATUS_ACCESS_DENIED, STATUS_INVALID_HANDLE, STATUS_INVALID_INFO_CLASS, or STATUS_INFO_LENGTH_MISMATCH.

Related Win32 Functions

SetVolumeLabel.

Remarks

None.

FS_INFORMATION_CLASS

```
                                            Query   Set
typedef enum _FSINFOCLASS {
    FileFsVolumeInformation = 1,     // 1    Y       N
    FileFsLabelInformation,          // 2    N       Y
    FileFsSizeInformation,           // 3    Y       N
    FileFsDeviceInformation,         // 4    Y       N
    FileFsAttributeInformation,      // 5    Y       N
    FileFsControlInformation,        // 6    Y       Y
    FileFsFullSizeInformation,       // 7    Y       N
    FileFsObjectIdInformation        // 8    Y       Y
} FS_INFORMATION_CLASS, *PFS_INFORMATION_CLASS;
```

FileFsVolumeInformation

```
typedef struct _FILE_FS_VOLUME_INFORMATION {
    LARGE_INTEGER VolumeCreationTime;
    ULONG VolumeSerialNumber;
    ULONG VolumeLabelLength;
    UCHAR Unknown;
    WCHAR VolumeLabel[1];
} FILE_FS_VOLUME_INFORMATION, *PFILE_FS_VOLUME_INFORMATION;
```

Members

VolumeCreationTime
The time when the volume was formatted in the standard time format (that is, the number of 100-nanosecond intervals since January 1, 1601).

VolumeSerialNumber
The volume serial number.

VolumeLabelLength
The size, in bytes, of the volume label.

Unknown
Interpretation unknown.

VolumeLabel
The volume label.

Remarks

None.

FileFsLabelInformation

```
typedef struct _FILE_FS_LABEL_INFORMATION {
    ULONG VolumeLabelLength;
    WCHAR VolumeLabel;
} FILE_FS_LABEL_INFORMATION, *PFILE_FS_LABEL_INFORMATION;
```

Members

VolumeLabelLength
The size, in bytes, of the volume label.

VolumeLabel
The volume label.

Remarks

None.

FileFsSizeInformation

```
typedef struct _FILE_FS_SIZE_INFORMATION {
    LARGE_INTEGER TotalAllocationUnits;
    LARGE_INTEGER AvailableAllocationUnits;
    ULONG SectorsPerAllocationUnit;
    ULONG BytesPerSector;
} FILE_FS_SIZE_INFORMATION, *PFILE_FS_SIZE_INFORMATION;
```

Members

TotalAllocationUnits
   The total number of allocation units on the volume.

AvailableAllocationUnits
   The number of free allocation units on the volume.

SectorsPerAllocationUnit
   The number of sectors per allocation unit.

BytesPerSector
   The number of bytes per sector.

Remarks

   None.

FileFsDeviceInformation

```
typedef struct _FILE_FS_DEVICE_INFORMATION {
    DEVICE_TYPE DeviceType;
    ULONG Characteristics;
} FILE_FS_DEVICE_INFORMATION, *PFILE_FS_DEVICE_INFORMATION;
```

Members

DeviceType
   The type of device on which the volume is stored. Possible values include:

```
FILE_DEVICE_CD_ROM
FILE_DEVICE_DFS
FILE_DEVICE_DISK
FILE_DEVICE_NETWORK_FILE_SYSTEM
FILE_DEVICE_VIRTUAL_DISK
```

Characteristics
   A bit array of flags describing characteristics of the volume. The defined characteristics
   include:

```
FILE_REMOVABLE_MEDIA
FILE_READ_ONLY_DEVICE
FILE_FLOPPY_DISKETTE
FILE_WRITE_ONCE_MEDIA
FILE_REMOTE_DEVICE
```

```
        FILE_DEVICE_IS_MOUNTED
        FILE_VIRTUAL_VOLUME
        FILE_AUTOGENERATED_DEVICE_NAME
```

Remarks

FILE_FS_DEVICE_INFORMATION is documented in the DDK.

FileFsAttributeInformation

```
typedef struct _FILE_FS_ATTRIBUTE_INFORMATION {
    ULONG FileSystemFlags;
    ULONG MaximumComponentNameLength;
    ULONG FileSystemNameLength;
    WCHAR FileSystemName[1];
} FILE_FS_ATTRIBUTE_INFORMATION, *PFILE_FS_ATTRIBUTE_INFORMATION;
```

Members

FileSystemFlags

A bit array of flags describing properties of the file system. The defined properties include:

```
        FILE_CASE_SENSITIVE_SEARCH
        FILE_CASE_PRESERVED_NAMES
        FILE_UNICODE_ON_DISK
        FILE_PERSISTENT_ACLS
        FILE_FILE_COMPRESSION
        FILE_VOLUME_QUOTAS
        FILE_SUPPORTS_SPARSE_FILES
        FILE_SUPPORTS_REPARSE_POINTS
        FILE_SUPPORTS_REMOTE_STORAGE
        FILE_VOLUME_IS_COMPRESSED
        FILE_SUPPORTS_OBJECT_IDS
        FILE_SUPPORTS_ENCRYPTION
        FILE_NAMED_STREAMS
```

MaximumComponentNameLength

The maximum number of characters in a component of a filename.

FileSystemNameLength

The size, in bytes, of the file system name.

FileSystemName

The file system name.

Remarks

None.

FileFsControlInformation

```
typedef struct _FILE_FS_CONTROL_INFORMATION {
    LARGE_INTEGER Reserved[3];
    LARGE_INTEGER DefaultQuotaThreshold;
    LARGE_INTEGER DefaultQuotaLimit;
    ULONG QuotaFlags;
} FILE_FS_CONTROL_INFORMATION, *PFILE_FS_CONTROL_INFORMATION;
```

Members

DefaultQuotaThreshold
> The default number of bytes of disk space that may be used by a SID before a warning is issued.

DefaultQuotaLimit
> The default number of bytes of disk space that may be used by a SID.

QuotaFlags
> An array of flags indicating whether disk quotas are enabled on the volume and the actions to take when warning levels and quotas are exceeded.

Remarks

This information class can only be used in Windows 2000.

FileFsFullSizeInformation

```
typedef struct _FILE_FS_FULL_SIZE_INFORMATION {
    LARGE_INTEGER TotalQuotaAllocationUnits;
    LARGE_INTEGER AvailableQuotaAllocationUnits;
    LARGE_INTEGER AvailableAllocationUnits;
    ULONG SectorsPerAllocationUnit;
    ULONG BytesPerSector;
} FILE_FS_FULL_SIZE_INFORMATION, *PFILE_FS_FULL_SIZE_INFORMATION;
```

Members

TotalQuotaAllocationUnits
> The largest number of allocation units on the volume that could be owned by the TokenOwner of the primary token of the current process. If volume quotas are enabled, this is the smaller of the total number of allocation units on the volume and the volume quota for the TokenOwner of the primary token of the current process.

AvailableQuotaAllocationUnits
> The number of free allocation units on the volume that could be acquired by the TokenOwner of the primary token of the current process. If volume quotas are enabled, this is the smaller of the total number of free allocation units on the volume and the unused volume quota for the TokenOwner of the primary token of the current process.

AvailableAllocationUnits
The number of free allocation units on the volume.

SectorsPerAllocationUnit
The number of sectors per allocation unit.

BytesPerSector
The number of bytes per sector.

Remarks

This information class can only be used in Windows 2000.

FileFsObjectIdInformation

```
typedef struct _FILE_FS_OBJECT_ID_INFORMATION {
    UUID VolumeObjectId;
    ULONG VolumeObjectIdExtendedInfo[12];
} FILE_FS_OBJECT_ID_INFORMATION, *PFILE_FS_OBJECT_ID_INFORMATION;
```

Members

VolumeObjectId
The UUID of the volume.

VolumeObjectIdExtendedInfo
Interpretation unknown.

Remarks

This information class can only be used in Windows 2000.

ZwQueryQuotaInformationFile

ZwQueryQuotaInformationFile retrieves information about the disk quotas on a
volume.

```
NTSYSAPI
NTSTATUS
NTAPI
ZwQueryQuotaInformationFile(
    IN HANDLE FileHandle,
    OUT PIO_STATUS_BLOCK IoStatusBlock,
    OUT PFILE_USER_QUOTA_INFORMATION Buffer,
    IN ULONG BufferLength,
    IN BOOLEAN ReturnSingleEntry,
    IN PFILE_QUOTA_LIST_INFORMATION QuotaList OPTIONAL,
    IN ULONG QuotaListLength,
    IN PSID ResumeSid OPTIONAL,
    IN BOOLEAN RestartScan
    );
```

Parameters

FileHandle
> A handle to a file object representing a volume. The handle must grant FILE_READ_DATA access.

IoStatusBlock
> Points to a variable that receives the final completion status and information about the requested operation.

Buffer
> Points to a caller-allocated buffer or variable that receives the quota information. The data is a sequence of FILE_USER_QUOTA_INFORMATION structures.

BufferLength
> The size, in bytes, of Buffer.

ReturnSingleEntry
> Specifies whether a single entry should be returned; if false, as many entries as will fit in the buffer are returned.

QuotaList
> Optionally points to a caller-allocated buffer or variable that contains a sequence of FILE_QUOTA_LIST_INFORMATION structures specifying the SIDs to query.

QuotaListLength
> The size, in bytes, of QuotaList.

ResumeSid
> Optionally points to a variable which specifies the position from which the scan of volume disk quotas should be resumed.

RestartScan
> Specifies whether the scan of the volume disk quotas should be restarted.

Return Value

Returns STATUS_SUCCESS, STATUS_NO_MORE_ENTRIES or an error status, such as STATUS_ACCESS_DENIED, STATUS_INVALID_HANDLE, or STATUS_QUOTA_LIST_INCONSISTENT.

Related Win32 Functions

None.

Remarks

The routine **ZwQueryQuotaInformationFile** is only present in Windows 2000.

NTFS supports disk quotas.

ZwSetQuotaInformationFile

ZwSetQuotaInformationFile sets disk quota restrictions on a volume.

```
NTSYSAPI
NTSTATUS
NTAPI
ZwSetQuotaInformationFile(
    IN HANDLE FileHandle,
    OUT PIO_STATUS_BLOCK IoStatusBlock,
    IN PFILE_USER_QUOTA_INFORMATION Buffer,
    IN ULONG BufferLength
    );
```

Parameters

FileHandle

A handle to a file object representing a volume. The handle must grant
FILE_WRITE_DATA access.

IoStatusBlock

Points to a variable that receives the final completion status and information about the
requested operation.

Buffer

Points to a caller-allocated buffer or variable that specifies the extended attributes. The
data is a sequence of FILE_USER_QUOTA_INFORMATION structures.

BufferLength

The size, in bytes, of Buffer.

Return Value

Returns STATUS_SUCCESS or an error status, such as STATUS_ACCESS_DENIED,
STATUS_INVALID_HANDLE, or STATUS_QUOTA_LIST_INCONSISTENT.

Related Win32 Functions

None.

Remarks

The routine **ZwSetQuotaInformationFile** is only present in Windows 2000.

NTFS supports disk quotas.

FILE_USER_QUOTA_INFORMATION

```
typedef struct _FILE_USER_QUOTA_INFORMATION {
    ULONG NextEntryOffset;
    ULONG SidLength;
    LARGE_INTEGER ChangeTime;
    LARGE_INTEGER QuotaUsed;
    LARGE_INTEGER QuotaThreshold;
    LARGE_INTEGER QuotaLimit;
    SID Sid[1];
} FILE_USER_QUOTA_INFORMATION, *PFILE_USER_QUOTA_INFORMATION;
```

Members

NextEntryOffset
> The number of bytes that must be skipped to get to the next entry. A value of zero indicates that this is the last entry.

SidLength
> The size in bytes of `Sid`.

ChangeTime
> The time when the quota was last changed in the standard time format (that is, the number of 100-nanosecond intervals since January 1, 1601).

QuotaUsed
> The number of bytes of disk space used by files owned by `Sid`.

QuotaThreshold
> The number of bytes of disk space that `Sid` may use before a warning is issued.

QuotaLimit
> The number of bytes of disk space that `Sid` may use.

Sid
> A SID that identifies a potential owner of files on a volume.

Remarks

> None.

FILE_QUOTA_LIST_INFORMATION

```
typedef struct _FILE_QUOTA_LIST_INFORMATION {
    ULONG NextEntryOffset;
    ULONG SidLength;
    SID Sid[1];
} FILE_QUOTA_LIST_INFORMATION, *PFILE_QUOTA_LIST_INFORMATION;
```

Members

NextEntryOffset
> The number of bytes that must be skipped to get to the next entry. A value of zero indicates that this is the last entry.

SidLength
> The size in bytes of `Sid`.

Sid
> A SID that identifies a potential owner of files on a volume.

Remarks

> None.

ZwQueryAttributesFile

ZwQueryAttributesFile retrieves basic information about a file object.

```
NTSYSAPI
NTSTATUS
NTAPI
ZwQueryAttributesFile(
    IN POBJECT_ATTRIBUTES ObjectAttributes,
    OUT PFILE_BASIC_INFORMATION FileInformation
    );
```

Parameters

ObjectAttributes
Specifies the file whose attributes are to be queried.

FileInformation
Points to a caller-allocated buffer or variable that receives the file attributes.

Return Value

Returns STATUS_SUCCESS or an error status, such as STATUS_ACCESS_DENIED or STATUS_OBJECT_NAME_NOT_FOUND.

Related Win32 Functions

GetFileAttributes.

Remarks

None.

ZwQueryFullAttributesFile

ZwQueryFullAttributesFile retrieves extended information about a file object.

```
NTSYSAPI
NTSTATUS
NTAPI
ZwQueryFullAttributesFile(
    IN POBJECT_ATTRIBUTES ObjectAttributes,
    OUT PFILE_NETWORK_OPEN_INFORMATION FileInformation
    );
```

Parameters

ObjectAttributes
Specifies the file whose attributes are to be queried.

FileInformation
Points to a caller-allocated buffer or variable that receives the file attributes.

Return Value

Returns STATUS_SUCCESS or an error status, such as STATUS_ACCESS_DENIED or
STATUS_OBJECT_NAME_NOT_FOUND.

Related Win32 Functions

GetFileAttributesEx.

Remarks

None.

ZwQueryInformationFile

ZwQueryInformationFile retrieves information about a file object.

```
NTSYSAPI
NTSTATUS
NTAPI
ZwQueryInformationFile(
    IN HANDLE FileHandle,
    OUT PIO_STATUS_BLOCK IoStatusBlock,
    OUT PVOID FileInformation,
    IN ULONG FileInformationLength,
    IN FILE_INFORMATION_CLASS FileInformationClass
    );
```

Parameters

FileHandle
  A handle to a file object. The handle must grant FILE_READ_DATA or FILE_READ_EA
  access for some information classes.

IoStatusBlock
  Points to a variable that receives the final completion status and information about the
  requested operation.

FileInformation
  Points to a caller-allocated buffer or variable that receives the requested file
  information.

FileInformationLength
  The size in bytes of FileInformation, which the caller should set according to the
  given FileInformationClass.

FileInformationClass
  Specifies the type of file information to be queried. The permitted values are a subset
  of the enumeration FILE_INFORMATION_CLASS, described in the following section.

Return Value

Returns STATUS_SUCCESS or an error status, such as STATUS_ACCESS_DENIED,
STATUS_INVALID_HANDLE, STATUS_INVALID_INFO_CLASS, or STATUS_INFO_LENGTH_MISMATCH.

Related Win32 Functions

GetFileInformationByHandle, GetFileSize, GetCompressedFileSize, GetFileTime.

Remarks

ZwQueryInformationFile is documented in the DDK.

ZwSetInformationFile

ZwSetInformationFile sets information affecting a file object.

```
NTSYSAPI
NTSTATUS
NTAPI
ZwSetInformationFile(
    IN HANDLE FileHandle,
    OUT PIO_STATUS_BLOCK IoStatusBlock,
    IN PVOID FileInformation,
    IN ULONG FileInformationLength,
    IN FILE_INFORMATION_CLASS FileInformationClass
    );
```

Parameters

FileHandle
A handle to a file object. The handle must grant FILE_WRITE_DATA, FILE_WRITE_EA, FILE_WRITE_ATTRIBUTES, or DELETE access for some information classes.

IoStatusBlock
Points to a variable that receives the final completion status and information about the requested operation.

FileInformation
Points to a caller-allocated buffer or variable that contains the file information to be set.

FileInformationLength
The size in bytes of FileInformation, which the caller should set according to the given FileInformationClass.

FileInformationClass
Specifies the type of file information to be set. The permitted values are a subset of the enumeration FILE_INFORMATION_CLASS, described in the following section.

Return Value

Returns STATUS_SUCCESS or an error status, such as STATUS_ACCESS_DENIED, STATUS_INVALID_HANDLE, STATUS_INVALID_INFO_CLASS, or STATUS_INFO_LENGTH_MISMATCH.

Related Win32 Functions

SetFileAttributes, SetEndOfFile, SetFilePointer, SetFileTime, DeleteFile.

Remarks

ZwSetInformationFile is documented in the DDK.

ZwQueryDirectoryFile

ZwQueryDirectoryFile retrieves information about the contents of a directory.

```
NTSYSAPI
NTSTATUS
NTAPI
ZwQueryDirectoryFile(
    IN HANDLE FileHandle,
    IN HANDLE Event OPTIONAL,
    IN PIO_APC_ROUTINE ApcRoutine OPTIONAL,
    IN PVOID ApcContext OPTIONAL,
    OUT PIO_STATUS_BLOCK IoStatusBlock,
    OUT PVOID FileInformation,
    IN ULONG FileInformationLength,
    IN FILE_INFORMATION_CLASS FileInformationClass,
    IN BOOLEAN ReturnSingleEntry,
    IN PUNICODE_STRING FileName OPTIONAL,
    IN BOOLEAN RestartScan
    );
```

Parameters

FileHandle

A handle to a file object representing a directory. The handle must grant
FILE_LIST_DIRECTORY access.

Event

Optionally specifies a handle to an event object to signal when the operation completes. The handle must grant EVENT_MODIFY_STATE access.

ApcRoutine

Optionally points to a routine to execute when the operation completes. The signature
of the routine is:

```
VOID (NTAPI *PIO_APC_ROUTINE)(PVOID ApcContext,
                              PIO_STATUS_BLOCK IoStatusBlock,
                              ULONG Reserved);
```

ApcContext

A void pointer that can be used to provide the **ApcRoutine** with contextual
information.

IoStatusBlock

Points to a variable that receives the final completion status and information about the
requested operation.

FileInformation

Points to a caller-allocated buffer or variable that receives the requested file
information.

FileInformationLength
> The size in bytes of `FileInformation`, which the caller should set according to the given `FileInformationClass`.

FileInformationClass
> Specifies the type of file information to be queried. The permitted values are a subset of the enumeration `FILE_INFORMATION_CLASS`, described in the following section.

ReturnSingleEntry
> Specifies whether a single entry should be returned. If false, as many entries as will fit in the `FileInformation` buffer are returned.

FileName
> Optionally specifies a filename pattern possibly containing "*" and "?" wildcards which is used to filter the files in the directory.

RestartScan
> Specifies whether the scan of the directory should be restarted, or should be resumed from the current directory file pointer position.

Return Value

> Returns `STATUS_SUCCESS` or an error status, such as `STATUS_ACCESS_DENIED`, `STATUS_INVALID_HANDLE`, `STATUS_INVALID_INFO_CLASS`, `STATUS_INFO_LENGTH_MISMATCH`, `STATUS_NO_SUCH_FILE`, or `STATUS_NO_MORE_FILES`.

Related Win32 Functions

> `FindFirstFile`, `FindFirstFileEx`, `FindNextFile`.

Remarks

> None.

ZwQueryOleDirectoryFile

The operation specified by **ZwQueryOleDirectoryFile** is not implemented by any of the supported file systems.

```
NTSYSAPI
NTSTATUS
NTAPI
ZwQueryOleDirectoryFile(
    IN HANDLE FileHandle,
    IN HANDLE Event OPTIONAL,
    IN PIO_APC_ROUTINE ApcRoutine OPTIONAL,
    IN PVOID ApcContext OPTIONAL,
    OUT PIO_STATUS_BLOCK IoStatusBlock,
    OUT PVOID Buffer,
    IN ULONG BufferLength,
    IN FILE_INFORMATION_CLASS FileInformationClass,
    IN BOOLEAN ReturnSingleEntry,
    IN PUNICODE_STRING FileName,
    IN BOOLEAN RestartScan
    );
```

Parameters

FileHandle

A handle to a file object representing a directory. The handle must grant `FILE_LIST_DIRECTORY` access.

Event

Optionally specifies a handle to an event object to signal when the operation completes. The handle must grant `EVENT_MODIFY_STATE` access.

ApcRoutine

Optionally points to a routine to execute when the operation completes. The signature of the routine is:

```
VOID (NTAPI *PIO_APC_ROUTINE)(PVOID ApcContext,
                              PIO_STATUS_BLOCK IoStatusBlock,
                              ULONG Reserved);
```

ApcContext

A void pointer that can be used to provide the `ApcRoutine` with contextual information.

IoStatusBlock

Points to a variable that receives the final completion status and information about the requested operation.

FileInformation

Points to a caller-allocated buffer or variable that receives the requested file information.

FileInformationLength

The size in bytes of `FileInformation`, which the caller should set according to the given `FileInformationClass`.

FileInformationClass

Specifies the type of file information to be queried. The permitted values are a subset of the enumeration `FILE_INFORMATION_CLASS`, described in the following section.

ReturnSingleEntry

Specifies whether a single entry should be returned. If false, as many entries as will fit in the `FileInformation` buffer are returned.

FileName

Optionally specifies a filename pattern possibly containing "*" and "?" wildcards, which is used to filter the files in the directory.

RestartScan

Specifies whether the scan of the directory should be restarted, or should be resumed from the current directory file pointer position.

Return Value

Returns STATUS_SUCCESS or an error status, such as STATUS_ACCESS_DENIED,
STATUS_INVALID_HANDLE, STATUS_INVALID_INFO_CLASS, STATUS_INFO_LENGTH_MISMATCH,
STATUS_NO_SUCH_FILE, or STATUS_NO_MORE_FILES.

Related Win32 Functions

None.

Remarks

ZwQueryOleDirectoryFile is only present in Windows NT 4.0.

The query OLE directory function is not implemented by the FAT or NTFS file
systems.

FILE_INFORMATION_CLASS

		Query	Set	File/Directory
typedef enum _FILE_INFORMATION_CLASS {				
FileDirectoryInformation = 1,	// 1	Y	N	D
FileFullDirectoryInformation,	// 2	Y	N	D
FileBothDirectoryInformation,	// 3	Y	N	D
FileBasicInformation,	// 4	Y	Y	F
FileStandardInformation,	// 5	Y	N	F
FileInternalInformation,	// 6	Y	N	F
FileEaInformation,	// 7	Y	N	F
FileAccessInformation,	// 8	Y	N	F
FileNameInformation,	// 9	Y	N	F
FileRenameInformation,	// 10	N	Y	F
FileLinkInformation,	// 11	N	Y	F
FileNamesInformation,	// 12	Y	N	D
FileDispositionInformation,	// 13	N	Y	F
FilePositionInformation,	// 14	Y	Y	F
FileModeInformation = 16,	// 16	Y	Y	F
FileAlignmentInformation,	// 17	Y	N	F
FileAllInformation,	// 18	Y	N	F
FileAllocationInformation,	// 19	N	Y	F
FileEndOfFileInformation,	// 20	N	Y	F
FileAlternateNameInformation,	// 21	Y	N	F
FileStreamInformation,	// 22	Y	N	F
FilePipeInformation,	// 23	Y	Y	F
FilePipeLocalInformation,	// 24	Y	N	F
FilePipeRemoteInformation,	// 25	Y	Y	F
FileMailslotQueryInformation,	// 26	Y	N	F
FileMailslotSetInformation,	// 27	N	Y	F
FileCompressionInformation,	// 28	Y	N	F
FileObjectIdInformation,	// 29	Y	Y	F
FileCompletionInformation,	// 30	N	Y	F
FileMoveClusterInformation,	// 31	N	Y	F
FileQuotaInformation,	// 32	Y	Y	F
FileReparsePointInformation,	// 33	Y	N	F
FileNetworkOpenInformation,	// 34	Y	N	F
FileAttributeTagInformation,	// 35	Y	N	F
FileTrackingInformation	// 36	N	Y	F
} FILE_INFORMATION_CLASS, *PFILE_INFORMATION_CLASS;				

FileDirectoryInformation

```
typedef struct _FILE_DIRECTORY_INFORMATION { // Information Class 1
    ULONG NextEntryOffset;
    ULONG Unknown;
    LARGE_INTEGER CreationTime;
    LARGE_INTEGER LastAccessTime;
    LARGE_INTEGER LastWriteTime;
    LARGE_INTEGER ChangeTime;
    LARGE_INTEGER EndOfFile;
    LARGE_INTEGER AllocationSize;
    ULONG FileAttributes;
    ULONG FileNameLength;
    WCHAR FileName[1];
} FILE_DIRECTORY_INFORMATION, *PFILE_DIRECTORY_INFORMATION;
```

Members

NextEntryOffset

The number of bytes that must be skipped to get to the next entry. A value of zero indicates that this is the last entry.

Unknown

Interpretation unknown.

CreationTime

The time when the file was created in the standard time format (that is, the number of 100-nanosecond intervals since January 1, 1601).

LastAccessTime

The time when the file was last accessed in the standard time format (that is, the number of 100-nanosecond intervals since January 1, 1601).

LastWriteTime

The time when the file was last written in the standard time format (that is, the number of 100-nanosecond intervals since January 1, 1601).

ChangeTime

The time when the file attributes were last changed in the standard time format (that is, the number of 100-nanosecond intervals since January 1, 1601).

EndOfFile

The number of bytes from the beginning to the end of the file.

AllocationSize

The number of bytes allocated to the file.

FileAttributes

The attributes of the file. Defined attributes include:

```
FILE_ATTRIBUTE_READONLY
FILE_ATTRIBUTE_HIDDEN
FILE_ATTRIBUTE_SYSTEM
```

```
FILE_ATTRIBUTE_DIRECTORY
FILE_ATTRIBUTE_ARCHIVE
FILE_ATTRIBUTE_DEVICE
FILE_ATTRIBUTE_NORMAL
FILE_ATTRIBUTE_TEMPORARY
FILE_ATTRIBUTE_SPARSE_FILE
FILE_ATTRIBUTE_REPARSE_POINT
FILE_ATTRIBUTE_COMPRESSED
FILE_ATTRIBUTE_OFFLINE
FILE_ATTRIBUTE_NOT_CONTENT_INDEXED
FILE_ATTRIBUTE_ENCRYPTED
```

FileNameLength
The size in bytes of the `FileName`.

FileName
The name of the file.

Remarks

None.

FileFullDirectoryInformation

```
typedef struct _FILE_FULL_DIRECTORY_INFORMATION { // Information Class 2
    ULONG NextEntryOffset;
    ULONG Unknown;
    LARGE_INTEGER CreationTime;
    LARGE_INTEGER LastAccessTime;
    LARGE_INTEGER LastWriteTime;
    LARGE_INTEGER ChangeTime;
    LARGE_INTEGER EndOfFile;
    LARGE_INTEGER AllocationSize;
    ULONG FileAttributes;
    ULONG FileNameLength;
    ULONG EaInformationLength;
    WCHAR FileName[1];
} FILE_FULL_DIRECTORY_INFORMATION, *PFILE_FULL_DIRECTORY_INFORMATION;
```

Members

NextEntryOffset
The number of bytes that must be skipped to get to the next entry. A value of zero indicates that this is the last entry.

Unknown
Interpretation unknown.

CreationTime
The time when the file was created in the standard time format (that is, the number of 100-nanosecond intervals since January 1, 1601).

LastAccessTime

The time when the file was last accessed in the standard time format (that is, the number of 100-nanosecond intervals since January 1, 1601).

LastWriteTime

The time when the file was last written in the standard time format (that is, the number of 100-nanosecond intervals since January 1, 1601).

ChangeTime

The time when the file attributes were last changed in the standard time format (that is, the number of 100-nanosecond intervals since January 1, 1601).

EndOfFile

The number of bytes from the beginning to the end of the file.

AllocationSize

The number of bytes allocated to the file.

FileAttributes

The attributes of the file. Defined attributes include:

```
FILE_ATTRIBUTE_READONLY
FILE_ATTRIBUTE_HIDDEN
FILE_ATTRIBUTE_SYSTEM
FILE_ATTRIBUTE_DIRECTORY
FILE_ATTRIBUTE_ARCHIVE
FILE_ATTRIBUTE_DEVICE
FILE_ATTRIBUTE_NORMAL
FILE_ATTRIBUTE_TEMPORARY
FILE_ATTRIBUTE_SPARSE_FILE
FILE_ATTRIBUTE_REPARSE_POINT
FILE_ATTRIBUTE_COMPRESSED
FILE_ATTRIBUTE_OFFLINE
FILE_ATTRIBUTE_NOT_CONTENT_INDEXED
FILE_ATTRIBUTE_ENCRYPTED
```

FileNameLength

The size in bytes of the name of the file.

EaInformationLength

The size in bytes of the extended attributes of the file.

FileName

The name of the file.

Remarks

None.

FileBothDirectoryInformation

```
typedef struct _FILE_BOTH_DIRECTORY_INFORMATION { // Information Class 3
    ULONG NextEntryOffset;
    ULONG Unknown;
    LARGE_INTEGER CreationTime;
    LARGE_INTEGER LastAccessTime;
    LARGE_INTEGER LastWriteTime;
    LARGE_INTEGER ChangeTime;
    LARGE_INTEGER EndOfFile;
    LARGE_INTEGER AllocationSize;
    ULONG FileAttributes;
    ULONG FileNameLength;
    ULONG EaInformationLength;
    UCHAR AlternateNameLength;
    WCHAR AlternateName[12];
    WCHAR FileName[1];
} FILE_BOTH_DIRECTORY_INFORMATION, *PFILE_BOTH_DIRECTORY_INFORMATION;
```

Members

NextEntryOffset

The number of bytes that must be skipped to get to the next entry. A value of zero indicates that this is the last entry.

Unknown

Interpretation unknown.

CreationTime

The time when the file was created in the standard time format (that is, the number of 100-nanosecond intervals since January 1, 1601).

LastAccessTime

The time when the file was last accessed in the standard time format (that is, the number of 100-nanosecond intervals since January 1, 1601).

LastWriteTime

The time when the file was last written in the standard time format (that is, the number of 100-nanosecond intervals since January 1, 1601).

ChangeTime

The time when the file attributes were last changed in the standard time format (that is, the number of 100-nanosecond intervals since January 1, 1601).

EndOfFile

The number of bytes from the beginning to the end of the file.

AllocationSize

The number of bytes allocated to the file.

FileAttributes

The attributes of the file. Defined attributes include:

```
FILE_ATTRIBUTE_READONLY
FILE_ATTRIBUTE_HIDDEN
FILE_ATTRIBUTE_SYSTEM
FILE_ATTRIBUTE_DIRECTORY
FILE_ATTRIBUTE_ARCHIVE
FILE_ATTRIBUTE_DEVICE
FILE_ATTRIBUTE_NORMAL
FILE_ATTRIBUTE_TEMPORARY
FILE_ATTRIBUTE_SPARSE_FILE
FILE_ATTRIBUTE_REPARSE_POINT
FILE_ATTRIBUTE_COMPRESSED
FILE_ATTRIBUTE_OFFLINE
FILE_ATTRIBUTE_NOT_CONTENT_INDEXED
FILE_ATTRIBUTE_ENCRYPTED
```

FileNameLength

The size in bytes of the name of the file.

EaInformationLength

The size in bytes of the extended attributes of the file.

AlternateNameLength

The size in bytes of the alternate (short DOS 8.3 alias) name of the file.

AlternateName

The alternate (short DOS 8.3 alias) name of the file.

FileName

The name of the file.

Remarks

None.

FileBasicInformation

```
typedef struct _FILE_BASIC_INFORMATION { // Information Class 4
    LARGE_INTEGER CreationTime;
    LARGE_INTEGER LastAccessTime;
    LARGE_INTEGER LastWriteTime;
    LARGE_INTEGER ChangeTime;
    ULONG FileAttributes;
} FILE_BASIC_INFORMATION, *PFILE_BASIC_INFORMATION;
```

Members

CreationTime

The time when the file was created in the standard time format (that is, the number of 100-nanosecond intervals since January 1, 1601).

LastAccessTime

The time when the file was last accessed in the standard time format (that is, the number of 100-nanosecond intervals since January 1, 1601).

LastWriteTime

The time when the file was last written in the standard time format (that is, the number of 100-nanosecond intervals since January 1, 1601).

ChangeTime

The time when the file attributes were last changed in the standard time format (that is, the number of 100-nanosecond intervals since January 1, 1601).

FileAttributes

The attributes of the file. Defined attributes include:

```
FILE_ATTRIBUTE_READONLY
FILE_ATTRIBUTE_HIDDEN
FILE_ATTRIBUTE_SYSTEM
FILE_ATTRIBUTE_DIRECTORY
FILE_ATTRIBUTE_ARCHIVE
FILE_ATTRIBUTE_DEVICE
FILE_ATTRIBUTE_NORMAL
FILE_ATTRIBUTE_TEMPORARY
FILE_ATTRIBUTE_SPARSE_FILE
FILE_ATTRIBUTE_REPARSE_POINT
FILE_ATTRIBUTE_COMPRESSED
FILE_ATTRIBUTE_OFFLINE
FILE_ATTRIBUTE_NOT_CONTENT_INDEXED
FILE_ATTRIBUTE_ENCRYPTED
```

Remarks

FILE_BASIC_INFORMATION is documented in the DDK.

FileStandardInformation

```
typedef struct _FILE_STANDARD_INFORMATION { // Information Class 5
    LARGE_INTEGER AllocationSize;
    LARGE_INTEGER EndOfFile;
    ULONG NumberOfLinks;
    BOOLEAN DeletePending;
    BOOLEAN Directory;
} FILE_STANDARD_INFORMATION, *PFILE_STANDARD_INFORMATION;
```

Members

AllocationSize

The number of bytes allocated to the file.

EndOfFile

The number of bytes from the beginning to the end of the file.

NumberOfLinks
The number of directories in which the file appears.

DeletePending
Indicates whether the file will be deleted when the last handle to it is closed.

Directory
Indicates whether the file is a directory.

Remarks

FILE_STANDARD_INFORMATION is documented in the DDK.

FileInternalInformation

```
typedef struct _FILE_INTERNAL_INFORMATION { // Information Class 6
    LARGE_INTEGER FileId;
} FILE_INTERNAL_INFORMATION, *PFILE_INTERNAL_INFORMATION;
```

Members

FileId
A numeric identifier for the file.

Remarks

The FileId can be used to open the file, when the FILE_OPEN_BY_FILE_ID
CreateOption is specified in a call to ZwCreateFile.

FileEaInformation

```
typedef struct _FILE_EA_INFORMATION { // Information Class 7
    ULONG EaInformationLength;
} FILE_EA_INFORMATION, *PFILE_EA_INFORMATION;
```

Members

EaInformationLength
The size in bytes of the extended attributes of the file.

Remarks

None.

FileAccessInformation

```
typedef struct _FILE_ACCESS_INFORMATION { // Information Class 8
    ACCESS_MASK GrantedAccess;
} FILE_ACCESS_INFORMATION, *PFILE_ACCESS_INFORMATION;
```

Members

GrantedAccess
The access granted to the file by the handle used to perform the query.

Remarks

None.

FileNameInformation

```
typedef struct _FILE_NAME_INFORMATION { // Information Classes 9 and 21
    ULONG FileNameLength;
    WCHAR FileName[1];
} FILE_NAME_INFORMATION, *PFILE_NAME_INFORMATION,
  FILE_ALTERNATE_NAME_INFORMATION, *PFILE_ALTERNATE_NAME_INFORMATION;
```

Members

FileNameLength
The size in bytes of the name of the file.

FileName
The name of the file.

Remarks

The alternate name of a file is its short DOS 8.3 alias.

FileRenameInformation and FileLinkInformation

```
typedef struct _FILE_LINK_RENAME_INFORMATION { // Info Classes 10 and 11
    BOOLEAN ReplaceIfExists;
    HANDLE RootDirectory;
    ULONG FileNameLength;
    WCHAR FileName[1];
} FILE_LINK_INFORMATION, *PFILE_LINK_INFORMATION,
  FILE_RENAME_INFORMATION, *PFILE_RENAME_INFORMATION;
```

Members

ReplaceIfExists
Indicates whether an existing file with the same name as FileName should be deleted.

RootDirectory
A handle to the directory to which the FileName is relative.

FileNameLength
The size in bytes of the FileName.

FileName
The name of the file.

Remarks

None.

FileNamesInformation

```
typedef struct _FILE_NAMES_INFORMATION { // Information Class 12
    ULONG NextEntryOffset;
    ULONG Unknown;
    ULONG FileNameLength;
    WCHAR FileName[1];
} FILE_NAMES_INFORMATION, *PFILE_NAMES_INFORMATION;
```

Members

NextEntryOffset
The number of bytes that must be skipped to get to the next entry. A value of zero indicates that this is the last entry.

Unknown
Interpretation unknown.

FileNameLength
The size in bytes of the `FileName`.

FileName
The name of the file.

Remarks

None.

FileDispositionInformation

```
typedef struct _FILE_DISPOSITION_INFORMATION { // Information Class 13
    BOOLEAN DeleteFile;
} FILE_DISPOSITION_INFORMATION, *PFILE_DISPOSITION_INFORMATION;
```

Members

DeleteFile
Indicates whether the file should be deleted.

Remarks

`FILE_DISPOSITION_INFORMATION` is documented in the DDK.

FilePositionInformation

```
typedef struct _FILE_POSITION_INFORMATION { // Information Class 14
    LARGE_INTEGER CurrentByteOffset;
} FILE_POSITION_INFORMATION, *PFILE_POSITION_INFORMATION;
```

Members

CurrentByteOffset
The offset, in bytes, of the file pointer from the beginning of the file.

Remarks

FILE_POSITION_INFORMATION is documented in the DDK.

FileModeInformation

```
typedef struct _FILE_MODE_INFORMATION { // Information Class 16
    ULONG Mode;
} FILE_MODE_INFORMATION, *PFILE_MODE_INFORMATION;
```

Members

Mode
The options associated with the file via the **ZwCreateFile** CreateOptions parameter or the **ZwOpenFile** OpenOptions parameter.

Remarks

The options FILE_WRITE_THROUGH, FILE_SEQUENTIAL_ONLY, FILE_SYNCHRONOUS_IO_ALERT and FILE_SYNCHRONOUS_IO_NONALERT can be set. Setting FILE_SYNCHRONOUS_IO_ALERT or FILE_SYNCHRONOUS_IO_NONALERT is only possible if the file was opened for synchronous I/O and just toggles the alertability of the file object.

FileAlignmentInformation

```
typedef struct _FILE_ALIGNMENT_INFORMATION { // Information Class 17
    ULONG AlignmentRequirement;
} FILE_ALIGNMENT_INFORMATION, *PFILE_ALIGNMENT_INFORMATION;
```

Members

AlignmentRequirement
The required buffer alignment. Possible values include:

```
FILE_BYTE_ALIGNMENT
FILE_WORD_ALIGNMENT
FILE_LONG_ALIGNMENT
FILE_QUAD_ALIGNMENT
FILE_OCTA_ALIGNMENT
FILE_32_BYTE_ALIGNMENT
FILE_64_BYTE_ALIGNMENT
FILE_128_BYTE_ALIGNMENT
FILE_512_BYTE_ALIGNMENT
```

Remarks

FILE_ALIGNMENT_INFORMATION is documented in the DDK.

FileAllInformation

```
typedef struct _FILE_ALL_INFORMATION { // Information Class 18
    FILE_BASIC_INFORMATION BasicInformation;
    FILE_STANDARD_INFORMATION StandardInformation;
    FILE_INTERNAL_INFORMATION InternalInformation;
    FILE_EA_INFORMATION EaInformation;
    FILE_ACCESS_INFORMATION AccessInformation;
    FILE_POSITION_INFORMATION PositionInformation;
    FILE_MODE_INFORMATION ModeInformation;
    FILE_ALIGNMENT_INFORMATION AlignmentInformation;
    FILE_NAME_INFORMATION NameInformation;
} FILE_ALL_INFORMATION, *PFILE_ALL_INFORMATION;
```

Remarks

FILE_ALL_INFORMATION is a collection of other information classes.

FileAllocationInformation

```
typedef struct _FILE_ALLOCATION_INFORMATION { // Information Class 19
    LARGE_INTEGER AllocationSize;
} FILE_ALLOCATION_INFORMATION, *PFILE_ALLOCATION_INFORMATION;
```

Members

AllocationSize
The number of bytes allocated to the file.

Remarks

None.

FileEndOfFileInformation

```
typedef struct _FILE_END_OF_FILE_INFORMATION { // Information Class 20
    LARGE_INTEGER EndOfFile;
} FILE_END_OF_FILE_INFORMATION, *PFILE_END_OF_FILE_INFORMATION;
```

Members

EndOfFile
The number of bytes from the beginning to the end of the file.

Remarks

FILE_END_OF_FILE_INFORMATION is documented in the DDK.

FileStreamInformation

```
typedef struct _FILE_STREAM_INFORMATION { // Information Class 22
    ULONG NextEntryOffset;
    ULONG StreamNameLength;
    LARGE_INTEGER EndOfStream;
    LARGE_INTEGER AllocationSize;
    WCHAR StreamName[1];
} FILE_STREAM_INFORMATION, *PFILE_STREAM_INFORMATION;
```

Members

NextEntryOffset
　　The number of bytes that must be skipped to get to the next entry. A value of zero
　　indicates that this is the last entry.

StreamNameLength
　　The size in bytes of the name of the stream.

EndOfStream
　　The number of bytes from the beginning to the end of the stream.

AllocationSize
　　The number of bytes allocated to the stream.

StreamName
　　The name of the stream.

Remarks

　　None.

FilePipeInformation

```
typedef struct _FILE_PIPE_INFORMATION { // Information Class 23
    ULONG ReadModeMessage;
    ULONG WaitModeBlocking;
} FILE_PIPE_INFORMATION, *PFILE_PIPE_INFORMATION;
```

Members

ReadModeMessage
　　A boolean specifying whether the pipe read mode is message (if true) or byte (if false).

WaitModeBlocking
　　A boolean specifying whether the pipe wait mode is blocking (if true) or no wait (if
　　false).

Remarks

　　The Win32 functions GetNamedPipeHandleState and SetNamedPipeHandleState use this
　　information class.

FilePipeLocalInformation

```
typedef struct _FILE_PIPE_LOCAL_INFORMATION { // Information Class 24
    ULONG MessageType;
    ULONG Unknown1;
    ULONG MaxInstances;
    ULONG CurInstances;
    ULONG InBufferSize;
    ULONG Unknown2;
    ULONG OutBufferSize;
    ULONG Unknown3[2];
    ULONG ServerEnd;
} FILE_PIPE_LOCAL_INFORMATION, *PFILE_PIPE_LOCAL_INFORMATION;
```

Members

MessageType
A boolean specifying whether the pipe is a message type pipe (if true) or a byte mode pipe (if false).

Unknown1
Interpretation unknown.

MaxInstances
The maximum number of instances of the pipe that are allowed.

CurInstances
The current number of instances of the pipe.

InBufferSize
The size in bytes of the pipe input buffer.

Unknown2
Interpretation unknown.

OutBufferSize
The size in bytes of the pipe output buffer.

Unknown3
Interpretation unknown.

ServerEnd
A boolean specifying whether the pipe handle refers to the server end (if true) or client end (if false) of the pipe.

Remarks

The Win32 functions `GetNamedPipeInfo` and `GetNamedPipeHandleState` use this information class.

FilePipeRemoteInformation

```
typedef struct _FILE_PIPE_REMOTE_INFORMATION { // Information Class 25
    LARGE_INTEGER CollectDataTimeout;
    ULONG MaxCollectionCount;
} FILE_PIPE_REMOTE_INFORMATION, *PFILE_PIPE_REMOTE_INFORMATION;
```

Members

CollectDataTimeout

The maximum time, in units of 100-nanoseconds, that can elapse before the data is transmitted over the network.

MaxCollectionCount

The maximum number of bytes that can be collected before the data is transmitted over the network.

Remarks

The Win32 functions `GetNamedPipeHandleState` and `SetNamedPipeHandleState` use this information class.

FileMailslotQueryInformation

```
typedef struct _FILE_MAILSLOT_QUERY_INFORMATION { // Information Class 26
    ULONG MaxMessageSize;
    ULONG Unknown;
    ULONG NextSize;
    ULONG MessageCount;
    LARGE_INTEGER ReadTimeout;
} FILE_MAILSLOT_QUERY_INFORMATION, *PFILE_MAILSLOT_QUERY_INFORMATION;
```

Members

MaxMessageSize

The maximum size, in bytes, of a single message that can be written to the mailslot.

Unknown

Interpretation unknown.

NextSize

The size in bytes of the next message to be read from the mailslot. If no message is available then `NextSize` is set to `MAILSLOT_NO_MESSAGE`.

MessageCount

The number of messages queued to the mailslot.

ReadTimeout

The maximum time, in units of 100-nanoseconds, that can elapse between starting to read from the mailslot and a message becoming available.

Remarks

The Win32 function `GetMailslotInfo` uses this information class.

FileMailslotSetInformation

```
typedef struct _FILE_MAILSLOT_SET_INFORMATION { // Information Class 27
    LARGE_INTEGER ReadTimeout;
} FILE_MAILSLOT_SET_INFORMATION, *PFILE_MAILSLOT_SET_INFORMATION;
```

Members

ReadTimeout

The maximum time, in units of 100-nanoseconds, that can elapse between starting to read from the mailslot and a message becoming available.

Remarks

The Win32 function `SetMailslotInfo` uses this information class.

FileCompressionInformation

```
typedef struct _FILE_COMPRESSION_INFORMATION { // Information Class 28
    LARGE_INTEGER CompressedSize;
    USHORT CompressionFormat;
    UCHAR CompressionUnitShift;
    UCHAR Unknown;
    UCHAR ClusterSizeShift;
} FILE_COMPRESSION_INFORMATION, *PFILE_COMPRESSION_INFORMATION;
```

Members

CompressedSize

The size in bytes of the space occupied by a compressed file.

CompressionFormat

The compression algorithm used to compress the file. Defined values include:

```
COMPRESSION_FORMAT_NONE
COMPRESSION_FORMAT_LZNT1
```

CompressionUnitShift

The size of a compression unit expressed as the logarithm to the base two of the number of bytes in a compression unit. This member is only valid when `CompressionFormat` is not `COMPRESSION_FORMAT_NONE`.

Unknown

Interpretation unknown. This member always contains the value 12 when `CompressionFormat` is not `COMPRESSION_FORMAT_NONE`. Possibly the logarithm to the base two of the number of bytes in a page.

ClusterSizeShift

The size of a cluster expressed as the logarithm to the base two of the number of bytes in a cluster. This member is only valid when `CompressionFormat` is not `COMPRESSION_FORMAT_NONE`.

Remarks

None.

FileObjectIdInformation

This information class is not implemented by any of the supported file systems. The file system control operations `FSCTL_SET_OBJECT_ID`, `FSCTL_GET_OBJECT_ID`, and `FSCTL_CREATE_OR_GET_OBJECT_ID` are possibly the preferred mechanisms for accessing this functionality.

FileCompletionInformation

```
typedef struct _FILE_COMPLETION_INFORMATION { // Information Class 30
    HANDLE IoCompletionHandle;
    ULONG CompletionKey;
} FILE_COMPLETION_INFORMATION, *PFILE_COMPLETION_INFORMATION;
```

Members

IoCompletionHandle

A handle to an I/O completion object. The handle must grant `IO_COMPLETION_MODIFY_STATE` access.

CompletionKey

A value to be returned to a caller of `ZwRemoveIoCompletion` via the `CompletionKey` parameter of that routine.

Remarks

None.

FileMoveClusterInformation

This information class is not implemented by any of the supported file systems. The file system control operation FSCTL_MOVE_FILE is possibly the preferred mechanism for accessing this functionality.

FileQuotaInformation

This information class is not implemented by any of the supported file systems. The native system services `ZwQueryQuotaInformationFile` and `ZwSetQuotaInformationFile` are possibly the preferred mechanisms for accessing this functionality.

FileReparsePointInformation

This information class is not implemented by any of the supported file systems. The file system control operations FSCTL_SET_REPARSE_POINT, FSCTL_GET_REPARSE_POINT, and FSCTL_DELETE_REPARSE_POINT are possibly the preferred mechanisms for accessing this functionality.

FileNetworkOpenInformation

```
typedef struct _FILE_NETWORK_OPEN_INFORMATION { // Information Class 34
    LARGE_INTEGER CreationTime;
    LARGE_INTEGER LastAccessTime;
    LARGE_INTEGER LastWriteTime;
    LARGE_INTEGER ChangeTime;
    LARGE_INTEGER AllocationSize;
    LARGE_INTEGER EndOfFile;
    ULONG FileAttributes;
} FILE_NETWORK_OPEN_INFORMATION, *PFILE_NETWORK_OPEN_INFORMATION;
```

Members

CreationTime

The time when the file was created in the standard time format (that is, the number of 100-nanosecond intervals since January 1, 1601).

LastAccessTime

The time when the file was last accessed in the standard time format (that is, the number of 100-nanosecond intervals since January 1, 1601).

LastWriteTime

The time when the file was last written in the standard time format (that is, the number of 100-nanosecond intervals since January 1, 1601).

ChangeTime

The time when the file attributes were last changed in the standard time format (that is, the number of 100-nanosecond intervals since January 1, 1601).

AllocationSize

The number of bytes allocated to the file.

EndOfFile

The number of bytes from the beginning to the end of the file.

FileAttributes

The attributes of the file. Defined attributes include:

```
FILE_ATTRIBUTE_READONLY
FILE_ATTRIBUTE_HIDDEN
FILE_ATTRIBUTE_SYSTEM
FILE_ATTRIBUTE_DIRECTORY
FILE_ATTRIBUTE_ARCHIVE
FILE_ATTRIBUTE_DEVICE
```

```
FILE_ATTRIBUTE_NORMAL
FILE_ATTRIBUTE_TEMPORARY
FILE_ATTRIBUTE_SPARSE_FILE
FILE_ATTRIBUTE_REPARSE_POINT
FILE_ATTRIBUTE_COMPRESSED
FILE_ATTRIBUTE_OFFLINE
FILE_ATTRIBUTE_NOT_CONTENT_INDEXED
FILE_ATTRIBUTE_ENCRYPTED
```

Remarks

None.

FileAttributeTagInformation

```
typedef struct _FILE_ATTRIBUTE_TAG_INFORMATION {// Information Class 35
    ULONG FileAttributes;
    ULONG ReparseTag;
} FILE_ATTRIBUTE_TAG_INFORMATION, *PFILE_ATTRIBUTE_TAG_INFORMATION;
```

Members

FileAttributes

The attributes of the file. Defined attributes include:

```
FILE_ATTRIBUTE_READONLY
FILE_ATTRIBUTE_HIDDEN
FILE_ATTRIBUTE_SYSTEM
FILE_ATTRIBUTE_DIRECTORY
FILE_ATTRIBUTE_ARCHIVE
FILE_ATTRIBUTE_DEVICE
FILE_ATTRIBUTE_NORMAL
FILE_ATTRIBUTE_TEMPORARY
FILE_ATTRIBUTE_SPARSE_FILE
FILE_ATTRIBUTE_REPARSE_POINT
FILE_ATTRIBUTE_COMPRESSED
FILE_ATTRIBUTE_OFFLINE
FILE_ATTRIBUTE_NOT_CONTENT_INDEXED
FILE_ATTRIBUTE_ENCRYPTED
```

ReparseTag

The reparse tag, if any, of the file. The format of reparse tags is defined in winnt.h.

Remarks

None.

Example 13.1: Opening a File by File Identifier

```
#include "ntdll.h"

int main(int argc, char *argv[])
{
    HANDLE hFile1 = CreateFile(argv[1], GENERIC_READ, FILE_SHARE_READ, 0,
                        OPEN_EXISTING, FILE_ATTRIBUTE_NORMAL, 0);
```

```
NT::IO_STATUS_BLOCK iosb;
NT::FILE_INTERNAL_INFORMATION fii;

NT::ZwQueryInformationFile(hFile1, &iosb, &fii, sizeof fii,
                           NT::FileInternalInformation);

NT::UNICODE_STRING name = {sizeof fii.FileId, sizeof fii.FileId,
                           PWSTR(&fii.FileId)};
NT::OBJECT_ATTRIBUTES oa = {sizeof oa, hFile1, &name};
HANDLE hFile2;


NT::ZwOpenFile(&hFile2, GENERIC_READ | SYNCHRONIZE, &oa, &iosb,
               FILE_SHARE_READ,
               FILE_SYNCHRONOUS_IO_NONALERT | FILE_OPEN_BY_FILE_ID);

CloseHandle(hFile1);

CHAR buf[400]; ULONG n;

ReadFile(hFile2, buf, sizeof buf, &n, 0);
WriteFile(GetStdHandle(STD_OUTPUT_HANDLE), buf, n, &n, 0);

CloseHandle(hFile2);

return 0;
}
```

When opening a file by file identifier, the `ObjectName` member of the
`ObjectAttributes` parameter to **ZwCreateFile** points to the file identifier, and the
`RootDirectory` member contains a handle that is used to identify the volume. This
handle can either be a handle to the volume or to any file on the volume. Not all file
systems support `FILE_OPEN_BY_FILE_ID`, but NTFS does.

14

Registry Keys

The system services described in this chapter create and manipulate registry key objects.

Key handles to registry keys on remote systems are implemented entirely in user mode and are not valid handles for the system services described in this chapter.

ZwCreateKey

ZwCreateKey creates or opens a registry key object.

```
NTSYSAPI
NTSTATUS
NTAPI
ZwCreateKey(
    OUT PHANDLE KeyHandle,
    IN ACCESS_MASK DesiredAccess,
    IN POBJECT_ATTRIBUTES ObjectAttributes,
    IN ULONG TitleIndex,
    IN PUNICODE_STRING Class OPTIONAL,
    IN ULONG CreateOptions,
    OUT PULONG Disposition OPTIONAL
    );
```

Parameters

KeyHandle
Points to a variable that will receive the key object handle if the call is successful.

DesiredAccess
Specifies the type of access that the caller requires to the key object. This parameter can be zero, or any combination of the following flags:

KEY_QUERY_VALUE	Values of key can be queried
KEY_SET_VALUE	Values of key can be set
KEY_CREATE_SUB_KEY	Subkeys can be created in the key
KEY_ENUMERATE_SUB_KEYS	Subkeys of key can be enumerated
KEY_NOTIFY	Key can be monitored
KEY_CREATE_LINK	Not used
KEY_ALL_ACCESS	All of the preceding + STANDARD_RIGHTS_REQUIRED

ObjectAttributes

> Points to a structure that specifies the object's attributes. OBJ_PERMANENT and OBJ_EXCLUSIVE are not valid attributes for a key object.

TitleIndex

> Not used.

Class

> Optionally points to a string that will be stored in the key.

CreateOptions

> Specifies options that affect the creation of the key. Permitted values are:

```
REG_OPTION_VOLATILE         0x00000001L
REG_OPTION_CREATE_LINK      0x00000002L
REG_OPTION_BACKUP_RESTORE   0x00000004L
REG_OPTION_OPEN_LINK        0x00000008L
```

Disposition

> Optionally points to a variable that receives an indication of whether the key was created or opened. The values returned are:

```
REG_CREATED_NEW_KEY         0x00000001L
REG_OPENED_EXISTING_KEY     0x00000002L
```

Return Value

Returns STATUS_SUCCESS or an error status, such as STATUS_ACCESS_DENIED, STATUS_INVALID_HANDLE, STATUS_OBJECT_TYPE_MISMATCH, STATUS_OBJECT_NAME_NOT_FOUND, STATUS_KEY_DELETED, STATUS_NO_LOG_SPACE, or STATUS_CHILD_MUST_BE_VOLATILE.

Related Win32 Functions

RegCreateKey, RegCreateKeyEx.

Remarks

ZwCreateKey is documented in the DDK.

A registry symbolic link is created by first creating a key with the option REG_OPTION_CREATE_LINK and then using **ZwSetValueKey** with a type of REG_LINK and value name of "SymbolicLinkValue" to point to another key. The link data should not include the zero-terminating character.

A symbolic link can be opened by specifying the attribute OBJ_OPENLINK in ObjectAttributes. REG_OPTION_OPEN_LINK appears to have no effect.

ZwOpenKey

ZwOpenKey opens a registry key object.

NTSYSAPI
NTSTATUS
NTAPI

```
ZwOpenKey(
    OUT PHANDLE KeyHandle,
    IN ACCESS_MASK DesiredAccess,
    IN POBJECT_ATTRIBUTES ObjectAttributes
    );
```

Parameters

KeyHandle
Points to a variable that will receive the key object handle if the call is successful.

DesiredAccess
Specifies the type of access that the caller requires to the key object. This parameter can be zero, or any combination of the following flags:

KEY_QUERY_VALUE	Values of key can be queried
KEY_SET_VALUE	Values of key can be set
KEY_CREATE_SUB_KEY	Subkeys can be created in the key
KEY_ENUMERATE_SUB_KEYS	Subkeys of key can be enumerated
KEY_NOTIFY	Key can be monitored
KEY_CREATE_LINK	Not used
KEY_ALL_ACCESS	All of the preceding + STANDARD_RIGHTS_REQUIRED

ObjectAttributes
Points to a structure that specifies the object's attributes. OBJ_PERMANENT and OBJ_EXCLUSIVE are not valid attributes for a key object.

Return Value

Returns STATUS_SUCCESS or an error status, such as STATUS_ACCESS_DENIED, STATUS_INVALID_HANDLE, STATUS_OBJECT_TYPE_MISMATCH, STATUS_OBJECT_NAME_NOT_FOUND, or STATUS_KEY_DELETED.

Related Win32 Functions

RegOpenKey, RegOpenKeyEx.

Remarks

ZwOpenKey is documented in the DDK.

ZwDeleteKey

ZwDeleteKey deletes a key in the registry.

```
NTSYSAPI
NTSTATUS
NTAPI
ZwDeleteKey(
    IN HANDLE KeyHandle
    );
```

Parameters

KeyHandle
   A handle to a key object. The handle must grant DELETE access.

Return Value

   Returns STATUS_SUCCESS or an error status, such as STATUS_ACCESS_DENIED,
   STATUS_INVALID_HANDLE, or STATUS_CANNOT_DELETE.

Related Win32 Functions

   RegDeleteKey.

Remarks

   ZwDeleteKey is documented in the DDK.

ZwFlushKey

ZwFlushKey flushes changes to a key to disk.

```
NTSYSAPI
NTSTATUS
NTAPI
ZwFlushKey(
    IN HANDLE KeyHandle
    );
```

Parameters

KeyHandle
   A handle to a key object. The handle need not grant any specific access.

Return Value

   Returns STATUS_SUCCESS or an error status, such as STATUS_ACCESS_DENIED,
   STATUS_INVALID_HANDLE, STATUS_KEY_DELETED, or STATUS_REGISTRY_IO_FAILED.

Related Win32 Functions

   RegFlushKey.

Remarks

   ZwFlushKey is documented in the DDK.

ZwSaveKey

ZwSaveKey saves a copy of a key and its subkeys in a file.

```
NTSYSAPI
NTSTATUS
NTAPI
```

```
ZwSaveKey(
    IN HANDLE KeyHandle,
    IN HANDLE FileHandle
    );
```

Parameters

KeyHandle
A handle to a key object. The handle need not grant any specific access.

FileHandle
A handle to the file object in which the key is to be saved. The handle should grant
FILE_GENERIC_WRITE access.

Return Value

Returns STATUS_SUCCESS or an error status, such as STATUS_ACCESS_DENIED,
STATUS_INVALID_HANDLE, STATUS_PRIVILEGE_NOT_HELD, STATUS_REGISTRY_IO_FAILED, or
STATUS_KEY_DELETED.

Related Win32 Functions

RegSaveKey.

Remarks

SeBackupPrivilege is required to save a key.

ZwSaveMergedKeys

ZwSaveMergedKeys merges two keys and their subkeys and saves the result in a file.

```
NTSYSAPI
NTSTATUS
NTAPI
ZwSaveMergedKeys(
    IN HANDLE KeyHandle1,
    IN HANDLE KeyHandle2,
    IN HANDLE FileHandle
    );
```

Parameters

KeyHandle1
A handle to a key object. The handle need not grant any specific access.

KeyHandle2
A handle to a key object. The handle need not grant any specific access.

FileHandle
A handle to the file object in which the key is to be saved. The handle should grant
FILE_GENERIC_WRITE access.

Return Value

Returns STATUS_SUCCESS or an error status, such as STATUS_ACCESS_DENIED, STATUS_INVALID_HANDLE, STATUS_PRIVILEGE_NOT_HELD, STATUS_REGISTRY_IO_FAILED, or STATUS_KEY_DELETED.

Related Win32 Functions

None.

Remarks

SeBackupPrivilege is required to save a key.

The keys identified by KeyHandle1 and KeyHandle2 must be stored in separate hives.

The routine **ZwSaveMergedKeys** is only present in Windows 2000.

ZwRestoreKey

ZwRestoreKey restores a key saved in a file to the registry.

```
NTSYSAPI
NTSTATUS
NTAPI
ZwRestoreKey(
    IN HANDLE KeyHandle,
    IN HANDLE FileHandle,
    IN ULONG Flags
    );
```

Parameters

KeyHandle
A handle to a key object. The handle need not grant any specific access.

FileHandle
A handle to the file object in which the key is to be saved. The handle should grant FILE_GENERIC_READ access.

Flags
Specifies options that affect the restoration of the key. Permitted values are:

```
REG_WHOLE_HIVE_VOLATILE
REG_REFRESH_HIVE
REG_FORCE_RESTORE          // Windows 2000 only
```

Return Value

Returns STATUS_SUCCESS or an error status, such as STATUS_ACCESS_DENIED, STATUS_INVALID_HANDLE, STATUS_PRIVILEGE_NOT_HELD, STATUS_REGISTRY_IO_FAILED, STATUS_CANNOT_DELETE, STATUS_KEY_DELETED, STATUS_INSUFFICIENT_RESOURCES, or STATUS_REGISTRY_CORRUPT.

Related Win32 Functions

RegRestoreKey.

Remarks

SeRestorePrivilege is required to restore a key.

ZwLoadKey

ZwLoadKey mounts a key hive in the registry.

```
NTSYSAPI
NTSTATUS
NTAPI
ZwLoadKey(
    IN POBJECT_ATTRIBUTES KeyObjectAttributes,
    IN POBJECT_ATTRIBUTES FileObjectAttributes
    );
```

Parameters

KeyObjectAttributes
Points to a structure that specifies the key object's attributes. OBJ_PERMANENT and
OBJ_EXCLUSIVE are not valid attributes for a key object.

FileObjectAttributes
Points to a structure that specifies the file object's attributes. OBJ_PERMANENT,
OBJ_EXCLUSIVE and OBJ_OPENLINK are not valid attributes for a file object.

Return Value

Returns STATUS_SUCCESS or an error status, such as STATUS_ACCESS_DENIED,
STATUS_INVALID_HANDLE, STATUS_PRIVILEGE_NOT_HELD, STATUS_REGISTRY_IO_FAILED,
STATUS_INSUFFICIENT_RESOURCES, or STATUS_REGISTRY_CORRUPT.

Related Win32 Functions

RegLoadKey.

Remarks

SeRestorePrivilege is required to load a key.

ZwLoadKey is equivalent to **ZwLoadKey2** with a flags argument of zero.

ZwLoadKey2

ZwLoadKey2 mounts a key hive in the registry.

```
NTSYSAPI
NTSTATUS
NTAPI
```

```
ZwLoadKey2(
    IN POBJECT_ATTRIBUTES KeyObjectAttributes,
    IN POBJECT_ATTRIBUTES FileObjectAttributes
    IN ULONG Flags
    );
```

Parameters

KeyObjectAttributes
> Points to a structure that specifies the key object's attributes. `OBJ_PERMANENT` and `OBJ_EXCLUSIVE` are not valid attributes for a key object.

FileObjectAttributes
> Points to a structure that specifies the file object's attributes. `OBJ_PERMANENT`, `OBJ_EXCLUSIVE`, and `OBJ_OPENLINK` are not valid attributes for a file object.

Flags
> Specifies options that affect the restoration of the key. Permitted values are:
>> `REG_NO_LAZY_FLUSH`

Return Value

> Returns `STATUS_SUCCESS` or an error status, such as `STATUS_ACCESS_DENIED`, `STATUS_INVALID_HANDLE`, `STATUS_PRIVILEGE_NOT_HELD`, `STATUS_REGISTRY_IO_FAILED`, `STATUS_INSUFFICIENT_RESOURCES`, or `STATUS_REGISTRY_CORRUPT`.

Related Win32 Functions

> None.

Remarks

> `SeRestorePrivilege` is required to load a key.

ZwUnloadKey

`ZwUnloadKey` dismounts a key hive in the registry.

```
NTSYSAPI
NTSTATUS
NTAPI
ZwUnloadKey(
    IN POBJECT_ATTRIBUTES KeyObjectAttributes
    );
```

Parameters

KeyObjectAttributes
> Points to a structure that specifies the key object's attributes. `OBJ_PERMANENT` and `OBJ_EXCLUSIVE` are not valid attributes for a key object.

Return Value

Returns STATUS_SUCCESS or an error status, such as STATUS_ACCESS_DENIED, STATUS_INVALID_HANDLE, STATUS_PRIVILEGE_NOT_HELD, or STATUS_REGISTRY_IO_FAILED.

Related Win32 Functions

RegUnloadKey.

Remarks

SeRestorePrivilege is required to unload a key.

ZwQueryOpenSubKeys

ZwQueryOpenSubKeys reports on the number of open keys in a hive.

```
NTSYSAPI
NTSTATUS
NTAPI
ZwQueryOpenSubKeys(
    IN POBJECT_ATTRIBUTES KeyObjectAttributes,
    OUT PULONG NumberOfKeys
    );
```

Parameters

KeyObjectAttributes

Points to a structure that specifies the key object's attributes. OBJ_PERMANENT and OBJ_EXCLUSIVE are not valid attributes for a key object. The key referred to by KeyObjectAttributes must be the root of a hive.

NumberOfKeys

Points to a variable that receives the number of open keys in the hive.

Return Value

Returns STATUS_SUCCESS or an error status, such as STATUS_INVALID_PARAMETER.

Related Win32 Functions

None.

Remarks

The routine **ZwQueryOpenSubKeys** is only present in Windows 2000.

ZwReplaceKey

ZwReplaceKey replaces a mounted key hive with another.

```
NTSYSAPI
NTSTATUS
NTAPI
ZwReplaceKey(
    IN POBJECT_ATTRIBUTES NewFileObjectAttributes,
    IN HANDLE KeyHandle,
    IN POBJECT_ATTRIBUTES OldFileObjectAttributes
    );
```

Parameters

NewFileObjectAttributes
Points to a structure that specifies the file object's attributes. OBJ_PERMANENT,
OBJ_EXCLUSIVE, and OBJ_OPENLINK are not valid attributes for a file object.

KeyHandle
A handle to a key object. The handle need not grant any specific access.

OldFileObjectAttributes
Points to a structure that specifies the file object's attributes. OBJ_PERMANENT,
OBJ_EXCLUSIVE, and OBJ_OPENLINK are not valid attributes for a file object.

Return Value

Returns STATUS_SUCCESS or an error status, such as STATUS_ACCESS_DENIED,
STATUS_INVALID_HANDLE, STATUS_PRIVILEGE_NOT_HELD, STATUS_REGISTRY_IO_FAILED,
STATUS_INSUFFICIENT_RESOURCES, or STATUS_REGISTRY_CORRUPT.

Related Win32 Functions

RegReplaceKey.

Remarks

SeRestorePrivilege is required to replace a key.

ZwSetInformationKey

ZwSetInformationKey sets information affecting a key object.

```
NTSYSAPI
NTSTATUS
NTAPI
ZwSetInformationKey(
    IN HANDLE KeyHandle,
    IN KEY_SET_INFORMATION_CLASS KeyInformationClass,
    IN PVOID KeyInformation,
    IN ULONG KeyInformationLength
    );
```

Parameters

KeyHandle
   A handle to a key object. The handle must grant KEY_SET_VALUE access.

KeyInformationClass
   Specifies the type of key object information to be set. The permitted values are drawn
   from the enumeration KEY_SET_INFORMATION_CLASS, described in the following section.

KeyInformation
   Points to a caller-allocated buffer or variable that receives the key object information
   to be set.

KeyInformationLength
   The size in bytes of KeyInformation, which the caller should set according to the given
   KeyInformationClass.

Return Value

   Returns STATUS_SUCCESS or an error status, such as STATUS_ACCESS_DENIED,
   STATUS_INVALID_HANDLE, STATUS_INVALID_INFO_CLASS, or STATUS_INFO_LENGTH_MISMATCH.

Related Win32 Functions

   None.

Remarks

   None.

KEY_SET_INFORMATION_CLASS

```
typedef enum _KEY_SET_INFORMATION_CLASS {
    KeyLastWriteTimeInformation
} KEY_SET_INFORMATION_CLASS;
```

KeyLastWriteTimeInformation

```
typedef struct _KEY_LAST_WRITE_TIME_INFORMATION {
    LARGE_INTEGER LastWriteTime;
} KEY_LAST_WRITE_TIME_INFORMATION, *PKEY_LAST_WRITE_TIME_INFORMATION;
```

Members

LastWriteTime
   The last time the key or any of its values changed in the standard time format (that is,
   the number of 100-nanosecond intervals since January 1, 1601).

Remarks

   None.

ZwQueryKey

`ZwQueryKey` retrieves information about a key object.

```
NTSYSAPI
NTSTATUS
NTAPI
ZwQueryKey(
    IN HANDLE KeyHandle,
    IN KEY_INFORMATION_CLASS KeyInformationClass,
    OUT PVOID KeyInformation,
    IN ULONG KeyInformationLength,
    OUT PULONG ResultLength
    );
```

Parameters

KeyHandle

A handle to a key object. The handle must grant KEY_QUERY_VALUE access, except when querying KeyNameInformation when no specific access is required.

KeyInformationClass

Specifies the type of key object information to be queried. The permitted values are drawn from the enumeration KEY_INFORMATION_CLASS, described in the following section.

KeyInformation

Points to a caller-allocated buffer or variable that receives the requested key object information.

KeyInformationLength

The size in bytes of KeyInformation, which the caller should set according to the given KeyInformationClass.

ReturnLength

Points to a variable that receives the number of bytes actually returned to KeyInformation if the call was successful.

Return Value

Returns STATUS_SUCCESS or an error status, such as STATUS_ACCESS_DENIED, STATUS_INVALID_HANDLE, STATUS_INVALID_PARAMETER, or STATUS_BUFFER_TOO_SMALL.

Related Win32 Functions

RegQueryInfoKey.

Remarks

`ZwQueryKey` is documented in the DDK.

ZwEnumerateKey

ZwEnumerateKey enumerates the subkeys of a key object.

```
NTSYSAPI
NTSTATUS
NTAPI
ZwEnumerateKey(
    IN HANDLE KeyHandle,
    IN ULONG Index,
    IN KEY_INFORMATION_CLASS KeyInformationClass,
    OUT PVOID KeyInformation,
    IN ULONG KeyInformationLength,
    OUT PULONG ResultLength
    );
```

Parameters

KeyHandle
A handle to a key object. The handle must grant KEY_ENUMERATE_SUB_KEYS access.

Index
Specifies the zero-based index of the subkey for which the information is requested.

KeyInformationClass
Specifies the type of key object information to be queried. The permitted values are drawn from the enumeration KEY_INFORMATION_CLASS, described in the following section.

KeyInformation
Points to a caller-allocated buffer or variable that receives the requested key object information.

KeyInformationLength
The size in bytes of KeyInformation, which the caller should set according to the given KeyInformationClass.

ReturnLength
Points to a variable that receives the number of bytes actually returned to KeyInformation if the call was successful.

Return Value

Returns STATUS_SUCCESS or an error status, such as STATUS_ACCESS_DENIED, STATUS_INVALID_HANDLE, STATUS_INVALID_PARAMETER, STATUS_BUFFER_TOO_SMALL, or STATUS_NO_MORE_ENTRIES.

Related Win32 Functions

RegEnumKey, RegEnumKeyEx.

Remarks

ZwEnumerateKey is documented in the DDK.

KEY_INFORMATION_CLASS

```
typedef enum _KEY_INFORMATION_CLASS {
    KeyBasicInformation,
    KeyNodeInformation,
    KeyFullInformation,
    KeyNameInformation
} KEY_INFORMATION_CLASS;
```

KeyBasicInformation

```
typedef struct _KEY_BASIC_INFORMATION {
    LARGE_INTEGER LastWriteTime;
    ULONG TitleIndex;
    ULONG NameLength;
    WCHAR Name[1];              // Variable length string
} KEY_BASIC_INFORMATION, *PKEY_BASIC_INFORMATION;
```

Members

LastWriteTime

The last time the key or any of its values changed in the standard time format (that is, the number of 100-nanosecond intervals since January 1, 1601).

TitleIndex

Not used.

NameLength

The size in bytes of Name, including the zero-terminating character.

Name

A zero-terminated Unicode string naming the key.

Remarks

KEY_BASIC_INFORMATION is documented in the DDK.

KeyNodeInformation

```
typedef struct _KEY_NODE_INFORMATION {
    LARGE_INTEGER LastWriteTime;
    ULONG TitleIndex;
    ULONG ClassOffset;
    ULONG ClassLength;
    ULONG NameLength;
    WCHAR Name[1];              // Variable length string
    //    Class[1];             // Variable length string not declared
} KEY_NODE_INFORMATION, *PKEY_NODE_INFORMATION;
```

Members

LastWriteTime
   The last time the key or any of its values changed in the standard time format (that is, the number of 100-nanosecond intervals since January 1, 1601).

TitleIndex
   Not used.

ClassOffset
   The offset in bytes from the start of the KEY_NODE_INFORMATION structure to the class name string.

ClassLength
   The size in bytes of Class, including the zero-terminating character.

NameLength
   The size in bytes of Name, including the zero-terminating character.

Name
   A zero-terminated Unicode string naming the key.

Class
   A zero-terminated Unicode string naming the key class.

Remarks

KEY_NODE_INFORMATION is documented in the DDK.

KeyFullInformation

```
typedef struct _KEY_FULL_INFORMATION {
    LARGE_INTEGER LastWriteTime;
    ULONG TitleIndex;
    ULONG ClassOffset;
    ULONG ClassLength;
    ULONG SubKeys;
    ULONG MaxNameLen;
    ULONG MaxClassLen;
    ULONG Values;
    ULONG MaxValueNameLen;
    ULONG MaxValueDataLen;
    WCHAR Class[1];              // Variable length string
} KEY_FULL_INFORMATION, *PKEY_FULL_INFORMATION;
```

Members

LastWriteTime
   The last time the key or any of its values changed in the standard time format (that is, the number of 100-nanosecond intervals since January 1, 1601).

TitleIndex
Not used.

ClassOffset
The offset in bytes from the start of the KEY_NODE_INFORMATION structure to the class name string.

ClassLength
The size in bytes of Class, including the zero-terminating character.

SubKeys
The number of subkeys for the key.

MaxNameLen
The length of the longest subkey name.

MaxClassLen
The length of the longest subkey class name.

Values
The number of value entries for the key.

MaxValueNameLen
The length of the longest value entry name.

MaxValueDataLen
The length of the longest value entry data.

Class
A zero-terminated Unicode string naming the key class.

Remarks

KEY_FULL_INFORMATION is documented in the DDK.

KeyNameInformation

```
typedef struct _KEY_NAME_INFORMATION {
    ULONG NameLength;
    WCHAR Name[1];              // Variable length string
} KEY_NAME_INFORMATION, *PKEY_NAME_INFORMATION;
```

Members

NameLength
The size in bytes of Name, including the zero-terminating character.

Name
A zero-terminated Unicode string naming the key.

Remarks

This information class is only available in Windows 2000.

ZwNotifyChangeKey

ZwNotifyChangeKey monitors a key for changes.

```
NTSYSAPI
NTSTATUS
NTAPI
ZwNotifyChangeKey(
    IN HANDLE KeyHandle,
    IN HANDLE EventHandle OPTIONAL,
    IN PIO_APC_ROUTINE ApcRoutine OPTIONAL,
    IN PVOID ApcContext OPTIONAL,
    OUT PIO_STATUS_BLOCK IoStatusBlock,
    IN ULONG NotifyFilter,
    IN BOOLEAN WatchSubtree,
    IN PVOID Buffer,
    IN ULONG BufferLength,
    IN BOOLEAN Asynchronous
    );
```

Parameters

KeyHandle
  A handle to a key object. The handle must grant KEY_NOTIFY access.

EventHandle
  Optionally specifies a handle to an event object to signal when the operation completes. The handle must grant EVENT_MODIFY_STATE access.

ApcRoutine
  Optionally points to a routine to execute when the operation completes. The signature of the routine is:

```
VOID (NTAPI *PIO_APC_ROUTINE)(PVOID ApcContext,
                              PIO_STATUS_BLOCK IoStatusBlock,
                              ULONG Reserved);
```

ApcContext
  A void pointer that can be used to provide the ApcRoutine with contextual information.

IoStatusBlock
  Points to a caller-allocated buffer or variable that receives the status of the change notification in the member IoStatusBlock.Status.

NotifyFilter

Specifies the types of changes to be monitored. This parameter can be any combination of the following flags:

```
REG_NOTIFY_CHANGE_NAME
REG_NOTIFY_CHANGE_ATTRIBUTES
REG_NOTIFY_CHANGE_LAST_SET
REG_NOTIFY_CHANGE_SECURITY
```

WatchSubtree

Specifies whether changes to all the keys in the subtree below `KeyHandle` should also be monitored.

Buffer

Not used.

BufferLength

Not used. Must be zero.

Asynchronous

Specifies whether `ZwNotifyChangeKey` should return immediately.

Return Value

Returns STATUS_SUCCESS, STATUS_PENDING, STATUS_NOTIFY_CLEANUP, STATUS_NOTIFY_ENUM_DIR, or an error status, such as STATUS_ACCESS_DENIED, STATUS_INVALID_HANDLE, or STATUS_KEY_DELETED.

Related Win32 Functions

RegNotifyChangeKeyValue.

Remarks

None.

ZwNotifyChangeMultipleKeys

`ZwNotifyChangeMultipleKeys` monitors one or two keys for changes.

```
NTSYSAPI
NTSTATUS
NTAPI
ZwNotifyChangeMultipleKeys (
    IN HANDLE KeyHandle,
    IN ULONG Flags,
    IN POBJECT_ATTRIBUTES KeyObjectAttributes,
    IN HANDLE EventHandle OPTIONAL,
    IN PIO_APC_ROUTINE ApcRoutine OPTIONAL,
    IN PVOID ApcContext OPTIONAL,
    OUT PIO_STATUS_BLOCK IoStatusBlock,
    IN ULONG NotifyFilter,
    IN BOOLEAN WatchSubtree,
    IN PVOID Buffer,
    IN ULONG BufferLength,
    IN BOOLEAN Asynchronous
    );
```

Parameters

KeyHandle

A handle to a key object. The handle must grant KEY_NOTIFY access.

Flags

Specifies options that affect the monitoring of the keys. Permitted values are:

```
REG_MONITOR_SINGLE_KEY    0x00
REG_MONITOR_SECOND_KEY    0x01
```

KeyObjectAttributes

Points to a structure that specifies a key object's attributes. OBJ_PERMANENT and OBJ_EXCLUSIVE are not valid attributes for a key object. If Flags specifies REG_MONITOR_SECOND_KEY, the key identified by KeyObjectAttributes is opened for REG_NOTIFY access and is monitored; otherwise KeyObjectAttributes may be a null pointer.

EventHandle

Optionally specifies a handle to an event object to signal when the operation completes. The handle must grant EVENT_MODIFY_STATE access.

ApcRoutine

Optionally points to a routine to execute when the operation completes. The signature of the routine is:

```
VOID (NTAPI *PIO_APC_ROUTINE)(PVOID ApcContext,
                              PIO_STATUS_BLOCK IoStatusBlock,
                              ULONG Reserved);
```

ApcContext

A void pointer that can be used to provide the ApcRoutine with contextual information.

IoStatusBlock

Points to a caller-allocated buffer or variable that receives the change of the notification in the member IoStatusBlock.Status.

NotifyFilter

Specifies the types of changes to be monitored. This parameter can be any combination of the following flags:

```
REG_NOTIFY_CHANGE_NAME
REG_NOTIFY_CHANGE_ATTRIBUTES
REG_NOTIFY_CHANGE_LAST_SET
REG_NOTIFY_CHANGE_SECURITY
```

WatchSubtree

Specifies whether changes to all the keys in the subtree below KeyHandle should also be monitored.

Buffer
Not used.

BufferLength
Not used. Must be zero.

Asynchronous
Specifies whether **ZwNotifyChangeMultipleKeys** should return immediately.

Return Value

Returns STATUS_SUCCESS, STATUS_PENDING, STATUS_NOTIFY_CLEANUP, STATUS_NOTIFY_ENUM_DIR, or an error status, such as STATUS_ACCESS_DENIED, STATUS_INVALID_HANDLE, or STATUS_KEY_DELETED.

Related Win32 Functions

None.

Remarks

The keys identified by KeyHandle and KeyObjectAttributes must be stored in separate hives.

The routine **ZwNotifyChangeMultipleKeys** is only present in Windows 2000.

ZwDeleteValueKey

ZwDeleteValueKey deletes a value from a key.

```
NTSYSAPI
NTSTATUS
NTAPI
ZwDeleteValueKey(
    IN HANDLE KeyHandle,
    IN PUNICODE_STRING ValueName
    );
```

Parameters

KeyHandle
A handle to a key object. The handle must grant KEY_SET_VALUE access.

ValueName
The name of the value to be deleted.

Return Value

Returns STATUS_SUCCESS or an error status, such as STATUS_ACCESS_DENIED, STATUS_INVALID_HANDLE, STATUS_OBJECT_NAME_NOT_FOUND, STATUS_KEY_DELETED, or STATUS_NO_LOG_SPACE.

Related Win32 Functions

RegDeleteValue.

Remarks

None.

ZwSetValueKey

ZwSetValueKey updates or adds a value to a key.

```
NTSYSAPI
NTSTATUS
NTAPI
ZwSetValueKey(
    IN HANDLE KeyHandle,
    IN PUNICODE_STRING ValueName,
    IN ULONG TitleIndex,
    IN ULONG Type,
    IN PVOID Data,
    IN ULONG DataSize
    );
```

Parameters

KeyHandle
  A handle to a key object. The handle must grant KEY_SET_VALUE access.

ValueName
  The name of the value to be set.

TitleIndex
  Not used.

Type
  Specifies the data type of the value to be set. Permitted values are:

```
        REG_NONE
        REG_SZ
        REG_EXPAND_SZ
        REG_BINARY
        REG_DWORD
        REG_DWORD_LITTLE_ENDIAN
        REG_DWORD_BIG_ENDIAN
        REG_LINK
        REG_MULTI_SZ
        REG_RESOURCE_LIST
        REG_FULL_RESOURCE_DESCRIPTOR
        REG_RESOURCE_REQUIREMENTS_LIST
        REG_QWORD
        REG_QWORD_LITTLE_ENDIAN
```

Data
  Points to a caller-allocated buffer or variable that contains the data of the value.

DataSize
The size in bytes of `Data`.

Return Value

Returns STATUS_SUCCESS or an error status, such as STATUS_ACCESS_DENIED, STATUS_INVALID_HANDLE, STATUS_KEY_DELETED, or STATUS_NO_LOG_SPACE.

Related Win32 Functions

RegSetValue, RegSetValueEx.

Remarks

ZwSetValueKey is documented in the DDK.

ZwQueryValueKey

ZwQueryValueKey retrieves information about a key value.

```
NTSYSAPI
NTSTATUS
NTAPI
ZwQueryValueKey(
    IN HANDLE KeyHandle,
    IN PUNICODE_STRING ValueName,
    IN KEY_VALUE_INFORMATION_CLASS KeyValueInformationClass,
    OUT PVOID KeyValueInformation,
    IN ULONG KeyValueInformationLength,
    OUT PULONG ResultLength
    );
```

Parameters

KeyHandle
A handle to a key object. The handle must grant KEY_QUERY_VALUE access.

ValueName
The name of the value to be deleted.

KeyValueInformationClass
Specifies the type of key object value information to be queried. The permitted values are drawn from the enumeration KEY_VALUE_INFORMATION_CLASS, described in the following section.

KeyValueInformation
Points to a caller-allocated buffer or variable that receives the requested key object value information.

KeyValueInformationLength
Specifies the size in bytes of KeyValueInformation, which the caller should set according to the given KeyValueInformationClass.

ReturnLength

Points to a variable that receives the number of bytes actually returned to KeyValueInformation if the call was successful.

Return Value

Returns STATUS_SUCCESS or an error status, such as STATUS_ACCESS_DENIED, STATUS_INVALID_HANDLE, STATUS_OBJECT_NAME_NOT_FOUND, STATUS_KEY_DELETED, or STATUS_BUFFER_TOO_SMALL.

Related Win32 Functions

RegQueryValue, RegQueryValueEx.

Remarks

ZwQueryValueKey is documented in the DDK.

ZwEnumerateValueKey

ZwEnumerateValueKey enumerates the values of a key.

```
NTSYSAPI
NTSTATUS
NTAPI
ZwEnumerateValueKey(
    IN HANDLE KeyHandle,
    IN ULONG Index,
    IN KEY_VALUE_INFORMATION_CLASS KeyValueInformationClass,
    OUT PVOID KeyValueInformation,
    IN ULONG KeyValueInformationLength,
    OUT PULONG ResultLength
    );
```

Parameters

KeyHandle

A handle to a key object. The handle must grant KEY_QUERY_VALUE access.

Index

Specifies the zero-based index of the value for which the information is requested.

KeyValueInformationClass

Specifies the type of key object value information to be queried. The permitted values are drawn from the enumeration KEY_VALUE_INFORMATION_CLASS, described in the following section.

KeyValueInformation

Points to a caller-allocated buffer or variable that receives the requested key object value information.

KeyValueInformationLength

Specifies the size in bytes of KeyValueInformation, which the caller should set according to the given KeyValueInformationClass.

ReturnLength
Points to a variable that receives the number of bytes actually returned to
KeyValueInformation if the call was successful.

Return Value

Returns STATUS_SUCCESS or an error status, such as STATUS_ACCESS_DENIED,
STATUS_INVALID_HANDLE, STATUS_OBJECT_NAME_NOT_FOUND, STATUS_KEY_DELETED,
STATUS_BUFFER_TOO_SMALL, or STATUS_NO_MORE_ENTRIES.

Related Win32 Functions

RegEnumValue.

Remarks

ZwEnumerateValueKey is documented in the DDK.

KEY_VALUE_INFORMATION_CLASS

```
typedef enum _KEY_VALUE_INFORMATION_CLASS {    KeyValueBasicInformation,
    KeyValueFullInformation,
    KeyValuePartialInformation,
    KeyValueFullInformationAlign64
} KEY_VALUE_INFORMATION_CLASS;
```

KeyValueBasicInformation

```
typedef struct _KEY_VALUE_BASIC_INFORMATION {
    ULONG TitleIndex;
    ULONG Type;
    ULONG NameLength;
    WCHAR Name[1];              // Variable length string
} KEY_VALUE_BASIC_INFORMATION, *PKEY_VALUE_BASIC_INFORMATION;
```

Members

TitleIndex
Not used.

Type
The data type of the value. The defined values are:
```
REG_NONE
REG_SZ
REG_EXPAND_SZ
REG_BINARY
REG_DWORD
REG_DWORD_LITTLE_ENDIAN
REG_DWORD_BIG_ENDIAN
REG_LINK
REG_MULTI_SZ
REG_RESOURCE_LIST
REG_FULL_RESOURCE_DESCRIPTOR
REG_RESOURCE_REQUIREMENTS_LIST
```

```
REG_QWORD
REG_QWORD_LITTLE_ENDIAN
```

NameLength
  The size in bytes of Name, including the zero-terminating character.

Name
  A zero-terminated Unicode string naming the value.

Remarks

KEY_VALUE_BASIC_INFORMATION is documented in the DDK.

KeyValueFullInformation and KeyValueFullInformationAlign64

```
typedef struct _KEY_VALUE_FULL_INFORMATION {
    ULONG TitleIndex;
    ULONG Type;
    ULONG DataOffset;
    ULONG DataLength;
    ULONG NameLength;
    WCHAR Name[1];              // Variable length string
    //   Data[1];              // Variable length data not declared
} KEY_VALUE_FULL_INFORMATION, *PKEY_VALUE_FULL_INFORMATION;
```

Members

TitleIndex
  Not used.

Type
  The data type of the value. The defined values are:

```
REG_NONE
REG_SZ
REG_EXPAND_SZ
REG_BINARY
REG_DWORD
REG_DWORD_LITTLE_ENDIAN
REG_DWORD_BIG_ENDIAN
REG_LINK
REG_MULTI_SZ
REG_RESOURCE_LIST
REG_FULL_RESOURCE_DESCRIPTOR
REG_RESOURCE_REQUIREMENTS_LIST
REG_QWORD
REG_QWORD_LITTLE_ENDIAN
```

DataOffset
  The offset in bytes from the start of the KEY_VALUE_FULL_INFORMATION structure to the value's data.

DataLength

The size in bytes of Data.

NameLength

The size in bytes of Name, including the zero-terminating character.

Name

A zero-terminated Unicode string naming the value.

Data

The data of the value.

Remarks

KEY_VALUE_FULL_INFORMATION is documented in the DDK.

KeyValueFullInformationAlign64 is only available in Windows 2000 and ensures that the Data is aligned on a 64-bit boundary.

KeyValuePartialInformation

```
typedef struct _KEY_VALUE_PARTIAL_INFORMATION {
    ULONG TitleIndex;
    ULONG Type;
    ULONG DataLength;
    UCHAR Data[1];                // Variable length data
} KEY_VALUE_PARTIAL_INFORMATION, *PKEY_VALUE_PARTIAL_INFORMATION;
```

Members

TitleIndex

Not used.

Type

The data type of the value. The defined values are:

```
REG_NONE
REG_SZ
REG_EXPAND_SZ
REG_BINARY
REG_DWORD
REG_DWORD_LITTLE_ENDIAN
REG_DWORD_BIG_ENDIAN
REG_LINK
REG_MULTI_SZ
REG_RESOURCE_LIST
REG_FULL_RESOURCE_DESCRIPTOR
REG_RESOURCE_REQUIREMENTS_LIST
REG_QWORD
REG_QWORD_LITTLE_ENDIAN
```

DataLength

The size in bytes of Data.

Data
The data of the value.

Remarks

KEY_VALUE_PARTIAL_INFORMATION is documented in the DDK.

ZwQueryMultipleValueKey

ZwQueryMultipleValueKey retrieves information about multiple key values.

```
NTSYSAPI
NTSTATUS
NTAPI
ZwQueryMultipleValueKey(
    IN HANDLE KeyHandle,
    IN OUT PKEY_VALUE_ENTRY ValueList,
    IN ULONG NumberOfValues,
    OUT PVOID Buffer,
    IN OUT PULONG Length,
    OUT PULONG ReturnLength
    );
```

Parameters

KeyHandle
A handle to a key object. The handle must grant KEY_QUERY_VALUE access.

ValueList
Points to a caller-allocated buffer or variable that contains an array of value names to
be queried and that receives information about the data of the values.

NumberOfValues
The number of elements in the ValueList.

Buffer
Points to a caller-allocated buffer or variable that receives the data of the values.

Length
Points to a variable that specifies the size in bytes of Buffer and that receives the
number of bytes actually returned to Buffer if the call was successful.

ReturnLength
Points to a variable that receives the number of bytes actually returned to Buffer if the
call was successful, or the number of bytes needed to contain the available data if the
call fails with STATUS_BUFFER_TOO_SMALL.

Return Value

Returns STATUS_SUCCESS or an error status, such as STATUS_ACCESS_DENIED,
STATUS_INVALID_HANDLE, STATUS_OBJECT_NAME_NOT_FOUND, STATUS_KEY_DELETED, or
STATUS_BUFFER_TOO_SMALL.

Related Win32 Functions

RegQueryMultipleValues.

Remarks

None.

KEY_VALUE_ENTRY

```
typedef struct _KEY_VALUE_ENTRY {
    PUNICODE_STRING ValueName;
    ULONG DataLength;
    ULONG DataOffset;
    ULONG Type;
} KEY_VALUE_ENTRY, *PKEY_VALUE_ENTRY;
```

Members

ValueName
Specifies the name of the value whose data is to be retrieved.

DataLength
Receives the length in bytes of the data of the value.

DataOffset
Receives the offset in bytes from the start of the Buffer to the value's data.

Type
Receives the data type of the value.

Remarks

None.

ZwInitializeRegistry

ZwInitializeRegistry initializes the registry.

```
NTSYSAPI
NTSTATUS
NTAPI
ZwInitializeRegistry(
    IN BOOLEAN Setup
    );
```

Parameters

Setup
Specifies whether the system was booted for system setup.

Return Value

Returns STATUS_SUCCESS or an error status, such as STATUS_ACCESS_DENIED.

Related Win32 Functions

None.

Remarks

The Session Manager processes (smss.exe) calls **ZwInitializeRegistry** to initialize the registry during system startup. Once the registry has been initialized, subsequent calls to **ZwInitializeRegistry** fail with STATUS_ACCESS_DENIED.

15

Security and Auditing

The system services described in this chapter are used to implement access checks and auditing for private objects.

ZwPrivilegeCheck

ZwPrivilegeCheck checks whether a set of privileges are enabled in a token.

```
NTSYSAPI
NTSTATUS
NTAPI
ZwPrivilegeCheck(
    IN HANDLE TokenHandle,
    IN PPRIVILEGE_SET RequiredPrivileges,
    OUT PBOOLEAN Result
    );
```

Parameters

TokenHandle
A handle to a token object. The handle must grant TOKEN_QUERY access.

RequiredPrivileges
Points to a structure specifying the privileges required.

Result
Points to a variable that receives the result of the privilege check.

Return Value

Returns STATUS_SUCCESS or an error status, such as STATUS_ACCESS_DENIED, STATUS_INVALID_HANDLE, or STATUS_BAD_IMPERSONATION_LEVEL.

Related Win32 Functions

PrivilegeCheck.

Remarks

PrivilegeCheck exposes the full functionality of **ZwPrivilegeCheck**.

ZwPrivilegeObjectAuditAlarm

ZwPrivilegeObjectAuditAlarm generates an audit alarm describing the use of privileges in conjunction with a handle to an object.

```
NTSYSAPI
NTSTATUS
NTAPI
ZwPrivilegeObjectAuditAlarm(
    IN PUNICODE_STRING SubsystemName,
    IN PVOID HandleId,
    IN HANDLE TokenHandle,
    IN ACCESS_MASK DesiredAccess,
    IN PPRIVILEGE_SET Privileges,
    IN BOOLEAN AccessGranted
    );
```

Parameters

SubsystemName

Points to a name identifying the subsystem generating the audit alarm.

HandleId

A value representing the client's handle to the object. If the access is denied, this parameter is ignored.

TokenHandle

A handle to the token object representing the client requesting the operation. The handle must grant TOKEN_QUERY access.

DesiredAccess

Specifies the access requested. This mask must have been mapped by the MapGenericMask or RtlMapGenericMask function to contain no generic access rights.

Privileges

Points to a PRIVILEGE_SET structure that specifies the set of privileges required for the access.

AccessGranted

Points to a variable that receives an indication of whether access was granted or denied.

Return Value

Returns STATUS_SUCCESS or an error status, such as STATUS_ACCESS_DENIED, STATUS_INVALID_HANDLE, STATUS_PRIVILEGE_NOT_HELD, STATUS_BAD_IMPERSONATION_LEVEL, or STATUS_GENERIC_NOT_MAPPED.

Related Win32 Functions

ObjectPrivilegeAuditAlarm.

Remarks

SeAuditPrivilege is required to generate an audit alarm.

ObjectPrivilegeAuditAlarm exposes the full functionality of **ZwPrivilegeObjectAuditAlarm**.

ZwPrivilegedServiceAuditAlarm

ZwPrivilegedServiceAuditAlarm generates an audit alarm describing the use of privileges.

```
NTSYSAPI
NTSTATUS
NTAPI
ZwPrivilegedServiceAuditAlarm(
    IN PUNICODE_STRING SubsystemName,
    IN PUNICODE_STRING ServiceName,
    IN HANDLE TokenHandle,
    IN PPRIVILEGE_SET Privileges,
    IN BOOLEAN AccessGranted
    );
```

Parameters

SubsystemName
Points to a name identifying the subsystem generating the audit alarm.

ServiceName
Points to a string specifying the name of the service to which the client gained access or attempted to gain access.

TokenHandle
A handle to the token object representing the client requesting the operation. The handle must grant TOKEN_QUERY access.

Privileges
Points to a PRIVILEGE_SET structure that specifies the set of privileges required for the access.

AccessGranted
Points to a variable that receives an indication of whether access was granted or denied.

Return Value

Returns STATUS_SUCCESS or an error status, such as STATUS_ACCESS_DENIED, STATUS_INVALID_HANDLE, STATUS_PRIVILEGE_NOT_HELD, or STATUS_BAD_IMPERSONATION_LEVEL.

Related Win32 Functions

PrivilegedServiceAuditAlarm.

Remarks

SeAuditPrivilege is required to generate an audit alarm.

PrivilegedServiceAuditAlarm exposes the full functionality of
ZwPrivilegedServiceAuditAlarm.

ZwAccessCheck

ZwAccessCheck checks whether a security descriptor grants the requested access to an agent represented by a token object.

```
NTSYSAPI
NTSTATUS
NTAPI
ZwAccessCheck(
    IN PSECURITY_DESCRIPTOR SecurityDescriptor,
    IN HANDLE TokenHandle,
    IN ACCESS_MASK DesiredAccess,
    IN PGENERIC_MAPPING GenericMapping,
    IN PPRIVILEGE_SET PrivilegeSet,
    IN PULONG PrivilegeSetLength,
    OUT PACCESS_MASK GrantedAccess,
    OUT PBOOLEAN AccessStatus
    );
```

Parameters

SecurityDescriptor
Points to a SECURITY_DESCRIPTOR structure against which access is checked.

TokenHandle
A handle to the token object representing the client requesting the operation.
The handle must grant TOKEN_QUERY access.

DesiredAccess
Specifies the access mask to be requested. This mask must have been mapped by the MapGenericMask or RtlMapGenericMask function to contain no generic access rights.

GenericMapping
Points to the GENERIC_MAPPING structure associated with the object for which access is being checked.

PrivilegeSet
Points to a PRIVILEGE_SET structure that the function fills with any privileges used to perform the access validation.

PrivilegeSetLength
Specifies the size, in bytes, of PrivilegeSet.

GrantedAccess
Points to a variable that receives the granted access mask.

AccessStatus
Points to a variable that receives the result of the access check.

Return Value

Returns STATUS_SUCCESS or an error status, such as STATUS_ACCESS_DENIED,
STATUS_INVALID_HANDLE, STATUS_BUFFER_TOO_SMALL,
STATUS_NO_IMPERSONATION_TOKEN, STATUS_INVALID_SECURITY_DESCR,
STATUS_BAD_IMPERSONATION_LEVEL, or STATUS_GENERIC_NOT_MAPPED.

Related Win32 Functions

AccessCheck.

Remarks

AccessCheck exposes the full functionality of **ZwAccessCheck**.

ZwAccessCheckAndAuditAlarm

ZwAccessCheckAndAuditAlarm checks whether a security descriptor grants the
requested access to an agent represented by the impersonation token of the current
thread. If the security descriptor has a SACL with ACEs that apply to the agent, any
necessary audit messages are generated.

```
NTSYSAPI
NTSTATUS
NTAPI
ZwAccessCheckAndAuditAlarm(
    IN PUNICODE_STRING SubsystemName,
    IN PVOID HandleId,
    IN PUNICODE_STRING ObjectTypeName,
    IN PUNICODE_STRING ObjectName,
    IN PSECURITY_DESCRIPTOR SecurityDescriptor,
    IN ACCESS_MASK DesiredAccess,
    IN PGENERIC_MAPPING GenericMapping,
    IN BOOLEAN ObjectCreation,
    OUT PACCESS_MASK GrantedAccess,
    OUT PBOOLEAN AccessStatus,
    OUT PBOOLEAN GenerateOnClose
    );
```

Parameters

SubsystemName
Points to a name identifying the subsystem generating the audit alarm.

HandleId
A value representing the client's handle to the object. If the access is denied, this
parameter is ignored.

ObjectTypeName
Points to a string specifying the type of object to which the client is requesting access.

ObjectName
>   Points to a string specifying the name of the object to which the client gained access or attempted to gain access.

SecurityDescriptor
>   Points to the SECURITY_DESCRIPTOR structure for the object being accessed.

DesiredAccess
>   Specifies the access requested. This mask must have been mapped by the MapGenericMask or RtlMapGenericMask function to contain no generic access rights.

GenericMapping
>   Points to the GENERIC_MAPPING structure associated with the object for which access is being checked.

ObjectCreation
>   Specifies whether a new object will be created or an existing object will be opened.

GrantedAccess
>   Points to a variable that receives the access granted.

AccessStatus
>   Points to a variable that receives an indication of whether access was granted or denied.

GenerateOnClose
>   Points to a variable that receives an indication of whether an audit alarm should be generated when the handle is closed.

Return Value

Returns STATUS_SUCCESS or an error status, such as STATUS_PRIVILEGE_NOT_HELD, STATUS_INVALID_SECURITY_DESCR, or STATUS_GENERIC_NOT_MAPPED.

Related Win32 Functions

AccessCheckAndAuditAlarm.

Remarks

SeAuditPrivilege is required to generate an audit alarm.

AccessCheckAndAuditAlarm exposes the full functionality of **ZwAccessCheckAndAuditAlarm**.

ZwAccessCheckByType

ZwAccessCheckByType checks whether a security descriptor grants the requested access to an agent represented by a token object.

```
NTSYSAPI
NTSTATUS
NTAPI
ZwAccessCheckByType(
    IN PSECURITY_DESCRIPTOR SecurityDescriptor,
    IN PSID PrincipalSelfSid,
    IN HANDLE TokenHandle,
    IN ULONG DesiredAccess,
    IN POBJECT_TYPE_LIST ObjectTypeList,
    IN ULONG ObjectTypeListLength,
    IN PGENERIC_MAPPING GenericMapping,
    IN PPRIVILEGE_SET PrivilegeSet,
    IN PULONG PrivilegeSetLength,
    OUT PACCESS_MASK GrantedAccess,
    OUT PULONG AccessStatus
    );
```

Parameters

SecurityDescriptor
 Points to a SECURITY_DESCRIPTOR structure against which access is checked.

PrincipalSelfSid
 Points to a SID that is used to replace any occurrence in SecurityDescriptor of the well-known SID PRINCIPAL_SELF.

TokenHandle
 A handle to the token object representing the client requesting the operation. The handle must grant TOKEN_QUERY access.

DesiredAccess
 Specifies the access mask to be requested. This mask must have been mapped by the MapGenericMask or RtlMapGenericMask function to contain no generic access rights.

ObjectTypeList
 Points to an array of OBJECT_TYPE_LIST structures that identify the hierarchy of object types for which to check access.

ObjectTypeListLength
 The number of elements in the ObjectTypeList array.

GenericMapping
 Points to the GENERIC_MAPPING structure associated with the object for which access is being checked.

PrivilegeSet
 Points to a PRIVILEGE_SET structure that the function fills with any privileges used to perform the access validation.

PrivilegeSetLength
Specifies the size, in bytes, of `PrivilegeSet`.

GrantedAccess
Points to a variable that receives the granted access mask.

AccessStatus
Points to a variable that receives the result of the access check.

Return Value

Returns `STATUS_SUCCESS` or an error status, such as `STATUS_ACCESS_DENIED`, `STATUS_INVALID_HANDLE`, `STATUS_BUFFER_TOO_SMALL`, `STATUS_NO_IMPERSONATION_TOKEN`, `STATUS_INVALID_SECURITY_DESCR`, `STATUS_BAD_IMPERSONATION_LEVEL`, or `STATUS_GENERIC_NOT_MAPPED`.

Related Win32 Functions

`AccessCheckByType`.

Remarks

`AccessCheckByType` exposes the full functionality of **ZwAccessCheckByType**.

The routine **ZwAccessCheckByType** is only present in Windows 2000.

ZwAccessCheckByTypeAndAuditAlarm

ZwAccessCheckByTypeAndAuditAlarm checks whether a security descriptor grants the requested access to an agent represented by the impersonation token of the current thread. If the security descriptor has a SACL with ACEs that apply to the agent, any necessary audit messages are generated.

```
NTSYSAPI
NTSTATUS
NTAPI
ZwAccessCheckByTypeAndAuditAlarm(
    IN PUNICODE_STRING SubsystemName,
    IN PVOID HandleId,
    IN PUNICODE_STRING ObjectTypeName,
    IN PUNICODE_STRING ObjectName,
    IN PSECURITY_DESCRIPTOR SecurityDescriptor,
    IN PSID PrincipalSelfSid,
    IN ACCESS_MASK DesiredAccess,
    IN AUDIT_EVENT_TYPE AuditType,
    IN ULONG Flags,
    IN POBJECT_TYPE_LIST ObjectTypeList,
    IN ULONG ObjectTypeListLength,
    IN PGENERIC_MAPPING GenericMapping,
    IN BOOLEAN ObjectCreation,
    OUT PACCESS_MASK GrantedAccess,
    OUT PULONG AccessStatus,
    OUT PBOOLEAN GenerateOnClose
    );
```

Parameters

SubsystemName
Points to a name identifying the subsystem generating the audit alarm.

HandleId
A value representing the client's handle to the object. If the access is denied, this parameter is ignored.

ObjectTypeName
Points to a string specifying the type of object to which the client is requesting access.

ObjectName
Points to a string specifying the name of the object to which the client gained access or attempted to gain access.

SecurityDescriptor
Points to the SECURITY_DESCRIPTOR structure for the object being accessed.

PrincipalSelfSid
Points to a SID that is used to replace any occurrence in SecurityDescriptor of the well-known SID PRINCIPAL_SELF.

DesiredAccess
Specifies the access requested. This mask must have been mapped by the MapGenericMask or RtlMapGenericMask function to contain no generic access rights.

AuditType
Specifies the type of audit to be generated. Permitted values are drawn from the enumeration AUDIT_EVENT_TYPE.

```
typedef enum _AUDIT_EVENT_TYPE {
    AuditEventObjectAccess,
    AuditEventDirectoryServiceAccess
} AUDIT_EVENT_TYPE, *PAUDIT_EVENT_TYPE;
```

Flags
A bit array of flags that affect the behavior of the routine. The following flags are defined:

```
AUDIT_ALLOW_NO_PRIVILEGE
```

ObjectTypeList
Points to an array of OBJECT_TYPE_LIST structures that identify the hierarchy of object types for which to check access.

ObjectTypeListLength
The number of elements in the ObjectTypeList array.

GenericMapping
Points to the GENERIC_MAPPING structure associated with the object for which access is being checked.

ObjectCreation
Specifies whether a new object will be created or an existing object will be opened.

GrantedAccess
Points to a variable that receives the access granted.

AccessStatus
Points to a variable that receives an indication of whether access was granted or denied.

GenerateOnClose
Points to a variable that receives an indication of whether an audit alarm should be generated when the handle is closed.

Return Value

Returns STATUS_SUCCESS or an error status, such as STATUS_PRIVILEGE_NOT_HELD, STATUS_INVALID_SECURITY_DESCR, or STATUS_GENERIC_NOT_MAPPED.

Related Win32 Functions

AccessCheckByTypeAndAuditAlarm.

Remarks

SeAuditPrivilege is required to generate an audit alarm.

AccessCheckByTypeAndAuditAlarm exposes the full functionality of **ZwAccessCheckByTypeAndAuditAlarm**.

The routine **ZwAccessCheckByTypeAndAuditAlarm** is only present in Windows 2000.

ZwAccessCheckByTypeResultList

ZwAccessCheckByTypeResultList checks whether a security descriptor grants the requested access to an agent represented by a token object.

```
NTSYSAPI
NTSTATUS
NTAPI
ZwAccessCheckByTypeResultList(
    IN PSECURITY_DESCRIPTOR SecurityDescriptor,
    IN PSID PrincipalSelfSid,
    IN HANDLE TokenHandle,
    IN ACCESS_MASK DesiredAccess,
    IN POBJECT_TYPE_LIST ObjectTypeList,
    IN ULONG ObjectTypeListLength,
    IN PGENERIC_MAPPING GenericMapping,
    IN PPRIVILEGE_SET PrivilegeSet,
    IN PULONG PrivilegeSetLength,
```

```
OUT PACCESS_MASK GrantedAccessList,
OUT PULONG AccessStatusList
);
```

Parameters

SecurityDescriptor

Points to a SECURITY_DESCRIPTOR structure against which access is checked.

PrincipalSelfSid

Points to a SID that is used to replace any occurrence in SecurityDescriptor of the well-known SID PRINCIPAL_SELF.

TokenHandle

A handle to the token object representing the client requesting the operation. The handle must grant TOKEN_QUERY access.

DesiredAccess

Specifies the access mask to be requested. This mask must have been mapped by the MapGenericMask or RtlMapGenericMask function to contain no generic access rights.

ObjectTypeList

Points to an array of OBJECT_TYPE_LIST structures that identify the hierarchy of object types for which to check access.

ObjectTypeListLength

The number of elements in the ObjectTypeList array.

GenericMapping

Points to the GENERIC_MAPPING structure associated with the object for which access is being checked.

PrivilegeSet

Points to a PRIVILEGE_SET structure that the function fills with any privileges used to perform the access validation.

PrivilegeSetLength

Specifies the size, in bytes, of PrivilegeSet.

GrantedAccessList

Points to a caller-allocated buffer or variable that receives an array of granted access masks, one per element in the ObjectTypeList.

AccessStatusList

Points to a caller-allocated buffer or variable that receives an array of the results of the access check, one per element in the ObjectTypeList.

Return Value

Returns STATUS_SUCCESS or an error status, such as STATUS_ACCESS_DENIED, STATUS_INVALID_HANDLE, STATUS_BUFFER_TOO_SMALL, STATUS_NO_IMPERSONATION_TOKEN, STATUS_INVALID_SECURITY_DESCR, STATUS_BAD_IMPERSONATION_LEVEL, or STATUS_GENERIC_NOT_MAPPED.

Related Win32 Functions

AccessCheckByTypeResultList.

Remarks

AccessCheckByTypeResultList exposes the full functionality of **ZwAccessCheckByTypeResultList**.

The routine **ZwAccessCheckByTypeResultList** is only present in Windows 2000.

ZwAccessCheckByTypeResultListAndAuditAlarm

ZwAccessCheckByTypeResultListAndAuditAlarm checks whether a security descriptor grants the requested access to an agent represented by the impersonation token of the current thread. If the security descriptor has a SACL with ACEs that apply to the agent, any necessary audit messages are generated.

```
NTSYSAPI
NTSTATUS
NTAPI
ZwAccessCheckByTypeResultListAndAuditAlarm(
    IN PUNICODE_STRING SubsystemName,
    IN PVOID HandleId,
    IN PUNICODE_STRING ObjectTypeName,
    IN PUNICODE_STRING ObjectName,
    IN PSECURITY_DESCRIPTOR SecurityDescriptor,
    IN PSID PrincipalSelfSid,
    IN ACCESS_MASK DesiredAccess,
    IN AUDIT_EVENT_TYPE AuditType,
    IN ULONG Flags,
    IN POBJECT_TYPE_LIST ObjectTypeList,
    IN ULONG ObjectTypeListLength,
    IN PGENERIC_MAPPING GenericMapping,
    IN BOOLEAN ObjectCreation,
    OUT PACCESS_MASK GrantedAccessList,
    OUT PULONG AccessStatusList,
    OUT PULONG GenerateOnClose
    );
```

Parameters

SubsystemName
Points to a name identifying the subsystem generating the audit alarm.

HandleId
A value representing the client's handle to the object. If the access is denied, this parameter is ignored.

ObjectTypeName
Points to a string specifying the type of object to which the client is requesting access.

ObjectName
Points to a string specifying the name of the object to which the client gained access or attempted to gain access.

SecurityDescriptor
Points to the SECURITY_DESCRIPTOR structure for the object being accessed.

PrincipalSelfSid
Points to a SID that is used to replace any occurrence in SecurityDescriptor of the well-known SID PRINCIPAL_SELF.

DesiredAccess
Specifies the access requested. This mask must have been mapped by the MapGenericMask or RtlMapGenericMask function to contain no generic access rights.

AuditType
Specifies the type of audit to be generated. Permitted values are drawn from the enumeration AUDIT_EVENT_TYPE.

```
typedef enum _AUDIT_EVENT_TYPE {
    AuditEventObjectAccess,
    AuditEventDirectoryServiceAccess
} AUDIT_EVENT_TYPE, *PAUDIT_EVENT_TYPE;
```

Flags
A bit array of flags that affect the behavior of the routine. The following flags are defined:

```
AUDIT_ALLOW_NO_PRIVILEGE
```

ObjectTypeList
Points to an array of OBJECT_TYPE_LIST structures that identify the hierarchy of object types for which to check access.

ObjectTypeListLength
The number of elements in the ObjectTypeList array.

GenericMapping
Points to the GENERIC_MAPPING structure associated with the object for which access is being checked.

ObjectCreation
Specifies whether a new object will be created or an existing object will be opened.

GrantedAccessList
Points to a caller-allocated buffer or variable that receives an array of granted access masks, one per element in the ObjectTypeList.

AccessStatusList
Points to a caller-allocated buffer or variable that receives an array of the results of the access check, one per element in the ObjectTypeList.

GenerateOnClose
Points to a variable that receives an indication of whether an audit alarm should be generated when the handle is closed.

Return Value

Returns STATUS_SUCCESS or an error status, such as STATUS_PRIVILEGE_NOT_HELD, STATUS_INVALID_SECURITY_DESCR, or STATUS_GENERIC_NOT_MAPPED.

Related Win32 Functions

AccessCheckByTypeResultListAndAuditAlarm.

Remarks

SeAuditPrivilege is required to generate an audit alarm.

AccessCheckByTypeResultListAndAuditAlarm exposes the full functionality of **ZwAccessCheckByTypeResultListAndAuditAlarm**.

The routine **ZwAccessCheckByTypeResultListAndAuditAlarm** is only present in Windows 2000.

ZwAccessCheckByTypeResultListAndAuditAlarmByHandle

ZwAccessCheckByTypeResultListAndAuditAlarmByHandle checks whether a security descriptor grants the requested access to an agent represented by a token. If the security descriptor has a SACL with ACEs that apply to the agent, any necessary audit messages are generated.

```
NTSYSAPI
NTSTATUS
NTAPI
ZwAccessCheckByTypeResultListAndAuditAlarmByHandle(
    IN PUNICODE_STRING SubsystemName,
    IN PVOID HandleId,
    IN HANDLE TokenHandle,
    IN PUNICODE_STRING ObjectTypeName,
    IN PUNICODE_STRING ObjectName,
    IN PSECURITY_DESCRIPTOR SecurityDescriptor,
    IN PSID PrincipalSelfSid,
    IN ACCESS_MASK DesiredAccess,
    IN AUDIT_EVENT_TYPE AuditType,
    IN ULONG Flags,
    IN POBJECT_TYPE_LIST ObjectTypeList,
    IN ULONG ObjectTypeListLength,
    IN PGENERIC_MAPPING GenericMapping,
    IN BOOLEAN ObjectCreation,
    OUT PACCESS_MASK GrantedAccessList,
    OUT PULONG AccessStatusList,
    OUT PULONG GenerateOnClose
    );
```

Parameters

SubsystemName
Points to a name identifying the subsystem generating the audit alarm.

HandleId
A value representing the client's handle to the object. If the access is denied, this parameter is ignored.

TokenHandle
A handle to a token object representing the client. The handle must grant `TOKEN_QUERY` access.

ObjectTypeName
Points to a string specifying the type of object to which the client is requesting access.

ObjectName
Points to a string specifying the name of the object to which the client gained access or attempted to gain access.

SecurityDescriptor
Points to the `SECURITY_DESCRIPTOR` structure for the object being accessed.

PrincipalSelfSid
Points to a SID that is used to replace any occurrence in `SecurityDescriptor` of the well-known SID `PRINCIPAL_SELF`.

DesiredAccess
Specifies the access requested. This mask must have been mapped by the `MapGenericMask` or `RtlMapGenericMask` function to contain no generic access rights.

AuditType
Specifies the type of audit to be generated. Permitted values are drawn from the enumeration `AUDIT_EVENT_TYPE`.

```
typedef enum _AUDIT_EVENT_TYPE {
    AuditEventObjectAccess,
    AuditEventDirectoryServiceAccess
} AUDIT_EVENT_TYPE, *PAUDIT_EVENT_TYPE;
```

Flags
A bit array of flags that affect the behavior of the routine. The following flags are defined:

```
AUDIT_ALLOW_NO_PRIVILEGE
```

ObjectTypeList
Points to an array of `OBJECT_TYPE_LIST` structures that identify the hierarchy of object types for which to check access.

ObjectTypeListLength
The number of elements in the `ObjectTypeList` array.

GenericMapping
Points to the `GENERIC_MAPPING` structure associated with the object for which access is being checked.

ObjectCreation
Specifies whether a new object will be created or an existing object will be opened.

GrantedAccessList
Points to a caller-allocated buffer or variable that receives an array of granted access masks, one per element in the `ObjectTypeList`.

AccessStatusList
Points to a caller-allocated buffer or variable that receives an array of the results of the access check, one per element in the `ObjectTypeList`.

GenerateOnClose
Points to a variable that receives an indication of whether an audit alarm should be generated when the handle is closed.

Return Value

Returns STATUS_SUCCESS or an error status, such as STATUS_PRIVILEGE_NOT_HELD, STATUS_INVALID_SECURITY_DESCR, or STATUS_GENERIC_NOT_MAPPED.

Related Win32 Functions

AccessCheckByTypeResultListAndAuditAlarmByHandle.

Remarks

SeAuditPrivilege is required to generate an audit alarm.

AccessCheckByTypeResultListAndAuditAlarmByHandle exposes the full functionality of **ZwAccessCheckByTypeResultListAndAuditAlarmByHandle**.

The routine **ZwAccessCheckByTypeResultListAndAuditAlarmByHandle** is only present in Windows 2000.

ZwOpenObjectAuditAlarm

ZwOpenObjectAuditAlarm generates an audit alarm describing the opening of a handle to an object.

```
NTSYSAPI
NTSTATUS
NTAPI
ZwOpenObjectAuditAlarm(
    IN PUNICODE_STRING SubsystemName,
    IN PVOID *HandleId,
    IN PUNICODE_STRING ObjectTypeName,
    IN PUNICODE_STRING ObjectName,
    IN PSECURITY_DESCRIPTOR SecurityDescriptor,
    IN HANDLE TokenHandle,
    IN ACCESS_MASK DesiredAccess,
    IN ACCESS_MASK GrantedAccess,
    IN PPRIVILEGE_SET Privileges OPTIONAL,
    IN BOOLEAN ObjectCreation,
    IN BOOLEAN AccessGranted,
    OUT PBOOLEAN GenerateOnClose
    );
```

Parameters

SubsystemName
    Points to a name identifying the subsystem generating the audit alarm.

HandleId
    Points to a value representing the client's handle to the object. If the access is denied, this parameter is ignored.

ObjectTypeName
    Points to a string specifying the type of object to which the client is requesting access.

ObjectName
    Points to a string specifying the name of the object to which the client gained access or attempted to gain access.

SecurityDescriptor
    Points to the SECURITY_DESCRIPTOR structure for the object being accessed.

TokenHandle
    A handle to the token object representing the client requesting the operation. The handle must grant TOKEN_QUERY access.

DesiredAccess
    Specifies the access requested. This mask must have been mapped by the MapGenericMask or RtlMapGenericMask function to contain no generic access rights.

GrantedAccess
    Specifies the access granted.

Privileges
    Optionally points to a PRIVILEGE_SET structure that specifies the set of privileges required for the access. This parameter can be a null pointer.

ObjectCreation
    Specifies whether a new object was created or an existing object was opened.

AccessGranted
    Specifies whether access was granted or denied.

GenerateOnClose
    Points to a variable that receives an indication of whether an audit alarm should be generated when the handle is closed.

Return Value

Returns STATUS_SUCCESS or an error status, such as STATUS_ACCESS_DENIED, STATUS_INVALID_HANDLE, STATUS_PRIVILEGE_NOT_HELD, STATUS_INVALID_SECURITY_DESCR, STATUS_BAD_IMPERSONATION_LEVEL, or STATUS_GENERIC_NOT_MAPPED.

Related Win32 Functions

ObjectOpenAuditAlarm.

Remarks

SeAuditPrivilege is required to generate an audit alarm.

ObjectOpenAuditAlarm exposes the full functionality of **ZwOpenObjectAuditAlarm**.

ZwCloseObjectAuditAlarm

ZwCloseObjectAuditAlarm generates an audit alarm describing the closing of a handle to an object.

```
NTSYSAPI
NTSTATUS
NTAPI
ZwCloseObjectAuditAlarm(
    IN PUNICODE_STRING SubsystemName,
    IN PVOID HandleId,
    IN BOOLEAN GenerateOnClose
    );
```

Parameters

SubsystemName
Points to a name identifying the subsystem generating the audit alarm.

HandleId
Specifies a value representing the client's handle to the object.

GenerateOnClose
Specifies whether an audit alarm should be generated when the handle is closed.

Return Value

Returns STATUS_SUCCESS or an error status, such as STATUS_PRIVILEGE_NOT_HELD.

Related Win32 Functions

ObjectCloseAuditAlarm.

Remarks

SeAuditPrivilege is required to generate an audit alarm.

ObjectCloseAuditAlarm exposes the full functionality of **ZwCloseObjectAuditAlarm**.

ZwDeleteObjectAuditAlarm

ZwDeleteObjectAuditAlarm generates an audit alarm describing the deletion of an object.

```
NTSYSAPI
NTSTATUS
NTAPI
ZwDeleteObjectAuditAlarm(
    IN PUNICODE_STRING SubsystemName,
    IN PVOID HandleId,
    IN BOOLEAN GenerateOnClose
    );
```

Parameters

SubsystemName
Points to a name identifying the subsystem generating the audit alarm.

HandleId
Specifies a value representing the client's handle to the object.

GenerateOnClose
Specifies whether an audit alarm should be generated when the handle is closed.

Return Value

Returns STATUS_SUCCESS or an error status, such as STATUS_PRIVILEGE_NOT_HELD.

Related Win32 Functions

ObjectDeleteAuditAlarm.

Remarks

SeAuditPrivilege is required to generate an audit alarm.

ObjectDeleteAuditAlarm exposes the full functionality of **ZwDeleteObjectAuditAlarm**.

16

Plug and Play and Power Management

The system services described in this chapter support plug and play and power management.

ZwRequestWakeupLatency

ZwRequestWakeupLatency controls the speed with which the system should be able to enter the working state.

```
NTSYSAPI
NTSTATUS
NTAPI
ZwRequestWakeupLatency(
    IN LATENCY_TIME Latency
    );
```

Parameters

Latency
Specifies the desired latency requirement. The permitted values are drawn from the enumeration LATENCY_TIME:

```
typedef enum {
    LT_DONT_CARE,
    LT_LOWEST_LATENCY
} LATENCY_TIME;
```

Return Value

Returns STATUS_SUCCESS or an error status.

Related Win32 Functions

RequestWakeupLatency.

Remarks

RequestWakeupLatency exposes the full functionality of ZwRequestWakeupLatency.

The routine ZwRequestWakeupLatency is only present in Windows 2000.

ZwRequestDeviceWakeup

ZwRequestDeviceWakeup issues a wakeup request to a device.

```
NTSYSAPI
NTSTATUS
NTAPI
ZwRequestDeviceWakeup(
    IN HANDLE DeviceHandle
    );
```

Parameters

DeviceHandle
A handle to a file object representing a device. The handle need not grant any specific access.

Return Value

Returns STATUS_SUCCESS or an error status, such as STATUS_INVALID_HANDLE or STATUS_NOT_IMPLEMENTED.

Related Win32 Functions

RequestDeviceWakeup.

Remarks

RequestDeviceWakeup exposes the full functionality of **ZwRequestDeviceWakeup**.

The routine **ZwRequestDeviceWakeup** is only present in Windows 2000.

Device wakeup requests are not implemented in early versions of Windows 2000.

ZwCancelDeviceWakeupRequest

ZwCancelDeviceWakeupRequest cancels a previously issued device wakeup request.

```
NTSYSAPI
NTSTATUS
NTAPI
ZwCancelDeviceWakeupRequest(
    IN HANDLE DeviceHandle
    );
```

Parameters

DeviceHandle
A handle to a file object representing a device. The handle need not grant any specific access.

Return Value

Returns STATUS_SUCCESS or an error status, such as STATUS_INVALID_HANDLE or STATUS_NOT_IMPLEMENTED.

Related Win32 Functions

CancelDeviceWakeupRequest.

Remarks

CancelDeviceWakeupRequest exposes the full functionality of **ZwCancelDeviceWakeupRequest**.

The routine **ZwCancelDeviceWakeupRequest** is only present in Windows 2000.

Device wakeup requests are not implemented in early versions of Windows 2000.

ZwIsSystemResumeAutomatic

ZwIsSystemResumeAutomatic reports whether the system was resumed to handle a scheduled event or was resumed in response to user activity.

```
NTSYSAPI
BOOLEAN
NTAPI
ZwIsSystemResumeAutomatic(
    VOID
    );
```

Parameters

None.

Return Value

Returns TRUE or FALSE.

Related Win32 Functions

IsSystemResumeAutomatic.

Remarks

IsSystemResumeAutomatic exposes the full functionality of **ZwIsSystemResumeAutomatic**.

The routine **ZwIsSystemResumeAutomatic** is only present in Windows 2000.

ZwSetThreadExecutionState

`ZwSetThreadExecutionState` sets the execution requirements of the current thread.

```
NTSYSAPI
NTSTATUS
NTAPI
ZwSetThreadExecutionState(
    IN EXECUTION_STATE ExecutionState,
    OUT PEXECUTION_STATE PreviousExecutionState
    );
```

Parameters

ExecutionState

Specifies the execution requirements of the current thread. The permitted values are any combination of the following flags:

```
ES_SYSTEM_REQUIRED
ES_DISPLAY_REQUIRED
ES_CONTINUOUS
```

PreviousExecutionState

Points to a variable that receives the previous execution requirements of the current thread. The value returned is zero or a combination of the following flags:

```
ES_SYSTEM_REQUIRED
ES_DISPLAY_REQUIRED
ES_USER_PRESENT
ES_CONTINUOUS
```

Return Value

Returns STATUS_SUCCESS or an error status.

Related Win32 Functions

SetThreadExecutionState.

Remarks

SetThreadExecutionState exposes the full functionality of **ZwSetThreadExecutionState**.

The routine **ZwSetThreadExecutionState** is only present in Windows 2000.

ZwGetDevicePowerState

`ZwGetDevicePowerState` retrieves the power state of a device.

```
NTSYSAPI
NTSTATUS
NTAPI
ZwGetDevicePowerState(
    IN HANDLE DeviceHandle,
    OUT PDEVICE_POWER_STATE DevicePowerState
    );
```

Parameters

DeviceHandle

A handle to a file object representing a device. The handle need not grant any specific access.

DevicePowerState

Points to a variable that receives the power state of the device. The values are drawn from the enumeration DEVICE_POWER_STATE:

```
typedef enum _DEVICE_POWER_STATE {
    PowerDeviceUnspecified = 0,
    PowerDeviceD0,
    PowerDeviceD1,
    PowerDeviceD2,
    PowerDeviceD3
} DEVICE_POWER_STATE, *PDEVICE_POWER_STATE;
```

Return Value

Returns STATUS_SUCCESS or an error status, such as STATUS_INVALID_HANDLE.

Related Win32 Functions

GetDevicePowerState.

Remarks

GetDevicePowerState exposes most of the functionality of **ZwGetDevicePowerState**.

The routine **ZwGetDevicePowerState** is only present in Windows 2000.

ZwSetSystemPowerState

ZwSetSystemPowerState sets the power state of the system.

```
NTSYSAPI
NTSTATUS
NTAPI
ZwSetSystemPowerState(
    IN POWER_ACTION SystemAction,
    IN SYSTEM_POWER_STATE MinSystemState,
    IN ULONG Flags
    );
```

Parameters

SystemAction

Specifies the power action to perform. The permitted values are drawn from the enumeration POWER_ACTION:

```
typedef enum _POWER_ACTION {
    PowerActionNone,
    PowerActionReserved,
    PowerActionSleep,
    PowerActionHibernate,
    PowerActionShutdown,
```

```
        PowerActionShutdownReset,
        PowerActionShutdownOff
    } POWER_ACTION, *PPOWER_ACTION;
```

MinSystemState

Specifies the minimum power state to enter as a result of performing the action. The permitted values are drawn from the enumeration SYSTEM_POWER_STATE:

```
        typedef enum _SYSTEM_POWER_STATE {
            PowerSystemUnspecified = 0,
            PowerSystemWorking,
            PowerSystemSleeping1,
            PowerSystemSleeping2,
            PowerSystemSleeping3,
            PowerSystemHibernate,
            PowerSystemShutdown
        } SYSTEM_POWER_STATE, *PSYSTEM_POWER_STATE;
```

Flags

Qualifies the SystemAction. Defined values include:

```
        POWER_ACTION_QUERY_ALLOWED
        POWER_ACTION_UI_ALLOWED
        POWER_ACTION_OVERRIDE_APPS
        POWER_ACTION_LOCK_CONSOLE
        POWER_ACTION_DISABLE_WAKES
        POWER_ACTION_CRITICAL
```

Return Value

Returns STATUS_SUCCESS or an error status, such as STATUS_PRIVILEGE_NOT_HELD, STATUS_ALREADY_COMMITTED, or STATUS_CANCELLED.

Related Win32 Functions

None.

Remarks

The routine **ZwSetSystemPowerState** is only present in Windows 2000.

SeShutdownPrivilege is required to set the system power state.

ZwInitiatePowerAction

ZwInitiatePowerAction initiates a power action.

```
NTSYSAPI
NTSTATUS
NTAPI
ZwInitiatePowerAction(
    IN POWER_ACTION SystemAction,
    IN SYSTEM_POWER_STATE MinSystemState,
    IN ULONG Flags,
    IN BOOLEAN Asynchronous
    );
```

Parameters

SystemAction

Specifies the power action to perform. The permitted values are drawn from the enumeration POWER_ACTION:

```
typedef enum _POWER_ACTION {
    PowerActionNone,
    PowerActionReserved,
    PowerActionSleep,
    PowerActionHibernate,
    PowerActionShutdown,
    PowerActionShutdownReset,
    PowerActionShutdownOff
} POWER_ACTION, *PPOWER_ACTION;
```

MinSystemState

Specifies the minimum power state to enter as a result of performing the action. The permitted values are drawn from the enumeration SYSTEM_POWER_STATE:

```
typedef enum _SYSTEM_POWER_STATE {
    PowerSystemUnspecified = 0,
    PowerSystemWorking,
    PowerSystemSleeping1,
    PowerSystemSleeping2,
    PowerSystemSleeping3,
    PowerSystemHibernate,
    PowerSystemShutdown
} SYSTEM_POWER_STATE, *PSYSTEM_POWER_STATE;
```

Flags

Qualifies the SystemAction. Defined values include:

```
POWER_ACTION_QUERY_ALLOWED
POWER_ACTION_UI_ALLOWED
POWER_ACTION_OVERRIDE_APPS
POWER_ACTION_LOCK_CONSOLE
POWER_ACTION_DISABLE_WAKES
POWER_ACTION_CRITICAL
```

Asynchronous

Specifies whether the routine should return immediately.

Return Value

Returns STATUS_SUCCESS or an error status, such as STATUS_PRIVILEGE_NOT_HELD.

Related Win32 Functions

None.

Remarks

The routine **ZwInitiatePowerAction** is only present in Windows 2000.

SeShutdownPrivilege is required to initiate a power action.

ZwPowerInformation

ZwPowerInformation sets or queries power information.

```
NTSYSAPI
NTSTATUS
NTAPI
ZwPowerInformation(
    IN POWER_INFORMATION_LEVEL PowerInformationLevel,
    IN PVOID InputBuffer OPTIONAL,
    IN ULONG InputBufferLength,
    OUT PVOID OutputBuffer OPTIONAL,
    IN ULONG OutputBufferLength
    );
```

Parameters

PowerInformationLevel

The code for the information level to be queried or set. Permitted values are drawn from the enumeration POWER_INFORMATION_LEVEL, described in the following section.

InputBuffer

Points to a caller-allocated buffer or variable that contains the data required to perform the operation. This parameter can be null if the PowerInformationLevel parameter specifies a level that does not require input data.

InputBufferLength

The size in bytes of InputBuffer.

OutputBuffer

Points to a caller-allocated buffer or variable that receives the operation's output data. This parameter can be null if the PowerInformationLevel parameter specifies a level that does not produce output data.

OutputBufferLength

The size in bytes of OutputBuffer.

Return Value

Returns STATUS_SUCCESS or an error status, such as STATUS_PRIVILEGE_NOT_HELD or STATUS_BUFFER_TOO_SMALL.

Related Win32 Functions

None.

Remarks

The routine **ZwPowerInformation** is only present in Windows 2000.

SeCreatePagefilePrivilege is required to set the SystemReserveHiberFile. SeShutdownPrivilege is required to set any other settable information level.

POWER_INFORMATION_LEVEL

```
typedef enum {
    SystemPowerPolicyAc,
    SystemPowerPolicyDc,
    VerifySystemPolicyAc,
    VerifySystemPolicyDc,
    SystemPowerCapabilities,
    SystemBatteryState,
    SystemPowerStateHandler,
    ProcessorStateHandler,
    SystemPowerPolicyCurrent,
    AdministratorPowerPolicy,
    SystemReserveHiberFile,
    ProcessorInformation,
    SystemPowerInformation
} POWER_INFORMATION_LEVEL;
```

SystemPowerPolicyAc, SystemPowerPolicyDc, SystemPowerPolicyCurrent

```
typedef struct _SYSTEM_POWER_POLICY {
    ULONG Revision;
    POWER_ACTION_POLICY PowerButton;
    POWER_ACTION_POLICY SleepButton;
    POWER_ACTION_POLICY LidClose;
    SYSTEM_POWER_STATE LidOpenWake;
    ULONG Reserved1;
    POWER_ACTION_POLICY Idle;
    ULONG IdleTimeout;
    UCHAR IdleSensitivity;
    UCHAR Reserved2[3];
    SYSTEM_POWER_STATE MinSleep;
    SYSTEM_POWER_STATE MaxSleep;
    SYSTEM_POWER_STATE ReducedLatencySleep;
    ULONG WinLogonFlags;
    ULONG Reserved3;
    ULONG DozeS4Timeout;
    ULONG BroadcastCapacityResolution;
    SYSTEM_POWER_LEVEL DischargePolicy[NUM_DISCHARGE_POLICIES];
    ULONG VideoTimeout;
    ULONG VideoReserved[4];
    ULONG SpindownTimeout;
    BOOLEAN OptimizeForPower;
    UCHAR FanThrottleTolerance;
    UCHAR ForcedThrottle;
    UCHAR MinThrottle;
    POWER_ACTION_POLICY OverThrottled;
} SYSTEM_POWER_POLICY, *PSYSTEM_POWER_POLICY;
```

SystemPowerCapabilities

```
typedef struct _SYSTEM_POWER_CAPABILITIES {
    BOOLEAN PowerButtonPresent;
    BOOLEAN SleepButtonPresent;
    BOOLEAN LidPresent;
    BOOLEAN SystemS1;
    BOOLEAN SystemS2;
```

```
        BOOLEAN SystemS3;
        BOOLEAN SystemS4;
        BOOLEAN SystemS5;
        BOOLEAN HiberFilePresent;
        BOOLEAN FullWake;
        UCHAR Reserved1[3];
        BOOLEAN ThermalControl;
        BOOLEAN ProcessorThrottle;
        UCHAR ProcessorMinThrottle;
        UCHAR ProcessorThrottleScale;
        UCHAR Reserved2[4];
        BOOLEAN DiskSpinDown;
        UCHAR Reserved3[8];
        BOOLEAN SystemBatteriesPresent;
        BOOLEAN BatteriesAreShortTerm;
        BATTERY_REPORTING_SCALE BatteryScale[3];
        SYSTEM_POWER_STATE AcOnLineWake;
        SYSTEM_POWER_STATE SoftLidWake;
        SYSTEM_POWER_STATE RtcWake;
        SYSTEM_POWER_STATE MinDeviceWakeState;
        SYSTEM_POWER_STATE DefaultLowLatencyWake;
} SYSTEM_POWER_CAPABILITIES, *PSYSTEM_POWER_CAPABILITIES;
```

SystemBatteryState

```
typedef struct _SYSTEM_BATTERY_STATE {_
    BOOLEAN AcOnLine;
    BOOLEAN BatteryPresent;
    BOOLEAN Charging;
    BOOLEAN Discharging;
    BOOLEAN Reserved[4];
    ULONG MaxCapacity;
    ULONG RemainingCapacity;
    ULONG Rate;
    ULONG EstimatedTime;
    ULONG DefaultAlert1;
    ULONG DefaultAlert2;
} SYSTEM_BATTERY_STATE, *PSYSTEM_BATTERY_STATE;
```

SystemPowerStateHandler

```
typedef struct _POWER_STATE_HANDLER {
    POWER_STATE_HANDLER_TYPE Type;
    BOOLEAN RtcWake;
    UCHAR Reserved[3];
    PENTER_STATE_HANDLER Handler;
    PVOID Context;
} POWER_STATE_HANDLER, *PPOWER_STATE_HANDLER;
```

ProcessorStateHandler

```
typedef struct _PROCESSOR_STATE_HANDLER {
    UCHAR ThrottleScale;
    BOOLEAN ThrottleOnIdle;
    PSET_PROCESSOR_THROTTLE SetThrottle;
```

```
    ULONG NumIdleHandlers;
    PROCESSOR_IDLE_HANDLER_INFO IdleHandler[MAX_IDLE_HANDLERS];
} PROCESSOR_STATE_HANDLER, *PPROCESSOR_STATE_HANDLER;
```

AdministratorPowerPolicy

```
typedef struct _ADMINISTRATOR_POWER_POLICY {
    SYSTEM_POWER_STATE MinSleep;
    SYSTEM_POWER_STATE MaxSleep;
    ULONG MinVideoTimeout;
    ULONG MaxVideoTimeout;
    ULONG MinSpindownTimeout;
    ULONG MaxSpindownTimeout;
} ADMINISTRATOR_POWER_POLICY, *PADMINISTRATOR_POWER_POLICY;
```

ProcessorInformation

```
typedef struct _PROCESSOR_POWER_INFORMATION {
    ULONG Number;
    ULONG MaxMhz;
    ULONG CurrentMhz;
    ULONG MhzLimit;
    ULONG MaxIdleState;
    ULONG CurrentIdleState;
} PROCESSOR_POWER_INFORMATION, *PPROCESSOR_POWER_INFORMATION;
```

SystemPowerInformation

```
typedef struct _SYSTEM_POWER_INFORMATION {
    ULONG MaxIdlenessAllowed;
    ULONG Idleness;
    ULONG TimeRemaining;
    UCHAR CoolingMode;
} SYSTEM_POWER_INFORMATION, *PSYSTEM_POWER_INFORMATION;
```

ZwPlugPlayControl

ZwPlugPlayControl performs a plug and play control operation.

```
NTSYSAPI
NTSTATUS
NTAPI
ZwPlugPlayControl(
    IN ULONG ControlCode,
    IN OUT PVOID Buffer,
    IN ULONG BufferLength
    );
```

Parameters

ControlCode
    The control code for operation to be performed.

Buffer
   Points to a caller-allocated buffer or variable that contains the data required to perform
   the operation and receives the result of the operation.

Length
   The size, in bytes, of the buffer pointed to by Buffer.

Return Value

Returns STATUS_SUCCESS or an error status, such as STATUS_NOT_IMPLEMENTED,
STATUS_PRIVILEGE_NOT_HELD, STATUS_BUFFER_TOO_SMALL, or
STATUS_INVALID_PARAMETER_MIX.

Related Win32 Functions

None.

Remarks

SeTcbPrivilege is required to perform a plug and play control operation.

Windows NT 4.0 has a version of ZwPlugPlayControl that does not require
SeTcbPrivilege and that has an additional (optional) parameter.

ZwGetPlugPlayEvent

ZwGetPlugPlayEvent gets a plug and play event.

```
NTSYSAPI
NTSTATUS
NTAPI
ZwGetPlugPlayEvent(
    IN ULONG Reserved1,
    IN ULONG Reserved2,
    OUT PVOID Buffer,
    IN ULONG BufferLength
    );
```

Parameters

Reserved1
   Not used.

Reserved2
   Not used.

Buffer
   Points to a caller-allocated buffer or variable that receives the plug and play event. The
   information return to the buffer begins with a PLUGPLAY_NOTIFICATION_HEADER structure:

```
typedef struct _PLUGPLAY_NOTIFICATION_HEADER {
    USHORT Version;
    USHORT Size;
    GUID Event;
} PLUGPLAY_NOTIFICATION_HEADER, *PPLUGPLAY_NOTIFICATION_HEADER;
```

BufferLength
    The size in bytes of Buffer.

Return Value

Returns STATUS_SUCCESS or an error status, such as STATUS_PRIVILEGE_NOT_HELD.

Related Win32 Functions

None.

Remarks

SeTcbPrivilege is required to get plug and play events.

17
Miscellany

This chapter describes the system services that do not appear in any other chapter.

ZwRaiseException

ZwRaiseException raises an exception.

```
NTSYSAPI
NTSTATUS
NTAPI
ZwRaiseException(
    IN PEXCEPTION_RECORD ExceptionRecord,
    IN PCONTEXT Context,
    IN BOOLEAN SearchFrames
    );
```

Parameters

ExceptionRecord
> Points to a structure that describes the exception.

Context
> Points to a structure that describes the execution state at the time of the exception.

SearchFrames
> Specifies whether frame-based exception handlers should be given a chance to handle the exception.

Return Value

Returns an error status or does not return at all.

Related Win32 Functions

RaiseException.

Remarks

If any of the pointer arguments are invalid, **ZwRaiseException** returns an error status; otherwise, the subsequent flow of control is dependent on the actions of exception handlers and debuggers.

Exceptions are discussed further in Appendix C, "Exceptions and Debugging."

ZwContinue

ZwContinue resumes execution of a saved execution context.

```
NTSYSAPI
NTSTATUS
NTAPI
ZwContinue(
    IN PCONTEXT Context,
    IN BOOLEAN TestAlert
    );
```

Parameters

Context

Points to a structure describing the execution state that should be restored prior to continuing execution.

TestAlert

Specifies whether **ZwTestAlert** should be called to clear the alerted flag and to allow the delivery of user APCs.

Return Value

Returns an error status or does not return at all.

Related Win32 Functions

None.

Remarks

If any of the pointer arguments are invalid, **ZwContinue** returns an error status; otherwise, execution will continue from the execution context specified by the `Context` argument.

Exceptions are discussed further in Appendix C.

ZwW32Call

ZwW32Call calls one of a predefined set of user mode functions.

```
NTSYSAPI
NTSTATUS
NTAPI
ZwW32Call(
    IN ULONG RoutineIndex,
```

```
IN PVOID Argument,
IN ULONG ArgumentLength,
OUT PVOID *Result OPTIONAL,
OUT PULONG ResultLength OPTIONAL
);
```

Parameters

RoutineIndex
Specifies an index into an array of routines pointed to by a field in the PEB.

Argument
Points to a caller-allocated buffer or variable that contains data to be passed as an argument to the routine. This data will be copied to the user mode stack.

ArgumentLength
The size, in bytes, of the data pointed to by Argument.

Result
Optionally points to a caller-allocated buffer or variable that receives results from the routine.

ResultLength
Optionally points to a variable that specifies the size, in bytes, of the data pointed to by Result and receives the size of the data actually returned.

Return Value

Returns an error status, such as STATUS_NOT_IMPLEMENTED, or the value returned by the called routine.

Related Win32 Functions

None.

Remarks

The calling thread must have initialized its Win32 state; otherwise, ZwW32Call returns STATUS_NOT_IMPLEMENTED.

ZwW32Call is only present in Windows NT 4.0.

If the process is a client of win32k.sys, ZwW32Call saves the current state (on the CallbackStack) and arranges that upon return to user mode; the routine NTDLL!_KiUserCallbackDispatcher@12 will be run with the arguments RoutineIndex, Argument and ArgumentLength. This routine uses the RoutineIndex as an index into a dispatch table stored in the PEB and invokes the callback routine found there with two arguments: Argument and ArgumentLength.

If this routine returns, NTDLL!_KiUserCallbackDispatcher@12 invokes ZwCallbackReturn with a zero length result and whatever NTSTATUS value the callback routine returned. ZwCallbackReturn restores the state from the CallbackStack so that when the system service returns, it will return to its original caller.

Most callback routines do not return, but instead invoke **ZwCallbackReturn** explicitly so that they can return a pointer to a buffer of results to their caller (via Result and ResultLength).

ZwCallbackReturn

ZwCallbackReturn returns from a function called by **ZwW32Call**.

```
NTSYSAPI
NTSTATUS
NTAPI
ZwCallbackReturn(
    IN PVOID Result OPTIONAL,
    IN ULONG ResultLength,
    IN NTSTATUS Status
    );
```

Parameters

Result

Optionally points to a caller-allocated buffer or variable that contains the results to be returned to the caller of **ZwW32Call**.

ResultLength

The size, in bytes, of the data pointed to by Result.

Status

Specifies a status value to be returned to the caller of **ZwW32Call** as the return value.

Return Value

Returns an error status, such as STATUS_NO_CALLBACK_ACTIVE, or does not return at all.

Related Win32 Functions

None.

Remarks

If the process is a client of win32k.sys, **ZwW32Call** saves the current state (on the CallbackStack) and arranges that upon return to user mode the routine. NTDLL!_KiUserCallbackDispatcher@12 will be run with the arguments RoutineIndex, Argument and ArgumentLength. This routine uses the RoutineIndex as an index into a dispatch table stored in the PEB and invokes the callback routine found there with two arguments: Argument and ArgumentLength.

If this routine returns, NTDLL!_KiUserCallbackDispatcher@12 invokes **ZwCallbackReturn** with a zero length result and whatever NTSTATUS value the callback routine returned. **ZwCallbackReturn** restores the state from the CallbackStack so that when the system service returns, it will return to its original caller.

Most callback routines do not return, but instead invoke **ZwCallbackReturn** explicitly so that they can return a pointer to a buffer of results to their caller (via Result and ResultLength).

ZwSetLowWaitHighThread

ZwSetLowWaitHighThread effectively invokes **ZwSetLowWaitHighEventPair** on the event pair of the thread.

```
NTSYSAPI
NTSTATUS
NTAPI
ZwSetLowWaitHighThread(
    VOID
    );
```

Parameters

None.

Return Value

Returns STATUS_SUCCESS or an error status, such as STATUS_NO_EVENT_PAIR.

Related Win32 Functions

None.

Remarks

ZwSetLowWaitHighThread is only present in Windows NT 4.0.

Even in Windows NT 4.0 it is difficult to call **ZwSetLowWaitHighThread** because three of the four entry points purporting to refer to this system service actually invoke a different routine.

NTDLL!**ZwSetLowWaitHighThread**, NTDLL!NtSetLowWaitHighThread and NTOSKRNL!**ZwSetLowWaitHighThread** all execute software interrupt 0x2c (KiSetLowWaitHighThread), which goes through the motions of system service dispatching but always returns STATUS_NO_EVENT_PAIR.

NTOSKRNL!NtSetLowWaitHighThread is equivalent to calling **ZwSetLowWaitHighEventPair** on the event pair previously associated with the current thread via a call to **ZwSetInformationThread**.

ZwSetHighWaitLowThread

ZwSetHighWaitLowThread effectively invokes **ZwSetHighWaitLowEventPair** on the event pair of the thread.

```
NTSYSAPI
NTSTATUS
NTAPI
ZwSetHighWaitLowThread(
    VOID
    );
```

Parameters

None.

Return Value

Returns STATUS_SUCCESS or an error status, such as STATUS_NO_EVENT_PAIR.

Related Win32 Functions

None.

Remarks

ZwSetHighWaitLowThread is only present in Windows NT 4.0.

Even in Windows NT 4.0 it is difficult to call **ZwSetHighWaitLowThread** because three of the four entry points purporting to refer to this system service actually invoke a different routine.

NTDLL!**ZwSetHighWaitLowThread**, NTDLL!NtSetHighWaitLowThread and NTOSKRNL!**ZwSetHighWaitLowThread** all execute software interrupt 0x2b (KiCallbackReturn).

NTOSKRNL!NtSetHighWaitLowThread is equivalent to calling **ZwSetLowWaitHighEventPair** on the event pair previously associated with the current thread via a call to **ZwSetInformationThread**.

ZwLoadDriver

ZwLoadDriver loads a device driver.

```
NTSYSAPI
NTSTATUS
NTAPI
ZwLoadDriver(
    IN PUNICODE_STRING DriverServiceName
    );
```

Parameters

DriverServiceName
Specifies the registry key name where the driver configuration information is stored.

Return Value

Returns STATUS_SUCCESS or an error status, such as STATUS_PRIVILEGE_NOT_HELD, STATUS_CONFLICTING_ADDRESSES, STATUS_INVALID_IMAGE_FORMAT, STATUS_PROCEDURE_NOT_FOUND, STATUS_IMAGE_ALREADY_LOADED, STATUS_IMAGE_CHECKSUM_MISMATCH, STATUS_IMAGE_MP_UP_MISMATCH, STATUS_DRIVER_ORDINAL_NOT_FOUND, STATUS_DRIVER_ENTRYPOINT_NOT_FOUND, STATUS_DRIVER_UNABLE_TO_LOAD, or STATUS_ILL_FORMED_SERVICE_ENTRY.

Related Win32 Functions

None.

Remarks

SeLoadDriverPrivilege is required to load a driver.

The Win32 function StartService directs the Service Control Manager process to execute this function on behalf of the caller.

The Service Control Manager process provides a DriverServiceName of the form "\Registry\Machine\System\CurrentControlSet\Services\Tcpip."

ZwUnloadDriver

ZwUnloadDriver unloads a device driver.

```
NTSYSAPI
NTSTATUS
NTAPI
ZwUnloadDriver(
    IN PUNICODE_STRING DriverServiceName
    );
```

Parameters

DriverServiceName
Specifies the registry key name where the driver configuration information is stored.

Return Value

Returns STATUS_SUCCESS or an error status, such as STATUS_PRIVILEGE_NOT_HELD, STATUS_ILL_FORMED_SERVICE_ENTRY, or STATUS_OBJECT_NAME_NOT_FOUND.

Related Win32 Functions

None.

Remarks

SeLoadDriverPrivilege is required to unload a driver.

The Win32 function ControlService directs the Service Control Manager process to execute this function on behalf of the caller.

The Service Control Manager process provides a DriverServiceName of the form "\Registry\Machine\System\CurrentControlSet\Services\Tcpip."

ZwFlushInstructionCache

`ZwFlushInstructionCache` flushes the instruction cache of a process.

```
NTSYSAPI
NTSTATUS
NTAPI
ZwFlushInstructionCache(
    IN HANDLE ProcessHandle,
    IN PVOID BaseAddress OPTIONAL,
    IN ULONG FlushSize
    );
```

Parameters

ProcessHandle
A handle to a process. The handle must grant `PROCESS_VM_WRITE` access.

BaseAddress
Optionally specifies the base of the region to be flushed.

FlushSize
The size of the region to be flushed if `BaseAddress` is not a null pointer.

Return Value

Returns `STATUS_SUCCESS` or an error status, such as `STATUS_ACCESS_DENIED` or `STATUS_INVALID_HANDLE`.

Related Win32 Functions

`FlushInstructionCache`.

Remarks

None.

ZwFlushWriteBuffer

`ZwFlushWriteBuffer` flushes the write buffer.

```
NTSYSAPI
NTSTATUS
NTAPI
ZwFlushWriteBuffer(
    VOID
    );
```

Parameters

None.

Return Value

Returns `STATUS_SUCCESS`.

Related Win32 Functions

None.

Remarks

ZwFlushWriteBuffer invokes `HAL!_KeFlushWriteBuffer@0` which, in the default HAL, just returns.

ZwQueryDefaultLocale

ZwQueryDefaultLocale retrieves the default locale.

```
NTSYSAPI
NTSTATUS
NTAPI
ZwQueryDefaultLocale(
    IN BOOLEAN ThreadOrSystem,
    OUT PLCID Locale
    );
```

Parameters

ThreadOrSystem
Specifies whether the thread (if true) or system (if false) locale identifier should be queried.

Locale
Points to a variable that receives the locale identifier.

Return Value

Returns STATUS_SUCCESS or an error status.

Related Win32 Functions

None.

Remarks

None.

ZwSetDefaultLocale

ZwSetDefaultLocale sets the default locale.

```
NTSYSAPI
NTSTATUS
NTAPI
ZwSetDefaultLocale(
    IN BOOLEAN ThreadOrSystem,
    IN LCID Locale
    );
```

Parameters

ThreadOrSystem
>   Specifies whether the thread (if true) or system (if false) locale identifier should be set.

Locale
>   The locale identifier.

Return Value

>   Returns STATUS_SUCCESS or an error status.

Related Win32 Functions

>   None.

Remarks

>   None.

ZwQueryDefaultUILanguage

ZwQueryDefaultUILanguage retrieves the default user interface language identifier.

```
NTSYSAPI
NTSTATUS
NTAPI
ZwQueryDefaultUILanguage(
    OUT PLANGID LanguageId
    );
```

Parameters

LanguageId
>   Points to a variable that receives the language identifier.

Return Value

>   Returns STATUS_SUCCESS or an error status.

Related Win32 Functions

>   None.

Remarks

>   The routine **ZwQueryDefaultUILanguage** is only present in Windows 2000.

ZwSetDefaultUILanguage

ZwSetDefaultUILanguage sets the default user interface language identifier.

```
NTSYSAPI
NTSTATUS
NTAPI
ZwSetDefaultUILanguage(
    IN LANGID LanguageId
    );
```

Parameters

LanguageId
The language identifier.

Return Value

Returns STATUS_SUCCESS or an error status.

Related Win32 Functions

None.

Remarks

The routine **ZwSetDefaultUILanguage** is only present in Windows 2000.

ZwQueryInstallUILanguage

ZwQueryInstallUILanguage retrieves the installation user interface language identifier.

```
NTSYSAPI
NTSTATUS
NTAPI
ZwQueryInstallUILanguage(
    OUT PLANGID LanguageId
    );
```

Parameters

LanguageId
Points to a variable that receives the language identifier.

Return Value

Returns STATUS_SUCCESS or an error status.

Related Win32 Functions

None.

Remarks

The routine **ZwQueryInstallUILanguage** is only present in Windows 2000.

ZwAllocateLocallyUniqueId

ZwAllocateLocallyUniqueId allocates a locally unique identifier.

```
NTSYSAPI
NTSTATUS
NTAPI
ZwAllocateLocallyUniqueId(
    OUT PLUID Luid
    );
```

Parameters

Luid
Points to a caller-allocated buffer or variable that receives the locally unique identifier.

Return Value

Returns STATUS_SUCCESS or an error status.

Related Win32 Functions

AllocateLocallyUniqueId.

Remarks

None.

ZwAllocateUuids

ZwAllocateUuids allocates some of the components of a universally unique identifier.

```
NTSYSAPI
NTSTATUS
NTAPI
ZwAllocateUuids(
    OUT PLARGE_INTEGER UuidLastTimeAllocated,
    OUT PULONG UuidDeltaTime,
    OUT PULONG UuidSequenceNumber,
    OUT PUCHAR UuidSeed
    );
```

Parameters

UuidLastTimeAllocated
Points to a variable that receives the time when a Uuid was last allocated.

UuidDeltaTime
Points to a variable that receives the time since a Uuid was last allocated.

UuidSequenceNumber
Points to a variable that receives the Uuid allocation sequence number.

UuidSeed
Points to a variable that receives the six bytes of Uuid seed.

Return Value

Returns STATUS_SUCCESS or an error status.

Related Win32 Functions

UuidCreate.

Remarks

The Windows NT 4.0 version of **ZwAllocateUuids** does not have a UuidSeed parameter.

ZwSetUuidSeed

ZwSetUuidSeed sets the universally unique identifier seed.

```
NTSYSAPI
NTSTATUS
NTAPI
ZwSetUuidSeed(
    IN PUCHAR UuidSeed
    );
```

Parameters

UuidSeed
Points to a caller–allocated buffer or variable that contains six bytes of seed.

Return Value

Returns STATUS_SUCCESS or an error status, such as STATUS_ACCESS_DENIED.

Related Win32 Functions

None.

Remarks

The routine **ZwSetUuidSeed** is only present in Windows 2000.

The UuidSeed is normally the hardware address of a network interface card.

The token of the calling thread must have an AuthenticationId of SYSTEM_LUID.

ZwRaiseHardError

ZwRaiseHardError displays a message box containing an error message.

```
NTSYSAPI
NTSTATUS
NTAPI
ZwRaiseHardError(
    IN NTSTATUS Status,
    IN ULONG NumberOfArguments,
    IN ULONG StringArgumentsMask,
    IN PULONG Arguments,
    IN HARDERROR_RESPONSE_OPTION ResponseOption,
    OUT PHARDERROR_RESPONSE Response
    );
```

Parameters

Status

The error status that is to be raised.

NumberOfArguments

The number of substitution directives in the string associated with the error status.

StringArgumentMask

Specifies which of the substitution directives indicate a string substitution.

Arguments

Points to an array of substitution values; the values are either ULONGs or
PUNICODE_STRINGs.

ResponseOption

Specifies the type of the message box. Permitted values are drawn from the enumeration HARDERROR_RESPONSE_OPTION:

```
typedef enum _HARDERROR_RESPONSE_OPTION {
    OptionAbortRetryIgnore,
    OptionOk,
    OptionOkCancel,
    OptionRetryCancel,
    OptionYesNo,
    OptionYesNoCancel,
    OptionShutdownSystem
} HARDERROR_RESPONSE_OPTION, *PHARDERROR_RESPONSE_OPTION;
```

Response

Points to a variable that receives the result of the user interaction with the message box. Possible values received are drawn from the enumeration HARDERROR_RESPONSE:

```
typedef enum _HARDERROR_RESPONSE {
    ResponseReturnToCaller,
    ResponseNotHandled,
    ResponseAbort,
    ResponseCancel,
    ResponseIgnore,
    ResponseNo,
```

```
        ResponseOk,
        ResponseRetry,
        ResponseYes
    } HARDERROR_RESPONSE, *PHARDERROR_RESPONSE;
```

Return Value

Returns STATUS_SUCCESS or an error status.

Related Win32 Functions

None.

Remarks

SeShutdownPrivilege is required to use the option OptionShutdownSystem.

The information on the number and type of arguments is needed to correctly pack the arguments into a message to be sent to the default hard error port. The recipient of the message uses the Status parameter to select a format string and then inserts the arguments (which should match the directives in the string).

An example of the use of **ZwRaiseHardError** is:

```
    UNICODE_STRING s = {16, 18, L"Recalled"};
    ULONG x, args[] = {0x11111111, 0x22222222, ULONG(&s)};

    ZwRaiseHardError(STATUS_ACCESS_VIOLATION, 3, 4, args, MB_OKCANCEL, &x);
```

ZwSetDefaultHardErrorPort

ZwSetDefaultHardErrorPort sets the default hard error port.

```
NTSYSAPI
NTSTATUS
NTAPI
ZwSetDefaultHardErrorPort(
    IN HANDLE PortHandle
    );
```

Parameters

PortHandle
A handle to a port. The handle need not grant any specific access.

Return Value

Returns STATUS_SUCCESS or an error status, such as STATUS_PRIVILEGE_NOT_HELD.

Related Win32 Functions

None.

Remarks

SeTcbPrivilege is required to set the default hard error port.

ZwSetDefaultHardErrorPort sets the system wide port to which "Hard Error" messages will be sent. Normally csrss creates the hard error port. **ZwRaiseHardError** allows kernel mode components to display a message box and receive a result.

ZwDisplayString

ZwDisplayString displays a string.

```
NTSYSAPI
NTSTATUS
NTAPI
ZwDisplayString(
    IN PUNICODE_STRING String
    );
```

Parameters

String
Specifies a string to be displayed.

Return Value

Returns STATUS_SUCCESS or an error status, such as STATUS_PRIVILEGE_NOT_HELD.

Related Win32 Functions

None.

Remarks

SeTcbPrivilege is required to display a string.

ZwDisplayString only displays the string if the HAL still owns the display (before the display driver takes ownership) or if a crash dump is in progress.

ZwCreatePagingFile

ZwCreatePagingFile creates a paging file.

```
NTSYSAPI
NTSTATUS
NTAPI
ZwCreatePagingFile(
    IN PUNICODE_STRING FileName,
    IN PULARGE_INTEGER InitialSize,
    IN PULARGE_INTEGER MaximumSize,
    IN ULONG Reserved
    );
```

Parameters

FileName
The full path in the native NT format of the paging file to create.

InitialSize
　　The initial size, in bytes, of the paging file.

MaximumSize
　　The maximum size, in bytes, to which the paging file may grow.

Reserved
　　Not used.

Return Value

Returns STATUS_SUCCESS or an error status, such as STATUS_PRIVILEGE_NOT_HELD, STATUS_OBJECT_NAME_INVALID, STATUS_TOO_MANY_PAGING_FILES, or STATUS_FLOPPY_VOLUME.

Related Win32 Functions

None.

Remarks

SeCreatePagefilePrivilege is required to create a paging file.

ZwAddAtom

ZwAddAtom adds an atom to the global atom table.

```
NTSYSAPI
NTSTATUS
NTAPI
ZwAddAtom(
    IN PWSTR String,
    IN ULONG StringLength,
    OUT PUSHORT Atom
    );
```

Parameters

String
　　The string to add to the global atom table.

StringLength
　　The size in bytes of the string pointed to by String.

Atom
　　Points to a variable that receives the atom.

Return Value

Returns STATUS_SUCCESS or an error status, such as STATUS_ACCESS_DENIED or STATUS_OBJECT_NAME_INVALID.

Related Win32 Functions

GlobalAddAtom.

Remarks

The Windows NT 4.0 version of **ZwAddAtom** does not have a StringLength parameter.

ZwFindAtom

ZwFindAtom searches for an atom in the global atom table.

```
NTSYSAPI
NTSTATUS
NTAPI
ZwFindAtom(
    IN PWSTR String,
    IN ULONG StringLength,
    OUT PUSHORT Atom
    );
```

Parameters

String
The string to be searched for in the global atom table.

StringLength
The size in bytes of the string pointed to by String.

Atom
Points to a variable that receives the atom.

Return Value

Returns STATUS_SUCCESS or an error status, such as STATUS_ACCESS_DENIED, STATUS_OBJECT_NAME_INVALID, or STATUS_OBJECT_NAME_NOT_FOUND.

Related Win32 Functions

GlobalFindAtom.

Remarks

The Windows NT 4.0 version of **ZwFindAtom** does not have a StringLength parameter.

ZwDeleteAtom

ZwDeleteAtom deletes an atom from the global atom table.

```
NTSYSAPI
NTSTATUS
NTAPI
ZwDeleteAtom(
    IN USHORT Atom
    );
```

Atom

The atom that is to be deleted.

Return Value

Returns STATUS_SUCCESS or an error status, such as STATUS_ACCESS_DENIED or STATUS_INVALID_HANDLE.

Related Win32 Functions

GlobalDeleteAtom.

Remarks

None.

ZwQueryInformationAtom

ZwQueryInformationAtom retrieves information about an atom in the global atom table.

```
NTSYSAPI
NTSTATUS
NTAPI
ZwQueryInformationAtom(
    IN USHORT Atom,
    IN ATOM_INFORMATION_CLASS AtomInformationClass,
    OUT PVOID AtomInformation,
    IN ULONG AtomInformationLength,
    OUT PULONG ReturnLength OPTIONAL
    );
```

Parameters

Atom

The atom that is to be queried.

AtomInformationClass

Specifies the type of atom information to be queried. The permitted values are drawn from the enumeration ATOM_INFORMATION_CLASS, described in the following section.

AtomInformation

Points to a caller-allocated buffer or variable that receives the requested atom information.

AtomInformationLength

The size in bytes of AtomInformation, which the caller should set according to the given AtomInformationClass.

ReturnLength

Optionally points to a variable that receives the number of bytes actually returned to AtomInformation if the call was successful. If this information is not needed, ReturnLength may be a null pointer.

Return Value

Returns STATUS_SUCCESS or an error status, such as STATUS_ACCESS_DENIED, STATUS_INVALID_HANDLE, STATUS_INVALID_INFO_CLASS, or STATUS_INFO_LENGTH_MISMATCH.

Related Win32 Functions

GlobalGetAtomName.

Remarks

None.

ATOM_INFORMATION_CLASS

```
typedef enum _ATOM_INFORMATION_CLASS {
    AtomBasicInformation,
    AtomListInformation
} ATOM_INFORMATION_CLASS;
```

AtomBasicInformation

```
typedef struct _ATOM_BASIC_INFORMATION {
    USHORT ReferenceCount;
    USHORT Pinned;
    USHORT NameLength;
    WCHAR Name[1];
} ATOM_BASIC_INFORMATION, *PATOM_BASIC_INFORMATION;
```

Members

ReferenceCount
The reference count of the atom.

Pinned
Specifies whether the atom is pinned or not.

NameLength
The size, in bytes, of the atom name.

Name
The name of the atom.

Remarks

None.

AtomListInformation

```
typedef struct _ATOM_LIST_INFORMATION {
    ULONG NumberOfAtoms;
    ATOM Atoms[1];
} ATOM_LIST_INFORMATION, *PATOM_LIST_INFORMATION;
```

Members

NumberOfAtoms
The number of atoms in the global atom table.

Atoms
An array containing all the atoms in the global atom table.

Remarks

None.

ZwSetLdtEntries

ZwSetLdtEntries sets Local Descriptor Table (LDT) entries for a Virtual DOS Machine (VDM).

```
NTSYSAPI
NTSTATUS
NTAPI
ZwSetLdtEntries(
    IN ULONG Selector1,
    IN LDT_ENTRY LdtEntry1,
    IN ULONG Selector2,
    IN LDT_ENTRY LdtEntry2
    );
```

Parameters

Selector1
A local segment descriptor table entry selector.

LdtEntry1
A local segment descriptor table entry.

Selector2
A local segment descriptor table entry selector.

LdtEntry2
A local segment descriptor table entry.

Return Value

Returns STATUS_SUCCESS or an error status, such as STATUS_INVALID_LDT_DESCRIPTOR.

Related Win32 Functions

None.

Remarks

None.

ZwVdmControl

ZwVdmControl performs a control operation on a VDM.

```
NTSYSAPI
NTSTATUS
NTAPI
ZwVdmControl(
    IN ULONG ControlCode,
    IN PVOID ControlData
    );
```

Parameters

ControlCode
The control code for operation to be performed.

ControlData
Pointer to a caller-allocated buffer or variable that contains the data required to perform the operation.

Return Value

Returns STATUS_SUCCESS or an error status.

Related Win32 Functions

None.

Remarks

None.

Unimplemented System Services

The following system services all just return STATUS_NOT_IMPLEMENTED:

```
ZwCreateChannel
ZwListenChannel
ZwOpenChannel
ZwReplyWaitSendChannel
ZwSendWaitReplyChannel
ZwSetContextChannel
```

The following system services are only present in Windows 2000 and just return STATUS_NOT_IMPLEMENTED on the Intel platform:

```
ZwAllocateVirtualMemory64
ZwFreeVirtualMemory64
ZwProtectVirtualMemory64
ZwQueryVirtualMemory64
ZwReadVirtualMemory64
ZwWriteVirtualMemory64
ZwMapViewOfVlmSection
ZwUnmapViewOfVlmSection
ZwReadFile64
ZwWriteFile64
```

A
Calling System Services from Kernel Mode

As was stated in the Introduction, it is in principle possible to call all of the system services from kernel mode code running at IRQL PASSIVE_LEVEL. The documentation of the system services in the previous chapters is valid for kernel mode applications with the minor proviso that statements regarding the need for holding privileges can be ignored. There is, however, a practical difficulty: ntoskrnl.exe does not export all of the necessary entry points.

The following **ZwXxx** system service entry points are exported by ntoskrnl.exe in Windows 2000:

ZwAccessCheckAndAuditAlarm	ZwPowerInformation
ZwAdjustPrivilegesToken	ZwPulseEvent
ZwAlertThread	ZwQueryDefaultLocale
ZwAllocateVirtualMemory	ZwQueryDefaultUILanguage
ZwCancelIoFile	ZwQueryDirectoryFile
ZwCancelTimer	ZwQueryDirectoryObject
ZwClearEvent	ZwQueryEaFile
ZwClose	ZwQueryInformationFile
ZwCloseObjectAuditAlarm	ZwQueryInformationProcess
ZwConnectPort	ZwQueryInformationToken
ZwCreateDirectoryObject	ZwQueryInstallUILanguage
ZwCreateEvent	ZwQueryKey
ZwCreateFile	ZwQueryObject
ZwCreateKey	ZwQuerySection
ZwCreateSection	ZwQuerySecurityObject
ZwCreateSymbolicLinkObject	ZwQuerySymbolicLinkObject
ZwCreateTimer	ZwQuerySystemInformation
ZwDeleteFile	ZwQueryValueKey
ZwDeleteKey	ZwQueryVolumeInformationFile
ZwDeleteValueKey	ZwReadFile
ZwDeviceIoControlFile	ZwReplaceKey
ZwDisplayString	ZwRequestWaitReplyPort
ZwDuplicateObject	ZwResetEvent
ZwDuplicateToken	ZwRestoreKey
ZwEnumerateKey	ZwSaveKey
ZwEnumerateValueKey	ZwSetDefaultLocale
ZwFlushInstructionCache	ZwSetDefaultUILanguage
ZwFlushKey	ZwSetEaFile
ZwFlushVirtualMemory	ZwSetEvent
ZwFreeVirtualMemory	ZwSetInformationFile
ZwFsControlFile	ZwSetInformationObject
ZwInitiatePowerAction	ZwSetInformationProcess
ZwLoadDriver	ZwSetInformationThread
ZwLoadKey	ZwSetSecurityObject

ZwMakeTemporaryObject	ZwSetSystemInformation
ZwMapViewOfSection	ZwSetSystemTime
ZwNotifyChangeKey	ZwSetTimer
ZwOpenDirectoryObject	ZwSetValueKey
ZwOpenEvent	ZwSetVolumeInformationFile
ZwOpenFile	ZwTerminateProcess
ZwOpenKey	ZwUnloadDriver
ZwOpenProcess	ZwUnloadKey
ZwOpenProcessToken	ZwUnmapViewOfSection
ZwOpenSection	ZwWaitForMultipleObjects
ZwOpenSymbolicLinkObject	ZwWaitForSingleObject
ZwOpenThread	ZwWriteFile
ZwOpenThreadToken	ZwYieldExecution
ZwOpenTimer	

The following NtXxx system service entry points are exported by ntoskrnl.exe in Windows 2000:

NtAddAtom	NtQueryEaFile
NtAdjustPrivilegesToken	NtQueryInformationAtom
NtAllocateLocallyUniqueId	NtQueryInformationFile
NtAllocateUuids	NtQueryInformationProcess
NtAllocateVirtualMemory	NtQueryInformationToken
NtClose	NtQueryQuotaInformationFile
NtConnectPort	NtQuerySecurityObject
NtCreateEvent	NtQuerySystemInformation
NtCreateFile	NtQueryVolumeInformationFile
NtCreateSection	NtReadFile
NtDeleteAtom	NtRequestPort
NtDeleteFile	NtRequestWaitReplyPort
NtDeviceIoControlFile	NtSetEaFile
NtDuplicateObject	NtSetEvent
NtDuplicateToken	NtSetInformationFile
NtFindAtom	NtSetInformationProcess
NtFreeVirtualMemory	NtSetInformationThread
NtFsControlFile	NtSetQuotaInformationFile
NtLockFile	NtSetSecurityObject
NtMapViewOfSection	NtSetVolumeInformationFile
NtNotifyChangeDirectoryFile	NtUnlockFile
NtOpenFile	NtVdmControl
NtOpenProcess	NtWaitForSingleObject
NtOpenProcessToken	NtWriteFile
NtQueryDirectoryFile	

If the system service is exported in the ZwXxx form, it can be used straightforwardly by kernel mode code. If the service is only exported in the NtXxx form, the kernel mode code must consider the checks performed on pointers and access to objects, as described in the Introduction.

The following system services are not exported at all:

ZwAcceptConnectPort	ZwQueryInformationThread
ZwAccessCheck	ZwQueryIntervalProfile
ZwAccessCheckByType	ZwQueryIoCompletion
ZwAccessCheckByTypeAndAuditAlarm	ZwQueryMultipleValueKey
ZwAccessCheckByTypeResultList	ZwQueryMutant
ZwAccessCheckByTypeResultListAndAuditAlarm	ZwQueryPerformanceCounter
ZwAdjustGroupsToken	ZwQuerySemaphore
ZwAlertResumeThread	ZwQuerySystemEnvironmentValue
ZwAllocateUserPhysicalPages	ZwQuerySystemTime
ZwAllocateVirtualMemory64	ZwQueryTimer
ZwAreMappedFilesTheSame	ZwQueryTimerResolution
ZwAssignProcessToJobObject	ZwQueryVirtualMemory

ZwCallbackReturn
ZwCancelDeviceWakeupRequest
ZwCompleteConnectPort
ZwContinue
ZwCreateChannel
ZwCreateEventPair
ZwCreateIoCompletion
ZwCreateJobObject
ZwCreateMailslotFile
ZwCreateMutant
ZwCreateNamedPipeFile
ZwCreatePagingFile
ZwCreatePort
ZwCreateProcess
ZwCreateProfile
ZwCreateSemaphore
ZwCreateThread
ZwCreateToken
ZwCreateWaitablePort
ZwDelayExecution
ZwDeleteObjectAuditAlarm
ZwExtendSection
ZwFilterToken
ZwFlushBuffersFile
ZwFlushWriteBuffer
ZwFreeUserPhysicalPages
ZwFreeVirtualMemory64
ZwGetContextThread
ZwGetDevicePowerState
ZwGetPlugPlayEvent
ZwGetTickCount
ZwImpersonateAnonymousToken
ZwImpersonateClientOfPort
ZwImpersonateThread
ZwInitializeRegistry
ZwIsSystemResumeAutomatic
ZwListenChannel
ZwListenPort
ZwLoadKey2
ZwLockVirtualMemory
ZwMapUserPhysicalPages
ZwMapViewOfVlmSection
ZwNotifyChangeMultipleKeys
ZwOpenChannel
ZwOpenEventPair
ZwOpenIoCompletion
ZwOpenJobObject
ZwOpenMutant
ZwOpenObjectAuditAlarm
ZwOpenSemaphore
ZwPlugPlayControl
ZwPrivilegeCheck
ZwPrivilegeObjectAuditAlarm
ZwPrivilegedServiceAuditAlarm
ZwProtectVirtualMemory
ZwProtectVirtualMemory64
ZwQueryAttributesFile
ZwQueryEvent
ZwQueryFullAttributesFile
ZwQueryInformationJobObject
ZwQueryInformationPort

ZwQueryVirtualMemory64
ZwQueueApcThread
ZwRaiseException
ZwRaiseHardError
ZwReadFile64
ZwReadFileScatter
ZwReadRequestData
ZwReadVirtualMemory
ZwReadVirtualMemory64
ZwRegisterThreadTerminatePort
ZwReleaseMutant
ZwReleaseSemaphore
ZwRemoveIoCompletion
ZwReplyPort
ZwReplyWaitReceivePort
ZwReplyWaitReceivePortEx
ZwReplyWaitReplyPort
ZwReplyWaitSendChannel
ZwRequestDeviceWakeup
ZwRequestWakeupLatency
ZwResumeThread
ZwSaveMergedKeys
ZwSecureConnectPort
ZwSendWaitReplyChannel
ZwSetContextChannel
ZwSetContextThread
ZwSetDefaultHardErrorPort
ZwSetHighEventPair
ZwSetHighWaitLowEventPair
ZwSetInformationJobObject
ZwSetInformationKey
ZwSetInformationToken
ZwSetIntervalProfile
ZwSetIoCompletion
ZwSetLdtEntries
ZwSetLowEventPair
ZwSetLowWaitHighEventPair
ZwSetSystemEnvironmentValue
ZwSetSystemPowerState
ZwSetThreadExecutionState
ZwSetTimerResolution
ZwSetUuidSeed
ZwShutdownSystem
ZwSignalAndWaitForSingleObject
ZwStartProfile
ZwStopProfile
ZwSuspendThread
ZwSystemDebugControl
ZwTerminateJobObject
ZwTerminateThread
ZwTestAlert
ZwUnlockVirtualMemory
ZwUnmapViewOfVlmSection
ZwWaitHighEventPair
ZwWaitLowEventPair
ZwWriteFile64
ZwWriteFileGather
ZwWriteRequestData
ZwWriteVirtualMemory
ZwWriteVirtualMemory64

For some system services, there are exported and documented kernel routines with broadly comparable functionality; for example, KeQueryPerformanceCounter could be used in place of **ZwQueryPerformanceCounter**.

The internal format of some objects (events, mutants, semaphores, timers, and files) are defined in ntddk.h, and by combining some exported and documented object manager and kernel routines, it is possible to re-implement some system services. Example A.1 is a re-implementation of NtQueryEvent, stripped of parameter validation.

Example A.1: Re-Implementing NtQueryEvent

```
#include "ntdll.h"

NTSTATUS
NTAPI
MyQueryEvent(
    IN HANDLE EventHandle,
    IN NT::EVENT_INFORMATION_CLASS EventInformationClass,
    OUT PVOID EventInformation,
    IN ULONG EventInformationLength,
    OUT PULONG ResultLength OPTIONAL
    )
{
    if (ResultLength) *ResultLength = 0;

    if (EventInformationClass != NT::EventBasicInformation)
        return STATUS_INVALID_INFO_CLASS;

    if (EventInformationLength != sizeof (NT::EVENT_BASIC_INFORMATION))
        return STATUS_INFO_LENGTH_MISMATCH;

    NT::PKEVENT Event;

    NTSTATUS rv = NT::ObReferenceObjectByHandle(EventHandle,
                                                EVENT_MODIFY_STATE,
                                                *NT::ExEventObjectType,
                                                NT::ExGetPreviousMode(),
                                                (PVOID*)&Event, 0);
    if (NT_SUCCESS(rv)) {
        NT::PEVENT_BASIC_INFORMATION(EventInformation)->EventType
            = NT::EVENT_TYPE(Event->Header.Type);
        NT::PEVENT_BASIC_INFORMATION(EventInformation)->SignalState
            = NT::KeReadStateEvent(Event);

        NT::ObDereferenceObject(Event);

        if (ResultLength) *ResultLength
            = sizeof (NT::EVENT_BASIC_INFORMATION);
    }
    return rv;
}
```

The origin of many common error codes can be seen in Example A.1. ObReferenceObjectByHandle can return the following error status codes: STATUS_INVALID_HANDLE if EventHandle is not a valid handle, STATUS_OBJECT_TYPE_MISMATCH if EventHandle is a valid handle but not a handle to an event object, and STATUS_ACCESS_DENIED if the handle does not grant

EVENT_MODIFY_STATE access and the previous mode is user mode. The parameter validation performed on the pointer PreviousState can result in STATUS_ACCESS_VIOLATION or STATUS_DATATYPE_MISALIGNMENT being returned.

The example also shows that the object manager just wraps simple data structures such as KEVENT to provide services such as naming, ACLs, reference counting, and quotas.

For the remaining inaccessible system services, there is no good solution, but one possible hack is to dynamically link to ntdll.dll, which is mapped into the address space of every process and exports the **ZwXxx** entry point for every system service. The caveat with this technique is that ntdll.dll is mapped copy on write, and so individual processes could modify the ntdll.dll code that implements the **ZwXxx** stubs (but this should not be a problem for threads running in system processes.

Example A.2: Dynamically Binding to ntdll.dll

```
#include "ntdll.h"

PVOID FindNT()
{
    ULONG n;
    NT::ZwQuerySystemInformation(NT::SystemModuleInformation,
                                 &n, 0, &n);
    PULONG q = PULONG(NT::ExAllocatePool(NT::PagedPool, n));
    NT::ZwQuerySystemInformation(NT::SystemModuleInformation,
                                 q, n * sizeof *q, 0);

    NT::PSYSTEM_MODULE_INFORMATION p
        = NT::PSYSTEM_MODULE_INFORMATION(q + 1);
    PVOID ntdll = 0;

    for (ULONG i = 0; i < *q; i++)
        if (_stricmp(p[i].ImageName + p[i].ModuleNameOffset,
                     "ntdll.dll") == 0)
            ntdll = p[i].Base;

    NT::ExFreePool(q);
    return ntdll;
}

PVOID FindFunc(PVOID Base, PCSTR Name)
{
    PIMAGE_DOS_HEADER dos = PIMAGE_DOS_HEADER(Base);
    PIMAGE_NT_HEADERS nt = PIMAGE_NT_HEADERS(PCHAR(Base) + dos->e_lfanew);
    PIMAGE_DATA_DIRECTORY expdir
        = nt->OptionalHeader.DataDirectory + IMAGE_DIRECTORY_ENTRY_EXPORT;

    ULONG size = expdir->Size;
    ULONG addr = expdir->VirtualAddress;

    PIMAGE_EXPORT_DIRECTORY exports
        = PIMAGE_EXPORT_DIRECTORY(PCHAR(Base) + addr);

    PULONG functions = PULONG(PCHAR(Base) + exports->AddressOfFunctions);
    PSHORT ordinals  = PSHORT(PCHAR(Base) + exports->AddressOfNameOrdinals);
    PULONG names     = PULONG(PCHAR(Base) + exports->AddressOfNames);

    PVOID func = 0;
```

```
        for (ULONG i = 0; i < exports->NumberOfNames; i++) {
            ULONG ord = ordinals[i];

            if (functions[ord] < addr || functions[ord] >= addr + size) {
                if (strcmp(PSTR(PCHAR(Base) + names[i]), Name) == 0)
                    func = PCHAR(Base) + functions[ord];
            }
        }

        return func;
    }

VOID Unload(NT::PDRIVER_OBJECT)
{
}

typedef NTSTATUS (NTAPI *NtQueryPerformanceCounter)(PLARGE_INTEGER,
                                                    PLARGE_INTEGER);

extern "C"
NTSTATUS DriverEntry(NT::PDRIVER_OBJECT DriverObject, NT::PUNICODE_STRING)
{
    LARGE_INTEGER Count, Freq;

    NtQueryPerformanceCounter(FindFunc(FindNT(), "ZwQueryPerformanceCounter"))
        (&Count, &Freq);

    NT::DbgPrint("Freq = %lx, Count = %lx\n", Freq.LowPart, Count.LowPart);

    if (DriverObject) DriverObject->DriverUnload = Unload;

    return DriverObject ? STATUS_SUCCESS : STATUS_UNSUCCESSFUL;
}
```

Example A.2 first uses **ZwQuerySystemInformation** to obtain a list of kernel images (which includes ntdll.dll), and it extracts the base address of ntdll.dll from this information. The example then uses knowledge of the format of PE format images to locate the export directory and to search it for the desired entry point.

Example A.2 can be installed as a device driver and started with **ZwLoadDriver** or can be loaded directly by **ZwSetSystemInformation**.

B

Intel Platform-Specific Entry Points to Kernel Mode

On the Intel platform, a change from user mode to kernel mode can be effected either by calling a routine via a "Call Gate" or by using software interrupts.

Windows 2000 does not use call gates, but instead reimplements much of the functionality of call gates in software (such as the copying of parameters), using software interrupts to perform the mode change.

The ability to successfully execute a software interrupt is controlled by the Descriptor Privilege Level (DPL) of the Interrupt Descriptor Table (IDT) entry. Windows 2000 sets the DPLs on the IDT entries such that user mode code is only allowed to execute the following software interrupts:

```
03 : _KiTrap03 (int3)
04 : _KiTrap04 (into)
2A : _KiGetTickCount
2B : _KiCallbackReturn
2C : _KiSetLowWaitHighThread
2D : _KiDebugService
2E : _KiSystemService
```

KiTrap03

KiTrap03 is the handler for the breakpoint exception generated by the instruction int3.

It constructs an EXCEPTION_RECORD and then dispatches the exception. The EXCEPTION_RECORD contains:

```
ExceptionCode = STATUS_BREAKPOINT;
ExceptionFlags = 0;
ExceptionRecord = 0;
ExceptionAddress = Eip;
NumberParameters = 3;
ExceptionParameters[0] = 0;
ExceptionParameters[1] = Ecx;
ExceptionParameters[2] = Edx;
```

The Ecx and Edx registers can be used to convey contextual information to an exception-handling routine.

KiTrap04

KiTrap03 is the handler for the integer overflow exception generated by the instruction into. It dispatches the exception STATUS_INTEGER_OVERFLOW.

KiGetTickCount

KiGetTickCount is a third method of obtaining the number of milliseconds that have elapsed since the system was booted. It is faster than calling **ZwGetTickCount** but slightly slower than reading from the KUSER_SHARED_DATA page.

If KiGetTickCount is invoked from a Virtual DOS Machine, it invokes NtSetLdtEntries instead.

KiCallbackReturn

Invoking KiCallbackReturn is effectively the same as calling **ZwCallbackReturn**.

KiSetLowWaitHighThread

KiSetLowWaitHighThread establishes most of the environment needed to call a system service, but instead of actually calling a service, it just returns STATUS_NO_EVENT_PAIR.

KiDebugService

KiDebugService constructs an EXCEPTION_RECORD and then dispatches the exception. The EXCEPTION_RECORD contains:

```
ExceptionCode = STATUS_BREAKPOINT;
ExceptionFlags = 0;
ExceptionRecord = 0;
ExceptionAddress = Eip;
NumberParameters = 3;
ExceptionParameters[0] = Eax;
ExceptionParameters[1] = Ecx;
ExceptionParameters[2] = Edx;
```

Eax is set to the debug service code drawn from the enumeration DEBUG_SERVICE_CODE.

```
typedef enum _DEBUG_SERVICE_CODE {
    DebugPrint = 1,
    DebugPrompt,
    DebugLoadImageSymbols,
    DebugUnLoadImageSymbols
} DEBUG_SERVICE_CODE;
```

Ecx points to a STRING that contains either a string to print or the name of an image.

Edx contains or points to additional information, such as the base of an image or a prompt reply STRING.

When the kernel debugger is informed of a STATUS_BREAKPOINT exception, it checks ExceptionParameters[0]. If this value is zero, the exception was caused by an int3 instruction; otherwise, the value should be one of the enumerated values in DEBUG_SERVICE_CODE.

If no remote debugger is present, DebugPrint, DebugLoadImageSymbols, and DebugUnLoadImageSymbols exceptions are ignored; DebugPrompt and int3 exceptions are left to be handled by the standard exception-handling mechanisms.

KiSystemService

KiSystemService is the system service dispatcher; it is responsible for dispatching all of the system services described in the previous chapters. KiSystemService expects to find the system service code in the Eax register, and a pointer to the arguments of the system service in the Edx register. It checks that the system service code specifies a valid dispatch descriptor table and a valid entry within the table. If so, the descriptor table specifies both the number of bytes to be copied from the memory pointed to by Edx to the kernel stack and the address of the routine to be called (which will be one of the NtXxx routines).

C

Exceptions and Debugging

Exceptions can occur in both user mode and kernel mode code and can be generated by either the processor (such as "general protection," "divide by zero," or debug exceptions) or by calling **ZwRaiseException**. Almost all exceptions eventually result in the kernel mode routine KiDispatchException being called. This routine is at the heart of the exception-handling and debugging support provided by the system, and its pseudocode appears in Example C.1.

Example C.1: Pseudocode for KiDispatchException

```
enum CHANCE {
    FirstChance,
    LastChance
};

enum EVENT {
    ExceptionEvent,
    DebugEvent
};

VOID KiDispatchException(PEXCEPTION_RECORD Er, ULONG Reserved,
                         PKTRAP_FRAME Tf, MODE PreviousMode,
                         BOOLEAN SearchFrames)
{
    PCR->KeExceptionDispatchCount++;

    CONTEXT Context
        = {CONTEXT_FULL | (PreviousMode == UserMode ? CONTEXT_DEBUG : 0)};

    KeContextFromKframes(Tf, Reserved, &Context);

    if (Er->ExceptionCode == STATUS_BREAKPOINT) Context.Eip—;

    do {
        if (PreviousMode == KernelMode) {
            if (SearchFrames) {
                if (KiDebugRoutine &&
                    KiDebugRoutine(Tf, Reserved, Er, &Context,
                                   PreviousMode, FirstChance) != 0) break;
```

```
                        if (RtlDispatchException(Er, &Context) == 1) break;
                }
                if (KiDebugRoutine &&
                    KiDebugRoutine(Tf, Reserved, Er, &Context,
                                      PreviousMode, LastChance) != 0) break;
        }
        else {
            if (SearchFrames) {
                if (PsGetCurrentProcess()->DebugPort == 0
                      || KdIsThisAKdTrap(Tf, &Context)) {

                    if (KiDebugRoutine &&
                        KiDebugRoutine(Tf, Reserved, Er, &Context,
                                          PreviousMode, FirstChance) != 0) break;
                }
                if (DbgkForwardException(Tf, DebugEvent,
                                            FirstChance) != 0) return;

                if (valid_user_mode_stack_with_enough_space) {

                    // copy EXCEPTION_RECORD and CONTEXT to user mode stack;

                    // push addresses of EXCEPTION_RECORD and CONTEXT
                    // on user mode stack;

                    Tf->Eip = KeUserExceptionDispatcher;

                    return;
                }
            }

            if (DbgkForwardException(Tf, DebugEvent,
                                        LastChance) != 0) return;

            if (DbgkForwardException(Tf, ExceptionEvent,
                                        LastChance) != 0) return;

            ZwTerminateThread(NtCurrentThread(), Er->ExceptionCode);
        }

        KeBugCheckEx(KMODE_EXCEPTION_NOT_HANDLED, Er->ExceptionCode,
                    Er->ExceptionAddress, Er->ExceptionInformation[0],
                    Er->ExceptionInformation[1]);
    } while (false);

    KeContextToKframes(Tf, Reserved, &Context,
                        Context.ContextFlags, PreviousMode);
}
```

KiDebugRoutine is a pointer to a function, and normally takes one of two values, depending on whether the system was booted with kernel mode debugging enabled (for example, /DEBUG was specified in boot.ini).

There are two main paths through KiDispatchException that are selected according to the previous execution mode.

If the previous mode was kernel, the following steps are taken:

- If frame-based exception-handling is allowed (SearchFrames == TRUE), the kernel debugger is given a first chance to handle the exception.

- If the kernel debugger does not handle the exception, RtlDispatchException is invoked to search for and invoke a frame-based exception handler.

- If RtlDispatchException does not find a handler prepared to handle the exception or if SearchFrames is FALSE, the kernel debugger is given a last chance to handle the exception.

- Finally, if the exception has still not been handled, KeBugCheckEx is invoked to shut down the system with the bugcheck code KMODE_EXCEPTION_NOT_HANDLED.

If the previous mode was user, the following steps are taken:

- If frame-based exception-handling is allowed (SearchFrames == TRUE) and if the process is not being debugged by a user mode debugger (DebugPort == 0), the kernel debugger is given a first chance to handle the exception; otherwise, a description of the exception is forwarded to the user mode debugger via the LPC mechanism.

- If the exception is not handled by a debugger and the user mode stack appears to be still valid, the user mode context is adjusted so that upon return to user mode, the function KiUserExceptionDispatcher will be invoked.

- After returning to user mode, KiUserExceptionDispatcher invokes RtlDispatchException to search for a frame-based exception handler.

- If RtlDispatchException does not find a handler prepared to handle the exception, the exception is re-signaled, specifying SearchFrames as FALSE.

- KiDispatchException is entered again and, because SearchFrames is FALSE, the next step is to give a user mode debugger a last chance to handle the exception.

- If the debugger (if any) still does not handle the exception, a description of the exception is forwarded to the exception port (if any) of the process.

- The recipient (if any) of the message to the exception port can still handle the exception, but if it does not, **ZwTerminateThread** is called to terminate the current thread.

- If **ZwTerminateThread** fails for any reason, KeBugCheckEx is invoked to shut down the system with the bugcheck code KMODE_EXCEPTION_NOT_HANDLED.

Example C.2: Pseudocode for KiUserExceptionDispatcher

```
VOID KiUserExceptionDispatcher(PEXCEPTION_RECORD ExceptionRecord, PCONTEXT Context)
{
    NTSTATUS rv = RtlDispatchException(ExceptionRecord, Context) == 1
        ? ZwContinue(Context, FALSE)
        : ZwRaiseException(ExceptionRecord, Context, FALSE);
```

```
                 EXCEPTION_RECORD NestedExceptionRecord
                    = {rv, EXCEPTION_NONCONTINUABLE, ExceptionRecord};

                 RtlRaiseException(&NestedExceptionRecord);
             }
```

Example C.2 shows how KiUserExceptionDispatcher uses the two system services, **ZwContinue** and **ZwRaiseException.** As mentioned previously, KiUserExceptionDispatcher first calls RtlDispatchException to find and invoke a frame-based exception handler. An exception handler can modify the Context structure (which it accesses by calling GetExceptionInformation). Therefore, if RtlDispatchException finds a handler, upon return from the handler, **ZwContinue** is invoked to modify the execution context of the current thread to make it the one that is specified by the handler. If a handler is not found, **ZwRaiseException** is called to re-signal the exception. If either **ZwContinue** or **ZwRaiseException** return, a nested, noncontinuable exception is raised.

All threads created by Win32 functions have a top-level frame-based exception handler; the behavior of this handler can be influenced by calling the Win32 function SetUnhandledExceptionFilter. This functionality allows a last-chance handler to be defined, which handles the unhandled exceptions of all threads in a process. There is no mechanism defined to provide a first-chance handler (which would have the chance to handle the exceptions of all threads before searching the thread's stack for frame-based handlers), but by knowing how exception dispatching works, it is possible to provide this functionality by patching the binary code of KiUserExceptionDispatcher. (There are resource kit–like utilities that actually do this).

The Kernel Debugger

The principal link between the kernel debugger and the kernel itself are the call-outs to the kernel debugger (KiDebugRoutine) embedded in the kernel routine KiDispatchException. The only other essential link is the check performed by KeUpdateSystemTime for input from a remote debugger (for example, a Ctrl-C break-in); if input is detected, KeUpdateSystemTime generates an exception by calling DbgBreakPointWithStatus, which eventually results in the KiDispatchException kernel debugger call-outs being invoked.

Other kernel components that wish to inform the kernel debugger of some event call DebugService, which ultimately conveys the information to the kernel debugger by raising an exception.

Example C.3: Pseudocode for DebugService

```
typedef enum _DEBUG_SERVICE_CODE {
    DebugPrint = 1,
    DebugPrompt,
    DebugLoadImageSymbols,
    DebugUnLoadImageSymbols
} DEBUG_SERVICE_CODE;

NTSTATUS DebugService(DEBUG_SERVICE_CODE Opcode, PSTRING String, PVOID Data)
{
```

```
NTSTATUS rv;

__asm {
    mov     eax, Opcode
    mov     ecx, String
    mov     edx, Data
    int     0x2D
    int     0x03
    mov     rv, eax
}
return rv;
}
```

As was mentioned in Appendix B, "Intel Platform-Specific Entry Points to Kernel Mode," the instruction "int 0x2D" invokes KiDebugService, which saves the values of selected registers in an EXCEPTION_RECORD structure and then raises a STATUS_BREAK-POINT exception. When KiDispatchException is invoked to handle the exception and KiDebugRoutine is called, the kernel debugger recognizes the exception as coming from KiDebugService (because the EXCEPTION_RECORD member ExceptionParameters[0] is non-zero) and responds accordingly.

Two kernel routines that inform the kernel debugger of events using this mechanism are MmLoadSystemImage and MmUnloadSystemImage. (This is how the kernel debugger learns of the loading and unloading of device drivers).

As was mentioned earlier, KiDebugService is a pointer to a function, and it normally points at one of two routines. If kernel debugging is enabled (by specifying /DEBUG in boot.ini, for example), KiDebugService points to KdpTrap; otherwise, it points to KdpStub.

KdpStub checks whether the exception is a STATUS_BREAKPOINT with a recognized DEBUG_SERVICE_CODE that can be ignored (all except DebugPrompt can be ignored) and, if so, returns the value one to KiDispatchException, indicating that the exception has been handled. KdpStub also does what is necessary to support **ZwSystemDebugControl**.

KdpTrap implements the full kernel debugger functionality and can, if necessary, freeze the operation of the system and interact with a remote debugger via the serial line.

User Mode Debuggers

At five points in the kernel (as described below), a check is made as to whether the current process has a debug port; if it does, then an LPC message is constructed describing the event that has just occurred. All threads (except the current) are frozen and the message is sent to the debug port. When a reply is received, the frozen threads are thawed.

The five points in the kernel at which checks are made are:

- Thread creation routine
- Thread termination routine
- Executable image-mapping routine
- Executable image-unmapping routine
- Exception dispatching routine (KiDispatchException, described earlier)

The message sent to the debug port is a DEBUG_MESSAGE structure, which bears a resemblance to the Win32 DEBUG_EVENT structure.

DEBUG_MESSAGE

```
typedef struct _DEBUG_MESSAGE {
    PORT_MESSAGE PortMessage;
    ULONG EventCode;
    ULONG Status;
    union {
        struct {
            EXCEPTION_RECORD ExceptionRecord;
            ULONG FirstChance;
        } Exception;
        struct {
            ULONG Reserved;
            PVOID StartAddress;
        } CreateThread;
        struct {
            ULONG Reserved;
            HANDLE FileHandle;
            PVOID Base;
            ULONG PointerToSymbolTable;
            ULONG NumberOfSymbols;
            ULONG Reserved2;
            PVOID EntryPoint;
        } CreateProcess;
        struct {
            ULONG ExitCode;
        } ExitThread;
        struct {
            ULONG ExitCode;
        } ExitProcess;
        struct {
            HANDLE FileHandle;
            PVOID Base;
            ULONG PointerToSymbolTable;
            ULONG NumberOfSymbols;
        } LoadDll;
        struct {
            PVOID Base;
        } UnloadDll;
    } u;
} DEBUG_MESSAGE, *PDEBUG_MESSAGE;
```

Some of the messages include handles that are valid in the context of the debuggee. Example C.4 demonstrates how to implement debugger-type functionality by directly receiving and replying to these messages.

Debug Message Routing

The debug port of Win32 processes being debugged is normally the general function port for the Win32 subsystem process (the port named "\Windows\ApiPort") rather than a port created by the debugger itself.

There are routines in ntdll.dll intended for use by environment subsystems to perform the bulk of debug message processing. By default, these routines repackage the message slightly and forward it to the port named "\DbgSsApiPort," but they allow the subsystem to customize their behavior by registering callback functions. The Win32 subsystem process (csrss.exe) does not add any significant functionality to the forwarding process.

The process that listens to the port named "\DbgSsApiPort" is the Session Manager (smss.exe), which acts as a switch and monitor between applications and debuggers. Debuggers register with the Session Manager by connecting to the port named "\DbgUiApiPort."

The Session Manager receives messages from the port named "\DbgSsApiPort," repackages their contents again (duplicating any handles into the debugger) and forwards the message to the debugger.

When the debugger replies to the message specifying the "continue status," the Session Manager forwards the reply to Win32 subsystem process, which forwards it in turn to the debuggee.

Value Added by the Routing Process

When a variant of Example C.4 that uses the Win32 debugging API (rather than the native API) is run, a consequence of the routing of the debug messages through various processes is that the CPU load is roughly evenly divided between the debuggee, the Session Manager, the Win32 subsystem, and the debugger. So it is worthwhile considering the value that each process adds.

The Win32 subsystem process does not add any significant value when debugging a newly created process, but it does provide important functionality in support of the Win32 DebugActiveProcess function. It fabricates process and thread creation debug messages for the existing threads and image-mapping events for the loaded DLLs of the debuggee.

The Session Manager ensures that the debuggee is terminated if the debugger terminates. A debuggee waiting for a debugger to reply to a debug message cannot be terminated, so if the debugger were to terminate and the debuggee were allowed to continue running, the next debug event to occur (as a result of thread creation, DLL loading, or exception) would cause the debuggee to enter a state from which it could not be continued or terminated.

The Session Manager also signals the availability of messages to the debugger by signaling a semaphore; this allows a debugger to timeout a wait for a debug event. This was necessary in Windows NT 4.0, because, as conventional ports are not waitable objects, it is not possible to use **ZwWaitForSingleObject** to wait on them. The waitable ports introduced with Windows 2000 or the new **ZwReplyWaitReceivePortEx** system service could also be used to tackle this problem, but in practice the Windows NT 4.0 architecture has been retained.

OutputDebugString

OutputDebugString communicates its string to the debugger by raising an exception with a particular code (0x40010006); if not recognized and handled by a debugger, a frame-based exception handler is invoked, which makes the string available to debug string monitors (such as dbmon.exe) by copying it to a file mapping and signaling an event.

Tracing Calls to Routines Exported by DLLs

Example C.4 demonstrates the direct manipulation of the debug port of a process. The example traces calls to the exported routines of all the DLLs that are loaded in a process and runs in about 60 percent of the time required by a variant using the Win32 debugging API. The level of tracing is more detailed than that produced by utilities that patch the image export directories of the loaded DLLs, but the tracing consumes substantially more CPU time. An application being traced runs at about one twentieth of its normal speed.

Example C.4: A Trace Utility

```c
#include "ntdll.h"
#include <imagehlp.h>
#include <stdlib.h>
#include <stdio.h>
#include <vector>
#include <map>

#define elements(s) (sizeof (s) / sizeof *(s))

namespace NT {
    extern "C" {

typedef struct _DEBUG_MESSAGE {
    PORT_MESSAGE PortMessage;
    ULONG EventCode;
    ULONG Status;
    union {
        struct {
            EXCEPTION_RECORD ExceptionRecord;
            ULONG FirstChance;
        } Exception;
        struct {
            ULONG Reserved;
            PVOID StartAddress;
        } CreateThread;
        struct {
            ULONG Reserved;
            HANDLE FileHandle;
            PVOID Base;
            ULONG PointerToSymbolTable;
            ULONG NumberOfSymbols;
            ULONG Reserved2;
            PVOID EntryPoint;
        } CreateProcess;
        struct {
            ULONG ExitCode;
```

```
            } ExitThread;
            struct {
                ULONG ExitCode;
            } ExitProcess;
            struct {
                HANDLE FileHandle;
                PVOID Base;
                ULONG PointerToSymbolTable;
                ULONG NumberOfSymbols;
            } LoadDll;
            struct {
                PVOID Base;
            } UnloadDll;
        } u;
    } DEBUG_MESSAGE, *PDEBUG_MESSAGE;

    }
}

typedef struct _DEBUG_STATUS {
    ULONG B0 : 1;
    ULONG B1 : 1;
    ULONG B2 : 1;
    ULONG B3 : 1;
    ULONG    : 9;
    ULONG BD : 1;
    ULONG BS : 1;
    ULONG BT : 1;
    ULONG    : 16;
} DEBUG_STATUS, *PDEBUG_STATUS;

typedef struct _DEBUG_CONTROL {
    ULONG L0 : 1;
    ULONG G0 : 1;
    ULONG L1 : 1;
    ULONG G1 : 1;
    ULONG L2 : 1;
    ULONG G2 : 1;
    ULONG L3 : 1;
    ULONG G3 : 1;
    ULONG LE : 1;
    ULONG GE : 1;
    ULONG    : 3;
    ULONG GD : 1;
    ULONG    : 2;
    ULONG RWE0 : 2;
    ULONG LEN0 : 2;
    ULONG RWE1 : 2;
    ULONG LEN1 : 2;
    ULONG RWE2 : 2;
    ULONG LEN2 : 2;
    ULONG RWE3 : 2;
    ULONG LEN3 : 2;
} DEBUG_CONTROL, *PDEBUG_CONTROL;

struct Error {
    ULONG line;
    ULONG code;
    Error(ULONG line, ULONG code) : line(line), code(code) {}
};

struct enter {
    PCSTR name;
    BYTE  opcode;
```

```
        ULONG argc;
        enter() : name(0), opcode(0), argc(0) {}
        enter(PCSTR n, BYTE o = 0, ULONG a = 3) : name(n), opcode(o), argc(a) {}
    };

    struct leave {
        PVOID eip;
        ULONG esp;
        leave() : eip(0), esp(0) {}
        leave(PVOID ip, ULONG sp) : eip(ip), esp(sp) {}
    };

    #pragma warning(disable:4786)

    typedef std::map<ULONG, std::vector<leave>, std::less<ULONG> > leaves_t;
    typedef std::map<PVOID, enter, std::less<PVOID> > enters_t;
    typedef std::map<ULONG, PVOID, std::less<ULONG> > steps_t;

    enters_t enters;
    leaves_t leaves;
    steps_t steps;
    std::map<ULONG, HANDLE, std::less<ULONG> > threads;
    HANDLE hProcess;
    ULONG StartTime;
    BOOL Discard;
    const int EXECUTE = PAGE_EXECUTE | PAGE_EXECUTE_READ
                    | PAGE_EXECUTE_READWRITE | PAGE_EXECUTE_WRITECOPY;

    BYTE InsertBreakPoint(PVOID addr)
    {
        MEMORY_BASIC_INFORMATION mbi;
        ULONG rv;
        BYTE op, bp = 0xcc;

        rv = VirtualQueryEx(hProcess, addr, &mbi, sizeof mbi);
        if (rv != sizeof mbi) return bp;

        if ((mbi.Protect & EXECUTE) == 0) return bp;

        rv = ReadProcessMemory(hProcess, addr, &op, sizeof op, 0);
        if (rv == FALSE) return bp;

        rv = WriteProcessMemory(hProcess, addr, &bp, sizeof bp, 0);
        if (rv == FALSE) return bp;

        return op;
    }

    VOID ReinsertBreakPoint(PVOID addr)
    {
        BYTE bp = 0xcc;

        BOOL rv = WriteProcessMemory(hProcess, addr, &bp, sizeof bp, 0);
        if (rv != TRUE) throw Error(__LINE__, GetLastError());
    }

    VOID StepBreakPoint(PCONTEXT context, ULONG tid, PVOID addr, BYTE opcode)
    {
        BOOL rv = WriteProcessMemory(hProcess, addr, &opcode, sizeof opcode, 0);
        if (rv != TRUE) throw Error(__LINE__, GetLastError());

        steps[tid] = addr;
```

```
    context->EFlags |= 0x100;
    context->Eip -= 1;
}

ULONG ReturnBreak(PCONTEXT context, PVOID addr, ULONG tid)
{
    std::vector<leave>& stack = leaves[tid];

    while (!stack.empty() && stack.back().esp < context->Esp) {
        stack.pop_back();
        printf("#");
    }

    if (addr == 0) return 0;

    stack.push_back(leave(addr, context->Esp));

    PDEBUG_CONTROL dr7 = PDEBUG_CONTROL(&context->Dr7);
    PDEBUG_STATUS  dr6 = PDEBUG_STATUS(&context->Dr6);

    context->Dr0 = ULONG(addr);
    dr7->L0 = 1, dr7->RWE0 = 0, dr7->LEN0 = 0, dr6->B0 = 0;

    return stack.size() - 1;
}

VOID AddFPO(PVOID base, PSTR name)
{
    PIMAGE_DEBUG_INFORMATION idi
        = MapDebugInformation(0, name, getenv("_NT_SYMBOL_PATH"), 0);
    if (idi == 0) return;

    for (ULONG i = 0; i < idi->NumberOfFpoTableEntries; i++) {
        PVOID func = PVOID(PBYTE(base) + idi->FpoTableEntries[i].ulOffStart);

        enters_t::iterator entry = enters.find(func);

        if (entry != enters.end())
            entry->second.argc = idi->FpoTableEntries[i].cdwParams;
    }

    UnmapDebugInformation(idi);
}

VOID InsertBreakPoints(PVOID base)
{
    IMAGE_DOS_HEADER dos;
    IMAGE_NT_HEADERS nt;
    BOOL rv;

    rv = ReadProcessMemory(hProcess, base,
                            &dos, sizeof dos, 0);
    if (rv != TRUE) throw Error(__LINE__, GetLastError());

    rv = ReadProcessMemory(hProcess, PBYTE(base) + dos.e_lfanew,
                            &nt, sizeof nt, 0);
    if (rv != TRUE) throw Error(__LINE__, GetLastError());

    PIMAGE_DATA_DIRECTORY expdir
        = nt.OptionalHeader.DataDirectory + IMAGE_DIRECTORY_ENTRY_EXPORT;
    ULONG size = expdir->Size;
    ULONG addr = expdir->VirtualAddress;
```

```
        PIMAGE_EXPORT_DIRECTORY exports = PIMAGE_EXPORT_DIRECTORY(malloc(size));

        rv = ReadProcessMemory(hProcess, PBYTE(base) + addr, exports, size, 0);
        if (rv != TRUE) throw Error(__LINE__, GetLastError());

        PULONG functions =  PULONG(PBYTE(exports) - addr
                                    + ULONG(exports->AddressOfFunctions));
        PUSHORT ordinals = PUSHORT(PBYTE(exports) - addr
                                    + ULONG(exports->AddressOfNameOrdinals));
        PULONG fnames    =  PULONG(PBYTE(exports) - addr
                                    + ULONG(exports->AddressOfNames));

        for (ULONG i = 0; i < exports->NumberOfNames; i++) {
            ULONG ord = ordinals[i];

            if (functions[ord] < addr || functions[ord] >= addr + size) {
                PBYTE func = PBYTE(base) + functions[ord];

                PSTR name = PSTR(PBYTE(exports) - addr + fnames[i]);

                BYTE op = InsertBreakPoint(func);

                if (enters.find(func) == enters.end())
                    enters[func] = enter(name, op);
            }
        }

        AddFPO(base, PSTR(PBYTE(exports) - addr + exports->Name));
    }

    VOID RemoveDeadBreakPoints()
    {
        enters_t dead(enters);
        BYTE op;

        for (enters_t::iterator entry = dead.begin();
             entry != dead.end(); entry++)
            if (ReadProcessMemory(hProcess, entry->first,
                                  &op, sizeof op, 0) == FALSE)
                enters.erase(entry->first);
    }

    VOID ReportEntry(PCONTEXT context, NT::PDEBUG_MESSAGE dm)
    {
        ULONG stack[17];
        CHAR buf[512];

        PVOID addr = dm->u.Exception.ExceptionRecord.ExceptionAddress;

        enter& entry = enters[addr];

        PCSTR s = entry.name;

        if (*s == '?' && UnDecorateSymbolName(s, buf, sizeof buf - 1, 0) > 0)
            s = buf;

        ULONG argc = min(ULONG(elements(stack)) - 1, entry.argc);

        BOOL rv = ReadProcessMemory(hProcess, PVOID(context->Esp),
                                    stack, sizeof stack[0] * (1 + argc), 0);

        ULONG now = GetTickCount() - StartTime;
```

```
    ULONG n = rv ? ReturnBreak(context, PVOID(stack[0]),
                               ULONG(dm->PortMessage.ClientId.UniqueThread))
                 : 0;

    printf("\n%4d.%02d %4x %*s%s(",
           now / 1000, (now % 1000) / 10,
           ULONG(dm->PortMessage.ClientId.UniqueThread), n, "", s);

    if (rv == TRUE) {
        switch (argc) {
          case 0:  break;
          case 1:  printf("%x", stack[1]); break;
          case 2:  printf("%x, %x", stack[1], stack[2]); break;
          case 3:  printf("%x, %x, %x", stack[1], stack[2], stack[3]); break;

          default:
            printf("%x, %x, %x, %x", stack[1], stack[2], stack[3], stack[4]);
            for (ULONG i = 5; i <= argc; i++) printf(", %x", stack[i]);
        }
    }

    printf(")");
}

VOID ReportExit(PCONTEXT context)
{
    printf(" -> %x", context->Eax);
}

ULONG HandleBreakPoint(NT::PDEBUG_MESSAGE dm)
{
    PVOID addr = dm->u.Exception.ExceptionRecord.ExceptionAddress;

    enters_t::iterator entry = enters.find(addr);

    if (entry != enters.end() && entry->second.opcode != 0xcc) {
        HANDLE hThread
            = threads[ULONG(dm->PortMessage.ClientId.UniqueThread)];

        CONTEXT context;

        context.ContextFlags = CONTEXT_DEBUG_REGISTERS | CONTEXT_CONTROL;

        GetThreadContext(hThread, &context);

        ReportEntry(&context, dm);

        StepBreakPoint(&context, ULONG(dm->PortMessage.ClientId.UniqueThread),
                       addr, entry->second.opcode);

        SetThreadContext(hThread, &context);
    }
    else {
        if (entry != enters.end() && entry->second.name != 0)
            printf("\nDebug exception at %s\n", entry->second.name);
        else
            printf("\nDebug exception at %p\n", addr);
    }

    return DBG_CONTINUE;
}
```

```
ULONG HandleSingleStep(NT::PDEBUG_MESSAGE dm)
{
    CONTEXT context;

    steps_t::iterator step
        = steps.find(ULONG(dm->PortMessage.ClientId.UniqueThread));

    if (step != steps.end()) {
        if (!Discard) ReinsertBreakPoint(step->second);

        steps.erase(step);

        return DBG_CONTINUE;
    }

    PVOID eaddr = dm->u.Exception.ExceptionRecord.ExceptionAddress;

    std::vector<leave>& stack
        = leaves[ULONG(dm->PortMessage.ClientId.UniqueThread)];

    if (!stack.empty() && stack.back().eip == eaddr) stack.pop_back();

    PVOID iaddr = stack.empty() ? 0 : stack.back().eip;

    HANDLE hThread = threads[ULONG(dm->PortMessage.ClientId.UniqueThread)];

    context.ContextFlags
        = CONTEXT_DEBUG_REGISTERS | CONTEXT_CONTROL | CONTEXT_INTEGER;

    GetThreadContext(hThread, &context);

    PDEBUG_CONTROL dr7 = PDEBUG_CONTROL(&context.Dr7);
    PDEBUG_STATUS  dr6 = PDEBUG_STATUS(&context.Dr6);

    context.Dr0 = ULONG(iaddr);
    dr7->L0 = 1, dr7->RWE0 = 0, dr7->LEN0 = 0, dr6->B0 = 0;

    if (iaddr == eaddr) context.EFlags |= 0x100, dr7->L0 = 0;

    SetThreadContext(hThread, &context);

    ReportExit(&context);

    return DBG_CONTINUE;
}

ULONG HandleExceptionEvent(NT::PDEBUG_MESSAGE dm)
{
    switch (dm->u.Exception.ExceptionRecord.ExceptionCode) {
      case EXCEPTION_BREAKPOINT:
        return HandleBreakPoint(dm);

      case EXCEPTION_SINGLE_STEP:
        return HandleSingleStep(dm);

      default:
        printf("\nException %x at %p\n",
                dm->u.Exception.ExceptionRecord.ExceptionCode,
                dm->u.Exception.ExceptionRecord.ExceptionAddress);
    }

    return DBG_EXCEPTION_NOT_HANDLED;
}
```

```
ULONG HandleCreateProcessThreadEvent(NT::PDEBUG_MESSAGE dm)
{
    printf("\nProcess %x, Thread create %x\n",
            dm->PortMessage.ClientId.UniqueProcess,
            dm->PortMessage.ClientId.UniqueThread);

    NT::OBJECT_ATTRIBUTES oa = {sizeof oa};
    HANDLE hThread;

    NT::ZwOpenThread(&hThread, THREAD_ALL_ACCESS,
                    &oa, &dm->PortMessage.ClientId);

    threads[ULONG(dm->PortMessage.ClientId.UniqueThread)]
        = hThread;

    leaves[ULONG(dm->PortMessage.ClientId.UniqueThread)]
        = std::vector<leave>();

    return DBG_CONTINUE;
}

ULONG HandleExitThreadEvent(NT::PDEBUG_MESSAGE dm)
{
    printf("\nThread %x exit code %x\n",
            dm->PortMessage.ClientId.UniqueThread,
            dm->u.ExitThread.ExitCode);

    leaves.erase(ULONG(dm->PortMessage.ClientId.UniqueThread));

    return DBG_CONTINUE;
}

ULONG HandleExitProcessEvent(NT::PDEBUG_MESSAGE dm)
{
    printf("\nProcess %x exit code %x\n",
            dm->PortMessage.ClientId.UniqueProcess,
            dm->u.ExitProcess.ExitCode);

    leaves.erase(ULONG(dm->PortMessage.ClientId.UniqueThread));

    return DBG_CONTINUE;
}

ULONG HandleLoadDllEvent(NT::PDEBUG_MESSAGE dm)
{
    InsertBreakPoints(dm->u.LoadDll.Base);

    return DBG_CONTINUE;
}

ULONG HandleUnloadDllEvent(NT::PDEBUG_MESSAGE)
{
    RemoveDeadBreakPoints();

    return DBG_CONTINUE;
}

BOOL WINAPI HandlerRoutine(ULONG event)
{
    if (event != CTRL_C_EVENT || Discard == TRUE)
        TerminateProcess(hProcess, 0);
```

```
        if (event == CTRL_C_EVENT)
            Discard = TRUE;

        return TRUE;
    }

    HANDLE StartDebuggee(HANDLE hPort)
    {
        PROCESS_INFORMATION pi;
        STARTUPINFO si = {sizeof si};

        PSTR cmd = strchr(GetCommandLine(), ' ') + 1;

        CreateProcess(0, cmd, 0, 0, 0, CREATE_SUSPENDED, 0, 0, &si, &pi);

        NT::ZwSetInformationProcess(pi.hProcess, NT::ProcessDebugPort,
                                    &hPort, sizeof hPort);

        ResumeThread(pi.hThread);
        CloseHandle(pi.hThread);

        return pi.hProcess;
    }

    int main(int argc, wchar_t *argv[])
    {
        if (argc == 1) return 0;

        SetConsoleCtrlHandler(HandlerRoutine, TRUE);

        NT::OBJECT_ATTRIBUTES oa = {sizeof oa};
        HANDLE hPort;

        NT::ZwCreatePort(&hPort, &oa, 0, 0x78, 0);

        hProcess = StartDebuggee(hPort);

        StartTime = GetTickCount();

        NT::DEBUG_MESSAGE dm;

        do {
            NT::ZwReplyWaitReceivePort(hPort, 0, 0, &dm.PortMessage);

            try {
                switch (dm.EventCode + 1) {
                  case EXCEPTION_DEBUG_EVENT:
                    dm.Status = HandleExceptionEvent(&dm);
                    break;

                  case CREATE_THREAD_DEBUG_EVENT:
                  case CREATE_PROCESS_DEBUG_EVENT:
                    dm.Status = HandleCreateProcessThreadEvent(&dm);
                    break;

                  case EXIT_THREAD_DEBUG_EVENT:
                    dm.Status = HandleExitThreadEvent(&dm);
                    break;

                  case EXIT_PROCESS_DEBUG_EVENT:
                    dm.Status = HandleExitProcessEvent(&dm);
                    break;
```

```
            case LOAD_DLL_DEBUG_EVENT:
              dm.Status = HandleLoadDllEvent(&dm);
              break;

            case UNLOAD_DLL_DEBUG_EVENT:
              dm.Status = HandleUnloadDllEvent(&dm);
              break;

            default:
              dm.Status = DBG_CONTINUE;
              printf("\nUnusual event %lx\n", dm.EventCode);
              break;
          }
      }
      catch (Error e) {
          printf("Error %ld on line %ld\n", e.code, e.line);

          dm.EventCode = EXIT_PROCESS_DEBUG_EVENT - 1;
      }

      NT::ZwReplyPort(hPort, &dm.PortMessage);

  } while (dm.EventCode + 1 != EXIT_PROCESS_DEBUG_EVENT);

  return 0;
}
```

As a utility, Example C.4 is useful for understanding the relationship between Win32 functions and the native system services. By attempting to show the call nesting, this example makes it possible to see which system services are invoked during a call to a Win32 function.

Contrary to the advice of, "Don't document bugs—fix them!"—one known problem with Example C.4 is that it does not suspend all the other threads in the process while single stepping a thread over a breakpoint. This would potentially allow other threads to call an exported function when the breakpoint instruction at its entry point is temporarily removed.

D
NTFS On-Disk Structure

One of the interesting file system control operations defined in winioctl.h is
FSCTL_GET_NTFS_FILE_RECORD, which retrieves a file record from the Master File Table
(MFT) on an NTFS volume. When calling **ZwFsControlFile** (or the Win32 function
DeviceIoControl) with this control code, the InputBuffer parameter points to a
NTFS_FILE_RECORD_INPUT_BUFFER structure, and the OutputBuffer parameter points to a
buffer large enough to hold a NTFS_FILE_RECORD_OUTPUT_BUFFER structure and a file
record.

```
typedef struct {
    ULONGLONG FileReferenceNumber;
} NTFS_FILE_RECORD_INPUT_BUFFER, *PNTFS_FILE_RECORD_INPUT_BUFFER;

typedef struct {
    ULONGLONG FileReferenceNumber;
    ULONG FileRecordLength;
    UCHAR FileRecordBuffer[1];
} NTFS_FILE_RECORD_OUTPUT_BUFFER, *PNTFS_FILE_RECORD_OUTPUT_BUFFER;
```

Strictly speaking, a FileReferenceNumber consists of a 48-bit index into the Master File
Table and a 16-bit sequence number that records how many times the entry in the
table has been reused, but the sequence number is ignored when using
FSCTL_GET_NTFS_FILE_RECORD. Therefore, to retrieve the file record at index 30, the
value 30 should be assigned to FileReferenceNumber. If the table entry at index 30 is
empty, FSCTL_GET_NTFS_FILE_RECORD retrieves a nearby entry that is not empty. To verify that the intended table entry has been retrieved, it is necessary to compare the low
order 48 bits of FileReferenceNumber in the output buffer with that in the input
buffer.

The remainder of this chapter describes the data structures that represent the on-
disk structure of NTFS. It includes a sample utility that interprets the data structures
to recover the data of a deleted file. The descriptions of the on-disk data structures also
serve to explain the contents of the FileRecordBuffer returned by
FSCTL_GET_NTFS_FILE_RECORD.

NTFS_RECORD_HEADER

```
typedef struct {
    ULONG Type;
    USHORT UsaOffset;
    USHORT UsaCount;
    USN Usn;
} NTFS_RECORD_HEADER, *PNTFS_RECORD_HEADER;
```

Members

Type

The type of NTFS record. When the value of Type is considered as a sequence of four one-byte characters, it normally spells an acronym for the type. Defined values include:

```
'FILE'
'INDX'
'BAAD'
'HOLE'
'CHKD'
```

UsaOffset

The offset, in bytes, from the start of the structure to the Update Sequence Array.

UsaCount

The number of values in the Update Sequence Array.

Usn

The Update Sequence Number of the NTFS record.

Remarks

None.

FILE_RECORD_HEADER

```
typedef struct {
    NTFS_RECORD_HEADER Ntfs;
    USHORT SequenceNumber;
    USHORT LinkCount;
    USHORT AttributesOffset;
    USHORT Flags;                // 0x0001 = InUse, 0x0002 = Directory
    ULONG BytesInUse;
    ULONG BytesAllocated;
    ULONGLONG BaseFileRecord;
    USHORT NextAttributeNumber;
} FILE_RECORD_HEADER, *PFILE_RECORD_HEADER;
```

Members

Ntfs

An NTFS_RECORD_HEADER structure with a Type of 'FILE.'

SequenceNumber
    The number of times that the MFT entry has been reused.

LinkCount
    The number of directory links to the MFT entry.

AttributeOffset
    The offset, in bytes, from the start of the structure to the first attribute of the MFT entry.

Flags
    A bit array of flags specifying properties of the MFT entry. The values defined include:

```
InUse       0x0001  // The MFT entry is in use
Directory   0x0002  // The MFT entry represents a directory
```

BytesInUse
    The number of bytes used by the MFT entry.

BytesAllocated
    The number of bytes allocated for the MFT entry.

BaseFileRecord
    If the MFT entry contains attributes that overflowed a base MFT entry, this member contains the file reference number of the base entry; otherwise, it contains zero.

NextAttributeNumber
    The number that will be assigned to the next attribute added to the MFT entry.

Remarks

An entry in the MFT consists of a FILE_RECORD_HEADER followed by a sequence of attributes.

ATTRIBUTE

```
typedef struct {
    ATTRIBUTE_TYPE AttributeType;
    ULONG Length;
    BOOLEAN Nonresident;
    UCHAR NameLength;
    USHORT NameOffset;
    USHORT Flags;                // 0x0001 = Compressed
    USHORT AttributeNumber;
} ATTRIBUTE, *PATTRIBUTE;
```

Members

AttributeType

The type of the attribute. The following types are defined:

```
typedef enum {
    AttributeStandardInformation = 0x10,
    AttributeAttributeList = 0x20,
    AttributeFileName = 0x30,
    AttributeObjectId = 0x40,
    AttributeSecurityDescriptor = 0x50,
    AttributeVolumeName = 0x60,
    AttributeVolumeInformation = 0x70,
    AttributeData = 0x80,
    AttributeIndexRoot = 0x90,
    AttributeIndexAllocation = 0xA0,
    AttributeBitmap = 0xB0,
    AttributeReparsePoint = 0xC0,
    AttributeEAInformation = 0xD0,
    AttributeEA = 0xE0,
    AttributePropertySet = 0xF0,
    AttributeLoggedUtilityStream = 0x100
} ATTRIBUTE_TYPE, *PATTRIBUTE_TYPE;
```

Length

The size, in bytes, of the resident part of the attribute.

Nonresident

Specifies, when true, that the attribute value is nonresident.

NameLength

The size, in characters, of the name (if any) of the attribute.

NameOffset

The offset, in bytes, from the start of the structure to the attribute name. The attribute name is stored as a Unicode string.

Flags

A bit array of flags specifying properties of the attribute. The values defined include:

```
Compressed    0x0001   // The attribute is compressed
```

AttributeNumber

A numeric identifier for the instance of the attribute.

Remarks

None.

RESIDENT_ATTRIBUTE

```
typedef struct {
    ATTRIBUTE Attribute;
    ULONG ValueLength;
    USHORT ValueOffset;
    USHORT Flags;                // 0x0001 = Indexed
} RESIDENT_ATTRIBUTE, *PRESIDENT_ATTRIBUTE;
```

Members

Attribute

An ATTRIBUTE structure containing members common to resident and nonresident attributes.

ValueLength

The size, in bytes, of the attribute value.

ValueOffset

The offset, in bytes, from the start of the structure to the attribute value.

Flags

A bit array of flags specifying properties of the attribute. The values defined include:

```
        Indexed        0x0001  // The attribute is indexed
```

Remarks

None.

NONRESIDENT_ATTRIBUTE

```
typedef struct {
    ATTRIBUTE Attribute;
    ULONGLONG LowVcn;
    ULONGLONG HighVcn;
    USHORT RunArrayOffset;
    UCHAR CompressionUnit;
    UCHAR AlignmentOrReserved[5];
    ULONGLONG AllocatedSize;
    ULONGLONG DataSize;
    ULONGLONG InitializedSize;
    ULONGLONG CompressedSize;    // Only when compressed
} NONRESIDENT_ATTRIBUTE, *PNONRESIDENT_ATTRIBUTE;
```

Members

Attribute

An ATTRIBUTE structure containing members common to resident and nonresident attributes.

LowVcn

The lowest valid Virtual Cluster Number (VCN) of this portion of the attribute value. Unless the attribute value is very fragmented (to the extent that an attribute list is needed to describe it), there is only one portion of the attribute value, and the value of LowVcn is zero.

HighVcn

The highest valid VCN of this portion of the attribute value.

RunArrayOffset

The offset, in bytes, from the start of the structure to the run array that contains the mappings between VCNs and Logical Cluster Numbers (LCNs).

CompressionUnit

The compression unit for the attribute expressed as the logarithm to the base two of the number of clusters in a compression unit. If CompressionUnit is zero, the attribute is not compressed.

AllocatedSize

The size, in bytes, of disk space allocated to hold the attribute value.

DataSize

The size, in bytes, of the attribute value. This may be larger than the AllocatedSize if the attribute value is compressed or sparse.

InitializedSize

The size, in bytes, of the initialized portion of the attribute value.

CompressedSize

The size, in bytes, of the attribute value after compression. This member is only present when the attribute is compressed.

Remarks

None.

AttributeStandardInformation

```
typedef struct {
    ULONGLONG CreationTime;
    ULONGLONG ChangeTime;
    ULONGLONG LastWriteTime;
    ULONGLONG LastAccessTime;
    ULONG FileAttributes;
    ULONG AlignmentOrReservedOrUnknown[3];
    ULONG QuotaId;                           // NTFS 3.0 only
    ULONG SecurityId;                        // NTFS 3.0 only
    ULONGLONG QuotaCharge;                   // NTFS 3.0 only
    USN Usn;                                 // NTFS 3.0 only
} STANDARD_INFORMATION, *PSTANDARD_INFORMATION;
```

Members

CreationTime
   The time when the file was created in the standard time format (that is, the number of 100-nanosecond intervals since January 1, 1601).

ChangeTime
   The time when the file attributes were last changed in the standard time format (that is, the number of 100-nanosecond intervals since January 1, 1601).

LastWriteTime
   The time when the file was last written in the standard time format (that is, the number of 100-nanosecond intervals since January 1, 1601).

LastAccessTime
   The time when the file was last accessed in the standard time format (that is, the number of 100-nanosecond intervals since January 1, 1601).

FileAttributes
   The attributes of the file. Defined attributes include:

```
FILE_ATTRIBUTE_READONLY
FILE_ATTRIBUTE_HIDDEN
FILE_ATTRIBUTE_SYSTEM
FILE_ATTRIBUTE_DIRECTORY
FILE_ATTRIBUTE_ARCHIVE
FILE_ATTRIBUTE_NORMAL
FILE_ATTRIBUTE_TEMPORARY
FILE_ATTRIBUTE_SPARSE_FILE
FILE_ATTRIBUTE_REPARSE_POINT
FILE_ATTRIBUTE_COMPRESSED
FILE_ATTRIBUTE_OFFLINE
FILE_ATTRIBUTE_NOT_CONTENT_INDEXED
FILE_ATTRIBUTE_ENCRYPTED
```

AlignmentOrReservedOrUnknown
   Normally contains zero. Interpretation unknown.

QuotaId
   A numeric identifier of the disk quota that has been charged for the file (probably an index into the file "\$Extend\$Quota"). If quotas are disabled, the value of QuotaId is zero. This member is only present in NTFS 3.0. If a volume has been upgraded from an earlier version of NTFS to version 3.0, this member is only present if the file has been accessed since the upgrade.

SecurityId
   A numeric identifier of the security descriptor that applies to the file (probably an index into the file "\$Secure"). This member is only present in NTFS 3.0. If a volume has been upgraded from an earlier version of NTFS to version 3.0, this member is only present if the file has been accessed since the upgrade.

QuotaCharge

The size, in bytes, of the charge to the quota for the file. If quotas are disabled, the value of QuotaCharge is zero. This member is only present in NTFS 3.0. If a volume has been upgraded from an earlier version of NTFS to version 3.0, this member is only present if the file has been accessed since the upgrade.

Usn

The Update Sequence Number of the file. If journaling is not enabled, the value of Usn is zero. This member is only present in NTFS 3.0. If a volume has been upgraded from an earlier version of NTFS to version 3.0, this member is only present if the file has been accessed since the upgrade.

Remarks

The standard information attribute is always resident.

AttributeAttributeList

```
typedef struct {
    ATTRIBUTE_TYPE AttributeType;
    USHORT Length;
    UCHAR NameLength;
    UCHAR NameOffset;
    ULONGLONG LowVcn;
    ULONGLONG FileReferenceNumber;
    USHORT AttributeNumber;
    USHORT AlignmentOrReserved[3];
} ATTRIBUTE_LIST, *PATTRIBUTE_LIST;
```

Members

AttributeType

The type of the attribute.

Length

The size, in bytes, of the attribute list entry.

NameLength

The size, in characters, of the name (if any) of the attribute.

NameOffset

The offset, in bytes, from the start of the ATTRIBUTE_LIST structure to the attribute name. The attribute name is stored as a Unicode string.

LowVcn

The lowest valid Virtual Cluster Number (VCN) of this portion of the attribute value.

FileReferenceNumber

The file reference number of the MFT entry containing the NONRESIDENT_ATTRIBUTE structure for this portion of the attribute value.

AttributeNumber
A numeric identifier for the instance of the attribute.

Remarks

The attribute list attribute is always nonresident and consists of an array of
ATTRIBUTE_LIST structures.

An attribute list attribute is only needed when the attributes of a file do not fit in a
single MFT record. Possible reasons for overflowing a single MFT entry include:

- The file has a large numbers of alternate names (hard links)

- The attribute value is large, and the volume is badly fragmented

- The file has a complex security descriptor (does not affect NTFS 3.0)

- The file has many streams

AttributeFileName

```
typedef struct {
    ULONGLONG DirectoryFileReferenceNumber;
    ULONGLONG CreationTime;      // Saved when filename last changed
    ULONGLONG ChangeTime;        // ditto
    ULONGLONG LastWriteTime;     // ditto
    ULONGLONG LastAccessTime;    // ditto
    ULONGLONG AllocatedSize;     // ditto
    ULONGLONG DataSize;          // ditto
    ULONG FileAttributes;        // ditto
    ULONG AlignmentOrReserved;
    UCHAR NameLength;
    UCHAR NameType;              // 0x01 = Long, 0x02 = Short
    WCHAR Name[1];
} FILENAME_ATTRIBUTE, *PFILENAME_ATTRIBUTE;
```

Members

DirectoryFileReferenceNumber
The file reference number of the directory in which the filename is entered.

CreationTime
The time when the file was created in the standard time format (that is, the number
of 100-nanosecond intervals since January 1, 1601). This member is only updated
when the filename changes and may differ from the field of the same name in the
STANDARD_INFORMATION structure.

ChangeTime
The time when the file attributes were last changed in the standard time format (that
is, the number of 100-nanosecond intervals since January 1, 1601). This member is
only updated when the filename changes and may differ from the field of the same
name in the STANDARD_INFORMATION structure.

LastWriteTime

The time when the file was last written in the standard time format (that is, the number of 100-nanosecond intervals since January 1, 1601). This member is only updated when the filename changes and may differ from the field of the same name in the STANDARD_INFORMATION structure.

LastAccessTime

The time when the file was last accessed in the standard time format (that is, the number of 100-nanosecond intervals since January 1, 1601). This member is only updated when the filename changes and may differ from the field of the same name in the STANDARD_INFORMATION structure.

AllocatedSize

The size, in bytes, of disk space allocated to hold the attribute value. This member is only updated when the filename changes.

DataSize

The size, in bytes, of the attribute value. This member is only updated when the filename changes.

FileAttributes

The attributes of the file. This member is only updated when the filename changes and may differ from the field of the same name in the STANDARD_INFORMATION structure.

NameLength

The size, in characters, of the filename.

NameType

The type of the name. A type of zero indicates an ordinary name, a type of one indicates a long name corresponding to a short name, and a type of two indicates a short name corresponding to a long name.

Name

The name, in Unicode, of the file.

Remarks

The filename attribute is always resident.

AttributeObjectId

```
typedef struct {
    GUID ObjectId;
    union {
        struct {
            GUID BirthVolumeId;
            GUID BirthObjectId;
            GUID DomainId;
        } ;
        UCHAR ExtendedInfo[48];
    };
} OBJECTID_ATTRIBUTE, *POBJECTID_ATTRIBUTE;
```

Members

ObjectId
The unique identifier assigned to the file.

BirtVolumeId
The unique identifier of the volume on which the file was first created. Need not be present.

BirthObjectId
The unique identifier assigned to the file when it was first created. Need not be present.

DomainId
Reserved. Need not be present.

Remarks

The object identifier attribute is always resident.

AttributeSecurityDescriptor

The security descriptor attribute is stored on disk as a standard self-relative security descriptor. This attribute does not normally appear in MFT entries on NTFS 3.0 format volumes.

AttributeVolumeName

The volume name attribute just contains the volume label as a Unicode string.

AttributeVolumeInformation

```
typedef struct {
    ULONG Unknown[2];
    UCHAR MajorVersion;
    UCHAR MinorVersion;
    USHORT Flags;
} VOLUME_INFORMATION, *PVOLUME_INFORMATION;
```

Members

Unknown
Interpretation unknown.

MajorVersion
The major version number of the NTFS format.

MinorVersion
The minor version number of the NTFS format.

Flags

A bit array of flags specifying properties of the volume. The values defined include:

```
VolumeIsDirty    0x0001
```

Remarks

Windows 2000 formats new volumes as NTFS version 3.0. Windows NT 4.0 formats new volumes as NTFS version 2.1.

AttributeData

The data attribute contains whatever data the creator of the attribute chooses.

AttributeIndexRoot

```
typedef struct {
    ATTRIBUTE_TYPE Type;
    ULONG CollationRule;
    ULONG BytesPerIndexBlock;
    ULONG ClustersPerIndexBlock;
    DIRECTORY_INDEX DirectoryIndex;
} INDEX_ROOT, *PINDEX_ROOT;
```

Members

Type

The type of the attribute that is indexed.

CollationRule

A numeric identifier of the collation rule used to sort the index entries.

BytesPerIndexBlock

The number of bytes per index block.

ClustersPerIndexBlock

The number of clusters per index block.

DirectoryIndex

A `DIRECTORY_INDEX` structure.

Remarks

An `INDEX_ROOT` structure is followed by a sequence of `DIRECTORY_ENTRY` structures.

AttributeIndexAllocation

```
typedef struct {
    NTFS_RECORD_HEADER Ntfs;
    ULONGLONG IndexBlockVcn;
    DIRECTORY_INDEX DirectoryIndex;
} INDEX_BLOCK_HEADER, *PINDEX_BLOCK_HEADER;
```

Members

Ntfs

An NTFS_RECORD_HEADER structure with a Type of 'INDX.'

IndexBlockVcn

The VCN of the index block.

DirectoryIndex

A DIRECTORY_INDEX structure.

Remarks

The index allocation attribute is an array of index blocks. Each index block starts with an INDEX_BLOCK_HEADER structure, which is followed by a sequence of DIRECTORY_ENTRY structures.

DIRECTORY_INDEX

```
typedef struct {
    ULONG EntriesOffset;
    ULONG IndexBlockLength;
    ULONG AllocatedSize;
    ULONG Flags;          // 0x00 = Small directory, 0x01 = Large directory
} DIRECTORY_INDEX, *PDIRECTORY_INDEX;
```

Members

EntriesOffset

The offset, in bytes, from the start of the structure to the first DIRECTORY_ENTRY structure.

IndexBlockLength

The size, in bytes, of the portion of the index block that is in use.

AllocatedSize

The size, in bytes, of disk space allocated for the index block.

Flags

A bit array of flags specifying properties of the index. The values defined include:

```
SmallDirectory   0x0000  // Directory fits in index root
LargeDirectory   0x0001  // Directory overflows index root
```

Remarks

None.

DIRECTORY_ENTRY

```
typedef struct {
    ULONGLONG FileReferenceNumber;
    USHORT Length;
    USHORT AttributeLength;
    ULONG Flags;           // 0x01 = Has trailing VCN, 0x02 = Last entry
    // FILENAME_ATTRIBUTE Name;
    // ULONGLONG Vcn;      // VCN in IndexAllocation of earlier entries
} DIRECTORY_ENTRY, *PDIRECTORY_ENTRY;
```

Members

FileReferenceNumber

The file reference number of the file described by the directory entry.

Length

The size, in bytes, of the directory entry.

AttributeLength

The size, in bytes, of the attribute that is indexed.

Flags

A bit array of flags specifying properties of the entry. The values defined include:

```
HasTrailingVcn   0x0001  // A VCN follows the indexed attribute
LastEntry        0x0002  // The last entry in an index block
```

Remarks

Until NTFS version 3.0, only filename attributes were indexed.

If the HasTrailingVcn flag of a DIRECTORY_ENTRY structure is set, the last eight bytes of the directory entry contain the VCN of the index block that holds the entries immediately preceding the current entry.

AttributeBitmap

The bitmap attribute contains an array of bits. The file "\$Mft" contains a bitmap attribute that records which MFT table entries are in use, and directories normally contain a bitmap attribute that records which index blocks contain valid entries.

AttributeReparsePoint

```
typedef struct {
    ULONG ReparseTag;
    USHORT ReparseDataLength;
    USHORT Reserved;
    UCHAR ReparseData[1];
} REPARSE_POINT, *PREPARSE_POINT;
```

Members

ReparseTag

The reparse tag identifies the type of reparse point. The high order three bits of the tag indicate whether the tag is owned by Microsoft, whether there is a high latency in accessing the file data, and whether the filename is an alias for another object.

ReparseDataLength

The size, in bytes, of the reparse data in the ReparseData member.

ReparseData

The reparse data. The interpretation of the data depends upon the type of the reparse point.

Remarks

None.

AttributeEAInformation

```
typedef struct {
    ULONG EaLength;
    ULONG EaQueryLength;
} EA_INFORMATION, *PEA_INFORMATION;
```

Members

EaLength

The size, in bytes, of the extended attribute information.

EaQueryLength

The size, in bytes, of the buffer needed to query the extended attributes when calling ZwQueryEaFile.

Remarks

None.

AttributeEA

```
typedef struct {
    ULONG NextEntryOffset;
    UCHAR Flags;
    UCHAR EaNameLength;
    USHORT EaValueLength;
    CHAR EaName[1];
    // UCHAR EaData[];
} EA_ATTRIBUTE, *PEA_ATTRIBUTE;
```

Members

NextEntryOffset
The number of bytes that must be skipped to get to the next entry.

Flags
A bit array of flags qualifying the extended attribute.

EaNameLength
The size, in bytes, of the extended attribute name.

EaValueLength
The size, in bytes, of the extended attribute value.

EaName
The extended attribute name.

EaData
The extended attribute data.

Remarks

None.

AttributePropertySet

Intended to support Native Structured Storage (NSS)—a feature that was removed from NTFS 3.0 during beta testing.

AttributeLoggedUtilityStream

A logged utility stream attribute contains whatever data the creator of the attribute chooses, but operations on the attribute are logged to the NTFS log file just like NTFS metadata changes. It is used by the Encrypting File System (EFS).

Special Files

The first sixteen entries in the Master File Table (MFT) are reserved for special files. NTFS 3.0 uses only the first twelve entries.

\$MFT (entry 0)

The Master File Table. The data attribute contains the MFT entries, and the bitmap attribute records which entries are in use.

\$MFTMirr (entry 1)

A mirror (backup copy) of the first four entries of the MFT.

\$LogFile (entry 2)

The volume log file that records changes to the volume structure.

\$Volume (entry 3)

The data attribute of $Volume represents the whole volume. Opening the Win32 pathname "\\.\C:" opens the volume file on drive C: (presuming that C: is an NTFS–formatted volume).

The $Volume file also has volume name, volume information, and object identifier attributes.

\$AttrDef (entry 4)

The data attribute of $AttrDef contains an array of attribute definitions.

```
typedef struct {
    WCHAR AttributeName[64];
    ULONG AttributeNumber;
    ULONG Unknown[2];
    ULONG Flags;
    ULONGLONG MinimumSize;
    ULONGLONG MaximumSize;
} ATTRIBUTE_DEFINITION, *PATTRIBUTE_DEFINITION;
```

\ (entry 5)

The root directory of the volume.

\$Bitmap (entry 6)

The data attribute of $Bitmap is a bitmap of the allocated clusters on the volume.

\$Boot (entry 7)

The first sector of $Boot is also the first sector of the volume. Because it is used early in the system boot process (if the volume is bootable), space is at a premium and the data stored in it is not aligned on natural boundaries. The format of the first sector can be represented by a BOOT_BLOCK structure.

```
#pragma pack(push, 1)

typedef struct {
    UCHAR Jump[3];
```

```
    UCHAR Format[8];
    USHORT BytesPerSector;
    UCHAR SectorsPerCluster;
    USHORT BootSectors;
    UCHAR Mbz1;
    USHORT Mbz2;
    USHORT Reserved1;
    UCHAR MediaType;
    USHORT Mbz3;
    USHORT SectorsPerTrack;
    USHORT NumberOfHeads;
    ULONG PartitionOffset;
    ULONG Reserved2[2];
    ULONGLONG TotalSectors;
    ULONGLONG MftStartLcn;
    ULONGLONG Mft2StartLcn;
    ULONG ClustersPerFileRecord;
    ULONG ClustersPerIndexBlock;
    ULONGLONG VolumeSerialNumber;
    UCHAR Code[0x1AE];
    USHORT BootSignature;
} BOOT_BLOCK, *PBOOT_BLOCK;

#pragma pack(pop)
```

\$BadClus (entry 8)

Bad clusters are appended to the data attribute of this file.

\$Secure (entry 9)

The data attribute of $Secure contains the shared security descriptors. $Secure also has two indexes.

\$UpCase (entry 10)

The data attribute of $Upcase contains the uppercase equivalent of all 65536 Unicode characters.

\$Extend (entry 11)

$Extend is a directory that holds the special files used by some of the extended functionality of NTFS 3.0. The (semi-) special files that are stored in the directory include "$ObjId," "$Quota," "$Reparse," and "$UsnJrnl."

Opening Special Files

Although the special files are indeed files, they cannot normally be opened by calling **ZwOpenFile** or **ZwCreateFile** because even though the ACL on the special files grants read access to Administrators, ntfs.sys (the NTFS file system driver) always returns STATUS_ACCESS_DENIED. There are two variables in ntfs.sys that affect this behavior: NtfsProtectSystemFiles and NtfsProtectSystemAttributes. By default, both of these variables are set to TRUE.

If NtfsProtectSystemAttributes is set to FALSE (by a debugger, for example), the system attributes (such as the standard information attribute) can be opened, using the names of the form "filename::$STANDARD_INFORMATION."

If NtfsProtectSystemFiles is set to FALSE, the special files can be opened. There are, however, some drawbacks associated with attempting to do this: because many of the special files are opened in a special way when mounting the volume, they are not prepared to handle the IRP_MJ_READ requests resulting from a call to ZwReadFile, and the system crashes if such a request is received. These special files can be read by mapping the special file with ZwCreateSection and ZwMapViewOfSection and then reading the mapped data. A further problem is that a few of the special files are not prepared to handle the IRP_MJ_CLEANUP request that is generated when the last handle to a file object is closed, and the system crashes if such a request is received. The only option is to duplicate the open handle to the special file into a process that never terminates (such as the system process).

Recovering Data from Deleted Files

Example D.1 demonstrates how to recover data from the unnamed data attribute of a file identified by drive letter and MFT entry index—even if the MFT entry represents a deleted file. It can also display a list of the deleted files on the volume. MFT entries are allocated on a first-free basis, so the entries for deleted files are normally quickly reused. Therefore, the example is of little practical use for recovering deleted files, but it can be used to make copies of the unnamed data attributes of the special files.

If the file to be recovered is compressed, the recovered data remains compressed and can be decompressed by a separate utility; Example D.2 shows one way in which this can be done.

Example D.1: Recovering Data from a File

```c
#include <windows.h>
#include <stdlib.h>
#include <stdio.h>
#include "ntfs.h"

ULONG BytesPerFileRecord;
HANDLE hVolume;
BOOT_BLOCK bootb;
PFILE_RECORD_HEADER MFT;

template <class T1, class T2> inline
T1* Padd(T1* p, T2 n) { return (T1*)((char *)p + n); }

ULONG RunLength(PUCHAR run)
{
    return (*run & 0xf) + ((*run >> 4) & 0xf) + 1;
}

LONGLONG RunLCN(PUCHAR run)
{
    UCHAR n1 = *run & 0xf;
    UCHAR n2 = (*run >> 4) & 0xf;
    LONGLONG lcn = n2 == 0 ? 0 : CHAR(run[n1 + n2]);

    for (LONG i = n1 + n2 - 1; i > n1; i—)
        lcn = (lcn << 8) + run[i];
    return lcn;
}
```

```
ULONGLONG RunCount(PUCHAR run)
{
    UCHAR n = *run & 0xf;
    ULONGLONG count = 0;

    for (ULONG i = n; i > 0; i—)
        count = (count << 8) + run[i];
    return count;
}

BOOL FindRun(PNONRESIDENT_ATTRIBUTE attr, ULONGLONG vcn,
             PULONGLONG lcn, PULONGLONG count)
{
    if (vcn < attr->LowVcn || vcn > attr->HighVcn) return FALSE;

    *lcn = 0;
    ULONGLONG base = attr->LowVcn;

    for (PUCHAR run = PUCHAR(Padd(attr, attr->RunArrayOffset));
         *run != 0;
         run += RunLength(run)) {

        *lcn += RunLCN(run);
        *count = RunCount(run);

        if (base <= vcn && vcn < base + *count) {
            *lcn = RunLCN(run) == 0 ? 0 : *lcn + vcn - base;
            *count -= ULONG(vcn - base);

            return TRUE;
        }
        else
            base += *count;
    }

    return FALSE;
}

PATTRIBUTE FindAttribute(PFILE_RECORD_HEADER file,
                         ATTRIBUTE_TYPE type, PWSTR name)
{
    for (PATTRIBUTE attr = PATTRIBUTE(Padd(file, file->AttributesOffset));
         attr->AttributeType != -1;
         attr = Padd(attr, attr->Length)) {

        if (attr->AttributeType == type) {
            if (name == 0 && attr->NameLength == 0) return attr;

            if (name != 0 && wcslen(name) == attr->NameLength
                && _wcsicmp(name, PWSTR(Padd(attr, attr->NameOffset))) == 0)
                return attr;
        }
    }

    return 0;
}

VOID FixupUpdateSequenceArray(PFILE_RECORD_HEADER file)
{
    PUSHORT usa = PUSHORT(Padd(file, file->Ntfs.UsaOffset));
    PUSHORT sector = PUSHORT(file);
```

```
        for (ULONG i = 1; i < file->Ntfs.UsaCount; i++) {
            sector[255] = usa[i];
            sector += 256;
        }
}

VOID ReadSector(ULONGLONG sector, ULONG count, PVOID buffer)
{
    ULARGE_INTEGER offset;
    OVERLAPPED overlap = {0};
    ULONG n;

    offset.QuadPart = sector * bootb.BytesPerSector;
    overlap.Offset = offset.LowPart; overlap.OffsetHigh = offset.HighPart;

    ReadFile(hVolume, buffer, count * bootb.BytesPerSector, &n, &overlap);
}

VOID ReadLCN(ULONGLONG lcn, ULONG count, PVOID buffer)
{
    ReadSector(lcn * bootb.SectorsPerCluster,
               count * bootb.SectorsPerCluster, buffer);
}

VOID ReadExternalAttribute(PNONRESIDENT_ATTRIBUTE attr,
                           ULONGLONG vcn, ULONG count, PVOID buffer)
{
    ULONGLONG lcn, runcount;
    ULONG readcount, left;
    PUCHAR bytes = PUCHAR(buffer);

    for (left = count; left > 0; left -= readcount) {
        FindRun(attr, vcn, &lcn, &runcount);

        readcount = ULONG(min(runcount, left));

        ULONG n = readcount * bootb.BytesPerSector * bootb.SectorsPerCluster;

        if (lcn == 0)
            memset(bytes, 0, n);
        else
            ReadLCN(lcn, readcount, bytes);

        vcn += readcount;
        bytes += n;
    }
}

ULONG AttributeLength(PATTRIBUTE attr)
{
    return attr->Nonresident == FALSE
        ? PRESIDENT_ATTRIBUTE(attr)->ValueLength
        : ULONG(PNONRESIDENT_ATTRIBUTE(attr)->DataSize);
}

ULONG AttributeLengthAllocated(PATTRIBUTE attr)
{
    return attr->Nonresident == FALSE
        ? PRESIDENT_ATTRIBUTE(attr)->ValueLength
        : ULONG(PNONRESIDENT_ATTRIBUTE(attr)->AllocatedSize);
}
```

```
VOID ReadAttribute(PATTRIBUTE attr, PVOID buffer)
{
    if (attr->Nonresident == FALSE) {
        PRESIDENT_ATTRIBUTE rattr = PRESIDENT_ATTRIBUTE(attr);
        memcpy(buffer, Padd(rattr, rattr->ValueOffset), rattr->ValueLength);
    }
    else {
        PNONRESIDENT_ATTRIBUTE nattr = PNONRESIDENT_ATTRIBUTE(attr);
        ReadExternalAttribute(nattr, 0, ULONG(nattr->HighVcn) + 1, buffer);
    }
}

VOID ReadVCN(PFILE_RECORD_HEADER file, ATTRIBUTE_TYPE type,
            ULONGLONG vcn, ULONG count, PVOID buffer)
{
    PNONRESIDENT_ATTRIBUTE attr
        = PNONRESIDENT_ATTRIBUTE(FindAttribute(file, type, 0));

    if (attr == 0 || (vcn < attr->LowVcn || vcn > attr->HighVcn)) {
        // Support for huge files

        PATTRIBUTE attrlist = FindAttribute(file, AttributeAttributeList, 0);

        DebugBreak();
    }

    ReadExternalAttribute(attr, vcn, count, buffer);
}

VOID ReadFileRecord(ULONG index, PFILE_RECORD_HEADER file)
{
    ULONG clusters = bootb.ClustersPerFileRecord;
    if (clusters > 0x80) clusters = 1;

    PUCHAR p = new UCHAR[bootb.BytesPerSector
                        * bootb.SectorsPerCluster * clusters];

    ULONGLONG vcn = ULONGLONG(index) * BytesPerFileRecord
                / bootb.BytesPerSector / bootb.SectorsPerCluster;

    ReadVCN(MFT, AttributeData, vcn, clusters, p);

    LONG m = (bootb.SectorsPerCluster * bootb.BytesPerSector
            / BytesPerFileRecord) - 1;

    ULONG n = m > 0 ? (index & m) : 0;

    memcpy(file, p + n * BytesPerFileRecord, BytesPerFileRecord);

    delete [] p;

    FixupUpdateSequenceArray(file);
}

VOID LoadMFT()
{
    BytesPerFileRecord = bootb.ClustersPerFileRecord < 0x80
                    ? bootb.ClustersPerFileRecord
                        * bootb.SectorsPerCluster
                        * bootb.BytesPerSector
                    : 1 << (0x100 - bootb.ClustersPerFileRecord);
```

```
    MFT = PFILE_RECORD_HEADER(new UCHAR[BytesPerFileRecord]);

    ReadSector(bootb.MftStartLcn * bootb.SectorsPerCluster,
               BytesPerFileRecord / bootb.BytesPerSector, MFT);

    FixupUpdateSequenceArray(MFT);
}

BOOL bitset(PUCHAR bitmap, ULONG i)
{
    return (bitmap[i >> 3] & (1 << (i & 7))) != 0;
}

VOID FindDeleted()
{
    PATTRIBUTE attr = FindAttribute(MFT, AttributeBitmap, 0);
    PUCHAR bitmap = new UCHAR[AttributeLengthAllocated(attr)];

    ReadAttribute(attr, bitmap);

    ULONG n = AttributeLength(FindAttribute(MFT, AttributeData, 0))
            / BytesPerFileRecord;

    PFILE_RECORD_HEADER file
        = PFILE_RECORD_HEADER(new UCHAR[BytesPerFileRecord]);

    for (ULONG i = 0; i < n; i++) {
        if (bitset(bitmap, i)) continue;

        ReadFileRecord(i, file);

        if (file->Ntfs.Type == 'ELIF' && (file->Flags & 1) == 0) {
            attr = FindAttribute(file, AttributeFileName, 0);
            if (attr == 0) continue;

            PFILENAME_ATTRIBUTE name
                = PFILENAME_ATTRIBUTE(Padd(attr,
                                PRESIDENT_ATTRIBUTE(attr)->ValueOffset));

            printf("%8lu %.*ws\n", i, int(name->NameLength), name->Name);
        }
    }
}

VOID DumpData(ULONG index, PCSTR filename)
{
    PFILE_RECORD_HEADER file
        = PFILE_RECORD_HEADER(new UCHAR[BytesPerFileRecord]);
    ULONG n;

    ReadFileRecord(index, file);

    if (file->Ntfs.Type != 'ELIF') return;

    PATTRIBUTE attr = FindAttribute(file, AttributeData, 0);
    if (attr == 0) return;

    PUCHAR buf = new UCHAR[AttributeLengthAllocated(attr)];

    ReadAttribute(attr, buf);

    HANDLE hFile = CreateFile(filename, GENERIC_WRITE, 0, 0,
                             CREATE_ALWAYS, 0, 0);
```

```
            WriteFile(hFile, buf, AttributeLength(attr), &n, 0);

            CloseHandle(hFile);

            delete [] buf;
    }

    int main(int argc, char *argv[])
    {
        CHAR drive[] = "\\\\.\\C:";
        ULONG n;

        if (argc < 2) return 0;

        drive[4] = argv[1][0];

        hVolume = CreateFile(drive, GENERIC_READ,
                            FILE_SHARE_READ | FILE_SHARE_WRITE, 0,
                            OPEN_EXISTING, 0, 0);

        ReadFile(hVolume, &bootb, sizeof bootb, &n, 0);

        LoadMFT();

        if (argc == 2) FindDeleted();
        if (argc == 4) DumpData(strtoul(argv[2], 0, 0), argv[3]);

        CloseHandle(hVolume);

        return 0;
    }
```

Example D.2: Decompressing Recovered Data

```
    #include <windows.h>

    typedef ULONG NTSTATUS;

    extern "C"
    NTSTATUS
    NTAPI
    RtlDecompressBuffer(
        USHORT CompressionFormat,
        PVOID OutputBuffer,
        ULONG OutputBufferLength,
        PVOID InputBuffer,
        ULONG InputBufferLength,
        PULONG ReturnLength
        );

    int main(int argc, char *argv[])
    {
        if (argc != 3) return 0;

        HANDLE hFile1 = CreateFile(argv[1], GENERIC_READ,
                            FILE_SHARE_READ, 0, OPEN_EXISTING, 0, 0);
        HANDLE hFile2 = CreateFile(argv[2], GENERIC_READ | GENERIC_WRITE,
                            FILE_SHARE_READ, 0, CREATE_ALWAYS, 0, 0);
```

```
ULONG n = GetFileSize(hFile1, 0);

HANDLE hMapping1 = CreateFileMapping(hFile1, 0, PAGE_READONLY, 0, 0, 0);
HANDLE hMapping2 = CreateFileMapping(hFile2, 0, PAGE_READWRITE, 0, n, 0);

PCHAR p = PCHAR(MapViewOfFileEx(hMapping1, FILE_MAP_READ, 0, 0, 0, 0));
PCHAR q = PCHAR(MapViewOfFileEx(hMapping2, FILE_MAP_WRITE, 0, 0, 0, 0));

for (ULONG m, i = 0; i < n; i += m)
    RtlDecompressBuffer(COMPRESSION_FORMAT_LZNT1,
                        q + i, n - i, p + i, n - i, &m);

return 0;
}
```

Index

New Riders Professional Library

Michael Masterson, Herman Knief,
Scott Vinick, and Eric Roul:

Windows NT DNS
ISBN: 1-56205-943-2

Sandra Osborne:

Windows NT Registry
ISBN: 1-56205-941-6

Mark Edmead and Paul Hinsberg:

*Windows NT Performance: Monitoring,
Benchmarking, and Tuning*
ISBN: 1-56205-942-4

Karanjit Siyan:

Windows NT TCP/IP
ISBN: 1-56205-887-8

Ted Harwood:

*Windows NT Terminal Server and Citrix
MetaFrame*
ISBN: 1-56205-944-0

Anil Desai:

*Windows NT Network Management: Reducing
Total Cost of Ownership*
ISBN: 1-56205-946-7

Eric K. Cone, Jon Boggs,
and Sergio Perez:

Planning for Windows 2000
ISBN: 0-7357-0048-6

Doug Hauger, Marywynne Leon,
and William C. Wade III:

Implementing Exchange Server
ISBN: 1-56205-931-9

Janice Rice Howd:

Exchange System Administration
ISBN: 0-7357-0081-8

Sean Baird and Chris Miller:

SQL Server System Administration
ISBN: 1-56205-955-6

Stu Sjouwerman and Ed Tittel:

Windows NT Power Toolkit
ISBN: 0-7357-0922-X

The Circle Series from MTP

April 1998

Richard Puckett:

Windows NT Automated Deployment and Customization
ISBN: 1-57870-045-0

Tim Hill:

Windows NT Shell Scripting
ISBN: 1-57870-047-7

May 1998

Gene Henriksen:

Windows NT and UNIX Integration
ISBN: 1-57870-048-5

November 1998

Peter Viscarola/Anthony Mason:

Windows NT Device Driver Development
ISBN: 1-57870-058-2

Steve Thomas:

Windows NT Heterogeneous Networking
ISBN: 1-57870-064-7

Todd Mathers/Shawn Genoway:

*Windows NT Thin Client Solutions: Implementing
Terminal Server and Citrix MetaFrame*
ISBN: 1-57870-065-5

January 1999

David Roth:

Win32 Perl Programming: The Standard Extensions
ISBN: 1-57870-067-1

February 1999

Gregg Branham:

Windows NT Domain Architecture
ISBN: 1-57870-112-0

August 1999

Sean Deuby:

Windows 2000 Server: Planning and Migration
ISBN: 1-57870-023-X

September 1999

David Iseminger:

Windows 2000 Quality of Service
ISBN: 1-57870-115-5

October 1999

Tim Hill:

Windows Script Host
ISBN: 1-57870-139-2

Paul Hinsberg:

*Windows NT Applications: Measuring
and Optimizing Performance*
ISBN: 1-57870-176-7

William Zack:

Windows 2000 and Mainframe Integration
ISBN: 1-57870-200-3